Guide to
Company Law

Guide to Company Law

1999

Philip Goldenberg MA (Oxon) FRSA FSALS

CCH NEW LAW

Disclaimer

This publication is intended to provide accurate information in regard to the subject matter covered. Readers entering into transactions on the basis of such information should seek the services of a competent professional adviser as this publication is sold on the understanding that the publisher is not engaged in rendering legal or accounting advice or other professional services. The publisher, its editors and any authors, consultants or general editors expressly disclaim all and any liability and responsibility to any person, whether a purchaser or reader of this publication or not, in respect of anything and of the consequences of anything, done or omitted to be done by any such person in reliance, whether wholly or partially, upon the whole or any part of the contents of this publication.

Legislative and other material

While copyright in all statutory and other materials resides in the Crown or other relevant body, copyright in the remaining material in this publication is vested in the publisher. The publisher advises that any statutory or other materials issued by the Crown or other relevant bodies and reproduced in this publication are not the authorised official versions of those statutory or other materials. In their preparation, however, the greatest care has been taken to ensure exact conformity with the law as enacted or other materials as issued. Crown copyright material is reproduced with the permission of the Controller of HMSO.

Ownership of Trade Mark

The trade mark   *CCH*   is the property of

Commerce Clearing House Incorporated, Riverwoods, Illinois, USA
(CCH INCORPORATED)

British Library Cataloguing in Publication Data
A catalogue record for this book is available from the British Library.

ISBN 0 86325 535 3

ISSN 0268-9588

First published 1983 under the title *Guidebook to British Company Law*
Second edition 1987, by Leon Cane
Reprinted 1988
Third edition 1990
Reprinted 1991, 1993
Fourth edition 1997
Fifth edition 1999

Typeset and printed in the UK by CCH Editions Limited.
Bound in the UK by Information Press Limited, Eynsham, Oxfordshire.

Preface

Company law was not that long ago described by a leading academic as a 'MEGO' subject ('My Eyes Glaze Over'). It is difficult to imagine a better exemplar of the proposition that 'a week is a long time in politics' than the way in which Company Law Reform has moved to the opposite end of the spectrum, so that it now falls within the ambit of the equally well-known Chinese curse 'May you live in interesting times!'.

This sea change follows the publication, earlier this year, by the Department of Trade and Industry, which a year previously launched its Company Law Review programme, of its *Strategic Framework Consultation Document* as the first step in that review.

The words 'Strategic Framework Consultation Document' are not best calculated to lift the spirits and bring a sparkle to the eyes of the reader. But behind those words are radical and well-balanced proposals for company law reform, as part of a disciplined and orderly process which is intended, within five years, to bring company law into the modern world, and contribute to British economic success.

This reform of company law is a mammoth task, aiming as it does to provide modern company law for the competitive economy in which business now operates in increasingly global markets, and to be understandable to business people and not just lawyers. The challenge is to simplify that which is not simple, and moreover to do it in plain English. One of the interesting by-products of the UK's membership of the European Union has been to illustrate the differing methodologies of legal drafting as between the UK's common-law system and the civil code basis operating in other member states. This has been dramatically illustrated in the process of giving domestic legal effect to EU directives, where the common-law tradition has resulted in UK legislation which over-enforces and is over-prescriptive. The occasion of a new Companies Act is a rare opportunity consciously to adopt a basis of drafting which is nearer the mainland European model.

The consultation document starts by setting the context of European and international developments in company law, where it is particularly significant that the historic dominions of Canada, New Zealand and Australia, each with its company law founded on British precedent, have gone their own ways in recent years.

Shareholders and Stakeholders

The bogus adversarial argument of 'shareholders or stakeholders' has been exposed, with the document's concept of 'enlightened shareholder value'. The document recognises the crucial importance of shifting the corporate culture to the best practice of those companies – Tomorrow's Companies – which pursue the interests of shareholders in an enlightened and inclusive way, and look to long-term sustainable growth in value.

Preface

Coupled with this is a need for better understanding and accessibility of the law on directors' duties – the Law Commission's proposed 'Highway Code' for directors will surely be the way forward. In addition, the document argues that reporting and accounting must move on from mere historic financial information, both by expanding the range of topics covered to those (skills, training, management techniques, marketing and branding, key third-party relationships and intellectual property in its broader sense) more relevant in an increasingly knowledge-based economy, and by setting and benchmarking targets for future performance.

This combination of 'enlightened shareholder value' with transparency and accountability mirrors closely the key recommendations of the RSA's 1995 TOMORROW'S COMPANY Enquiry, whose work has since been carried forward by The Centre for Tomorrow's Company.

Simplification

The consultation document then turns to smaller companies, and reviews the options, including both a separate (optional) form of incorporation for owner-managed companies and an integrated approach within a single Companies Act regime, but one where the basic building block would be the private company. This will be a key area for consultation, to discover what the small and medium-sized enterprise (SME) sector really wants.

There is then a proposal for significant and welcome simplification of the law relating to company formation and capital maintenance, not least as regards the vexed issue of financial assistance, where the present legal constraints are argued to cost the business community some £20m each year.

Finally, the document deals with the inter-action between law and regulation. The present higgledy-piggledy mess is rightly regarded as unsustainable, with Pt. X of the *Companies Act* 1985 (on the enforcement of directors' duties) having grown like topsy over the years to reflect each passing scandal. The document rightly concludes that there is a need to start from first principles to produce a structure which is intellectually coherent, and also recognises that, with the degree of Stock Exchange regulation having developed over the years way beyond that prevailing at the time most of Pt. X was enacted, there is considerable scope for pruning from legislation those matters which really only apply to larger companies and are already covered by such regulation.

The process

The Strategic Framework Consultation Document is the first stage in a process which is intended to lead a wholesale new Companies Act (or Acts) in the next Parliament. This is a mammoth task, not least because the thought of such legislation going through the Parliamentary process without a significant measure of consensus on its contents is horrific.

Quite deliberately, the Steering Group of the Company Law Review is setting out on an inclusive process of building that consensus. So far, it's doing rather well.

Preface

Civil Procedure Rules

Although the infamous Civil Procedure Rules from 26 April 1999 (my birthday!) have sadly altered some of the hallowed terminology of civil litigation (e.g. a 'plaintiff' is now a 'claimant') the former wording has, for consistency been retained throughout the book.

Acknowledgements

The more lynx-eyed readers of this Edition will notice that I am now described as 'Consultant Editor'. This reflects the fact that, as CCH and I have worked together over a period, we have jointly concluded that producing text book material of this nature with the benefit of an experienced practitioner's overview is best achieved by CCH's technical staff producing the first draft, with a subsequent review by me. It is accordingly both my duty and my pleasure to place on record my debt to Peter Bailey as CCH's in-house company law editor, the standard of whose work has enormously lightened my task. I also wish to thank Anthony Shatz, who, as a result of devilling my Editorship of the Fourth Edition in 1996, is now a newly qualified Assistant Solicitor in my office – he has maintained a friendly interest in his work as it has been updated.

The law is stated as at 15 June 1999.

Philip Goldenberg
September 1999

About the Publisher

CCH New Law is a business unit of Croner Publications Limited, part of the Wolters Kluwer Group. Wolters Kluwer is the leading international professional publisher specialising in tax, business and law publishing throughout Europe, the US and the Asia Pacific. The group produces a wide range of books and reporting services in different media for the accounting and legal professions and for businesses. The Oxfordshire premises are the centre for all CCH UK and European operations.

All CCH publications are designed to provide practical, authoritative reference works, and useful guides, and are written by CCH's highly qualified and experienced editorial team and specialist outside authors.

CCH New Law publishes information packages including bound books, loose-leaf reporting services, newsletters and electronic products on UK and European legal topics for distribution world-wide. The UK operation also acts as distributor of the publications of the overseas affiliates.

CCH New Law
Telford Road
Bicester
Oxfordshire OX6 0XD
Telephone: (01869) 253300

A business unit of Croner Publications Limited,
Croner House, London Road, Kingston-upon-Thames,
Surrey, KT2 6SR, 020 8547 3333
Part of the Wolters Kluwer Group

About the Consultant Editor

The Consultant Editor, **Philip Goldenberg MA (Oxon) FRSA FSALS**, is a partner in City solicitors S J Berwin & Co. He has wide-ranging experience in UK domestic corporate finance and governance, with particular emphasis on mergers, acquisitions, flotations, issues and reconstructions and employee share ownership; he was involved in the conception and enactment of the profit-sharing provisions of the 1978 Finance Act. He is a member of the National Council of the CBI and of its Managing Committee, and was the legal adviser to the RSA's Tomorrow's Company Inquiry. He assisted the Department of Trade and Industry in the preparation of its Strategic Framework Consultation Document on Company Law Reform.

Abbreviations

The following abbreviations are used in this book:

AC	Law Reports, Appeal Cases, 1891–current
A-G	Attorney-General
AGM	annual general meeting
AIM	Alternative Investment Market
All ER	All England Law Reports, 1936–current
App Cas	Law Reports, Appeal Cases, 1875–1890
ARD	accounting reference date
ARP	accounting reference period
art.	Article
ASB	Accounting Standards Board
BCC	British Company Cases, 1983–current (CCH)
BCLC	Butterworths Company Law Cases
BNA 1985	Business Names Act 1985
CA 1985	Companies Act 1985
CA 1989	Companies Act 1989
CA	Court of Appeal
CC(CP)A 1985	Companies Consolidation (Consequential Provisions) Act 1985
CCH	CCH Editions Limited
CCRPPOS	convertible cumulative redeemable participating preferred ordinary shares
CDDA 1986	Company Directors Disqualification Act 1986
cf.	(confer) compare
ch. (Ch.)	chapter (Chapter of Act)
Ch	Law Reports, Chancery Division, 1891–current
Ch App	Law Reports, Chancery Appeals, 1865–1875
ChD	Law Reports, Chancery Division, 1875–1890
CJA 1993	Criminal Justice Act 1993
cl.	clause
CLR	Commonwealth Law Reports, 1903–current (Australia)
Cmnd	Command Paper
CPR	Civil Procedure Rules
CS(ID)A 1985	Company Securities (Insider Dealing) Act 1985
Ct Sess	Court of Session (Scotland)
CVA	company voluntary arrangement
DLR; (2d); (3d); (4th)	Dominion Law Reports (Canada), 1912–1922; (Second Series), 1923–1968; (Third Series), 1969–1984; (Fourth Series), 1984–current
DPP	Director of Public Prosecutions

Abbreviations

DTI	Department of Trade and Industry
E & B	Ellis and Blackburn's Reports, Queen's Bench, 1851–1858
EC	European Community
edn	edition
EEC	European Economic Community
EEIG	European Economic Interest Grouping
EGM	extraordinary general meeting
Eq	Equity Reports, 1853-1855
ER	English Reports, 1220–1865
EU	European Union
ExD	Law Reports, Exchequer Division, 1875–1880
F	Federal Reporter (USA)
FA 1998	Finance Act 1998
F(No. 2)A 1997	Finance (No. 2) Act 1997
ff.	following
FRC	Financial Reporting Council
FRRP	Financial Reporting Review Panel
FSA	Financial Services Authority
FSA 1986	Financial Services Act 1986
FTA 1973	Fair Trading Act 1973
Hare	Hare's Reports, Vice-Chancellor's Court, 1841—1853
HL	House of Lords
IA 1986	Insolvency Act 1986
ICR	Industrial Cases Reports, 1972–current
IMRO	Investment Management Regulatory Organisation
IPO	initial public offering
IVA	individual voluntary arrangement
J	Mr Justice
KB	Law Reports, King's Bench Division, 1900–1952
LC	Lord Chancellor
LCJ	Lord Chief Justice
LJ	Lord Justice
Ll L Rep	Lloyd's Reports, 1919–1950
Ll Rep	Lloyd's Reports, 1951–current
LR	Law Reports, from 1865
LSE	London Stock Exchange
LR Eq	Law Reports, Equity Cases, 1866–1875
LT	Law Times Reports, 1859–1947
Ltd	Limited
m	million

Abbreviations

Macq	Macqueen's Reports (Scotland), House of Lords, 1851–1865
M & S	Maule and Selwyn's Reports, King's Bench, 1813–1817
MMC	Monopolies and Mergers Commission
MR	Master of the Rolls
NZLR	New Zealand Law Reports, 1883–current
O.	Order
OECD	Organisation for Economic Co-operation and Development
OEIC	open-ended investment company
OFT	Office of Fair Trading
P	Law Reports, Probate, Divorce and Admiralty Division, 1891–1971
p.	page
para.	paragraph
PAYE	pay as you earn
PC	Privy Council
PIA	Personal Investment Authority
plc	public limited company
Pt.	Part
QB	Law Reports, Queen's Bench Division, 1891–1900; 1952–current
QBD	Law Reports, Queen's Bench Division, 1875–1890
QC	Queen's Counsel
R	Queen (regina); King (rex)
r.	rule
reg.	regulation
RSC	Rules of the Supreme Court
s.	section
SC	Court of Session Cases (Scotland), 1906–current
Sch.	Schedule
SFA	Securities and Futures Authority
SI	Statutory Instrument
SIB	Securities and Investments Board
SLT	Scots Law Times, 1893–current
SRO	Self-regulating Organisation
SSAP	Statement of Standard Accounting Practice
TLR	The Times Law Reports, 1884–1952
UITF	Urgent Issues Task Force
UK	United Kingdom

Abbreviations

US   United States of America

v   versus
VAT   value added tax
V-C   Vice-Chancellor

WLR   Weekly Law Reports, 1953–current

¶   Paragraph

Contents

INTRODUCTION •
INCORPORATION

Table of Contents

continued over

COMPANIES GENERALLY

¶20-000 Development of company registration

The concept of the commercial 'corporate enterprise' originated with merchant corporations of the fourteenth century. These were created by entrepreneurs, for exploitation of trading opportunities. Each member of such a corporation traded on his own account. It was not until the late seventeenth century that the 'joint stock' company emerged. This was a trading enterprise in which each member contributed to and benefited from the financial success of the venture as a single trading unit.

Companies were later incorporated by grant of a Royal Charter on advice of the Law Officers of the Crown (chartered companies), or by individual Acts of Parliament (statutory companies). These mechanisms of incorporation are now seldom used, except for charters granted for prestige purposes, and the nationalisation of certain industries by statute. The proliferation of commercial activity in the nineteenth century, and the suitability of the 'corporate entity' as a vehicle for enterprise, resulted in the introduction of a registration system for companies. This was the *Joint Stock Companies Act* 1844. As a consequence, a private Act of Parliament or Royal Charter was not required for each new company. The 1844 Act also called for disclosure of the affairs of companies registered under it for the first time.

Limited liability

The advantages of limited liability (i.e. that the liability of the owners for debts of the company be restricted to their initial capital contribution as far as it remained unpaid) were appreciated at this time but this privilege was not conferred upon companies registered under the *Joint Stock Companies Act* 1844. Four forms of 'corporate enterprise' then existed. These were private partnerships, chartered companies, statutory companies and companies registered under the 1844 Act.

Limited liability for registered companies was introduced by the *Limited Liability Act* 1855. The first Act which resembled the current companies legislation was the *Joint Stock Companies Act* 1856, which consolidated the various companies legislation in force at that time.

A high priority in the development of companies legislation subsequent to 1855 has been the imposition of duties and responsibilities upon shareholders and company officers as a cost of the privilege of limited liability. In more recent times, the drive for harmonisation of company law within the EU has proved an important influence in the reformation of companies legislation. The *Companies Act* 1985 was a consolidating statute of various Acts introduced since 1948. Much of the initiative and impetus for the more recent legislation has emanated from the UK's obligations under the EU Treaties, as witness Pt. I and II of the *Companies Act* 1989.

Public and private companies

A legacy of the early Companies Acts which has remained a part of English law is the monolithic approach to the regulation of companies, irrespective of size (however measured) or ownership (public or family). The need for a different regulatory code, which distinguishes companies by size, was recognised to a limited extent by the reformulation of rules applicable to companies in the 1980 and 1981 Companies Acts. The reformulation has resulted in different regulatory codes applying to public and private companies, with regard to particular matters, such as distributions and return of capital. Further, for disclosure purposes, certain exemptions are conferred upon private companies which fall within the 'small' or 'medium-sized' bracket.

Insolvency and director disqualification

The *Insolvency Act* 1986 and the *Company Directors Disqualification Act* 1986 consolidated the long-heralded *Insolvency Act* 1985 with provisions of the *Companies Act* 1985 relating to receivership and winding up. The *Insolvency Act* 1985 was partly based on the 'Cork Report' (*Review Committee on Insolvency Law and Practice* (June 1982, Cmnd 8558)) and, apart from a handful of provisions, never came into force. The *Insolvency Act* 1986 contained a new code for the law of bankruptcy together with far-reaching changes to the law of corporate insolvency (see ¶90-000ff.). The *Company Directors Disqualification Act* 1986 laid down a strict code of conduct on directors of both solvent and insolvent companies.

Financial Services Act 1986

The *Financial Services Act* 1986, based on the 'Gower Report' (*Review of Investor Protection* (January 1984, Cmnd 9125)), substantially came into force during 1987. It regulates the carrying on of investment business and increases protection for investors in companies.

Companies Act 1989

The *Companies Act* 1989, while originally only intended to implement the EU seventh and eighth company law directives on group accounts and the Regulation of Auditors, includes other piecemeal amendments. These involve provisions for the de-regulation of company law, for a pre-notification system of merger control and for increased investigative powers of Department of Trade and Industry (DTI) inspectors, and alterations to the *Financial Services Act* 1986. Very importantly, the Companies Act also implements, in part, the report of the review committee under the chairmanship of Sir Ronald Dearing on 'The Making of Accounting Standards', and the report of Dr Daniel Prentice on the 'Reform of the Ultra Vires Rule'.

¶20-000

TYPES OF REGISTERED COMPANY

¶20-100   General

There are various methods of incorporating a company. Each form of incorporation results in the creation of a corporate entity with its own separate legal personality (see ¶20-800). The early forms of incorporation, by Royal Charter or special Act of Parliament, are nowadays used only in special circumstances (see ¶20-000). Virtually all companies are now created by registration under the Companies Act of the day (see ¶22-000ff.).

There are various forms of registered company. The most common forms of incorporation are public and private companies with their members' liability limited to the amount (if any) unpaid on their shares. However it is also possible to incorporate companies limited by guarantee, companies where the liability of the members is unlimited and, under the *Companies Act* 1989, 'partnership companies' which are limited by shares intended to be held to a substantial extent by or on behalf of employees. The various forms of incorporation are considered at ¶22-000.

¶20-150   Public companies

A 'public company' is a company having the liability of its members limited by shares, or limited by guarantee and having a share capital, with a memorandum of association which provides that the company is to be public, and for which the requirements as to registration for public companies are complied with (*Companies Act* 1985 (CA 1985), s. 1(3)). These are as follows:

- the name of the company must end with the initials 'plc';

- the company must have an authorised share capital of at least £50,000 (of which at least £12,500 must actually be paid to the company by its shareholders); and

- the company's memorandum of association (which sets out the company's constitution) must also comply with the format stipulated for public companies under Table F of the *Companies (Tables A to F) Regulations* 1985 (SI 1985/805).

The special significance of public companies is that they are permitted to offer securities to the public. The distinction between public and private companies is important for certain regulatory provisions of the Companies Act, such as the presentation of accounts, the determination of distributable profits and the repurchase of shares from members. Where the distinction is not drawn in the legislation, the Act applies equally to both forms of company.

¶20-200   Private companies

A company incorporated under the *Companies Act* 1985 which does not register as public is a private company. The Act is less strict on certain regulatory requirements of private companies. For example, there is no requirement as to minimum authorised and paid-up share capital, and the rules as to distributable profits are eased. However a private company is not permitted to offer shares to the public.

Note that it is possible to convert from a private company to a public company, and vice versa (see ¶22-500 and ¶22-600, respectively).

The main contrasts between public and private companies are contained in the list below.

Public	*Private*
Share issues to public permitted	Share issues to public prohibited
Minimum issued share capital requirement	No minimum issued share capital requirement
Minimum paid up share capital requirement	No minimum paid up share capital requirement
Minimum number of members is two	Minimum number of members is one
Minimum number of directors is two	Minimum number of directors is one
Age limit applied to directors	No age limit applied
Pre-emption rights for existing shareholders may be disapplied for limited periods	Pre-emption rights may be waived generally and without time limit
Transactions by directors with the company closely regulated	Transaction by directors with the company less closely regulated
Expert's valuation report required on acquisition of non-cash assets	No valuation report required on acquisition of non-cash assets
Serious loss of capital requires extraordinary meeting of shareholders	No rules on serious loss of capital
Financial assistance for purchase of shares generally prohibited	Financial assistance for purchase of shares more widely permitted

Public	*Private*
Redemption or repurchase of shares out of capital prohibited	Redemption or repurchase of shares out of capital permitted
Full accounts must be filed, complying with accounting standards	Small or medium-sized companies need not file full accounts, and such accounts need not comply with accounting standards; very small companies can dispense with audit requirements
No elective regime for written resolutions	Elective regime for written resolutions

¶20-250   Companies limited by guarantee

A company limited by guarantee has the liability of its members limited by the memorandum to such an amount as they may undertake to contribute to the assets of the company in the event of its being wound up. Since 1980, it is not possible to form or convert to a company limited by guarantee and having a share capital. Most guarantee companies are clubs, societies and trade associations. The memorandum and articles (which are the company's internal regulatory code) of guarantee companies must comply with Table C of the *Companies (Tables A to F) Regulations* 1985. All the provisions of the *Companies Act* 1985 apply to guarantee companies, unless specifically excluded.

See further ¶20-900.

¶20-300   Companies limited by shares

These are by far the most common form of registered company in the UK. Such companies can be either public or private, as explained in ¶20-150 and ¶20-200 above. The liability of the members is limited to the amount, if any, unpaid on their shares. Once a member's shares are fully paid, then his liability to the company on them ceases, and he is not liable to make any contribution to the company's assets in respect of the shares in the event of the company being wound up.

The limited liability company is the classic vehicle into which the armchair investor, who does not wish to have a direct involvement in the day-to-day running of the enterprise, may apply his funds safe in the knowledge that his liability to the company will not exceed the amount of his investment.

The model form of articles of association for companies limited by shares is Table A in the *Companies (Tables A to F) Regulations* 1985. The Table is set out at ¶31-050. If such a company does not register articles (or, if it does register articles, in so far as these do not exclude Table A), then that Table will constitute the company's articles (CA 1985, s. 8(2)).

See further ¶20-900.

¶20-350 Single member private companies

In 1992 the government introduced regulations which allow for private companies limited by either shares or guarantee to have only one member. This type of business unit blurs the distinction between companies and sole trader business units, despite the fact that the latter carry unlimited liability. Difficulties can often arise in single member companies because the company is still an entirely separate legal personality. This was illustrated in *Neptune (Vehicle Washing Equipment) Ltd v Fitzgerald*.

> **Case example (1)**
> Fitzgerald, who was the sole director of the plaintiff company, purported to terminate his contract of employment and retire as director of the company. At the same time, he authorised payment to himself of approximately £100,000 which he argued was due to him under his contract of employment. The new director of the company disputed this, and the court agreed that Fitzgerald's conduct had breached the rule against self-dealing. Fitzgerald was duty-bound to declare any interest in a contract with the company (by virtue of s. 317 of the *Companies Act* 1985). Where the company had only one director, that director should make the declaration to himself and record the same in the minute book. *Neptune (Vehicle Washing Equipment) Ltd v Fitzgerald* [1996] Ch 274; [1995] BCC 474.

However this decision has been significantly criticised.

The difficulty in determining liability for negligent misstatement of the sole member of a one-man company was considered by the House of Lords in *Williams v Natural Life Health Foods Ltd*.

> **Case example (2)**
> The company advised on franchises for shops in the health food trade. Its sole shareholder was M and there were two employees. W approached the company for advice on a franchise. He received the company's brochure which described M as managing director and head of the franchising team and went on to describe his history in the health food business. Financial projections were supplied by the company to W for a proposed shop; the projections were not prepared by M although he approved them. M never dealt with W directly. The franchise went through but the projections were inaccurate. The company was liable to W for negligent misstatement but went into liquidation and W sought damages from M himself. The Court of Appeal held him liable, finding that special circumstances were established so that the fact of incorporation, even in the case of a one-man company, did not preclude the establishment of personal liability. The House of Lords disagreed, holding that on the facts there had been no assumption of liability by M: in a small one-man company the managing director would almost certainly be the one possessed of qualities essential to the functioning of the company but by itself this did not mean that the managing director was willing to be personally answerable to the customers of the company. The fact that there had been no personal dealings between M and W was highly relevant in the finding that M had assumed no liability to W. *Williams v Natural Life Health Foods Ltd* [1998] BCC 428.

¶20-400 Unlimited companies

An unlimited liability company is one which does not have any limitation on the contribution which can be called for from members to meet liabilities of the company. The members' liability will arise if the company is wound up and has an excess of liabilities over assets. The memorandum and articles of an unlimited liability company must comply with Table E of the *Companies (Tables A to F) Regulations* 1985. The advantages of unlimited liability are the exemption from filing accounts with the registrar of companies, from the need to maintain capital and the ability to repurchase its shares outside the regulatory code of the *Companies Act* 1985. Such a company can reduce its share capital without the sanction of the court (*Re Borough Commercial and Building Society* [1893] 2 Ch 242).

Note that a company may convert its members' liability from limited to unlimited, and vice versa.

¶20-450 Partnership companies

A partnership company is one which is limited by shares, where the shares are intended to be held to a substantial extent by or on behalf of its employees. This option is contained in s. 8A of the *Companies Act* 1985 and allows the Secretary of State to prescribe a Table G (in addition to the *Companies (Tables A to F) Regulations* 1985) which may be adopted in whole, or in part, by a company limited by shares. In contrast to the ordinary limited liability company, the day-to-day running of the whole enterprise is predominantly by the investors.

There has been a parallel development on partnerships, largely in response to legislation in the Channel Island of Jersey. In February 1997 the Department of Trade and Industry (DTI) published a consultation paper *Limited Liability Partnership – A New Form of Business Association for Professions*, proposing a new form of business association for professions. If enacted, this would involve many of the fundamental tenets of company law such as incorporation, separate legal personality, capacity to contract and to hold property and grant charges over it. The partners (or rather 'members') would have limited liability subject, in an insolvency situation, to a clawback of excessive drawings and a guarantee to contribute to the assets available to the liquidator. Like companies, limited liability partnerships would be subject to DTI investigation powers and compulsory filing of accounts giving a true and fair view, and the members could be disqualified if unfit. The name of the limited liability partnership would have to end with 'LLP'.

Although limited liability partnerships have proved popular in the US, the types of regulated profession which might appear most amenable to the format in the UK, mainly solicitors and accountants, although keen to obtain the benefits of limited liability, have shown no great enthusiasm for the disclosure requirements and transparency of the 'limited' nature of the members' liability. The DTI published a further consultation document on 17 September 1998 containing a draft Limited Liability Partnerships Bill for comment. The members' guarantee to contribute in insolvency was dropped. The ultimate legislation would incorporate large tracts from the Companies Act and insolvency legislation with appropriate modifications as necessary.

¶20-500   European Economic Interest Groupings

The increasing influence of the European Union (EU) on corporate structures resulted in the creation of the European Economic Interest Grouping (EEIG) from 1 July 1989 as a vehicle for the promotion of cross-border co-operation within the EU.

The legal basis of the EEIG in the UK is EC Regulation 2137/85 (OJ 1985 L199/1), together with a UK statutory instrument (*European Economic Interest Grouping Regulations* 1989 (SI 1989/638)).

In structure the EEIG is a hybrid of a partnership and an unlimited company in that an EEIG registered in the UK will have a separate legal personality as a body corporate while its members will retain unlimited joint and several liability for its debts. Most of the provisions of the EC regulation may be altered by the formation contract creating the EEIG; however there are a number of mandatory requirements. The constitutional organs must include:

(1) members acting collectively, in a similar manner to shareholders in a general meeting of a company; and

(2) individuals designated as managers, who are treated as directors under the Companies Acts for certain purposes.

The structure of the EEIG is flexible; a limited number of matters must be agreed by the members unanimously, while the formation contract may regulate the decision-making process on other matters. However EEIGs are specifically prevented from inviting investment from the public or having more than 500 employees. Further, only a subsidiary business interest may be pursued through an EEIG; the main business activities of a participant in an EEIG must be continued through its original enterprise. The members of an EEIG may be a company, a partnership or a sole trader, or a public body, provided that they are based in the EU and are from at least two member states.

According to the DTI, by 1996 there were 93 EEIGs registered in the UK. Architects, solicitors, and construction firms have utilised EEIGs in order to liaise with other firms in their fields of expertise. Notably, the operators of the Channel Tunnel set up an EEIG, as have a District Council in England and a Chamber of Commerce in France in order to promote their respective ports.

Special Companies

¶20-550   General

Limited liability companies all have the same fundamental characteristics. However particular features of a company necessitate special regulation under the Companies Acts in respect of certain matters. The most common of the special categories of company are identified at ¶20-575 to ¶20-675. The regulatory provisions which apply to them are referred to under the relevant headings throughout the commentary. The full relevance of each distinction is explained in these latter references.

¶20-575   Subsidiary companies and subsidiary undertakings

Prior to the *Companies Act* 1989, the term subsidiary (as then defined) was used for both accounting and non-accounting purposes. The previous emphasis on the ownership of equity share capital has been replaced by concentration on the exercise of voting rights. A 'subsidiary undertaking' is based on a similar concept, but is relevant for accounting purposes only (see ¶70-100).

The definition of a 'subsidiary' is contained in s. 736 of the Companies Act 1985. A company is deemed to be a subsidiary of another if (but only if):

(1) that other company either:

   (a) holds a majority of the voting rights in it; or

   (b) is a member of it and has the right to appoint or remove a majority of its board of directors; or

   (c) is a member of it and controls alone, pursuant to an agreement with other shareholders or members, a majority of the voting rights in it; or

(2) the first-mentioned company is a subsidiary of any company which is that other's subsidiary (CA 1985, s. 736(1)).

Voting rights

The above references to 'voting rights' in any company are to rights conferred on shareholders in respect of their shares. If the company does not have a share capital, then references to voting rights are to rights conferred on members to vote at general meetings of companies in all, or substantially all, matters (CA 1985, s. 736A(1), (2)).

A company's board of directors is deemed to be controlled by another company if that company can appoint or remove directors (to the board) holding the majority of voting rights at the board meetings by exercise of a power without the consent or concurrence of any other person (unless no other person has power so to appoint or remove). A power of appointment exists if:

(1) a person's appointment is an inevitable result of his directorship of the other company; or

(2) the directorship is held by the other company itself (CA 1985, s. 736A(3)).

The concept of 'rights' is defined for purposes of the definition of a subsidiary by s. 736A(4)–(10) of the *Companies Act* 1985. In particular, it is important to note that:

(1) rights held in a fiduciary capacity do not count in establishing control;

(2) rights held by a person as nominee are treated as rights of the person for whom they are held;

(3) rights which are exercisable only in certain circumstances count –

(a) where the circumstances have arisen, and for so long as they continue, or

(b) where the circumstances are within the control of the person having the rights;

(4) rights which are normally exercised, but are temporarily incapable of exercise, continue to be taken into account; and

(5) the voting rights in a company are reduced by any rights held by the company.

¶20-600 Oversea companies

An oversea company is:

(1) any company incorporated outside Great Britain, which, after 1 July 1985, establishes a 'place of business' (which includes a share transfer or share registration office) in Great Britain; and

(2) a company so incorporated which has before 1 July 1985 established a place of business and continued to have an established place of business in Great Britain at 1 July 1985 (CA 1985, s. 744).

The Court of Appeal considers that establishing a place of business requires a place at or from which a business activity is habitually carried out and effected. The mere fact that the company's directors have their matrimonial home in Great Britain is not enough to establish this (*Re Oriel Ltd* [1986] 1 WLR 180; (1985) 1 BCC 99,444).

Until the end of 1992, a 'place of business' registration scheme obliged oversea companies with a place of business in this country to register certain information with the registrar. That regime now only applies to unlimited companies incorporated outside Great Britain, companies incorporated in Northern Ireland and Gibraltar, and limited companies incorporated outside the UK that do not have a branch in Northern Ireland and whose presence in Great Britain is not sufficient to fall under the branch registration scheme.

Since 1992, every overseas limited company (i.e. outside the UK and Gibraltar) which opens a branch in the UK has been required to lodge certain documents with the registrar. For these purposes, 'branch' is defined as 'a part of a company which is organised so as to conduct business on behalf of the company'. Information that should be disclosed includes the company name, directors' particulars, and branch details. The registrar must also be notified of any changes.

¶20-625 Dormant companies

A company is dormant for an accounting period if no significant accounting transactions occur during that period. A significant accounting transaction is one which must be entered in the company's accounting records. However, excluded from this definition are transactions which arise from the taking of shares of the company by a subscriber to the memorandum in pursuance of an undertaking in the memorandum (CA 1985, s. 250).

¶20-650 Small companies

A small company is one which, for a financial year, satisfies at least two of the following conditions:

(1) turnover of not more than £2.8m,

(2) net assets, as disclosed on the balance sheet, of not more than £1.4m,

(3) the average number of persons employed during the year is not greater than 50.

¶20-675 Medium-sized companies

A medium-sized company is one which, in a financial year, satisfies at least two of the following conditions:

(1) turnover of not more than £11.2m,

(2) net assets of not more than £5.6m,

(3) the average number of persons employed during the year is not greater than 250.

Similar criteria apply in relation to small and medium-sized groups of companies. A company which is small or medium-sized in accordance with the above criteria is exempted from various requirements relating to the submission of accounts and the preparation of directors' reports (CA 1985, s. 246). A very small company is totally exempted from the audit regime.

¶20-700 Open-ended investment companies

Open-ended investment companies (OEICs) were introduced in Great Britain on 6 January 1997 by the *Open-Ended Investment Companies (Investment Companies with Variable Capital) Regulations* 1996 (SI 1996/2827). An OEIC is a company that is able to redeem its own shares for cash and manages a portfolio of investments on behalf of its members. A small number of this new form of investment vehicle, already popular in certain European countries, were created in the first year of operation of the above legislation. The momentum is continuing, particularly among the larger fund management groups converting the form in which their retail managed funds are held in one OEIC, particularly as a single 'umbrella' vehicle for a multitude of sub-funds.

¶20-800   The nature of a company

The very bedrock of British company law is that a registered company is a legal person in its own right, quite distinct from its officers and members. This fact that a company has a separate existence from its directors and shareholders has important, and sometimes unexpected, consequences. The feature of corporate existence enables the company to own property, to continue in existence despite changes in ownership and, most importantly, to keep the liability of the company separate from that of its members. The case of *Salomon v Salomon & Co Ltd*, which has proved a cornerstone of British company law, confirmed this principle.

> **Case example (1)**
> Salomon had been a successful boot and shoe manufacturer in London. He formed a company in which shares were issued to himself, his wife and five of his children. The Companies Act at that time required companies to have at least seven members. The new company contracted to buy the business from Salomon for £39,000 (although Lord Macnaghten later estimated its then value at about £10,000). A sum of £20,000 was paid to Salomon, which was returned to the company in return for shares. A further £10,000 was satisfied by the issue of debentures to Salomon. The balance was applied in payment of liabilities of the business prior to the transfer to the company. The company's business later ran into difficulties and went into liquidation. The liquidator claimed rescission of the transfer of the business and disputed the validity of the debenture issue. In the Court of Appeal, it was found that Salomon had used the company as his agent, and that it was therefore entitled to an indemnity from him. However the House of Lords upheld the separate legal identity of the company, which was explained to be a consequence of incorporation under the Companies Act. The company was a legal entity separate from Salomon. Thus Salomon was not responsible for its debts. The legal position was summarised by Lord Macnaghten as follows (at p. 51): 'The company is at law a different person altogether from the subscribers to the memorandum; and, though it may be that after incorporation the business is precisely the same as it was before, and the same persons are managers, and the same hands receive the profits, the company is not in law the agent of the subscribers or trustee for them. Nor are the subscribers as members liable, in any shape or form, except to the extent and in the manner provided by the Act.'
> *Salomon v Salomon & Co Ltd* [1897] AC 22.

A more striking example of application of the doctrine is illustrated by the case of *Lee v Lee's Air Farming Ltd*. This case shows that a majority shareholder can contract with the company he owns.

Case example (2)

Lee was a crop-duster in New Zealand. The business was conducted through a company in which Lee owned 2,999 of the 3,000 issued shares. He was the sole director of the company, and was employed at a salary. Lee subsequently died in an aeroplane crash while crop-dusting. His wife claimed compensation from the New Zealand Government, under a statutory scheme. A widow could only qualify for benefits under the scheme if her deceased husband was a 'worker', as opposed to being self-employed. It was held that Lee was an employee of his company and thus his widow was entitled to compensation. The company and Lee were separate legal persons, between whom there was a contract of service. Lord Morris of Borth-y-Gest explained (at p. 26): 'it is a logical consequence of the decision in *Salomon's* case that one person may function in dual capacities. There is no reason, therefore, to deny the possibility of a contractual relationship being created as between the deceased and the company.'

When faced with the objection that Lee both gave the orders and obeyed them, his Lordship explained (at p. 27): 'The fact that so long as the deceased continued to be governing director, with amplitude of powers, it would be for him to act as the agent of the company to give the orders does not alter the fact that the company and the deceased were two separate and distinct legal persons ... Just as the company and the deceased were separate legal entities so as to permit of contractual relations being established between them, so also were they separate legal entities so as to enable the company to give an order to the deceased.' *Lee v Lee's Air Farming Ltd* [1961] AC 12.

Another important feature of corporate personality was illustrated by the case of *Macaura v Northern Assurance Co Ltd*. This is the fact that it is the company which owns its property, not the shareholders or creditors.

Case example (3)

Macaura sold timber to a company, in exchange for all of its issued share capital. Insurance policies on the timber were then taken out by Macaura, but in his own name. The timber was later destroyed by fire, but Macaura could not recover under the policies as he had no insurable interest in it. (An 'insurable interest', a requirement of all valid insurance policies, means that the insured party must have such an interest in the subject-matter of the policy that he will suffer a direct loss or liability if the event insured against does occur.) Lord Sumner explained that Macaura stood in no legal or equitable relation to the timber. His relation was to the company, not its goods. *Macaura v Northern Assurance Co Ltd* [1925] AC 619.

The definition of 'subsidiary' has already been referred to above. Often, there is potential for a parent company to be found liable for a subsidiary's debts. The problem was illustrated in *Adams v Cape Industries plc*.

Case example (4)

Until 1979, Cape, an English company, mined asbestos and marketed it in the USA through an English subsidiary called Capasco and an American subsidiary called NAAC. In 1978 NAAC was wound up and new subsidiaries were set up to continue the marketing operation. In 1979 approximately 200 people gained default judgments in a US court against Cape and Capasco for personal injuries caused by asbestos. The plaintiffs sought to enforce the judgment in the UK. Cape and Capasco successfully argued that the Texan court had no jurisdiction over it or its subsidiaries. An oversea company would only be subject to the jurisdiction of the foreign court if it maintained a place of business there for more than a minimal amount of time. In this case, the new marketing subsidiary was not acting as an agent for Cape. Although this was a deliberate tactic, there was no attempt to conceal the true facts and therefore no justification for lifting the corporate veil. *Adams v Cape Industries plc* [1990] Ch 433; [1990] BCC 786.

¶20-900 Limited liability

Limitation of the liability of shareholders for the activities of a venture is a quintessential feature of companies registered under the Companies Act. The most common form of limited liability is by reference to the shares subscribed. The principle limits the liability of a company member to his commitment to pay for his shares. If the shares are issued 'at par', the member must meet calls up to their nominal amount. However it may be that the shares are issued at a premium, in which case the shareholder must meet calls up to this higher value.

A company registered under the Companies Act may also be limited by guarantee. In such a case, the members agree in the memorandum that they will act as guarantors of the company's liabilities. However a maximum sum per subscriber is stipulated in the memorandum. Under Tables C and D of the model sets of articles provided in the *Companies (Tables A to F) Regulations* 1985, this stands at £100 (before the 1985 regulations, the recommended figure was £10).

Liability limited by guarantee is most commonly used by clubs, associations and charities. Liability limited by shares is most commonly used by commercial enterprises. The latter form of corporate structure has facilitated investment in business ventures by persons who will have no control over the day-to-day running of the company. This concept is the backbone of modern commercial enterprise.

The facility for limitation of liability can result in abuse of the privilege, by persons who hide behind the corporate shield. The courts will 'lift the corporate veil' in certain circumstances to frustrate unfair exploitation of limited liability or to avoid extreme consequences of a strict application of the principle. Particular statutory enactments achieve the same result.

LIFTING THE VEIL

¶21-000   General

The concepts of the independent corporate existence of companies and of limited liability of shareholders are almost inviolate principles of company law. However the courts have, on rare occasions, attributed acts or omissions of a company to the shareholders, thereby identifying the company with its owners. This may have the effect of denying the shareholders the protection of limited liability.

Various legislative provisions also merge the identity of shareholders with that of the company. The relevant provisions are not confined to the Companies Act. Many examples are found in tax legislation. Thus the Inland Revenue may in certain circumstances collect unpaid corporation tax from the previous owners of the company, or from other companies previously under the same ownership, where the company is sold in circumstances intended to ensure that its tax liabilities arising before the sale are likely to remain uncollected (*Income and Corporation Taxes Act* 1988, s. 767A, 767B; *Finance Act* 1998, s. 114). Similarly, a transfer of value by a close company can be apportioned to the company's shareholders, etc. for inheritance tax purposes (*Inheritance Tax Act* 1984, s. 94–102).

However the House of Lords has made it quite clear that the veil of incorporation will only be lifted by statutory authority where this is the clear intention of the legislation (*Dimbleby & Sons Ltd v National Union of Journalists* [1984] 1 WLR 427).

See further ¶21-050 to ¶21-100.

¶21-050   'Lifting the veil' under the Companies Act

Some examples in which shareholders and their company are identified as one and the same under the Companies Act are as follows:

(1) Membership of a company falls below two persons for a continuous period of six months, after which time the company continues to carry on business (CA 1985, s. 24). The remaining shareholder becomes liable for the company's debts, if he knew that membership had so fallen. Section 24 will not apply if the company is a single member private company limited by shares or guarantee.

(2) Presentation of group accounts (CA 1985, s. 227). A parent company must file consolidated accounts, which show the results and financial position of the companies within the group, together with those of its subsidiary undertakings.

¶21-100   'Lifting the veil' by the courts

The courts have lifted the corporate veil in rare circumstances, usually in order to prevent the company being used as a cover for fraudulent acts of its owners.

There is also authority for the view that the separate legal existence of companies will be disregarded when companies are in a 'group' relationship, as defined under s. 736 of the *Companies Act* 1985. Disregarding the separate legal personality in a group of companies may reflect the realities of a situation more closely than a strict application of the 'corporate personality' principle. However later cases have cast doubt on the validity of the view that the courts will merge the identities of companies within a group in the absence of fraud. The following cases of *Gilford Motor Co Ltd v Horne* and *Re FG (Films) Ltd* illustrate the principles of lifting the corporate veil in cases of fraud.

Case example (1)

Horne was managing director of Gilford Motor Company. He left the company and commenced business in direct competition with it. This was contrary to a restraint of trade clause in his contract with the company. An attempt was made to avoid the clause by incorporation of a company, through which Horne conducted his business. The Gilford Motor Company sought an injunction to restrain breach of the covenant by both Horne and his company. Lord Hanworth MR granted the injunction and stated (at p. 956): 'I am quite satisfied that this company was formed as a device, a stratagem, in order to mask the effective carrying on of a business of Mr E B Horne. The purpose of it was to try to enable him, under what is a cloak or a sham, to engage in . . . a business in respect of which he had a fear that the plaintiffs might intervene and object.' *Gilford Motor Co Ltd v Horne* [1933] Ch 935.

Case example (2)

The import of foreign films was restricted by means of a licensing system. This entailed British films being registered as such with the Board of Trade. An American company incorporated a UK company, which was controlled by the American company's President. The UK company had no place of business or staff in the UK, but contrived to make an expensive film, which was financed by the US company. The Board of Trade refused to register the film as British. The refusal was upheld by the court. The reality of the situation was explained by Vaisey J as follows (at p. 486): 'It seems to me to be contrary, not only to all sense and reason, but to the proved and admitted facts of the case, to say or to believe that this insignificant company undertook in any real sense of that word the arrangements for the making of this film. I think that its participation in any such undertaking was so small as to be practically negligible, and that they acted, in so far as they acted at all in the matter, merely as the nominee of and agent for an American company . . .' *Re FG (Films) Ltd* [1953] 1 WLR 483.

It is to be noted that a finding of agency was made in the latter case, which enabled the judge to identify the shareholders with the company. For a principal is always accountable for acts of an agent which are undertaken with the actual or implied authority of that principal. A company acting as agent for its shareholders

¶21-100

is one method of effectively 'lifting the veil', but the agency relationship would have to be proved on the facts. If this were not possible, the identification of the shareholders with the company would have to be justified on other grounds. In practice, these are limited to cases of fraud.

Groups of companies

The *DHN Food Distributors* case is an example of the courts 'lifting the corporate veil' in order to treat a group of companies as one entity. Later cases have thrown doubt upon the validity of this application of the rule.

> **Case example (3)**
> DHN ran a business from premises owned by a subsidiary company. The premises were compulsorily acquired by the Tower Hamlets Council in 1970, and DHN thus ceased to trade. Compensation for disturbance of business was available to DHN, if it could be shown that this company had an interest in the land greater than that of a licensee. The Court of Appeal treated the group of companies as a single economic unit, and ordered that compensation should be paid. The position was summarised by Shaw LJ as follows (at pp. 867–868): 'If the strict legal differentiation between the two entities of parent and subsidiary must, even on the special facts of this case, be observed, the common factors in their identities must at the lowest demonstrate that the occupation of DHN would and could never be determined without the consent of DHN itself. If it was a licence at will, it was at the will of the licensee, DHN, that the licence subsisted . . . The President of the Lands Tribunal took a strict legalistic view of the respective positions of the companies concerned. It appears to me that it was too strict in its application to the facts of this case, which are, as I have said, of a very special character, for it ignored the realities of the respective roles which the companies filled.' *DHN Food Distributors Ltd v Tower Hamlets London Borough Council* [1976] 1 WLR 852.

Unification of the separate legal identities of group companies was later refused in *Woolfson v Strathclyde Regional Council* despite the fact that the circumstances were very similar to those in the *DHN* case.

> **Case example (4)**
> A company, C Ltd, occupied five premises and used them for its business. C Ltd was owned by Woolfson and his wife. Two of the sites which C Ltd occupied were owned by S Ltd, a company in which Woolfson owned two-thirds of the shares and his wife owned one-third. The other three sites were owned by Woolfson himself. A claim for compensation was entered when a compulsory purchase order was made on the properties. Woolfson sought to have C Ltd and S Ltd treated as a single entity embodied in himself. His argument was that the court should set aside the legalistic view that he, C Ltd and S Ltd were separate legal persons, and treat him as both the owner and occupier of the premises.
>
> His claim was turned down by the House of Lords. There were no grounds for treating the company structure as a façade. The facts of the DHN case were distinguished by Lord Keith, because the company which owned the land in the latter case was wholly owned by the company which carried on the business

> therein. However Lord Keith also expressed doubt (at p. 96) as to whether [in the
> DHN case] the 'Court of Appeal properly applied the principle that it is
> appropriate to pierce the corporate veil only where special circumstances exist
> indicating that is a mere façade concealing the true facts.' *Woolfson v Strathclyde*
> *Regional Council* 1978 SC (HL) 90.

The latter cases illustrate the unpredictability of just when the courts are
prepared to lift the veil of incorporation. In one decision on the subject, the Court
of Appeal was prepared to lift the veil 'if it is necessary to achieve justice
irrespective of the legal efficacy of the corporate structure under consideration' (*Re
a Company* (1985) 1 BCC 99,421). The Court of Appeal has disapproved the
concept of lifting the veil to do justice in the circumstances of the case in two
decisions (*Adams v Cape Industries plc* [1990] BCC 786 and *Ord v Belhaven Pubs
Ltd* [1998] BCC 607). Further uncertainty in this area may arise due to the new
definitions of 'subsdiary' and 'subsidiary undertaking' introduced by the
Companies Act 1989 (see ¶20-575, ¶70-100). This places much more emphasis on
control of a subsidiary company by its holding company, and therefore it could be
argued that a subsidiary has a closer relationship with its holding company. In
addition, the EU ninth company law directive may, in due course, give rise to UK
legislation dealing with the domination of a company by an undertaking, whether
de facto or by a 'control contract'; and this is foreshadowed in the definition of
'subsidiary undertaking' in the 1989 Act (see ¶70-100).

INCORPORATION

¶22-000 Obtaining a certificate of incorporation

A company commences its existence on the day that its certificate of incorporation is issued by the registrar of companies. A certificate will be issued after the procedure under s. 10 of the *Companies Act* 1985 has been completed. The steps which must be taken are the submission of the company's constitutional documents (the articles of association and the memorandum of association) to the registrar of companies, with the statutory registration fee (currently £20) and the following forms:

(1) *Companies Form 10* discloses the proposed address of the company's registered office, and the names, former names, addresses, date of birth, business occupations, nationalities and other directorships of the directors. The name, former name and address of the company secretary must also be disclosed. Each director and the company secretary are required to sign the form. The form is a consent to act in the capacity specified in it.

(2) *Companies Form 12* contains a statutory declaration by a director or company secretary named in Form 10, or by a solicitor engaged in the formation of the company, that all the requirements of the Companies Act in respect of the newly incorporated company have been met.

The documents and registration fee must be sent to the registrar of companies. The appropriate registrar is in Cardiff if the registered office of the company is to be in England or Wales, and Edinburgh if the registered office of the company is to be in Scotland.

The registrar will examine the documents which have been submitted. If they are in order, a number will be allocated to the company and a certificate of incorporation issued. The effect of registration is set out in s. 13 of the *Companies*

Act 1985, so that, from the date of incorporation mentioned in the certificate, the subscribers of the memorandum are a body corporate, by the name contained in the memorandum. The company is then capable of 'exercising all the functions of an incorporated company, but with such liability on the part of its members to contribute to its assets in the event of its being wound up as is provided by this Act'. In all cases other than those for which statute 'lifts the corporate veil' (see ¶21-000, ¶21-050) and certain penal provisions (such as fraudulent or wrongful trading: see ¶41-800), the members' liability will be restricted to the sum for which they agree to subscribe shares or which they undertake to pay on the company's winding up. A certificate of incorporation is conclusive (i.e. legally indisputable) evidence of the following facts (CA 1985, s. 13(7)):

(1) that the requirements of the Act in respect of registration and of matters precedent and incidental to it have been complied with, and that the association is a company authorised to be registered, and is duly registered, under the Act; and

(2) that, if the certificate contains a statement that the company is a public company, then the company is such a company.

¶22-100   'Off-the-shelf' companies

It is possible to shortcut the rather cumbersome procedure of company formation by the purchase of an 'off-the-shelf' company from company formation agents. The procedure in such a case is as follows.

The formation agents will have incorporated the company with two of themselves as first shareholders and as the first-named director and secretary. A change of name and of accounting reference date will usually be required. The proposed directors and company secretary return a form to the formation agents in which they accept their office (Form 288(a)). The agents then deal with the change of registered office, and also (if necessary) the change of name and of accounting reference date. The appointment of the new directors and company secretary are notified to the company registrar, and the agents resign as first-named director and company secretary (Form 288(b)). The purchasers are sent a share transfer form, by which the agents pass on their shares to the purchaser. The new owners will be sent a package which contains the articles of association and memorandum of association, and all the various registers the company is required to maintain. The company secretary will record the new owners of the shares in the register of shareholders, and issue the share certificates. Details of directors and the company secretary will also have to be entered into the appropriate register. If more shares are to be subscribed, the company secretary will have to submit a Form 88(2) to the registrar of companies. The memorandum of association provided by the formation agents will (hopefully!) be of a type appropriate for the business it is intended the company should conduct.

¶22-100

Audit exemptions

Originally, off-the-shelf companies failed to benefit from various audit exemptions for small turnover companies because they were also classified as subsidiary undertakings. This problem was remedied by the *Companies Act 1985 (Miscellaneous Accounting Amendments) Regulations* 1996 (SI 1996/189). Now, a company which is otherwise disqualified from claiming an audit exemption pursuant to s. 249A of the *Companies Act* 1985 because it is a subsidiary for any period during the financial year can do so provided that it is dormant for that period.

¶22-200 Incorporating an existing business

If it is intended to incorporate an existing business, it will be necessary to draw up a contract of sale between the new company and the proprietors of the business. It is likely that exemption from capital gains tax will be sought for disposal of assets to the company in exchange for shares (under the *Taxation of Chargeable Gains Act* 1992, s. 162). To secure this exemption, all the assets other than cash must be transferred to the new company in exchange for shares. Form 88(2) and the agreement for transfer must be submitted to the registrar of companies.

The transfer of a business to a company is a very significant step to take. There are advantages and disadvantages in incorporation. Most of the disadvantages flow from the formalities required of companies by the Companies Act, particularly in regard to disclosure. A comparative list is set out below.

Corporate	*Non-corporate*
Annual accounts must be filed	No disclosure requirements
Annual return must be filed	No annual return requirement
Annual registration fee must be paid	No annual registration fee
Books and records must be maintained in accordance with the Companies Act	No legal requirements as to books and records
Audited accounts must be laid before the shareholders in general meeting	No audit requirement
Liability may be limited	Liability may not be limited
Company can own property	Proprietors will own all business property
Capital structure is divided into shares which can be disposed of individually	Business structure more difficult to divide
Constraints on transactions with directors imposed by Companies Act	Proprietors may deal with business
Companies have perpetual succession	No perpetual succession
No limit on number of members	Most partnerships are restricted to 20 members
Formal dissolution required	Can be dissolved informally

¶22-300 Commencement of business

A private company can begin to trade from the first day of its existence, i.e. the date of registration, as disclosed on the certificate of incorporation. However a public company (see ¶20-150) must obtain a trading certificate in addition to a certificate of incorporation before it can commence business or exercise any borrowing powers (CA 1985, s. 117(1)). To obtain a trading certificate, the directors must make a statutory declaration which states (CA 1985, s. 117(3)):

(1) that the nominal amount of the company's allotted share capital is not less than the minimum prescribed by statute (currently £50,000 under s. 118);

(2) the amount of the allotted share capital actually paid up at the time of the application for the certificate (which must be at least £12,500);

(3) the amount of the company's preliminary expenses (or an estimate of them) and the identity of the persons by whom such expenses have been paid or are payable; and

(4) the amount paid or benefits provided (or intended to be paid or provided) to any promoter of the company, and the consideration given for the payment or the benefit.

The declaration is sent to the registrar of companies. The registrar will issue a trading certificate, if he is satisfied that the nominal amount of the company's issued share capital is not less than the authorised minimum.

When completing application form 117 for a trading certificate, only the share capital actually paid up at the time of the application can be included. A company share is deemed paid up (as to its nominal amount and any premium on it) in cash if the consideration is one of the following: cash, a cheque which the directors have no reason to believe will not be honoured, a discharge of a liquidated sum owed by the company or an undertaking to pay cash at a future date (CA 1985, s. 738(2)). According to Companies House, any such undertakings to pay cash in the future cannot be included in the total amount of allotted share capital when filing the application because the amounts have not yet 'been paid up at the time of the application'. A public company cannot allot a share except when it is paid up to at least one-quarter of its nominal amount and the whole of any premium (CA 1985, s. 101).

If a company has not been issued with a trading certificate within one year of the date of its original incorporation, a petition can be brought by an interested party to wind up the company (*Insolvency Act* 1986 (IA 1986), s. 122(1)(b)). In any event, a private company which re-registers as a public company does not require a trading certificate.

If a company starts business or borrows money before the certificate is issued, both the company and the officer responsible are liable to a fine (CA 1985, s. 117(7)). The transaction itself is not avoided. However the directors of the company can be held jointly and severally liable to indemnify other parties to the transaction for loss or damage they may suffer should the company fail to comply with its contractual obligations.

¶22-400   Pre-incorporation contracts

A company's existence begins on the date of the issue of the certificate of incorporation by the registrar of companies (see ¶22-000). It may be necessary to enter into contracts on the company's behalf prior to its incorporation, for example, to effect preliminary agreements for the purchase of a business or property. Further, persons responsible for the formation of the company may wish to recover expenses incurred in the course of doing so.

A company cannot be bound by a contract made on its behalf prior to incorporation as it is not then in existence. It is provided by s. 36C of the *Companies Act* 1985 that, where a contract purports to be made by a company, or by a person acting as agent for a company, at a time when the company has not been formed, the person purporting so to act is to be personally liable on the contract. The agent can clearly avoid personal liability, as application of the provision is expressly 'subject to any agreement to the contrary'. A company cannot be bound by a pre-incorporation contract, or enforce one. However the agent should be able to secure performance of the pre-incorporation contract on the company's behalf if, for example, he is a director of the company when formed.

Persons who wish to secure contractual rights for a company prior to its incorporation may do so without potentially incurring personal liability. This is achieved by acting as trustee for the company prior to its formation. The company later enters into a new contract in similar terms. However the original contract would include a term to the effect that liability of the trustee under the original contract determines once the company has itself entered into an agreement, and that, if the company does not enter into the subsequent agreement within a specified time, either party can rescind it.

Novation, etc.

If an agreement is drawn up informally, the agent should ensure that all personal liability thereunder is disclaimed. However it may be possible, on the facts of a particular case, to show that the company has entered into a new contract if it undertakes activities as if bound by the pre-incorporation contract. It is necessary to show that a new contract has been agreed, to which the company has joined itself as a party. This process is known as 'novation'.

If such a problem should arise, it may be instructive to compare the facts and judgments of two cases. In *Re Northumberland Avenue Hotel Co Ltd* (1886) 33 ChD 16 the court did not find evidence of a new contract. The activities undertaken in the course of fulfilling obligations under the first contract were attributable to the mistaken belief of the directors that the pre-incorporation contract was binding on the company. However sufficient evidence of a new contract was available in *Howard v Patent Ivory Manufacturing Co* (1888) 38 ChD 156, in which the company agreed to vary the terms of a contract made prior to incorporation. Consenting to the variations was sufficient evidence of an intention to be bound.

Provisional contracts

By contrast, provisional contracts are agreements entered into by public companies after the issue of a certificate of incorporation but before the grant of a trading certificate. Despite s. 117(1) of the *Companies Act* 1985 (see ¶22-300), provisional contracts will still be binding on companies even if a trading certificate is never granted. This is derived from s. 117(8) of the *Companies Act* 1985 which states that nothing in that section affects the validity of transactions entered into. If a public company enters into a provisional contract, a director may incur personal liability if the company fails to meet its obligations within 21 days of being asked to do so.

¶22-500   Re-registration of a private company as a public company

Incorporation under the Companies Act can be as a private or public company (see ¶20-150, ¶20-200). A private company is any company that is not a public company. It is possible for a private company to convert its status so as to become a public company. To achieve this, the company must re-register under the procedure set out in s. 43 of the *Companies Act* 1985. The re-registration must be passed by a special resolution of the shareholders (which requires a 75 per cent majority of the shares voted), and an application for re-registration (Form 43(3)) delivered to the registrar of companies. The special resolution must alter:

(1) the company's memorandum so that it states that the company is a public company; and

(2) the memorandum and articles to a form suitable for a public company.

Documents to be delivered with application

The following documents must be sent to the registrar of companies along with the application form for re-registration:

(1) a copy of the revised memorandum and articles;

(2) an unqualified, audited balance sheet of the company, prepared to a date not more than seven months before the application;

(3) a statement by the company's auditors that, in their opinion, the balance sheet shows the company has net assets which are not worth less than the called-up share capital and undistributable reserves;

(4) a copy of any report prepared on the value of non-cash assets accepted by the company in exchange for shares between the last balance sheet date and the date the special resolution was passed;

(5) a statutory declaration by a director or secretary of the company which states that:

(a) the special resolution has been passed;

(b) the company's net asset value has not fallen below the amount of the called-up share capital and non-distributable reserves, between the balance sheet date and the date of the application for re-registration;

(c) the minimum authorised and paid up share capital requirements for public companies are satisfied;

(d) any undertaking to provide services to the company, given as consideration for an issue of shares, has been satisfied;

(e) any undertaking to transfer non-cash assets to the company in exchange for shares has been satisfied, or that there is a binding contract for satisfaction of the undertaking within five years of the resolution to change status; and

(f) non-cash assets given for shares between the balance sheet date and the date of the resolution have been valued in accordance with s. 44 of the *Companies Act* 1985.

Certificate of re-registration

Once the registrar of companies is satisfied with the application, a certificate of incorporation will be issued, which states that the company is a public company (CA 1985, s. 47). The certificate is conclusive evidence that the requirements of the Companies Act in respect of re-registration have been satisfied.

¶22-600 Conversion from a public company to a private company

Re-registration of a public company as a private company is provided for under s. 53 of the *Companies Act* 1985. The company must pass a special resolution that the re-registration should be undertaken, and deliver an application for re-registration to the registrar of companies (Form 53). The application must be accompanied by copies of the memorandum of association and articles of association, as altered by the resolution.

Objections to a re-registration

It is possible for minority shareholders who oppose a re-registration from public to private to apply to the court for cancellation of the special resolution. The application must be made within 28 days of the resolution being passed (CA 1985, s. 54). The company cannot re-register within 28 days of the resolution being passed, so shareholders have an opportunity to object. Any objection which is made must be notified to the registrar of companies. The application to the court must be supported by either at least 50 shareholders, or shareholders with five per cent of the issued capital of any class of share, or at least five per cent of the members if the company is not limited by shares. However a shareholder who originally supported the resolution cannot later be numbered amongst the dissentients. The court will consider the application for re-registration. The application will either be cancelled or confirmed by the court. Terms may be imposed with the order for confirmation or cancellation. The Act specifically provides that the court may make an order for the shares of the minority to be purchased. This can be accompanied by an order for a reduction of capital so the shares can be repurchased from the minority by the company.

A copy of the court's order must be sent by the company seeking re-registration to the registrar of companies within 15 days of the order having been made. The company cannot subsequently alter any terms of its memorandum or articles which were amended pursuant to the court order without a further application to the court.

COMPANY NAMES

¶22-700   General

A company must be incorporated with a name. This is disclosed in the memorandum of association (see ¶30-000). Certain names are unacceptable and will not be registered by the registrar of companies (see ¶22-750). Others will be accepted only with the consent of the Secretary of State (see ¶22-800). The rules which govern selection of a company name are set out in a series of Companies House Guidance Notes (CHN 2, 3, 4 and 11) published by the Companies Registration Office.

¶22-750   Unacceptable names

Registration of certain names is prohibited by the *Companies Act* 1985 as follows.

(1) *Name already registered.* A register of company names is maintained at the Companies Registration Office. A company will not be permitted to use a name which is already on the register (s. 26(1)). Appendix D to CHN2 ('Choosing a company name') explains factors which will be taken into account to establish whether names are too similar.

(2) *Use of particular words.* A name which incorporates the words 'limited', 'unlimited', or 'public limited' or abbreviations thereof, other than at the end of the name, will not be accepted by the registrar for registration.

(3) *Use of name a criminal offence.* The unauthorised use of particular words or expressions as part of a name (for example 'Architect') will constitute a

¶22-700

criminal offence. Some of these words are set out in Appendix C of CHN2 together with the names and addresses of the relevant bodies who may confirm whether a word does not contravene the regulation involved. Use of such words will result in a refusal of registration.

(4) *Use of name offensive.* If, in the opinion of the Secretary of State, use of a particular name would be offensive, registration will be refused.

¶22-800 Names needing approval of Secretary of State

Certain names may not be registered without the approval of the Secretary of State for Trade and Industry:

(1) If the name is likely to give the impression that the company is connected with the government or a local authority, registration will be refused unless the Secretary of State's permission is obtained. Words which are likely to imply such a connection are set out in Appendix A of CHN2.

(2) Any word specified in the *Company and Business Names Regulations* 1981 (SI 1981/1685) (as amended by SI 1982/1653, SI 1992/1196, and SI 1995/3022) made pursuant to s. 29 of the *Companies Act* 1985 cannot be used as a company name until prior approval has been obtained from the appropriate Secretary of State.

(3) If the name includes a word set out in either Appendix A or Appendix B of CHN2, the Secretary of State's approval must be obtained before the name will be registered.

¶22-850 Misleading names

The Secretary of State may order a company to change its name if the name gives such a misleading view of the nature of the company's activities that it is likely to cause harm to the public (CA 1985, s. 32).

¶22-900 Name clashes

It is possible that a name is accepted for registration by the registrar which is the same as, or similar to, that of another company. In such circumstances, the Secretary of State can call for the company to change its name within 12 months of the registration (CA 1985, s. 28(2)). If the company provided misleading information in order to obtain the registration, the Secretary of State has five years from the date of registration in which to direct a change of name.

A company which is aggrieved at having its name copied, but which cannot persuade the Secretary of State to order a change, may seek a court order to restrain the new company using the name. This is called a 'passing off' action. It is intended to prevent a company from 'passing off' its goods or services as those of another company. It is necessary to show a real probability of deception from the use of the name, and damage to the originator of the name from its exploitation by the new company.

¶22-950   Change of name

The procedure for change of a company name is set out in s. 28 of the *Companies Act* 1985. A special resolution must be passed, which is sent to the registrar of companies within 15 days. A copy of the memorandum, as revised by the change of name, must accompany the resolution. The rules as to refusal of registration, order of a name change and direction for abandonment of a misleading name by the Secretary of State (see ¶22-700ff.) apply equally to the new name. The change of name is effective as from the date of issue of the altered certificate of incorporation by the registrar of companies. Where a company in the process of changing its name contracts in its new name before the date of issue of the altered certificate, this will not constitute a pre-incorporation contract (see ¶22-400) (*Oshkosh B'Gosh Inc v Dan Marbel Inc Ltd* (1988) 4 BCC 795).

¶23-000   Business names

A company can trade under a different name to that under which it is incorporated. The *Business Names Act* 1985 regulates the conduct of business under a name which differs from that of the owners. A company cannot use any of the words or expressions listed in the Companies and Business Names Regulations (made pursuant to s. 3 of the *Business Names Act* 1985, and which are currently identical to the regulations made under s. 29 of the *Companies Act* 1985: see ¶22-800), without the consent of the Secretary of State. Further, the registered name of the company which owns the business must be displayed at all premises to which the public have access, and also on all business letters, invoices, receipts and written demands. Contravention of these rules exposes the company to the possibility of a fine.

The company will not be allowed to enforce contractual rights if the other contracting party can show either that he has suffered loss as a consequence of the company's failure to comply with the statutory rules, or that he was unable to enforce rights against the company because of the failure to observe these rules.

¶23-050   Disclosure of a company name

A company must paint and affix its name outside each of its offices or places of business (CA 1985, s. 348), and disclose its name in business letters, notices and official publications, bills of exchange and promissory notes, invoices, receipts and letters of credit (CA 1985, s. 349). Failure to comply with these rules can give rise to a fine on the company and its officers.

A company officer who signs on behalf of the company or authorises a bill of exchange or promissory note or endorsement, cheque or order for money or goods on which the company's name is not mentioned as required above, is liable to a fine, and also may be made personally liable to the holder of the document (CA 1985, s. 349(4)).This applies where the word 'limited' is omitted (*Lindholst & Co A/S v Fowler* (1988) 4 BCC 776; *Blum v OCP Repartition SA* (1988) 4 BCC 771). Note that where a director signs a company cheque (on which its name is printed) he is not personally liable on it (*Bondina Ltd v Rollaway Shower Blinds Ltd* [1986] 1 WLR 517; (1985) 1 BCC 99,590). When a director of a company signs a cheque on which the company name is incorrectly printed, difficulties may arise. This was clearly illustrated in *Jenice Ltd v Dan*.

> **Case example**
> The defendant director of a company signed a number of cheques in the company's name. The cheques had printed on them 'Primkeen Ltd' rather than 'Primekeen Ltd'. The judge held that the defendant would not be personally liable for the cheques as this would defy both common sense and the purpose of the Act. An omission of a single letter in a word was distinguishable from the omission of a whole word, the transposition of words, or the unacceptable abbreviation of words. *Jenice Ltd v Dan* [1994] BCC 43.

¶23-150   The registered office

A company must have a registered office to which all communications and notices can be addressed (CA 1985, s. 287). A change of address must be notified to the registrar of companies within 14 days. A notice is then published in the *London Gazette*. However until this notice appears, documents served at the previous address are validly served unless the person seeking to deliver the document knew of the change (CA 1985, s. 42). The memorandum of association must disclose whether the registered office is situated in England, Wales or Scotland. A company will be domiciled in the country in which the registered office is situated. The address of the registered office will be disclosed in each annual return of a company, and on all business letters and order forms (CA 1985, s. 351). The registered office of a company is important because documents are served on the company by delivery to the registered office, and because the statutory registers are normally maintained there for inspection by outsiders and members.

A company may change the situation of its registered office from time to time by giving notice in the prescribed form to the registrar (CA 1985, s. 287). Although the change takes effect upon the notice being registered by the registrar, documents may be validly served at its previous registered office for up to 14 days after the date of registration of the change. Further, a company may maintain its registers at the old registered office or cite the old address in correspondence for the same period after notice has been given. Difficulty had arisen under the predecessor legislation when a company had unavoidably ceased to maintain its registered office before it was practicable to give formal notice of the change. It is now stated that a company will fulfil its statutory obligations if it resumes performance of its duties at the new registered office as soon as possible and gives notice to the registrar of the new office's situation within 14 days of moving (CA 1985, s. 287(6)).

¶23-250   Company seal and contracts

A company may now elect whether to have a common seal (CA 1985, s. 36A); if it does, then its name must be engraved in legible characters thereon (s. 350), and its articles of association will govern the procedure for affixing it. Whether or not a company has a common seal:

(1) a contract required to be in writing will be valid if signed on behalf of a company by a person having apparent or actual authority;

(2) a contract which may be concluded orally will bind a company if the person making it has apparent or actual authority;

(3) a document signed by a director and the secretary (or by two directors), and expressed to be executed by a company, will have effect as if executed under seal;

(4) such a document which indicates that it is to have effect upon delivery as a deed will have such effect and, unless a contrary intention is proved, delivery is presumed upon execution; and

(5) in favour of a purchaser for value in good faith, deeming provisions operate in respect of (3) and (4) above.

¶23-350   Obligations of audit, accounts and maintenance of registers and of accounting records

Significant administrative burdens are placed on company directors. Accounting records must be kept, which are sufficient to show and explain the company's transactions and financial position (CA 1985, s. 222). The legislation sets out more detailed requirements, which are considered at ¶70-000ff. The directors must present an audited profit and loss account and balance sheet in respect of each accounting reference period to the members in general meeting, and also group accounts where appropriate. The largest companies (including all public companies) must file copies of their accounts at Companies House, where they are available for public inspection. Small and medium-sized companies and groups have a less onerous burden of public disclosure placed upon them (CA 1985, s. 246–249).

Registers, etc. open to inspection

The registers and other documents which must be maintained by the company officers and kept for inspection at the registered office are as follows:

- register of members (CA 1985, s. 352), disclosing the shareholdings and the class to which each member belongs;

- register of directors and company secretaries (CA 1985, s. 288);

- register of directors' interests in shares and debentures of the company or of associated companies (CA 1985, s. 325);

¶23-250

- register of charges and copies of instruments which create charges (CA 1985, s. 407 and 408);
- minute books of general meetings (CA 1985, s. 383);
- copies of directors' service contracts (CA 1985, s. 318);
- register of 'substantial interests' in any class of voting shares in a public company (CA 1985, s. 211).

The register of members can be kept at the place where it is made up, if this is not the company's registered office. In such a case, the register of directors' interests, the register of substantial interests and copies of directors' service contracts may be kept at the same place.

¶23-450   The annual return

Every company must make a return to the registrar of companies at least once each year, which contains the following details (CA 1985, s. 363):

- the address of the company's registered office;
- the company's principal business activities;
- the address where the register of members and the register of debenture holders are kept, if this is not the registered office;
- names and addresses of the directors and company secretary;
- directors' particulars;
- a statement that the company has dispensed with the obligation to lay accounts/reports under s. 252 of the *Companies Act* 1985 or the holding of AGMs under s. 366A, if it has in fact done so;
- the total number of issued shares and their aggregate nominal amount;
- the nature of each class of share and the number/aggregate nominal amount of issued shares of each class as at the date of the return;
- the names and addresses of all members, and of all members that ceased to be so since the last return; and
- the number of shares held and transferred by each member.

A company must submit successive annual returns made up to, although not later than, the date which is from time to time the company's 'return date'.

The 'return date' is either:

- the anniversary of the company's incorporation; or
- if the company's last properly delivered return was made up to a different date, then the anniversary of that date.

Where a company maintains an overseas branch of its share register, the details contained in this register need not be provided in annual returns in so far as such details are not received at the company's registered office in time. However details of entries in overseas branch registers which arrive at the registered office too late for inclusion in any annual return must be included in the next annual return.

Each return must be signed by a director or the secretary of the company and delivered to the registrar of companies within 28 days after the date to which it is made up. Failure to deliver a properly drawn up annual return before the end of the 28-day period exposes the company and every officer in default to a maximum fine of £5,000, with a further potential fine of £500 for each day the return is overdue.

¶23-550   Official notification of events affecting a company's status

Section 711 of the *Companies Act* 1985 obliges the registrar to publish the issue or receipt by him of any document listed in that section. For example, the appointment of new directors, a change in the location of the registered office, or an alteration in the memorandum or articles of association will all be publicised. A company can only rely on the following events if proper and punctual notice was given to the registrar and the third party knew of the change at the relevant time (CA 1985, s. 42):

- a winding-up order being made, or the appointment of a liquidator in a voluntary winding up;
- a change in the memorandum or articles of association;
- a change of director(s); or,
- a change of registered office.

Further, a company will be disentitled from relying on these events where the event in question occurred within 15 days of the official notification date and the third party was unavoidably prevented from knowing about the event at the time.

Exclusion of deemed notice

The effect of registration of events affecting a company's status has altered due to the abolition of the doctrine of deemed notice under s. 711A of the *Companies Act* 1985. A person is not taken to have notice of any matter merely because it was disclosed in any document kept by the registrar of companies. However this does not affect the question of whether a person is affected by notice of any matter by reason of a failure to make such inquiries as ought reasonably to be made. In practice, therefore, third parties dealing with companies remain on inquiry as to registered documents.

REFORM OF COMPANY LAW AND FINANCIAL SERVICES REGULATION

¶23-650 General

There have been major developments in 1997 and 1998 which, when implemented, will have a significant effect on the regulation of financial services, and a potentially enormous effect on the whole structure of company law. These are dealt with below, together with brief comments on corporate governance and other future developments.

¶23-700 Financial services regulation

Within three weeks of the 1997 General Election the new Chancellor of the Exchequer, Gordon Brown, announced a major shake-up of financial services regulation. The self-regulatory scheme under the *Financial Services Act* 1986 was perceived as plagued with problems from its introduction and several high-profile financial scandals, including pensions mis-selling by High Street insurance companies which were then perceived to have dragged their feet in making forced reparations, resulted in a loss of confidence by the public.

The essence of the reforms involves a move away from self-regulation by sector regulators to regulation of the whole industry by a single regulator, akin to the position in the US with its Securities and Exchange Commission. Filling this role is the lead regulator, the Securities and Investments Board (SIB), renamed the Financial Services Authority (FSA) in October 1997. The FSA will have far wider regulatory powers than the SIB for, in addition to regulating financial services as understood under the 1986 Act, it will also be responsible for regulating banks, insurance companies, building societies, friendly societies, credit unions and others. The transfer of banking supervision (from the Bank of England) occurred on 1 June 1998 under the *Bank of England Act* 1998. The Financial Services and Markets Bill was published on 17 June 1999; when enacted, it is intended to replace the Financial Services Act in 2000.

The FSA is drafting (as at early 1999) a gargantuan handbook, to replace the plethora of rulebooks from the existing regulatory bodies, providing the detail for its industry-wide regulation to be grafted onto the framework to be supplied by the reforming legislation. The formation of the advisory group on the handbook was announced in December 1998 with members drawn from across the range of sectors to be affected by the proposed legislation.

Continuing the integration of financial services regulation was one of the priorities for the FSA in its budget and plan for 1999/2000, published on

3 February 1999. By that date all the regulatory bodies being subsumed into the FSA were operating under one roof at the new FSA headquarters, with the FSA supplying regulatory and other services under contract to various organisations including the Building Societies Commission and the three self-regulating organisations, IMRO, PIA and the SFA.

¶23-750   Corporate governance and the Hampel Report

High profile financial scandals of the late 1980s and years following (e.g. Polly Peck, Maxwell, Bank of Credit and Commerce International, the latter involving 'fraud on a hitherto unimaginable scale' according to a report by the now Lord Chief Justice), together with media-driven outrage at the massive increases in remuneration paid to some company chief executives (particularly in the recently-privatised public utilities) while the country was in economic recession, led to a series of reports on corporate governance. The Cadbury Committee's *Report on the Financial Aspects of Corporate Governance* (24 May 1995) and *Directors' Remuneration: Report of a Study Group Chaired by Sir Richard Greenbury* (17 July 1995) were subsumed into the Hampel Report, *Committee on Corporate Governance: Final Report*, published on 28 January 1998. The reports primarily relate to governance of listed public companies by their directors and how they are accountable. The emphasis is to have independent non-executive directors providing in-house supervision of the executive directors (the auditors provide external supervision). Importantly, directors' remuneration in relevant companies should be decided upon by a remuneration committee comprising non-executives, hopefully to prevent the obvious conflict of interest of the executives determining their own remuneration packages. The Hampel Committee produced a draft 'Combined Code' of Principles of Good Governance and Code of Best Practice which the London Stock Exchange has consulted upon and amended. This was issued on 25 June 1998 and has been appended to its *Listing Rules*, together with some amendments to the latter, in particular a new rule on disclosure of directors' remuneration (this goes far beyond the disclosure requirements of Sch. 6 to the *Companies Act* 1985). UK companies are required in respect of accounting periods ending on or after 31 December 1998 to disclose in their annual report and accounts how and to what extent they have applied the principles and complied with the detailed provisions of the Combined Code. Companies are encouraged to comment on their corporate governance arrangements with regard to the Combined Code in respect of accounting periods ending before 31 December 1998, although this is not mandatory.

¶23-800   Review of company law

On 4 March 1998 the DTI published a consultative document entitled *Modern Company Law for a Competitive Economy*. This heralded a fundamental review of company law, proclaimed to be the first overview of the whole of 'core' company law (i.e. without financial services and insolvency) since the 'modern' system of companies legislation was introduced in the mid-nineteenth century. The terms of reference for the review, which is being carried out by working groups overseen by a steering group, were to make recommendations having:

(1) considered how core company law can be modernised in order to provide a simple, efficient and cost-effective framework for carrying out business activity which provides the maximum freedom and flexibility while protecting those involved in the enterprise, and is drafted in clear, concise and unambiguous language that can be readily understood by those involved in business;

(2) considered whether company law, partnership law and other legislation together provide an adequate choice of legal vehicle for business at all levels;

(3) considered the proper relationship between company law and non-statutory standards of corporate behaviour; and

(4) reviewed the extent to which foreign companies operating in Great Britain should be regulated under British company law.

One of the important topics for this review will be that of directors' duties, not least in the context of the current shareholder/stakeholder debate. Its importance is not only intrinsic, but also exemplifies what should be one of the cardinal principles of the review, namely that, even where existing company law is perfectly adequate, it must also be made accessible to its consumers. For example, nothing in present company law prevents directors from looking to the long-term sustainable growth in value of their companies as opposed to the short-termism that is sadly too prevalent in British boardrooms; but it is manifest that this analysis is not widely understood. Its wider comprehension must be a key objective for the review. As part of the process of reform of directors' duties, the Law Commission and the Scottish Law Commission in September 1998 issued a joint consultation paper on regulating conflicts of directors' interests and formulating a statement of directors' duties.

The timetable for the review is lengthy. The steering group was launched in June 1998 and published a consultation document, *Modern Company Law for a Competitive Economy – The Strategic Framework*, on 25 February 1999.

¶23-850 Other future developments

The Neill Committee on Standards in Public Life on 28 April 1999 responded to the Department of Trade and Industry (DTI) consultative document on political donations by companies. The DTI issued that consultative document on 25 March 1999 in light of the Neill Committee's report of October 1998 on the funding of political parties. The consultative document adopted some of the Neill recommendations; it focused on a definition of 'political donation', a requirement for prior shareholder consent for such donations by companies and proper disclosure of political donations by companies, and set 3 April 1999 as the deadline for further comments.

Although not strictly a matter of company law as such, companies will also be significantly affected by other pending legislative changes. The incorporation into UK domestic law of the European Convention on Human Rights will significantly impinge upon the regulation of financial services and indeed more generally. The *Human Rights Act* 1998, enacted on 9 November 1998, will give direct access in the UK courts to rights and freedoms guaranteed under the Convention. A new Human Rights Task Force has been set up under the chairmanship of Lord Williams of Mostyn, the Home Office Minister, to help the government in the preparations for implementation. With regard to company law the Act may promote further litigation: art. 6(1) of the Convention (whereby every person is entitled to a fair and public hearing) has been invoked in a couple of cases (see ¶41-700). Full implementation of the Act is unlikely before 2000.

In addition, legislation pending (as at early 1999) on freedom of information will be of relevance to companies which, to judge from the US experience, will be major users of the legislation as both a sword and a shield.

CONSTITUTION AND ADMINISTRATION

Table of Contents

continued over

40

THE MEMORANDUM OF ASSOCIATION

¶30-000　General

A company's memorandum of association and articles of association are among the documents which must be submitted to the registrar of companies before a certificate of incorporation can be obtained (see ¶22-000). The memorandum defines a company's purpose whilst the articles regulate the way in which the company conducts its internal affairs.

The legal nature and effect of these constitutional documents is set out in s. 14 of the *Companies Act* 1985: the documents are to have effect as if signed and sealed by each member and as if they contained covenants on the part of each member to observe all their provisions (see further ¶30-250). The memorandum and articles are signed by each of the first subscribers of shares. The signature must be witnessed. Each subscriber of the memorandum must take at least one share in the company. The number of shares he takes will be entered alongside his name in the memorandum. At least two persons must subscribe to the memorandum unless the company is to be a single member private company limited by shares or guarantee (CA 1985, s. 1).

¶30-050　Requirements with respect to the memorandum

The details which the memorandum of association is to contain are as follows (CA 1985, s. 2):

(1) the company name (the rules governing choice of company name are set out at ¶22-700ff.);

(2) if the company is a public company, a statement to that effect;

(3) the registered office: whether the registered office is situated in England, Wales or Scotland (the registered office of a company is considered at ¶23-150);

(4) the objects of the company: this clause defines the capacity of the company, and acts of the company which are outside such objects are 'ultra vires' and void (the doctrine of ultra vires is considered at ¶30-650ff.);

(5) if a company is registered with limited liability: a statement that the liability of members is limited;

(6) companies limited by guarantee: the amount of the guarantee; and

(7) limited companies with a share capital: the amount of the authorised share capital with which the company will be registered, and its division into shares of a fixed amount.

The forms of memoranda for various classes of company are set out in the *Companies (Tables A to F) Regulations* 1985 (SI 1985/805). A private company should adopt the format set out in Table B of the regulations, and a public company the format of Table F.

General commercial companies

As part of a general reform of the 'ultra vires' rule, s. 3A of the *Companies Act* 1985 provides that, where a company's memorandum states that its object is to carry on business 'as a general commercial company':

(1) its object is to carry on any trade or business whatsoever; and

(2) it has power to do anything incidental or conducive to the carrying on of any trade or business by it.

The difference between 'objects' and 'powers' is discussed at ¶30-700.

THE ARTICLES OF ASSOCIATION

¶30-150   General

The articles of association govern the day-to-day administration of a company's affairs. A company's articles may be submitted with its memorandum on application to the registrar of companies for incorporation. However, if articles are not registered, s. 8 of the *Companies Act* 1985 provides that the relevant model contained in the *Companies (Tables A to F) Regulations* 1985 (SI 1985/805) is to apply (i.e. Table A, C, D or E). As the articles govern dealings between a company and its shareholders, they are often the focus for disputes. For this purpose, the articles are to be construed as a commercial document, to which a pragmatic interpretation should be applied in order to give business efficacy to the document.

Table A, the model articles for companies limited by shares, is reproduced at ¶31-050.

¶30-250   Effect of the articles

The articles can be regarded as a contract between the shareholders and the company and between the shareholders themselves (see ¶30-000), but several modifications and refinements have to be made to this analogy, for the articles bind the shareholders only in their capacity as members of the company. Thus, a shareholder cannot make the company abide by the articles in order to enforce rights which are not shared by all members. This principle is illustrated by a comparison of two cases. In the *Kent or Romney Marsh Sheepbreeders' Association* case, the petitioner succeeded because the dispute related to an issue in respect of which any shareholder could have complained. However, in the *Beattie* case, a director could not force the company to abide by the articles in order to resolve a dispute which he had with the company in his capacity as director.

Case example (1)
The plaintiff was a member of the defendant company. The company's articles provided that disputes between it and its members should be referred to arbitration. The plaintiff brought an action against the company, because he was dissatisfied with the way in which it was run. The company sought to have the issue referred to arbitration, as provided for by the articles. The arbitration requirement was found to be binding on both the company and the shareholders, so a stay of proceedings was granted. The judgment of Astbury J provided the classic statement, upon which much of the law as to the legal effect of a company's articles now rests (at p. 900): 'first, that no article can constitute a contract between the company and a third person; secondly, that no right merely purporting to be given by an article to a person, whether a member or not, in a capacity other than that of a member, as, for instance, as solicitor, promoter, director, can be enforced against the company; and, thirdly, that articles regulating the rights and obligations of the members generally as such do create rights and obligations between them and the company respectively . . .'

The judge then proceeded to apply these principles to the Association's application (at p. 902): 'In the present case, the plaintiff's action is, in substance, to enforce his rights as a member under the articles against the association. Article 49 is a general article applying to all the members as such, and . . . it would seem reasonable that the plaintiff ought not to be allowed in the absence of any evidence filed by him to proceed with an action to enforce his rights under the articles, seeing that the action is a breach of his obligation under article 49 to submit his disputes with the association to arbitration . . .' *Hickman v Kent or Romney Marsh Sheepbreeders' Association* [1915] 1 Ch 881.

Case example (2)
A company's articles provided for any dispute between it and a member to be referred to arbitration. A disagreement arose between a shareholder-director and the company. The director sought to have the issue referred to arbitration. The court refused his application on the ground that the shareholder was seeking to vindicate the rights of a director through the procedure provided under the articles. In the course of his judgment, Greene MR explained (at p. 722): 'the real matter which is here being litigated is a dispute between the company and the appellant in his capacity as a director, and when the appellant, relying on this clause, seeks to have that dispute referred to arbitration, it is that dispute and none other which he is seeking to have referred, and by seeking to have it referred he is not, in my judgment, seeking to enforce a right which is common to himself and all other members.' *Beattie v E & F Beattie Ltd* [1938] Ch 708.

Some commentators have argued that, had the director sued as a shareholder to have all of the provisions of the articles observed, he would have been successful.

Actions between shareholders

One shareholder can sue another on the basis of the contract created by s. 14 of the *Companies Act* 1985 (see ¶30-000). This can be done without involving the company in the action. An example of such an enforcement is provided by the case of *Rayfield v Hands*.

> **Case example (3)**
> The articles of a company stipulated that shareholders who wished to transfer their shares should inform the directors, who would then purchase the shares at a fair value. The directors, who were also shareholders, refused to accept a transfer from another shareholder, who then brought an action to compel the directors to purchase his shares. His action succeeded. The judge explained that the relationship contemplated by the article was 'between the plaintiff as a member and the defendants, not as directors, but as members.' *Rayfield v Hands* [1960] Ch 1.

Contracts incorporating provisions in the articles

Although a person who is not a shareholder (or who sues in a capacity other than as a shareholder) cannot enforce the contract under the articles, it is possible that a term in the articles could be included (expressly or impliedly) into a contract between the company and that third person. This principle was illustrated by the case of *Re New British Iron Co, ex parte Beckwith*.

> **Case example (4)**
> Directors' remuneration was fixed at one total lump sum of £1,000 under the articles. This was then to be divided between the directors as considered appropriate. Shareholders who had assumed the role of directors, without any express agreement with the company to this effect, then claimed the £1,000. Their claim was upheld. The status of the relevant article was explained by Wright J in the following terms (at p. 326): 'That article is not in itself a contract between the company and the directors; it is only part of the contract constituted by the articles of association between the members of the company inter se. But where on the footing of that article the directors are employed by the company and accept office the terms of [the article] are embodied in and form part of the contract between the company and the directors.' *Re New British Iron Co, ex parte Beckwith* [1898] 1 Ch 324.

Notably, although the articles of association are analogous to a contract, they are unusual in that the freedom of the parties will be curtailed if any of the terms are inconsistent with either the Companies Act (CA 1985, s. 14: see ¶30-000) or the memorandum of association (*Welton v Saffery* [1897] AC 299). Another unusual feature of the 'contract' is that it may be changed subsequent to its conclusion, as there is facility for alteration of the articles under s. 9 of the *Companies Act* 1985: see ¶30-500). Nor can the articles be rectified to reflect the true intention of the parties (*Scott v Frank F Scott (London) Ltd* [1940] Ch 794). If an act complained of as contrary to the articles could be ratified by a majority of shareholders or a general or extraordinary meeting, a complaint by an aggrieved shareholder would

¶30-250

not be upheld, provided that the act is not outside the company's powers as set out in the objects clause of its memorandum of association.

Shareholder's right to damages

Originally, no remedy in damages was available for shareholders when a company was in breach of an agreement under the articles (*Houldsworth v City of Glasgow Bank and Liquidators* (1880) 5 App Cas 317). This, however, has been seen as an inequitable principle, and its effect was amended by the Financial Services Act 1986, s. 152(9) in relation to a company paying compensation under s. 150 of that Act for misleading listing particulars (see ¶54-150ff.). Moreover, s. 111A of the *Companies Act* 1985 now provides that, in general, a person is not debarred from obtaining damages or other compensation from a company by reason only of being a member or having rights to apply for or subscribe its shares.

¶30-350   Shareholders' agreements

The memorandum and articles of association define the purpose of the company and the rights and obligations of its members. Separate shareholders' agreements are permissible in law and are often used to regulate matters such as management participation or dividend policy. A contractual agreement is drawn up and signed by the company's members. These agreements are frequently used in small 'family' companies to restrict share dealings in order to prevent outsiders gaining control, or where an outside investor seeks 'veto rights' on key management issues.

The terms of a shareholders' agreement may be declared invalid for a number of reasons. They may invalidly limit the power of a company to alter its articles (see ¶30-500) or may be either illegal or contrary to public policy. Obligations set out in the articles apply to present and future shareholders. Obligations derived from shareholders' agreements do not because they are personal and so only bind the contracting parties. Alteration of a shareholders' agreement will be subject to the law of contract, and such an agreement will usually prohibit the transfer of shares unless the transferee shall have acceded thereto.

ALTERATION OF THE MEMORANDUM AND ARTICLES

¶30-450   Alteration of the memorandum

A company may not alter the memorandum except in the cases, in the mode and to the extent that the Act expressly provides (CA 1985, s. 2(7)). The legislation closely defines some of the circumstances in which a change can be made.

A change of name can be made by special resolution (see ¶22-950). It is not possible to change the country in which the registered office is situated. A limited liability company may re-register as an unlimited company (CA 1985, s. 49), and vice versa (CA 1985, s. 51). See also s. 16 of the *Companies Act* 1985 at ¶30-500.

Alteration of share capital

It is also possible to alter the capital structure of a company, provided that this power is conferred under the articles (CA 1985, s. 121). This alteration may take the form of an increase in capital, a consolidation or subdivision of shares, or a cancellation of shares. If the capital structure of the company is so altered, the company should give notice to the registrar in the prescribed form within one month (CA 1985, s. 122). However, if the alteration in share capital will reduce the capital base of the company, it will be necessary to go before the court for confirmation (CA 1985, s. 135). Where a company does so attempt to alter its share capital, problems may arise if the shareholders have entered into a contrary agreement. This happened in *Russell v Northern Bank Development Corp Ltd.*

Case example
A shareholders' agreement was executed between the company and four of its shareholders, one of which was the plaintiff. One of the terms specified that no more share capital would be issued unless all the parties to the agreement consented in writing. When the company did call a meeting to discuss whether it should issue further share capital, the plaintiff applied for injunctions to prevent the other parties from voting on this issue. The court concluded that the agreement was unlawful in so far as it attempted to paralyse the company's power to increase its share capital. However, the agreement still bound the four individual shareholders and could be enforced. *Russell v Northern Bank Development Corp Ltd* [1992] 1 WLR 588; [1992] BCC 578.

Procedure for objecting to alteration

A company may alter its objects clause by special resolution (CA 1985, s. 4). However, shareholders of at least 15 per cent of the nominal amount of the company's aggregate issued share capital may apply within 21 days to have the resolution set aside (CA 1985, s. 5). Persons who originally voted for a change will be precluded from so applying. On such an application, the court may reject or confirm the alteration, in whole or in part, and on such terms as it thinks fit. The court may call for the purchase of the dissentients' shares, by either the majority proposing the alteration or the company itself. However, if no objection is forthcoming within the 21-day period from the passing of the resolution, the alteration cannot be challenged. Any changes to the memorandum which result in a change of class rights will be subject to the rules set out at ¶30-550.

Terms which could have been in articles

Any term in a company's memorandum which could have been included in the articles (i.e. any provision which is not within s. 2 of the *Companies Act* 1985: see ¶30-050) can be changed by a special resolution of the company, unless the memorandum provides otherwise (CA 1985, s. 17). The procedure for objecting to such an alteration is the same as for objecting to a change in the company's objects clause pursuant to s. 4 of the *Companies Act* 1985.

Amendments to be registered

Copies of any resolution which alters the memorandum of a company must be sent to the registrar of companies within 15 days of the resolution together with a copy of the altered memorandum (CA 1985, s. 18(2)).

¶30-500   Alteration of the articles

A company may alter its articles by special resolution (CA 1985, s. 9(1)). Such alterations are valid 'as if originally contained in [the articles] and are subject in like manner to alteration by special resolution'. However, it is possible for the shareholders to alter the articles without a meeting or the passing of a resolution, provided unanimous consent is obtained (*Cane v Jones* [1980] 1 WLR 1451). A company can never contract out of the ability to amend its articles in the future (*Bushell v Faith* [1969] 2 Ch 438: see ¶41-950). The power of alteration conferred under s. 9 is thus always available to a company.

Alterations not binding on members

Certain statutory provisions apply to restrict a company's power to alter the articles. A shareholder cannot be forced to accept more shares, or to contribute a greater sum to the company's capital than was originally required of him (unless the shareholder agrees), as a consequence of an alteration of the articles (CA 1985, s. 16).

Case law restrictions

A further restriction on a company's power to alter its articles is that the power should be exercised 'bona fide for the benefit of the company as a whole'. This stipulation prevents the majority shareholders from exercising their vote to alter the articles to the prejudice of a minority. Although a shareholder's vote can be exploited for his own self-interest, a check is placed on the exercise of this power. There is considerable practical difficulty in identification of the correct balance between an amendment of the articles 'bona fide for the benefit of the company as a whole', and an alteration motivated by an individual shareholder's own self-interest. The problem was highlighted by Dixon J in the Australian case of *Peters' American Delicacy Co v Heath* (1939) 31 CLR 45 as follows:

> 'No one supposes that in voting each shareholder is to assume an inhuman altruism and consider only the intangible notion of the benefit of the vague abstraction called . . . "the company as an institution". An investigation of the thought and motives of each shareholder voting would be an impossible proceeding.'

However, in certain circumstances, the change may be so blatantly prejudicial that the court will not hesitate to interfere. Two examples of such cases are *Dafen*

Tinplate Co Ltd v Llanelly Steel Co (1907) Ltd and *Brown v British Abrasive Wheel Co.*

Case example (1)
A company altered its articles to enable a majority of the shareholders to force minority shareholders to sell out at a fair value. The minority successfully opposed the alteration. In the course of his judgment, Peterson J explained (at p. 141): 'The question of fact ... which I have to consider is whether the alteration of the articles which enables the majority of the shareholders to compel any shareholder to transfer his shares, can properly be said to be for the benefit of the company. It may be for the benefit of the majority of the shareholders to acquire the shares of the minority, but how can it be said to be for the benefit of the company that any shareholder, against whom no charge of acting to the detriment of the company can be urged, and who is in every respect a desirable member of the company, and for whose expropriation there is no reason except the will of the majority, should be forced to transfer his shares to the majority or to anyone else? ... In my view it cannot be said that a power on the part of the majority to expropriate any shareholder they may think proper at their will and pleasure is for the benefit of the company as a whole.' *Dafen Tinplate Co Ltd v Llanelly Steel Co (1907) Ltd* [1920] 2 Ch 124.

Case example (2)
The company was in need of further capital. There were two groups of shareholders, one of which was prepared to provide more funds if the other (a minority of two per cent) sold out. The minority refused, and an alteration of the articles was proposed. The revision was to the effect that any member may be forced to sell his shares at a fair value if called to do so by 90 per cent of the other shareholders. The minority successfully opposed the alteration. The revision was not just or equitable or for the benefit of the company as a whole, it was introduced for the benefit of the majority alone, to facilitate expropriation of the minority. *Brown v British Abrasive Wheel Co Ltd* [1919] 1 Ch 290.

Amendments to be registered

Any alteration in the company's articles must be notified to the registrar of companies within 15 days of the amendment.

Use of weighted voting rights

Although a company cannot contract out of the ability to alter its articles, it may be possible to achieve the same effect through the use of weighted voting rights. Such a scheme accords extra votes to a particular shareholder when particular issues are decided upon. The scheme operates by making it impossible to pass a resolution on a particular issue. The principle is illustrated by the case of *Bushell v Faith*.

Case example (3)
A father left the shares in his company to his children in three equal parts. Two of the children then sought to remove the other as director. A resolution was proposed at the general meeting to this effect. However, the company's articles provided

that, on any resolution to remove a director, that director's shares should carry three votes each. Consequently, the attempt to remove the director was frustrated.

The conflict of this scheme with what is now s. 9 of the *Companies Act* 1985 was addressed by Russell LJ in the Court of Appeal (at p. 448A) as follows: 'An article purporting to do this [deprive the company of the power to alter its articles] is ineffective. But a provision as to voting rights which has the effect of making a special resolution incapable of being passed, if a particular shareholder or group of shareholders exercises his or their voting rights against a proposed alteration, is not such a provision. An article in terms providing that no alteration shall be made without the consent of X is contrary to [what is now CA 1985, s. 9] and ineffective. But the provision as to voting rights that I have mentioned is wholly different, and it does not serve to say that it can have the same result.' *Bushell v Faith* [1969] 2 Ch 438; [1970] AC 1099.

¶30-550   Alteration of class rights

Where a proposal is made to alter the rights which attach to a particular class of shares, complicated procedures set out in s. 125 of the *Companies Act* 1985 must be followed. These procedures ultimately depend on the source of the class rights (i.e. whether they arise from the memorandum or articles) and whether the company has declared the variation permissible.

Generally, the alteration can only take effect either with the written support of holders of shares constituting at least 75 per cent of the issued shares of the class, or where an extraordinary resolution in support of the variation is passed at a general meeting of that class.

When employing this 'statutory scheme' for the alteration of class rights, the shareholders must take account of that class's interests. This point was highlighted in *Re Holders Investment Trust Ltd.*

Case example
Members holding cumulative redeemable preference shares brought a petition to confirm a reduction in share capital. A proposal had been made to achieve this by cancelling the preference shares and giving the holders an equivalent amount of unsecured loan stock. The court held that the majority of the preference shareholders who had agreed to the change had voted in their own favour and had not considered the interests of that class. Megarry J sought to consider 'whether the majority were honestly endeavouring to decide and act for the benefit of the class as a whole, rather than with a view to the interests of some of the class and against that of others'. In this case, the majority had failed to meet their obligations. Confirming the petition would cause prejudice to the minority and was therefore refused. *Re Holders Investment Trust* [1971] 1 WLR 583.

Alteration of class rights is discussed in more detail in ¶50-250ff.

ULTRA VIRES

¶30-650   General

The objects clause in a company's memorandum delimits the acts that a company is permitted to undertake. Agreements or transactions entered into by a company for purposes which are beyond the scope of the objects are consequently void and unenforceable. This simple formulation of the ultra vires rule has now been substantially restricted by statute.

For the distinction between a company's objects and powers, and the rules that the courts have developed in order to interpret objects clauses in memoranda of association, see ¶30-700. For the statutory provisions and other remedies that are used to mitigate the effect of the ultra vires rule, see ¶30-750ff.

¶30-700   When is an act ultra vires?

The desire to ensure that the company has the widest possible scope for exploitation of any opportunity which may arise has resulted in registration of memoranda that are extremely lengthy and comprehensive. This practice was not universally approved of and introduced new complications when determining whether acts were ultra vires. In particular, a confusion between objects and powers arose which was succinctly explained by Lord Wrenbury in *Cotman v Brougham* [1918] AC 514 at p. 523:

'There has grown up a pernicious practice of registering memoranda of association which, under the clause relating to objects, contain paragraph after paragraph not specifying or delimiting the proposed trade or purpose, but confusing power with purpose and indicating every class of act which the corporation is to have power to do.'

Despite this, the courts are prepared to accept that acts which are reasonably incidental to the attainment of the express objects will also be within the company's capacity. The ultra vires doctrine ought 'to be reasonably, and not unreasonably, understood and applied, and ... whatever may fairly be regarded as incidental to, or consequential upon, those things which the Legislature has authorised, ought not (unless expressly prohibited) to be held, by judicial construction, to be ultra vires' (*A-G v Great Eastern Railway Co* (1880) 5 App Cas 473, per Lord Selborne LC).

It is not permissible to define a company's objects by reference to the contents of another document. The company must set out fully each of its objects in the memorandum (*Royal Exchange Buildings Glasgow* 1919 SLT 88).

¶30-650

Subjective clauses

The scope of the objects can be drafted to confer upon the company a very large measure of freedom, by inclusion of a 'subjective' clause. This clause provides that the company can 'carry on any other trade or business whatsoever which can, in the opinion of the board of directors, be advantageously carried on by the company in connection with or as ancillary to ... the general business of the company'. If such a clause appeared as the main object of the company, it is unlikely that the registrar would accept the memorandum for registration (but see ¶30-050 as to 'general commercial companies'). The validity of the 'subjective' clause as ancillary to the main objects clause has been confirmed by the English courts (*Bell Houses Ltd v City Wall Properties Ltd* [1966] 1 QB 207).

Objects and powers

The courts developed a rule of interpretation by which what appeared to be the main objects were singled out in the objects clause. The other clauses were then treated as ancillary to the main objects. To guarantee the company's capacity to perform 'powers' as well as substantive objects, 'separate and independent objects' clauses were included into memoranda. These clauses provide that 'each paragraph is to constitute a separate and independent object not limited by references in other paragraphs'. Such clauses are now common in the memoranda of companies. The validity of such clauses was upheld reluctantly by the House of Lords in *Cotman v Brougham*, but a limitation on the effectiveness of such clauses was illustrated by *Re Introductions Ltd*.

> **Case example (1)**
> The issue was whether or not it was intra vires for one company to underwrite an issue of shares in another. The objects clause of the company permitted a large number of activities to be validly undertaken, and also provided that (per Lord Finlay at p. 517): 'The objects set forth in any sub-clause of this clause shall not, except when the context expressly so requires, be in any wise limited or restricted by reference to or inference from the terms of any other sub-clause, or by the name of the company. None of such sub-clauses or the objects therein specified or the powers thereby conferred shall be deemed subsidiary or auxiliary merely to the objects mentioned in the first sub-clause of this clause, but the company shall have full power to exercise all or any of the powers conferred by any part of this clause in any part of the world, and notwithstanding that the business, undertaking, property or acts proposed to be transacted, acquired, dealt with or performed do not fall within the objects of the first sub-clause of this clause.' *Cotman v Brougham* [1918] AC 514.

Because the objects clause expressly permitted dealing in shares, the activities in question were upheld. The registrar of companies had accepted the memorandum of association upon application. Consequently, the House of Lords had no jurisdiction to determine the validity of the document according to companies legislation at that time (CA 1985, s. 13(7) now states that the certificate of incorporation is conclusive evidence that the requirements of the Act in respect of registration have been complied with). However, the court noted that the memorandum should delimit a company's intended activities. It should not attempt to cover every conceivable business act.

> **Case example (2)**
> A company was incorporated with the object of hosting visitors from abroad at the Festival of Britain. Some years later, it became involved in a pig-breeding business. In the course of the latter venture, two debentures over the company's assets were issued to a bank, to secure a large overdraft. The bank was provided with a copy of the company's memorandum. The objects clause stated that the company could borrow by debenture and secure loans by a charge. There was also a clause which provided that 'each of the preceding sub-clauses shall be construed independently of and shall be in no way limited by reference to any other sub-clause and that the objects set out in each sub-clause are independent objects of the company'. The bank thus alleged that the loan and charge were valid. The Court of Appeal decided that the ability to borrow money was a power, not an object. Further, the power to borrow could not be elevated into an object by the 'independent objects' clause. Harman LJ explained that 'it is a necessarily implied addition to a power to borrow, whether express or implied, that you should add "for the purposes of the company". This borrowing was not for a legitimate purpose of the company: the bank knew it, and therefore cannot rely on its debentures.' *Re Introductions Ltd* [1970] Ch 199.

An implied power cannot be used for an ultra vires purpose. It can only be employed in connection with furtherance of the objects of the company (*Hutton v West Cork Railway Co* (1883) 23 ChD 654). If an express power is used for an ultra vires purpose, it is not void (*Rolled Steel Products (Holdings) Ltd v British Steel Corporation* [1986] Ch 246; (1984) 1 BCC 99,158). However, such an act will expose the directors to a liability for breach of fiduciary duty. Further, if the other party to the transaction knows that the power has been exercised for an ultra vires purpose, rights arising under it cannot be enforced. If the third party has received company property as a consequence of the exercise of the power for an ultra vires purpose, it will be accountable for this property as a constructive trustee.

Accordingly, it is first necessary to establish the status of a term in the objects clause. The most recent exposition of the rule of construction for classification of a term in the objects clause appears in the judgment of Slade LJ in the *Rolled Steel* case. The clause is to stand as an express object unless it is incapable by its nature of constituting a 'substantive object' (for example, the power to borrow money) or the wording of the memorandum shows expressly or by implication that the clause was intended merely to constitute an ancillary power. Having established the status of the clause, a third party will be precluded from enforcing any rights acquired only if the clause is classified as a power, and the third party knew that the power was exercised for an ultra vires purpose.

There is no reason why a company should not have the express power to confer gratuitous benefit upon employees or third parties. As Buckley LJ said in *Re Horsley & Weight Ltd* [1982] Ch 442 at p. 450E:

¶30-700

'The objects of a company do not need to be commercial; they can be charitable or philanthropic; indeed, they can be whatever the original incorporators wish, provided that they are legal. Nor is there any reason why a company should not part with its funds gratuitously or for non-commercial reasons if to do so is within its declared objects.'

However, if the power or object is used to effect a return of capital to shareholders (albeit disguised as something else), thus circumventing the statutory rules on return of capital, the court will impugn the transaction and order repayment of the money (*Re Halt Garage (1964) Ltd* [1982] 3 All ER 1016). A similar problem arose in *Re Aveling Barford Ltd*.

Case example (3)
Both A and P were companies controlled by L, a Japanese businessman. A sold an asset to P for £350,000 even though it was valued by A at £650,000 and by P's mortgagees at £1.15m. P later sold the asset for £1.5m. A motion was brought where the question arose as to whether P held the proceeds of sale on trust for A. The court held that the sale was not a genuine exercise of A's power to dispose of assets. The transaction was an attempt to benefit L, and constituted a return of capital. This was an ultra vires act that could not be approved by shareholder ratification. *Re Aveling Barford Ltd* [1989] 1 WLR 360; (1988) 4 BCC 548.

General commercial companies

Reference was made in ¶30-050 to a company having the object of carrying on business as a 'general commercial company' pursuant to s. 3A of the *Companies Act* 1985. The intention of this provision was to enable a company to dispense with the traditional long objects clause (which, as noted above, should more properly be seen as a mixture of objects and powers) by giving it express powers 'to do all such things as are incidental or conducive to the carrying on of any trade or business by it'. However, s. 35 of the *Companies Act* 1985 (discussed in ¶30-800) states that the 'validity of an act done by a company shall not be called into question on the ground of lack of capacity by reason of anything in the company's memorandum'. It may therefore be imprudent to rely on an implicit power pursuant to s. 3A of the *Companies Act* 1985 which by definition is not in the memorandum. Where s. 3A is used, lawyers still advise companies to include explicit powers (i.e. for support for group borrowings) so as to err on the side of caution.

¶30-750   Effect of ultra vires rule

An ultra vires transaction (see ¶30-700) is void and unenforceable as against the company. However, the effect of the rule has been mitigated by both statute (see ¶30-800) and other remedies which seek to redress any imbalance caused by a transaction being declared void (see ¶30-850).

¶30-800   Mitigation of the ultra vires rule by statute

The *Companies Act* 1985 separates the twin questions of invalidity of transactions due to the lack of capacity of the company on the one hand ('corporate ultra vires'), and limitations imposed on the board of directors on the other ('director ultra vires'). These questions are linked but considered separately.

Corporate ultra vires

The Act (CA 1985, s. 35) provides that:

(1) the validity of an act done by a company shall not be called into question on the ground of lack of capacity by reason of anything in its memorandum of association; but

(2) a member of a company may bring proceedings to restrain the doing of an act which, but for (1), would be beyond the company's capacity; but no such proceedings shall lie in respect of an act to be done in fulfilment of a legal obligation arising from a previous act of the company; and

(3) an act by the directors which, but for (1), would be beyond the company's capacity, is a breach of duty by them, and may only be ratified by special resolution (with a separate special resolution dealing with any proposed relief in respect of their liability arising from such breach of duty).

It is for consideration whether the principle that the validity of an act shall not be called into question on the ground of lack of capacity means that an ultra vires contract may now be enforced, not only by the third party, but also by the company itself.

Director ultra vires

In favour of a person dealing with a company in good faith, the power of the board of directors to bind the company, or authorise others to do so, shall be free of any limitation under the company's constitution (CA 1985, s. 35A(1)). The powers of directors are those outlined in the memorandum and articles of association as discussed in ¶30-700, together with any limitations contained in a valid resolution of the company in general meeting, or in a unanimous resolution of members.

A third party transacting with a company is not obliged to examine the registered documents of the company to see if the proposed transaction is within the capacity of the company, or within the powers of the board of directors to bind the company (CA 1985, s. 35B).

Beneficiaries from gratuitous dispositions of company property should now be protected if a disposition is outside the powers of the directors, because 'dealing' has been defined (CA 1985, s. 35A(2)(b)) to include any transaction or other act to which the company is a party. The 'dealing' must be the result of a quorate decision of the directors, or a decision of others authorised to bind the company. This would seem to include any person or group of persons (directors or otherwise) who are authorised, expressly, implied or ostensibly, to act on the board's behalf. Previous difficulty centred around the phrase 'transaction decided upon by the directors' in the predecessor legislation.

Invalidity of transactions involving directors, etc.

However, there is a special regime under s. 322A of the *Companies Act* 1985 relating to transactions by a company with parties including any of its directors, any director of its holding company, or any of their associates. In such a case, if the limitations on the powers of the directors under the company's memorandum and articles are exceeded, the transaction is voidable at the instance of the company. Any such invalidity does not affect transactions with genuine third parties, where s. 35A above will still apply. In such a case, the court may decide to sever the different parts of a transaction, or set aside parts of a transaction, on such terms as it thinks just.

¶30-850   Mitigation of the ultra vires rule by other remedies

Other remedies used by third parties in order to recover assets lost in transactions declared ultra vires include the following.

Equitable tracing remedies

Although an ultra vires act was void, it might be possible for claimants to exercise equitable remedies in order to recover from the company. If the company's directors or agents had received the money or assets of the claimant for an ultra vires purpose, the claimant might be able to trace his asset into the hands of the company. This meant that the claimant asserted a right of property over the asset (an equitable lien). If the claimant was seeking to recover specific and identifiable property, the remedy of common law tracing would be available.

However, if (as is more likely) the claimant was seeking to trace money into a mixed fund, it would be necessary for the tracing claim to be based upon equitable principles (*Taylor v Plumer* (1815) 3 M & S 562). In order to establish the right to an equitable tracing claim, the company's directors or agent must have received the money in the capacity of a fiduciary. This would arise, for example, where the purposes for which the claimant parted with his assets were, by law, incapable of fulfilment (*Sinclair v Brougham* [1914] AC 398), as with receipt of money for an ultra vires purpose.

Complex rules govern identification and recovery of money under the equitable tracing principles. It is possible, in certain circumstances, to follow the money out of the company into the hands of third parties. There are also defences available to defeat an equitable tracing claim.

Subrogation

The next technique which may afford redress to a party engaged in an ultra vires transaction is subrogation. This right arises where money received for an ultra vires purpose is used by the company to meet claims maintainable against it. The party to the ultra vires transaction cannot recover the money by assertion of any right which may have arisen from that act, but can be substituted to the position of person whose claim was met. To establish the rights to subrogation, it is first necessary to identify how the claimant's money was employed.

The remedy of subrogation is correlative with that of tracing (see above). In the latter, the claimant seeks to recover in respect of a positive form of enrichment of the company, and establishes a lien over an asset. In the former, the claimant seeks to counter a negative form of enrichment, by standing in the shoes of the relevant creditor. The two remedies are not therefore different; rather it is the nature of the assets which calls for a different mode of effecting restitution. Circumstances in which the courts will allow a claim for subrogation to succeed are difficult to define. For 'it is impossible ... to formulate any narrower principle than that the doctrine will be applied only when the courts are satisfied that reason and justice demand that it should be' (*Orakpo v Manson Investments Ltd* [1978] AC 95 per Lord Salmon at p. 110E).

Remedies against the company's agents

It may also be worth considering availability of a remedy against the agents of the company who were responsible for the ultra vires act. This could be on the grounds of breach of warranty of authority (*Collen v Wright* (1857) 8 E & B 647), or possibly fraudulent misrepresentation (*Derry v Peek* (1889) 14 App Cas 337), or common law negligence (*Hedley Byrne and Co Ltd v Heller and Partners Ltd* [1964] AC 465).

Remedies for a company seeking redress

It is possible that the company wishes to recover under an ultra vires contract. If the company has parted with money, for which no benefit has been conferred, and in respect of which no inconvenience or forbearance has been suffered by the other party, the money can be recovered on the grounds of a total failure of consideration. If, however, the company has conferred a benefit under an ultra vires contract, and the other party relies upon avoidance of the contract on grounds of ultra vires to evade liability to pay, the company may recover on a quantum meruit claim. It will be necessary to show free acceptance of the benefits by the other party to the contract, in order to enforce the restitutionary claim.

The company will also be able to recover against the directors or agents who were responsible for its involvement in the ultra vires act, for any loss sustained thereunder. If third parties have obtained benefits from the company in the course of an ultra vires act, with knowledge that the act was outside the company's capacity, they are deemed to hold those benefits as constructive trustees. The company can therefore recover from them.

TABLE A

¶31-000   General

The *Companies (Tables A to F) Regulations* 1985 (SI 1985/805) contain model memoranda and articles of association for the various types of companies. Previously the Table A articles of association had been included in the First Schedule to the *Companies Act* 1948. Presumably the intention of including them in regulations, rather than in the Companies Act itself, is to facilitate future amendment although only minor revisions have in fact been made to the current Table A.

Table A (regulations for management of a company limited by shares) in the 1985 regulations is different in content in several ways from earlier versions of Table A. It contains some regulations which did not appear previously (in particular relating to alternate directors, to permission for directors to attend and speak at class and general meetings without having to be a member, and to the issue of redeemable shares of any class and the purchase by a company of its own shares). Some of the former regulations are omitted (largely because they were repetitive, unnecessary or had become obsolete), whilst others have been revised.

It should be noted that Table A in the 1985 regulations will not apply automatically to companies incorporated before the consolidation in 1985 (see the *Companies Consolidation (Consequential Provisions) Act* 1985), but they may of course resolve to adopt it.

¶31-050   Table A articles

Set out below is Table A from the *Companies (Tables A to F) Regulations* 1985 (SI 1985/805) as amended.

Regulations for Management of a Company Limited by Shares

INTERPRETATION

1 In these regulations –

'the Act' means the Companies Act 1985 including any statutory modification or re-enactment thereof for the time being in force.

'the articles' means the articles of the company.

'clear days' in relation to the period of a notice means that period excluding the day when the notice is given or deemed to be given and the day for which it is given or on which it is to take effect.

'executed' includes any mode of execution.

'office' means the registered office of the company.

'**the holder**' in relation to shares means the member whose name is entered in the register of members as the holder of the shares.

'**the seal**' means the common seal of the company.

'**secretary**' means the secretary of the company or any other person appointed to perform the duties of the secretary of the company, including a joint, assistant or deputy secretary.

'**the United Kingdom**' means Great Britain and Northern Ireland.

Unless the context otherwise requires, words or expressions contained in these regulations bear the same meaning as in the Act but excluding any statutory modification thereof not in force when these regulations become binding on the company.

SHARE CAPITAL

2 Subject to the provisions of the Act and without prejudice to any rights attached to any existing shares, any share may be issued with such rights or restrictions as the company may by ordinary resolution determine.

3 Subject to the provisions of the Act, shares may be issued which are to be redeemed or are to be liable to be redeemed at the option of the company or the holder on such terms and in such manner as may be provided by the articles.

4 The company may exercise the powers of paying commissions conferred by the Act. Subject to the provisions of the Act, any such commission may be satisfied by the payment of cash or by the allotment of fully or partly paid shares or partly in one way and partly in the other.

5 Except as required by law, no person shall be recognised by the company as holding any share upon any trust and (except as otherwise provided by the articles or by law) the company shall not be bound by or recognise any interest in any share except an absolute right to the entirety thereof in the holder.

SHARE CERTIFICATES

6 Every member, upon becoming the holder of any shares, shall be entitled without payment to one certificate for all the shares of each class held by him (and, upon transferring a part of his holding of shares of any class, to a certificate for the balance of such holding) or several certificates each for one or more of his shares upon payment for every certificate after the first of such reasonable sum as the directors may determine. Every certificate shall be sealed with the seal and shall specify the number, class and distinguishing numbers (if any) of the shares to which it relates and the amount or respective amounts paid up thereon. The company shall not be bound to issue more than one certificate for shares held jointly by several persons and delivery of a certificate to one joint holder shall be a sufficient delivery to all of them.

7 If a share certificate is defaced, worn-out, lost or destroyed, it may be renewed on such terms (if any) as to evidence and indemnity and payment of the expenses reasonably incurred by the company in investigating evidence as the directors may

determine but otherwise free of charge, and (in the case of defacement or wearing-out) on delivery up of the old certificate.

LIEN

8 The company shall have a first and paramount lien on every share (not being a fully paid share) for all moneys (whether presently payable or not) payable at a fixed time or called in respect of that share. The directors may at any time declare any share to be wholly or in part exempt from the provisions of this regulation. The company's lien on a share shall extend to any amount payable in respect of it.

9 The company may sell in such manner as the directors determine any shares on which the company has a lien if a sum in respect of which the lien exists is presently payable and is not paid within fourteen clear days after notice has been given to the holder of the share or to the person entitled to it in consequence of the death or bankruptcy of the holder, demanding payment and stating that if the notice is not complied with the shares may be sold.

10 To give effect to a sale the directors may authorise some person to execute an instrument of transfer of the shares sold to, or in accordance with the directions of, the purchaser. The title of the transferee to the shares shall not be affected by any irregularity in or invalidity of the proceedings in reference to the sale.

11 The net proceeds of the sale, after payment of the costs, shall be applied in payment of so much of the sum for which the lien exists as is presently payable, and any residue shall (upon surrender to the company for cancellation of the certificate for the shares sold and subject to a like lien for any moneys not presently payable as existed upon the shares before the sale) be paid to the person entitled to the shares at the date of the sale.

CALLS ON SHARES AND FORFEITURE

12 Subject to the terms of allotment, the directors may make calls upon the members in respect of any moneys unpaid on their shares (whether in respect of nominal value or premium) and each member shall (subject to receiving at least fourteen clear days' notice specifying when and where payment is to be made) pay to the company as required by the notice the amount called on his shares. A call may be required to be paid by instalments. A call may, before receipt by the company of any sum due thereunder, be revoked in whole or part and payment of a call may be postponed in whole or part. A person upon whom a call is made shall remain liable for calls made upon him notwithstanding the subsequent transfer of the shares in respect whereof the call was made.

13 A call shall be deemed to have been made at the time when the resolution of the directors authorising the call was passed.

14 The joint holders of a share shall be jointly and severally liable to pay all calls in respect thereof.

15 If a call remains unpaid after it has become due and payable the person from whom it is due and payable shall pay interest on the amount unpaid from the day it became due and payable until it is paid at the rate fixed by the terms of allotment of the share or in the notice of the call or, if no rate is fixed, at the appropriate rate (as defined by the Act) but the directors may waive payment of the interest wholly or in part.

16 An amount payable in respect of a share on allotment or at any fixed date, whether in respect of nominal value or premium or as an instalment of a call, shall be deemed to be a call and if it is not paid the provisions of the articles shall apply as if that amount had become due and payable by virtue of a call.

17 Subject to the terms of allotment, the directors may make arrangements on the issue of shares for a difference between the holders in the amounts and times of payment of calls on their shares.

18 If a call remains unpaid after it has become due and payable the directors may give to the person from whom it is due not less than fourteen clear days' notice requiring payment of the amount unpaid together with any interest which may have accrued. The notice shall name the place where payment is to be made and shall state that if the notice is not complied with the shares in respect of which the call was made will be liable to be forfeited.

19 If the notice is not complied with any share in respect of which it was given may, before the payment required by the notice has been made, be forfeited by a resolution of the directors and the forfeiture shall include all dividends or other moneys payable in respect of the forfeited shares and not paid before the forfeiture.

20 Subject to the provisions of the Act, a forfeited share may be sold, re-allotted or otherwise disposed of on such terms and in such manner as the directors determine either to the person who was before the forfeiture the holder or to any other person and at any time before sale, re-allotment or other disposition, the forfeiture may be cancelled on such terms as the directors think fit. Where for the purposes of its disposal a forfeited share is to be transferred to any person the directors may authorise some person to execute an instrument of transfer of the share to that person.

21 A person any of whose shares have been forfeited shall cease to be a member in respect of them and shall surrender to the company for cancellation the certificate for the shares forfeited but shall remain liable to the company for all moneys which at the date of forfeiture were presently payable by him to the company in respect of those shares with interest at the rate at which interest was payable on those moneys before the forfeiture or, if no interest was so payable, at the appropriate rate (as defined in the Act) from the date of forfeiture until payment but the directors may waive payment wholly or in part or enforce payment without any allowance for the value of the shares at the time of forfeiture or for any consideration received on their disposal.

22 A statutory declaration by a director or the secretary that a share has been forfeited on a specified date shall be conclusive evidence of the facts stated in it as against all persons claiming to be entitled to the share and the declaration shall (subject to the execution of an instrument of transfer if necessary) constitute a good title to the share and the person to whom the share is disposed of shall not be bound to see to the application of the consideration, if any, nor shall his title to the share be affected by any irregularity in or invalidity of the proceedings in reference to the forfeiture or disposal of the share.

TRANSFER OF SHARES

23 The instrument of transfer of a share may be in any usual form or in any other form which the directors may approve and shall be executed by or on behalf of the transferor and, unless the share is fully paid, by or on behalf of the transferee.

24 The directors may refuse to register the transfer of a share which is not fully paid to a person of whom they do not approve and they may refuse to register the transfer of a share on which the company has a lien. They may also refuse to register a transfer unless –

    (a) it is lodged at the office or at such other place as the directors may appoint and is accompanied by the certificate for the shares to which it relates and such other evidence as the directors may reasonably require to show the right of the transferor to make the transfer;

    (b) it is in respect of only one class of shares; and

    (c) it is in favour of not more than four transferees.

25 If the directors refuse to register a transfer of a share, they shall within two months after the date on which the transfer was lodged with the company send to the transferee notice of the refusal.

26 The registration of transfers of shares or of transfers of any class of shares may be suspended at such times and for such periods (not exceeding thirty days in any year) as the directors may determine.

27 No fee shall be charged for the registration of any instrument of transfer or other document relating to or affecting the title to any share.

28 The company shall be entitled to retain any instrument of transfer which is registered, but any instrument of transfer which the directors refuse to register shall be returned to the person lodging it when notice of the refusal is given.

TRANSMISSION OF SHARES

29 If a member dies the survivor or survivors where he was a joint holder, and his personal representatives where he was a sole holder or the only survivor of joint holders, shall be the only persons recognised by the company as having any title to his interest; but nothing herein contained shall release the estate of a deceased member from any liability in respect of any share which had been jointly held by him.

30 A person becoming entitled to a share in consequence of the death or bankruptcy of a member may, upon such evidence being produced as the directors may properly require, elect either to become the holder of the share or to have some person nominated by him registered as the transferee. If he elects to become the holder he shall give notice to the company to that effect. If he elects to have another person registered he shall execute an instrument of transfer of the share to that person. All the articles relating to the transfer of shares shall apply to the notice or instrument of transfer as if it were an instrument of transfer executed by the member and the death or bankruptcy of the member had not occurred.

31 A person becoming entitled to a share in consequence of the death or bankruptcy of a member shall have the rights to which he would be entitled if he were the holder of the share, except that he shall not, before being registered as the holder of the share, be entitled in respect of it to attend or vote at any meeting of the company or at any separate meeting of the holders of any class of shares in the company.

ALTERATION OF SHARE CAPITAL

32 The company may by ordinary resolution –

(a) increase its share capital by new shares of such amount as the resolution prescribes;

(b) consolidate and divide all or any of its share capital into shares of larger amount than its existing shares;

(c) subject to the provisions of the Act, sub-divide its shares, or any of them, into shares of smaller amount and the resolution may determine that, as between the shares resulting from the sub-division, any of them may have any preference or advantage as compared with the others; and

(d) cancel shares which, at the date of the passing of the resolution, have not been taken or agreed to be taken by any person and diminish the amount of its share capital by the amount of the shares so cancelled.

33 Whenever as a result of a consolidation of shares any members would become entitled to fractions of a share, the directors may, on behalf of those members, sell the shares representing the fractions for the best price reasonably obtainable to any person (including, subject to the provisions of the Act, the company) and distribute the net proceeds of sale in due proportion among those members, and the directors may authorise some person to execute an instrument of transfer of the shares to, or in accordance with the directions of, the purchaser. The transferee shall not be bound to see to the application of the purchase money nor shall his title to the shares be affected by any irregularity in or invalidity of the proceedings in reference to the sale.

34 Subject to the provisions of the Act, the company may by special resolution reduce its share capital, any capital redemption reserve and any share premium account in any way.

PURCHASE OF OWN SHARES

35 Subject to the provisions of the Act, the company may purchase its own shares (including any redeemable shares) and, if it is a private company, make a payment in respect of the redemption or purchase of its own shares otherwise than out of distributable profits of the company or the proceeds of a fresh issue of shares.

GENERAL MEETINGS

36 All general meetings other than annual general meetings shall be called extraordinary general meetings.

37 The directors may call general meetings and, on the requisition of members pursuant to the provisions of the Act, shall forthwith proceed to convene an extraordinary general meeting for a date not later than eight weeks after receipt of the requisition. If there are not within the United Kingdom sufficient directors to call a general meeting, any director or any member of the company may call a general meeting.

NOTICE OF GENERAL MEETINGS

38 An annual general meeting and an extraordinary general meeting called for the passing of a special resolution or a resolution appointing a person as a director shall be called by at least twenty-one clear days' notice. All other extraordinary general meetings shall be called by at least fourteen clear days' notice but a general meeting may be called by shorter notice if it is so agreed –

(a) in the case of an annual general meeting, by all the members entitled to attend and vote thereat; and

(b) in the case of any other meeting by a majority in number of the members having a right to attend and vote being a majority together holding not less than ninety-five per cent in nominal value of the shares giving that right.

The notice shall specify the time and place of the meeting and the general nature of the business to be transacted and, in the case of an annual general meeting, shall specify the meeting as such.

Subject to the provisions of the articles and to any restrictions imposed on any shares, the notice shall be given to all the members, to all persons entitled to a share in consequence of the death or bankruptcy of a member and to the directors and auditors.

39 The accidental omission to give notice of a meeting to, or the non-receipt of notice of a meeting by, any person entitled to receive notice shall not invalidate the proceedings at that meeting.

PROCEEDINGS AT GENERAL MEETINGS

40 No business shall be transacted at any meeting unless a quorum is present. Two persons entitled to vote upon the business to be transacted, each being a member or a proxy for a member or a duly authorised representative of a corporation, shall be a quorum.

41 If such a quorum is not present within half an hour from the time appointed for the meeting, or if during a meeting such a quorum ceases to be present, the meeting shall stand adjourned to the same day in the next week at the same time and place or to such time and place as the directors may determine.

42 The chairman, if any, of the board of directors or in his absence some other director nominated by the directors shall preside as chairman of the meeting, but if neither the chairman nor such other director (if any) be present within fifteen minutes after the time appointed for holding the meeting and willing to act, the directors present shall elect one of their number to be chairman and, if there is only one director present and willing to act, he shall be chairman.

43 If no director is willing to act as chairman, or if no director is present within fifteen minutes after the time appointed for holding the meeting, the members present and entitled to vote shall choose one of their number to be chairman.

44 A director shall, notwithstanding that he is not a member, be entitled to attend and speak at any general meeting and at any separate meeting of the holders of any class of shares in the company.

45 The chairman may, with the consent of a meeting at which a quorum is present (and shall if so directed by the meeting), adjourn the meeting from time to time and from place to place, but no business shall be transacted at an adjourned meeting other than business which might properly have been transacted at the meeting had the adjournment not taken place. When a meeting is adjourned for fourteen days or more, at least seven clear days' notice shall be given specifying the time and place of the adjourned meeting and the general nature of the business to be transacted. Otherwise it shall not be necessary to give any such notice.

46 A resolution put to the vote of a meeting shall be decided on a show of hands unless before, or on the declaration of the result of, the show of hands a poll is duly demanded. Subject to the provisions of the Act, a poll may be demanded –

(a) by the chairman; or

(b) by at least two members having the right to vote at the meeting; or

(c) by a member or members representing not less than one-tenth of the total voting rights of all the members having the right to vote at the meeting; or

(d) by a member or members holding shares conferring a right to vote at the meeting being shares on which an aggregate sum has been paid up equal to not less than one-tenth of the total sum paid up on all the shares conferring that right;

and a demand by a person as proxy for a member shall be the same as a demand by the member.

47 Unless a poll is duly demanded a declaration by the chairman that a resolution has been carried or carried unanimously, or by a particular majority, or lost, or not carried by a particular majority and an entry to that effect in the minutes of the meeting shall be conclusive evidence of the fact without proof of the number or proportion of the votes recorded in favour of or against the resolution.

48 The demand for a poll may, before the poll is taken, be withdrawn but only with the consent of the chairman and a demand so withdrawn shall not be taken to have invalidated the result of a show of hands declared before the demand was made.

49 A poll shall be taken as the chairman directs and he may appoint scrutineers (who need not be members) and fix a time and place for declaring the result of the poll. The result of the poll shall be deemed to be the resolution of the meeting at which the poll was demanded.

50 In the case of an equality of votes, whether on a show of hands or on a poll, the chairman shall be entitled to a casting vote in addition to any other vote he may have.

51 A poll demanded on the election of a chairman or on a question of adjournment shall be taken forthwith. A poll demanded on any other question shall be taken either forthwith or at such time and place as the chairman directs not being more than thirty days after the poll is demanded. The demand for a poll shall not prevent the continuance of a meeting for the transaction of any business other than the question on which the poll was demanded. If a poll is demanded before the declaration of the result of a show of hands and the demand is duly withdrawn, the meeting shall continue as if the demand had not been made.

52 No notice need be given of a poll not taken forthwith if the time and place at which it is to be taken are announced at the meeting at which it is demanded. In any other case at least seven clear days' notice shall be given specifying the time and place at which the poll is to be taken.

53 A resolution in writing executed by or on behalf of each member who would have been entitled to vote upon it if it had been proposed at a general meeting at which he was present shall be as effectual as if it had been passed at a general meeting duly convened and held and may consist of several instruments in the like form each executed by or on behalf of one or more members.

VOTES OF MEMBERS

54 Subject to any rights or restrictions attached to any shares, on a show of hands every member who (being an individual) is present in person or (being a corporation) is present by a duly authorised representative, not being himself a member entitled to vote, shall have one vote and on a poll every member shall have one vote for every share of which he is the holder.

55 In the case of joint holders the vote of the senior who tenders a vote, whether in person or by proxy, shall be accepted to the exclusion of the votes of the other joint holders; and seniority shall be determined by the order in which the names of the holders stand in the register of members.

56 A member in respect of whom an order has been made by any court having jurisdiction (whether in the United Kingdom or elsewhere) in matters concerning mental disorder may vote, whether on a show of hands or on a poll, by his receiver, curator bonis or other person authorised in that behalf appointed by that court, and any such receiver, curator bonis or other person may, on a poll, vote by proxy. Evidence to the satisfaction of the directors of the authority of the person claiming to exercise the right to vote shall be deposited at the office, or at such other place as is specified in accordance with the articles for the deposit of instruments of proxy, not less than 48 hours before the time appointed for holding the meeting or adjourned meeting at which the right to vote is to be exercised and in default the right to vote shall not be exercisable.

57 No member shall vote at any general meeting or at any separate meeting of the holders of any class of shares in the company, either in person or by proxy, in respect of any share held by him unless all moneys presently payable by him in respect of that share have been paid.

58 No objection shall be raised to the qualification of any voter except at the meeting or adjourned meeting at which the vote objected to is tendered, and every vote not disallowed at the meeting shall be valid. Any objection made in due time shall be referred to the chairman whose decision shall be final and conclusive.

59 On a poll votes may be given either personally or by proxy. A member may appoint more than one proxy to attend on the same occasion.

60 An instrument appointing a proxy shall be in writing, executed by or on behalf of the appointor and shall be in the following form (or in a form as near thereto as circumstances allow or in any other form which is usual or which the directors may approve) —

> '   PLC/Limited
> I/We,   , of   , being a member/members of the above-named company, hereby appoint   of   , or failing him,   of   , as my/our proxy to vote in my/our name[s] and on my/our behalf at the annual/extraordinary general meeting of the company to be held on   19   and at any adjournment thereof.
> Signed on   19   .'

61 Where it is desired to afford members an opportunity of instructing the proxy how he shall act the instrument appointing a proxy shall be in the following form (or in a form as near thereto as circumstances allow or in any other form which is usual or which the directors may approve) —

> '   PLC/Limited
> I/We,   , of   , being a member/members of the above-named company, hereby appoint   of   , or failing him,   of   , as my/our proxy to vote in my/our name[s] and on my/our behalf at the annual/extraordinary general meeting of the company to be held on   19   and at any adjournment thereof.

> This form is to be used in respect of the resolutions mentioned below as follows:

>> Resolution No. 1 *for *against
>> Resolution No. 2 *for *against.

> * Strike out whichever is not desired.

> Unless otherwise instructed, the proxy may vote as he thinks fit or abstain from voting.

> Signed this   day of   19   .'

62 The instrument appointing a proxy and any authority under which it is executed or a copy of such authority certified notarially or in some other way approved by the directors may –

(a) be deposited at the office or at such other place within the United Kingdom as is specified in the notice convening the meeting or in any instrument of proxy sent out by the company in relation to the meeting not less than 48 hours before the time for holding the meeting or adjourned meeting at which the person named in the instrument proposes to vote; or

(b) in the case of a poll taken more than 48 hours after it is demanded, be deposited as aforesaid after the poll has been demanded and not less than 24 hours before the time appointed for the taking of the poll; or

(c) where the poll is not taken forthwith but is taken not more than 48 hours after it was demanded, be delivered at the meeting at which the poll was demanded to the chairman or to the secretary or to any director;

and an instrument of proxy which is not deposited or delivered in a manner so permitted shall be invalid.

63 A vote given or poll demanded by proxy or by the duly authorised representative of a corporation shall be valid notwithstanding the previous determination of the authority of the person voting or demanding a poll unless notice of the determination was received by the company at the office or at such other place at which the instrument of proxy was duly deposited before the commencement of the meeting or adjourned meeting at which the vote is given or the poll demanded or (in the case of a poll taken otherwise than on the same day as the meeting or adjourned meeting) the time appointed for taking the poll.

NUMBER OF DIRECTORS

64 Unless otherwise determined by ordinary resolution, the number of directors (other than alternate directors) shall not be subject to any maximum but shall be not less than two.

ALTERNATE DIRECTORS

65 Any director (other than an alternate director) may appoint any other director, or any other person approved by resolution of the directors and willing to act, to be an alternate director and may remove from office an alternate director so appointed by him.

66 An alternate director shall be entitled to receive notice of all meetings of directors and of all meetings of committees of directors of which his appointor is a member, to attend and vote at any such meeting at which the director appointing him is not personally present, and generally to perform all the functions of his appointor as a director in his absence but shall not be entitled to receive any remuneration from the company for his services as an alternate director. But it shall not be necessary to give notice of such a meeting to an alternate director who is absent from the United Kingdom.

67 An alternate director shall cease to be an alternate director if his appointor ceases to be a director; but, if a director retires by rotation or otherwise but is reappointed or deemed to have been reappointed at the meeting at which he retires, any appointment of an alternate director made by him which was in force immediately prior to his retirement shall continue after his reappointment.

68 Any appointment or removal of an alternate director shall be by notice to the company signed by the director making or revoking the appointment or in any other manner approved by the directors.

69 Save as otherwise provided in the articles, an alternate director shall be deemed for all purposes to be a director and shall alone be responsible for his own acts and defaults and he shall not be deemed to be the agent of the director appointing him.

POWERS OF DIRECTORS

70 Subject to the provisions of the Act, the memorandum and the articles and to any directions given by special resolution, the business of the company shall be managed by the directors who may exercise all the powers of the company. No alteration of the memorandum or articles and no such direction shall invalidate any prior act of the directors which would have been valid if that alteration had not been made or that direction had not been given. The powers given by this regulation shall not be limited by any special power given to the directors by the articles and a meeting of directors at which a quorum is present may exercise all powers exercisable by the directors.

71 The directors may, by power of attorney or otherwise, appoint any person to be the agent of the company for such purposes and on such conditions as they determine, including authority for the agent to delegate all or any of his powers.

DELEGATION OF DIRECTORS' POWERS

72 The directors may delegate any of their powers to any committee consisting of one or more directors. They may also delegate to any managing director or any director holding any other executive office such of their powers as they consider desirable to be exercised by him. Any such delegation may be made subject to any conditions the directors may impose, and either collaterally with or to the exclusion of their own powers and may be revoked or altered. Subject to any such conditions, the proceedings of a committee with two or more members shall be governed by the articles regulating the proceedings of directors so far as they are capable of applying.

APPOINTMENT AND RETIREMENT OF DIRECTORS

73 At the first annual general meeting all the directors shall retire from office, and at every subsequent annual general meeting one-third of the directors who are subject to retirement by rotation or, if their number is not three or a multiple of three, the number nearest to one-third shall retire from office; but, if there is only one director who is subject to retirement by rotation, he shall retire.

74 Subject to the provisions of the Act, the directors to retire by rotation shall be those who have been longest in office since their last appointment or reappointment, but as between persons who became or were last reappointed directors on the same day those to retire shall (unless they otherwise agree among themselves) be determined by lot.

75 If the company, at the meeting at which a director retires by rotation, does not fill the vacancy the retiring director shall, if willing to act, be deemed to have been reappointed unless at the meeting it is resolved not to fill the vacancy or unless a resolution for the reappointment of the director is put to the meeting and lost.

76 No person other than a director retiring by rotation shall be appointed or reappointed a director at any general meeting unless –

(a) he is recommended by the directors; or

(b) not less than fourteen nor more than thirty-five clear days before the date appointed for the meeting, notice executed by a member qualified to vote at the meeting has been given to the company of the intention to propose that person for appointment or reappointment stating the particulars which would, if he were so appointed or reappointed, be required to be included in the company's register of directors together with notice executed by that person of his willingness to be appointed or reappointed.

77 Not less than seven nor more than twenty-eight clear days before the date appointed for holding a general meeting notice shall be given to all who are entitled to receive notice of the meeting of any person (other than a director retiring by rotation at the meeting) who is recommended by the directors for appointment or reappointment as a director at the meeting or in respect of whom notice has been duly given to the company of the intention to propose him at the meeting for appointment or reappointment as a director. The notice shall give the particulars of that person which would, if he were so appointed or reappointed, be required to be included in the company's register of directors.

78 Subject as aforesaid, the company may by ordinary resolution appoint a person who is willing to act to be a director either to fill a vacancy or as an additional director and may also determine the rotation in which any additional directors are to retire.

79 The directors may appoint a person who is willing to act to be a director, either to fill a vacancy or as an additional director, provided that the appointment does not cause the number of directors to exceed any number fixed by or in accordance with the articles as the maximum number of directors. A director so appointed shall hold office only until the next following annual general meeting and shall not be taken into account in determining the directors who are to retire by rotation at the meeting. If not reappointed at such annual general meeting, he shall vacate office at the conclusion thereof.

80 Subject as aforesaid, a director who retires at an annual general meeting may, if willing to act, be reappointed. If he is not reappointed, he shall retain office until the meeting appoints someone in his place, or if it does not do so, until the end of the meeting.

DISQUALIFICATION AND REMOVAL OF DIRECTORS

81 The office of a director shall be vacated if –

(a) he ceases to be a director by virtue of any provision of the Act or he becomes prohibited by law from being a director; or

(b) he becomes bankrupt or makes any arrangement or composition with his creditors generally; or

(c) he is, or may be, suffering from mental disorder and either –

  (i) he is admitted to hospital in pursuance of an application for admission for treatment under the Mental Health Act 1983 or, in Scotland, an application for admission under the Mental Health (Scotland) Act 1960, or

  (ii) an order is made by a court having jurisdiction (whether in the United Kingdom or elsewhere) in matters concerning mental disorder for his detention or for the appointment of a receiver, curator bonis or other person to exercise powers with respect to his property or affairs; or

(d) he resigns his office by notice to the company; or

(e) he shall for more than six consecutive months have been absent without permission of the directors from meetings of directors held during that period and the directors resolve that his office be vacated.

REMUNERATION OF DIRECTORS

82 The directors shall be entitled to such remuneration as the company may by ordinary resolution determine and, unless the resolution provides otherwise, the remuneration shall be deemed to accrue from day to day.

DIRECTORS' EXPENSES

83 The directors may be paid all travelling, hotel, and other expenses properly incurred by them in connection with their attendance at meetings of directors or committees of directors or general meetings or separate meetings of the holders of any class of shares or of debentures of the company or otherwise in connection with the discharge of their duties.

DIRECTORS' APPOINTMENTS AND INTERESTS

84 Subject to the provisions of the Act, the directors may appoint one or more of their number to the office of managing director or to any other executive office under the company and may enter into an agreement or arrangement with any director for his employment by the company or for the provision by him of any services outside the scope of the ordinary duties of a director. Any such appointment, agreement or arrangement may be made upon such terms as the directors determine and they may remunerate any such director for his services as they think fit. Any appointment of a director to an executive office shall terminate if he ceases to be a director but without prejudice to any claim to damages for breach of the contract of service between the director and the company. A managing director and a director holding any other executive office shall not be subject to retirement by rotation.

85 Subject to the provisions of the Act, and provided that he has disclosed to the directors the nature and extent of any material interest of his, a director notwithstanding his office –

(a) may be a party to, or otherwise interested in, any transaction or arrangement with the company or in which the company is otherwise interested;

(b) may be a director or other officer of, or employed by, or a party to any transaction or arrangement with, or otherwise interested in, any body corporate promoted by the company or in which the company is otherwise interested; and

(c) shall not, by reason of his office, be accountable to the company for any benefit which he derives from any such office or employment or from any such transaction or arrangement or from any interest in any such body corporate and no such transaction or arrangement shall be liable to be avoided on the ground of any such interest or benefit.

86 For the purposes of regulation 85 –

(a) a general notice given to the directors that a director is to be regarded as having an interest of the nature and extent specified in the notice in any transaction or arrangement in which a specified person or class of persons is interested shall be deemed to be a disclosure that the director has an interest in any such transaction of the nature and extent so specified; and

(b) an interest of which a director has no knowledge and of which it is unreasonable to expect him to have knowledge shall not be treated as an interest of his.

DIRECTORS' GRATUITIES AND PENSIONS

87 The directors may provide benefits, whether by the payment of gratuities or pensions or by insurance or otherwise, for any director who has held but no longer holds any executive office or employment with the company or with any body corporate which is or has been a subsidiary of the company or a predecessor in business of the company or of any such subsidiary, and for any member of his family (including a spouse and a former spouse) or any person who is or was dependent on him, and may (as well before as after he ceases to hold such office or employment) contribute to any fund and pay premiums for the purchase or provision of any such benefit.

PROCEEDINGS OF DIRECTORS

88 Subject to the provisions of the articles, the directors may regulate their proceedings as they think fit. A director may, and the secretary at the request of a director shall, call a meeting of the directors. It shall not be necessary to give notice of a meeting to a director who is absent from the United Kingdom. Questions arising at a meeting shall be decided by a majority of votes. In the case of an equality of votes, the chairman shall have a second or casting vote. A director who is also an alternate director shall be entitled in the absence of his appointor to a separate vote on behalf of his appointor in addition to his own vote.

89 The quorum for the transaction of the business of the directors may be fixed by the directors and unless so fixed at any other number shall be two. A person who holds office only as an alternate director shall, if his appointor is not present, be counted in the quorum.

90 The continuing directors or a sole continuing director may act notwithstanding any vacancies in their number, but, if the number of directors is less than the number fixed as the quorum, the continuing directors or director may act only for the purpose of filling vacancies or of calling a general meeting.

91 The directors may appoint one of their number to be the chairman of the board of directors and may at any time remove him from that office. Unless he is unwilling to do so, the director so appointed shall preside at every meeting of directors at which he is present. But if there is no director holding that office, or if the director holding it is unwilling to preside or is not present within five minutes after the time appointed for the meeting, the directors present may appoint one of their number to be chairman of the meeting.

92 All acts done by a meeting of directors, or of a committee of directors, or by a person acting as a director shall, notwithstanding that it be afterwards discovered that there was a defect in the appointment of any director or that any of them were disqualified from holding office, or had vacated office, or were not entitled to vote, be as valid as if every such person had been duly appointed and was qualified and had continued to be a director and had been entitled to vote.

93 A resolution in writing signed by all the directors entitled to receive notice of a meeting of directors or of a committee of directors shall be as valid and effectual as if it had been passed at a meeting of directors or (as the case may be) a committee of directors duly convened and held and may consist of several documents in the like form each signed by one or more directors; but a resolution signed by an alternate director need not also be signed by his appointor and, if it is signed by a director who has appointed an alternate director, it need not be signed by the alternate director in that capacity.

94 Save as otherwise provided by the articles, a director shall not vote at a meeting of directors or of a committee of directors on any resolution concerning a matter in which he has, directly or indirectly, an interest or duty which is material and which conflicts or may conflict with the interests of the company unless his interest or duty arises only because the case falls within one or more of the following paragraphs –

(a) the resolution relates to the giving to him of a guarantee, security, or indemnity in respect of money lent to, or an obligation incurred by him for the benefit of, the company or any of its subsidiaries;

(b) the resolution relates to the giving to a third party of a guarantee, security, or indemnity in respect of an obligation of the company or any of its subsidiaries for which the director has assumed responsibility in whole or part and whether alone or jointly with others under a guarantee or indemnity or by the giving of security;

(c) his interest arises by virtue of his subscribing or agreeing to subscribe for any shares, debentures or other securities of the company or any of its subsidiaries, or by virtue of his being, or intending to become, a participant in the underwriting or sub-underwriting of an offer of any such shares, debentures, or other securities by the company or any of its subsidiaries for subscription, purchase or exchange;

(d) the resolution relates in any way to a retirement benefits scheme which has been approved, or is conditional upon approval, by the Board of Inland Revenue for taxation purposes.

For the purposes of this regulation, an interest of a person who is, for any purpose of the Act (excluding any statutory modification thereof not in force when this regulation becomes binding on the company) , connected with a director shall be treated as an interest of the director and, in relation to an alternate director, an interest of his appointor shall be treated as an interest of the alternate director without prejudice to any interest which the alternate director has otherwise.

95 A director shall not be counted in the quorum present at a meeting in relation to a resolution on which he is not entitled to vote.

96 The company may by ordinary resolution suspend or relax to any extent, either generally or in respect of any particular matter, any provision of the articles prohibiting a director from voting at a meeting of directors or of a committee of directors.

97 Where proposals are under consideration concerning the appointment of two or more directors to offices or employments with the company or any body corporate in which the company is interested the proposals may be divided and considered in relation to each director separately and (provided he is not for another reason precluded from voting) each of the directors concerned shall be entitled to vote and be counted in the quorum in respect of each resolution except that concerning his own appointment.

98 If a question arises at a meeting of directors or of a committee of directors as to the right of a director to vote, the question may, before the conclusion of the meeting, be referred to the chairman of the meeting and his ruling in relation to any director other than himself shall be final and conclusive.

SECRETARY

99 Subject to the provisions of the Act, the secretary shall be appointed by the directors for such term, at such remuneration and upon such conditions as they may think fit; and any secretary so appointed may be removed by them.

MINUTES

100 The directors shall cause minutes to be made in books kept for the purpose –

(a) of all appointments of officers made by the directors; and

(b) of all proceedings at meetings of the company, of the holders of any class of shares in the company, and of the directors, and of committees of directors, including the names of the directors present at each such meeting.

THE SEAL

101 The seal shall only be used by the authority of the directors or of a committee of directors authorised by the directors. The directors may determine who shall sign any instrument to which the seal is affixed and unless otherwise so determined it shall be signed by a director and by the secretary or by a second director.

DIVIDENDS

102 Subject to the provisions of the Act, the company may by ordinary resolution declare dividends in accordance with the respective rights of the members, but no dividend shall exceed the amount recommended by the directors.

103 Subject to the provisions of the Act, the directors may pay interim dividends if it appears to them that they are justified by the profits of the company available for distribution. If the share capital is divided into different classes, the directors may pay interim dividends on shares which confer deferred or non-preferred rights with regard to dividend as well as on shares which confer preferential rights with regard to dividend, but no interim dividend shall be paid on shares carrying deferred or non-preferred rights if, at the time of payment, any preferential dividend is in arrear. The directors may also pay at intervals settled by them any dividend payable at a fixed rate if it appears to them that the profits available for distribution justify the payment. Provided the directors act in good faith they shall not incur any liability to the holders of shares conferring preferred rights for any loss they may suffer by the lawful payment of an interim dividend on any shares having deferred or non-preferred rights.

104 Except as otherwise provided by the rights attached to shares, all dividends shall be declared and paid according to the amounts paid up on the shares on which the dividend is paid. All dividends shall be apportioned and paid proportionately to the amounts paid up on the shares during any portion or portions of the period in respect of which the dividend is paid; but, if any share is issued on terms providing that it shall rank for dividend as from a particular date, that share shall rank for dividend accordingly.

105 A general meeting declaring a dividend may, upon the recommendation of the directors, direct that it shall be satisfied wholly or partly by the distribution of assets and, where any difficulty arises in regard to the distribution, the directors may settle the same and in particular may issue fractional certificates and fix the value for distribution of any assets and may determine that cash shall be paid to any member upon the footing of the value so fixed in order to adjust the rights of members and may vest any assets in trustees.

106 Any dividend or other moneys payable in respect of a share may be paid by cheque sent by post to the registered address of the person entitled or, if two or more persons are the holders of the share or are jointly entitled to it by reason of the death or bankruptcy of the holder, to the registered address of that one of those persons who is first named in the register of members or to such person and to such address as the person or persons entitled may in writing direct. Every cheque shall be made payable to the order of the person or persons entitled or to such other person as the person or persons entitled may in writing direct and payment of the cheque shall be a good discharge to the company. Any joint holder or other person jointly entitled to a share as aforesaid may give receipts for any dividend or other moneys payable in respect of the share.

107 No dividend or other moneys payable in respect of a share shall bear interest against the company unless otherwise provided by the rights attached to the share.

108 Any dividend which has remained unclaimed for twelve years from the date when it became due for payment shall, if the directors so resolve, be forfeited and cease to remain owing by the company.

ACCOUNTS

109 No member shall (as such) have any right of inspecting any accounting records or other book or document of the company except as conferred by statute or authorised by the directors or by ordinary resolution of the company.

CAPITALISATION OF PROFITS

110 The directors may with the authority of an ordinary resolution of the company –

(a) subject as hereinafter provided, resolve to capitalise any undivided profits of the company not required for paying any preferential dividend (whether or not they are available for distribution) or any sum standing to the credit of the company's share premium account or capital redemption reserve;

(b) appropriate the sum resolved to be capitalised to the members who would have been entitled to it if it were distributed by way of dividend and in the same proportions and apply such sum on their behalf either in or towards paying up the amounts, if any, for the time being unpaid on any shares held by them respectively, or in paying up in full unissued shares or debentures of the company of a nominal amount equal to that sum, and allot the shares or debentures credited as fully paid to those members, or as they may direct, in those proportions, or partly in one way and partly in the other: but the share premium account, the capital redemption reserve, and any profits which are not available for distribution may, for the purposes of this regulation, only be applied in paying up unissued shares to be allotted to members credited as fully paid;

(c) make such provision by the issue of fractional certificates or by payment in cash or otherwise as they determine in the case of shares or debentures becoming distributable under this regulation in fractions; and

(d) authorise any person to enter on behalf of all the members concerned into an agreement with the company providing for the allotment to them respectively, credited as fully paid, of any shares or debentures to which they are entitled upon such capitalisation, any agreement made under such authority being binding on all such members.

NOTICES

111 Any notice to be given to or by any person pursuant to the articles shall be in writing except that a notice calling a meeting of the directors need not be in writing.

112 The company may give any notice to a member either personally or by sending it by post in a prepaid envelope addressed to the member at his registered address or by leaving it at that address. In the case of joint holders of a share, all notices shall be given to the joint holder whose name stands first in the register of members in respect of the joint holding and notice so given shall be sufficient notice to all the joint holders. A member whose registered address is not within the United Kingdom and who gives to the company an address within the United Kingdom at which notices may be given to him shall be entitled to have notices given to him at that address, but otherwise no such member shall be entitled to receive any notice from the company.

113 A member present, either in person or by proxy, at any meeting of the company or of the holders of any class of shares in the company shall be deemed to have received notice of the meeting and, where requisite, of the purposes for which it was called.

114 Every person who becomes entitled to a share shall be bound by any notice in respect of that share which, before his name is entered in the register of members, has been duly given to a person from whom he derives his title.

115 Proof that an envelope containing a notice was properly addressed, prepaid and posted shall be conclusive evidence that the notice was given. A notice shall be deemed to be given at the expiration of 48 hours after the envelope containing it was posted.

116 A notice may be given by the company to the persons entitled to a share in consequence of the death or bankruptcy of a member by sending or delivering it, in any manner authorised by the articles for the giving of notice to a member, addressed to them by name, or by the title of representatives of the deceased, or trustee of the bankrupt or by any like description at the address, if any, within the United Kingdom supplied for that purpose by the persons claiming to be so entitled. Until such an address has been supplied, a notice may be given in any manner in which it might have been given if the death or bankruptcy had not occurred.

WINDING UP

117 If the company is wound up, the liquidator may, with the sanction of an extraordinary resolution of the company and any other sanction required by the

Act, divide among the members in specie the whole or any part of the assets of the company and may, for that purpose, value any assets and determine how the division shall be carried out as between the members or different classes of members. The liquidator may, with the like sanction, vest the whole or any part of the assets in trustees upon such trusts for the benefit of the members as he with the like sanction determines, but no member shall be compelled to accept any assets upon which there is a liability.

INDEMNITY

118 Subject to the provisions of the Act but without prejudice to any indemnity to which a director may otherwise be entitled, every director or other officer or auditor of the company shall be indemnified out of the assets of the company against any liability incurred by him in defending any proceedings, whether civil or criminal, in which judgment is given in his favour or in which he is acquitted or in connection with any application in which relief is granted to him by the court from liability for negligence, default, breach of duty or breach of trust in relation to the affairs of the company.

DIRECTORS, OFFICERS ● INSIDER DEALING

Table of Contents

continued over

continued over

COMPANY OFFICERS

¶40-000   Who are company officers?

Company officers are identified by s. 744 of the *Companies Act* 1985. They include a director, manager or secretary. A company's statutory auditor is also an officer, as he is appointed under the Companies Act 'to hold office'. To establish the nature and extent of an individual's duties to his company, it is necessary to identify the office he holds.

A director is somebody appointed to carry out the day-to-day running and control of a business. Anybody 'occupying the position of director, by whatever name called', is also classified as a director under s. 741 of the *Companies Act* 1985.

'Shadow directors', etc.

The Act identifies 'shadow directors' for the purpose, among other things, of regulating loans made by companies. These are persons 'in accordance with whose directions or instructions the directors of a company are accustomed to act'; depending upon the terms of a loan agreement and the facts of a particular case, a creditor may become a 'shadow director' (*Re a Company No. 005009 of 1987* (1988) 4 BCC 424) but cf. *Re M C Bacon Ltd* [1991] Ch 127; [1990] BCC 78.

In addition, a person appointed as a 'company doctor' may be deemed a director of that company if his duties include monitoring the company's trading, controlling its bank account or becoming involved in the company's operational strategy (*Re Tasbian Ltd (No. 3)* [1992] BCC 358). De facto directorships may also arise where a person assumes the status and functions of a director without any formal appointment to that position (*Secretary of State for Trade and Industry v Tjolle* [1998] BCC 282). There is no one test of de facto directorship, but there are many relevant factors to consider (*Potier v Secretary of State for Trade and Industry* [1999] BCC 390). Such directors may be subject to the regime of the *Company Directors Disqualification Act* 1986 but this will depend on whether there was evidence that the de facto director was the only person directing the company's affairs or, where other directors were appointed, that he acted on an equal footing with them in controlling the company (see *Re Richborough Furniture Ltd* [1996] BCC 155 and ¶41-700).

Both executive and non-executive directors are company officers. Whereas the former are primarily concerned with the day-to-day affairs of the company, the latter are involved in the overall strategy and direction of the company. Successive reports on corporate governance (see ¶23-750) have stressed the need for non-executive directors to sit on the boards of all listed public companies. The London Stock Exchange has issued the 'Combined Code' (principles of good governance and code of best practice) of which para. 3 of Section 1 of the Principles of Good Governance provides that the board should include a balance of executive and non-executive directors (including independent non-executives) such that no individual or small group of individuals can dominate the board's decision taking. The Combined Code has been appended to the Stock Exchange's *Listing Rules* and for financial years ending on or after 31 December 1998 listed companies must disclose in their annual report and accounts how and to what extent they have applied the principles and detailed provisions of the Combined Code.

Managers, employees

A manager is a person to whom supervisory control over the affairs of the company is delegated (*Re a Company* [1980] Ch 138). A manager's duties to his company resemble those of a director, but are usually more onerous than those of employees. Employees' duties 'consist only of respect for trade secrets and confidentiality of customer lists' (*Canadian Aero Service v O'Malley* (1973) 40 DLR (3rd) 371), unless expressly extended by contract.

Auditors

A company's auditors are appointed by the shareholders in general meeting. The primary duty of the auditors is not to the company as an independent legal entity, but to the members, as it is the members to whom the auditors' report is addressed (CA 1985, s. 236). The role of the auditors is defined by statute. See further ¶44-300ff.

¶40-100　The company secretary

Every company must appoint a company secretary (CA 1985, s. 283). A sole director cannot also hold office as company secretary; however, if there is more than one director, it is possible for any of them to fulfil the office of company secretary. The Act prevents circumvention of this rule by preventing a company from making the following appointments:

(1) company A to the post of secretary of company B where the sole director of A is also the sole director of B; or

(2) company A as sole director of company B where the sole director of A is also the secretary of B.

The company secretary undertakes administrative work, such as the preparation and submission of returns, the preparation of the agenda for directors' meetings and company general meetings, and the compilation of the minutes of those meetings. The articles of association may specify particular tasks for which the secretary is to assume responsibility. It is possible for more than one person to hold office as secretary of a company.

¶40-100

In the event of a vacancy in the office of company secretary, the duties must be fulfilled by an assistant or deputy secretary, or by an officer authorised by the directors (CA 1985, s. 283).

Qualifications of company secretaries

The *Companies Act* 1985 sets out the qualifications which the company secretary of a public company must have, and imposes a duty upon the directors to take responsible steps to secure that the secretary (or joint secretaries) has the requisite knowledge and experience to discharge his duties, and is suitably qualified (CA 1985, s. 286).

Status, etc. of company secretaries

The office of company secretary undoubtedly carries significant authority and responsibilities. Lord Esher expressed the view of the courts in the nineteenth century as follows:

'A secretary is a mere servant; his position is that he is to do what he is told, and no person can assume that he has any authority to represent anything at all; nor can any one assume that statements made by him are necessarily to be accepted as trustworthy without further inquiry.' (*Barnett Hoares and Co v South London Tramways Co* (1887) 18 QBD 815 at p. 817).

The status of the company secretary has undergone a significant transformation. This fact was highlighted by the judgment in *Panorama Developments (Guildford) Ltd v Fidelis Furnishing Fabrics Ltd* [1971] 2 QB 711. In this case the company secretary was described (at p. 716H) as,

'a much more important person nowadays than he was in 1887. He is an officer of the company with extensive duties and responsibilities. This appears not only in the modern Companies Act, but also in the role which he plays in the day-to-day business of companies. He is no longer a mere clerk.'

The power of the secretary to make representations and enter into contracts on behalf of the company is accordingly extended. This power is certainly wide in respect of administrative matters.

The company secretary is an office holder who may be prosecuted for fraudulent trading (CA 1985, s. 458) and/or made liable to contribute to the company's assets for his involvement (IA 1986, s. 213). He may also fall within the disqualification provisions of s. 10(1) of the *Company Directors Disqualification Act* 1986 where he has been ordered to make a contribution under s. 213 of the *Insolvency Act* 1986 (fraudulent trading provisions). However, s. 214 of the *Insolvency Act* 1986 (wrongful trading provisions) only applies to directors and shadow directors.

Indemnification of secretary

For a company's power to indemnify its secretary against liability for negligence, etc., see ¶41-000.

¶40-200   Registers of directors and secretaries

All companies are required to maintain a register of directors (CA 1985, s. 288), in which the following details must be entered.

Where the director is an individual:

- full present name and any former names used (a former name does not include either a name changed at least 20 years ago or before the person was aged 18, or a maiden name of a married woman or, for those with titles, their previous ordinary names);

- date of birth;

- residential address;

- nationality;

- business occupation;

- particulars of any other directorships held (not including any held at least five years previously, or those held in a dormant company or another company in the same group).

Where the director is a company:

- the name of the company; and

- the address of its registered office.

This register must be open for inspection by shareholders, and for inspection by other persons. In this latter case a fee may be charged for inspection.

A company must also keep a register of its company secretaries (CA 1985, s. 288). If the secretary is a person, his/her present/former names and addresses should be recorded. If the secretary is a company, its name and registered office address should be recorded (CA 1985, s. 290).

DIRECTORS' DUTIES

Duties and powers of company officers .... ¶40-500	Nature of directors' fiduciary duty .... ¶40-900
Directors' duties of care .... ¶40-600	Indemnification of directors,
Directors' fiduciary duty ... ¶40-700	etc. .... ¶41-000
To whom fiduciary duty is owed .... ¶40-800	

¶40-500   Duties and powers of company officers

A significant body of case law has developed over the issue of directors' duties and powers. Problems of duties and powers arise less frequently in relation to other corporate officers. Managers will have duties consonant with their seniority and the trust reposed in them. A company secretary fulfils a senior administrative role which carries statutory responsibilities and fiduciary obligations (see ¶40-100).

The liability of the company for acts of its directors, managers and of the secretary is determined by agency principles. While it is possible for the company to invest managers and the secretary with a significant measure of apparent or actual authority, the usual authority of these officers is often less than that of the directors.

The duties owed by directors to the company fall into two distinct classes: a duty of care, and a fiduciary duty (see ¶40-600ff.).

¶40-600 Directors' duties of care

The extent of a director's duty of care and skill was comprehensively examined by Romer J in *Re City Equitable Fire Insurance Co Ltd* [1925] Ch 407. This statement of the law draws on previous authorities and runs as follows:

(1) A director need not exhibit in the performance of his duties a greater degree of skill than may reasonably be expected from a person of his knowledge and experience. If directors act within their powers, if they act with such care as is reasonably to be expected from them, having regard to their knowledge and experience, and if they act honestly for the benefit of the company they represent, they discharge both their equitable as well as their legal duty to the company. It is perhaps only another way of stating the same proposition to say that directors are not liable for errors of judgment.

(2) A director is not bound to give continuous attention to the affairs of his company. He is not bound to attend all such meetings, though he ought to attend whenever, in the circumstances, he is reasonably able to do so (see *Winkworth v Edward Baron Development Co Ltd* [1986] 1 WLR 1512, where one of two directors of a company failed to ensure that the company's activities were properly conducted).

(3) In respect of all duties that, having regard to the exigencies of business, and the articles of association, may be properly left to some other official, a director is, in the absence of grounds for suspicion, justified in trusting that official to perform such duties honestly.

These guidelines were fundamentally changed in *Re D'Jan of London Ltd*.

Case example (1)

A director of the company signed a fire insurance document in which he declared that he had never been a director of a company that had gone into liquidation. In actual fact, he had been. The insurance company discovered this and repudiated liability when the company made a claim under the agreement. Later, the company went into liquidation. The court held that the director had been negligent in filling in the form. Hoffmann LJ commented that a director's duty of care was accurately stated in s. 214(4) of the *Insolvency Act* 1986 (provisions regarding wrongful trading). *Re D'Jan of London Ltd* [1993] BCC 646.

The conduct required is that of a reasonably diligent person having both the knowledge and experience that may reasonably be expected of a director carrying out the same functions as are carried out by that director (a test targeted primarily at executive directors), and the knowledge and experience that the director actually has (targeted more at non-executive directors) (IA 1986, s. 214). Because the test is both objective and subjective, the duty of care owed by directors will consequently be more difficult to satisfy. If a director is found to have acted within the foregoing parameters, there is no liability for negligence. However, a higher standard of care is expected from a professional person who occupies the office of director than from a person with little or no business experience. This was illustrated in the case of *Dorchester Finance v Stebbing*.

Case example (2)

Dorchester Finance had three directors. Two of the directors were chartered accountants, and the other had a large measure of accounting experience. The company suffered significant losses as a consequence of a failure to take security on loans. The directors were sued for negligence. Foster J decided that a professionally qualified director could be expected to show a greater measure of understanding and control of the company's affairs than one not so qualified. He said, 'For a chartered accountant and an experienced accountant to put forward the proposition that a non-executive director has no duties to perform I find quite alarming.' *Dorchester Finance Co Ltd v Stebbing* [1989] BCLC 498 at p. 505F.

Waiver of right of recovery

A company can waive the right to recover from directors for negligent acts, by subsequent adoption of those acts (*Multinational Gas and Petrochemical Co v Multinational Gas and Petrochemical Services Ltd* [1983] Ch 258). For the directors' acts then become acts of the company itself. Even if an attempt to recover from the directors were to be made, it is the company itself who must sue under the rule in *Foss v Harbottle* (see ¶61-700ff.). However, if the refusal by the company to pursue the claim amounts to unfairly prejudicial conduct on the minority shareholders, a remedy will lie under s. 459 of the *Companies Act* 1985 (see ¶62-550).

In the *Multinational* case, the negligent acts resulted in loss to the company itself. If the directors' negligent acts (as opposed to acts they negligently cause the company to do) cause loss to the shareholders, the shareholders may recover from the directors, if a duty of care and causation can be established (*Heron International Ltd v Lord Grade* [1983] BCLC 244).

¶40-700   Directors' fiduciary duty

The fact that directors are placed in a position of trust and responsibility has resulted in the imposition of fiduciary duties upon them. It is important to establish to whom the duties are owed (see ¶40-800), and also the nature and extent of those duties (see ¶40-900).

¶40-700

¶40-800 To whom fiduciary duty is owed

In the normal course of the governance of the company's affairs, the fiduciary duties of the directors are owed to the company alone. This means the company as a separate legal entity, not the shareholders. This is clearly shown by *R v Philippou* (1989) 5 BCC 665, where directors, who were also shareholders, misappropriated money from the company; this constituted theft from the company rather than from the other shareholders. Further, in *Percival v Wright* [1902] 2 Ch 421 when directors were asked to purchase shares from shareholders, the directors were under no obligation to disclose to the vendor shareholders an anticipated sale of part of the company's undertaking. However, it is possible for the directors to accept an obligation to represent fairly the interests of shareholders. This could apply, for example, when the shareholders undertake a particular course of action on the advice of the directors (*Allen v Hyatt* (1914) 30 TLR 444).

Creation of a collateral duty to shareholders will depend on the facts and circumstances of a particular case. If, for example, shareholder directors are considering the merits of the terms of rival take-over bids, they would be obliged to advise the other shareholders as to the best bid reasonably obtainable (*Heron International Ltd v Lord Grade* [1983] BCLC 244). The directors should also remain impartial as between different groups of shareholders in the same company (*Mills v Mills* (1938) 60 CLR 150). However, the directors cannot place the interests of the group of which their company is a member above those of the company itself (*Bell v Lever Bros Ltd* [1932] AC 161).

Duties towards creditors and employees

While a company is solvent, its directors do not owe strictly defined fiduciary duties to the company's creditors (*Multinational Gas and Petrochemical Co v Multinational Gas and Petrochemical Services Ltd* [1983] Ch 258), but are placed under a statutory obligation to consider the interests of employees (CA 1985, s. 309). The duty of directors to take into account the interests of creditors is indirectly enforced through the rules which call for the directors to maintain capital levels, and which impose personal liability for fraudulent trading and wrongful trading immediately before liquidation. However, when the company is insolvent to the knowledge of the directors, there is a common law fiduciary duty owed to the creditors (*Liquidator of West Mercia Safetywear Ltd v Dodd* (1988) 4 BCC 30).

¶40-900 Nature of directors' fiduciary duty

The nature of the fiduciary duty of directors has many facets. The directors should act bona fide in the interests of the company, and not for any collateral purpose. There is scope for subjectivity in the fulfilment of this duty. For the directors must exercise their discretion bona fide in what they consider, not what a court may consider, is in the interests of the company (per Greene MR, in *Re Smith and Fawcett Ltd* [1942] Ch 304). The courts are reluctant to interfere with the honest exercise of directors' discretion.

Although directors owe no direct fiduciary duty to shareholders (see ¶40-800) the interests of the company are identified as those of the members as a whole. This embraces both current and future members, and necessitates the balancing of current and future benefits to the company. The use of powers for a 'collateral purpose' means utilisation of powers conferred under the articles for purposes other than those for which they were intended. An obvious example of such an abuse is the issue of shares to maintain control of the board and not to raise capital (*Piercy v S Mills & Co Ltd* [1920] 1 Ch 77). The principle was further considered in *Punt v Symonds & Co Ltd*, and *Howard Smith Ltd v Ampol Petroleum Ltd*.

Case example (1)
Directors were found to have issued shares with the immediate object of gaining control of the company. Byrne J explained (at pp. 515–516): 'the meaning, object and intention of the issue of these shares was to enable the shareholders holding the smaller amount of shares to control the holders of a very considerable majority. A power of the kind exercised by the directors in this case, is one which must be exercised for the benefit of the company: primarily it is given them for the purpose of enabling them to raise capital when required for the purposes of the company. There may be occasions when the directors may fairly and properly issue shares in the case of a company constituted like the present for other reasons. For instance, it would not be at all an unreasonable thing to create a sufficient number of shareholders to enable statutory powers to be exercised; but when I find a limited issue of shares to persons who are obviously meant and intended to secure the necessary statutory majority in a particular interest, I do not think that is a fair and bona fide exercise of the power.' *Punt v Symons & Co Ltd* [1903] 2 Ch 506.

Case example (2)
A company (R W Miller (Holdings) Ltd) was the target for many takeover bids. Ampol controlled 55 per cent of the target's shares, but the directors of the company favoured Howard Smith's offer. Their preference was founded upon legitimate commercial reasons. The terms of the Howard Smith offer were more generous, and there was some uncertainty as to the future of Miller if it passed into Ampol's hands. Thus, Miller's directors engineered a share issue to Howard Smith. The target company was in need of cash, and Miller's directors sought to justify their acts by reference to this fact. The judgment of the Privy Council was delivered by Lord Wilberforce. He explained that the exercise of powers by directors, conferred upon them under the company's articles, would clearly not be in the interests of the company if the directors thereby served their own interests. However, absence of self-interest did not necessarily mean the directors' acts were in accordance with the purposes for which the powers were conferred. For self-interest is only one example of improper motive. Before it is possible to conclude that a fiduciary power was exercised for the purpose to which it was conferred, it may be necessary to have a close look at the surrounding circumstances. The Privy Council were reluctant to define those circumstances and purposes where directors could validly make a share issue. Lord Wilberforce expressed this as follows (at p. 835C–H): 'To define in advance exact limits beyond which directors must not pass is, in their Lordships' view, impossible ...

¶40-900

In their Lordships' opinion, it is necessary to start with a consideration of the power whose exercise is in question ... Having ascertained, on a fair view, the nature of this power, and having defined as can best be done in the light of modern conditions the, or some, limits within which it may be exercised, it is then necessary for the court, if a particular exercise of it is challenged, to examine the substantial purpose for which it was exercised, and to reach a conclusion whether that purpose was proper or not. In doing so it will necessarily give credit to the bona fide opinion of the directors, if such is found to exist, and will respect their judgment as to matters of management; having done this, the ultimate conclusion has to be as to the side of a fairly broad line on which the case falls.' *Howard Smith Ltd v Ampol Petroleum Ltd* [1974] AC 821.

Directors profiting from their position

An important consequence of a director's fiduciary duty to his company is the prohibition placed upon him from profiting from this position. In cases where the courts have found the director to have done so, he has made liable to account. However, it is possible for the company to agree to a director profiting from his position. Such agreement will be effective only if made after full disclosure to the company of the terms of the proposed transaction. The duty to account, and the power to exonerate a director from this duty, are illustrated by the cases of *Regal (Hastings) Ltd v Gulliver* and *New Zealand Netherlands Society 'Oranje' Inc v Kuys.*

Case example (3)

Regal had incorporated a subsidiary ('Amalgamated') to lease two cinemas, but needed to increase the issued share capital of Amalgamated to exploit this opportunity. Regal itself was unable to provide the necessary finance. Thus, directors of Regal, the company secretary, and some outside parties, subscribed for the shares in Amalgamated.

The shares in both companies were then sold. The shareholders in Amalgamated realised a profit on the share sale. The purchasers of the Regal shares caused Regal to apply to the courts for recovery of the profit. The House of Lords explained the principles of directors' liability to account for profits made in the course of their office, as follows (per Lord Russell of Killowen at p. 144G): 'The rule of equity which insists on those, who by use of a fiduciary position make a profit, being liable to account for that profit, in no way depends on fraud, or absence of bona fides; or upon such questions or considerations as whether the profit would or should otherwise have gone to the plaintiff, or whether the profiteer was under a duty to obtain the source of the profit for the plaintiff, or whether he took a risk or acted as he did for the benefit of the plaintiff, or whether the plaintiff has in fact been damaged or benefited by his action. The liability arises from the mere fact of a profit having, in the stated circumstances, been made. The profiteer, however honest and well-intentioned, cannot escape the risk of being called upon to account.'

The directors were therefore required to repay their profit to Regal. However, the company solicitor was not held liable to account, as he was not a director. An important lesson to be learned from this case is that, had the company consented to the directors making a profit, by shareholder approval in general meeting, they could not have been forced to account. *Regal (Hastings) Ltd v Gulliver* [1967] 2 AC 134.

Case example (4)

Kuys worked as the secretary of the New Zealand Netherlands Society. He agreed to publish a newspaper independently to which the Society would subscribe, for distribution to its members. Kuys left the Society, and the Society introduced a new, competitor, newspaper with the same name. Kuys successfully applied for an injunction, restraining the Society from producing the new magazine. It was alleged that Kuys acquired ownership of the newspaper as a consequence of his fiduciary relationship with the Society and was therefore in a position of trust. It was admitted that the Society could release Kuys from accountability, and allow him to retain ownership, but only by 'an arrangement, freely arrived at, after disclosure of all the relevant matters'.

However, there was no agreement that the newspaper should revert to the Society. Further, the only possible conclusion from the facts was that ownership should remain with Kuys. The House of Lords therefore decided that, in the circumstances, the agreement between the parties had displaced any potential fiduciary obligation, and that the injunction should stand. *New Zealand Netherlands Society 'Oranje' Inc v Kuys* [1973] 1 WLR 1126.

Conflicts of interest

Directors must be careful to avoid conflicts of interest with the company. This could arise where, for example, a director concludes a contract with the company (though Table A, art. 85 (see ¶31-050) may often be incorporated into the articles of association in order to regulate situations where directors are parties to, or are interested in, transactions in which the company is interested). In such circumstances, the temptation for the director may be to place his personal interests above those of the company and, if this does occur, the company may have the contract set aside if the interest is not disclosed (*Aberdeen Railway Co v Blaikie Bros* (1854) 1 Macq 461).

This principle does not impose an absolute prohibition on contracts between a company and its directors, but such transactions must comply with the Companies Act rules on contracts with directors (see ¶43-450ff.), and company approval should be secured (*Movitex Ltd v Bulfield* (1986) 2 BCC 99,403). Further, under s. 317 of the *Companies Act* 1985, such contracts must be disclosed at the first board meeting possible. Inadequate disclosure leads, on conviction or indictment, to an unlimited fine (or on conviction on a summary charge, to a fine not exceeding the statutory maximum); see also, for the civil consequences of failure to disclose, *Hely-Hutchinson v Brayhead Ltd* [1968] 1 QB 549 and *Guinness plc v Saunders* [1990] 2 AC 663; [1990] BCC 205 (in the *Hely-Hutchinson* case, the court concluded that contracts made between a director and his company were voidable

¶40-900

at the instance of the company unless approved of at a meeting or by the articles of association).

¶41-000 Indemnification of directors, etc.

As originally enacted, s. 310 of the *Companies Act* 1985 limited the power of a company to indemnify any officer or auditor against, or exempt him from, liability for negligence, default, breach of duty or breach of trust to the defence of any proceedings (civil or criminal) in which judgment was given in favour of such person or he was acquitted, or relief was granted to him under s. 144(3) or (4) of the *Companies Act* 1985 (acquisition of shares by company's nominee) or s. 727 of the *Companies Act* 1985.

As a matter of law, a company could not pay insurance premiums against risks where it could not give an indemnity. Nevertheless, such premiums were widely accepted by insurance companies, often on a notional 90/10 split with the director paying ten per cent as a (theoretically) appropriate proportion to cover the unindemnifiable risks.

Section 310 (as amended by the *Companies Act* 1989) now provides a full power of insurance to companies in respect of the liability of any officer or auditor.

APPOINTMENT, DISQUALIFICATION AND REMOVAL OF DIRECTORS

¶41-300 Appointment of directors

The Companies Act requires disclosure of the first directors and the company secretary of any company, on registration (CA 1985, s. 10). This statement must accompany the memorandum of association, and contain the directors' 'consent to accept office'.

The company must notify the registrar of companies within 14 days of any change in its directors, or in the details set out in the register of directors. Any notification to the registrar of a change in the composition of the board of directors must be accompanied by a signed consent for the new director to act as such (CA 1985, s. 288(2)). Changes in a company's directors must be recorded in the register of directors and also publicised by the registrar in the *London Gazette* (CA 1985, s. 711(1)(c)). Appointment of the first directors is sometimes made in the articles of association. Subsequent directors are appointed in accordance with the terms of the articles.

Appointment of directors to public companies

There are statutory rules for appointing directors to public companies. Individual votes are taken for the appointment of each director, unless waived by unanimous consent (CA 1985, s. 292). An appointment made without the necessary vote is void. However, acts undertaken by the individual whilst acting in the capacity of director are not invalidated (CA 1985, s. 285).

¶41-400   Retirement and appointment under Table A

The model articles provided for limited companies in the *Companies (Tables A to F) Regulations* 1985 (SI 1985/805: see ¶31-050) include the following regulations as to election, retirement and re-election of directors. These rules are included in the articles of association of most limited companies.

(1)   Retirement at first general meeting

All directors appointed under the articles of association, in the course of registration of the company, must retire at the first general meeting, and seek election (Table A, reg. 73). It is the company (i.e. the shareholders) who elect the directors.

(2)   Retirement by rotation

At every subsequent general meeting, one-third of the directors (or however many nearest approximates to one-third) must retire. Directors who should retire are selected by reference to length of time since previous retirement. Retiring directors may be re-elected. If the shareholders fail to re-elect retiring directors or to replace them, but do not positively reject their re-election, they are deemed to have been re-elected (Table A, reg. 73 and 80).

(3)   Appointment of new directors

It is not possible to appoint a director at a general meeting who is other than a director retiring by rotation unless he is recommended by the current directors, or requirements as to notice are satisfied. The notice requirements are that the company is informed of the intention to propose the appointment and given such details of the nominated director as would have to appear in the register of directors by a member of the company who is qualified to vote at the meeting. This notice must be received by the company not less than 14 and not more than 35 clear days before the meeting. The proposed director must also give notice of his willingness to accept appointment (Table A, reg. 76 and 77).

(4)   Filling a casual vacancy

Both the company (by ordinary resolution) and the directors can appoint a director to fill a casual vacancy. If the appointment is made by the directors, he must retire at the next general meeting, and seek election by the shareholders. Such a director is not counted as one who has retired by rotation (Table A, reg. 78 and 79).

¶41-400

(5) Appointment of additional directors

Both the company by ordinary resolution and the directors can appoint additional directors. However, in the latter case, the person appointed must stand for election. Again, such directors are not considered to have retired by rotation (Table A, reg. 78 and 79).

(6) Alternate directors

There is a facility for the appointment of alternate directors by existing directors. The functions and responsibilities of office are then accepted by the appointee. The alternate director must be approved by resolution of the directors (Table A, reg. 65). An alternate director is entitled to receive notice of all meetings and vote when his appointor is not present (Table A, reg. 66). If the appointor ceases to be a director, so will the alternate director appointed by him (Table A, reg. 67). In any event, the appointee will be responsible for his own acts; in other words, he is not deemed the agent of the appointor (Table A, reg. 69).

It is important to appreciate that the above rules may be omitted from a company's articles by choice. For example, it is common for small private companies to exclude the requirement for retirement of directors by rotation.

¶41-500 Qualification of directors

Although there are very few statutory rules as to qualifications of directors, it is open to the company to impose such conditions as are deemed necessary in the articles of association.

A shareholding qualification for directors is sometimes included in the articles. If the directors are called upon to hold shares, they must be obtained within two months of appointment, or such shorter time as is provided in the articles (CA 1985, s. 291(1)). Further, failure to acquire the shares or sustain the stipulated level of holding will result in vacation of the office (CA 1985, s. 291(3)). It should be borne in mind that the articles of association may make the acquisition of shares a condition precedent to the holding of office. This question will be determined as a matter of construction. If the articles make acquisition of qualification shares a condition precedent, failure to comply will avoid any appointment from the assumed commencement of office, as opposed to annulment after any period of grace under the articles or the two months under s. 291(3) above.

Age limit for directors

There is no minimum age below which a person cannot accept office as a director. Nor is there a maximum age limit for private companies. However, unless the articles of association of the company otherwise provide, a public company (or a private company which is a subsidiary of a public company) cannot appoint a director who is 70 years old or over (CA 1985, s. 293), unless that appointment is approved in a general meeting by special notice of a resolution stating the age of the director to be appointed (CA 1985, s. 293(5)). Further, anybody who is 70 or has reached retiring age as defined by the company's articles, and who is appointed to or proposed for office of director, must give notice to the company of this age (CA 1985, s. 294).

Directors who attain the age of 70 must vacate office at the next general meeting (CA 1985, s. 293). In this case, the director will not be automatically reappointed in default of appointment under the rules in Table A (reg. 75 of Table A in the *Companies (Tables A to F) Regulations* 1985: see ¶31-050).

DISQUALIFICATION OF DIRECTORS

¶41-600   General

Although there are virtually no statutory regulations as to the qualifications of directors (see ¶41-500), disqualification from office may arise under the *Company Directors Disqualification Act* 1986 (CDDA 1986). Disqualifications often relate to 'phoenix' companies (new companies deliberately established to avoid the debts of insolvent predecessors). A disqualification order is made by the court, and the 1986 Act provides three 'divisions' of disqualification. There are disqualifications for general misconduct in connection with companies (CDDA 1986, s. 2–5: see ¶41-650), disqualifications for unfitness either where a company has become insolvent or where it has been investigated (CDDA 1986, s. 6–9: see ¶41-700) and other cases of disqualification (CDDA 1986, s. 10–12: see ¶41-800). The consequences of a contravention of a disqualification order are set out in CDDA 1986, s. 13–15 (see ¶41-850).

¶41-650   Disqualification for general misconduct in connection with companies

If a person is convicted of an indictable offence in connection with the promotion, formation, management or liquidation of a company, or with the receivership or management of a company's property, a disqualification order may be made against him (CDDA 1986, s. 2). The maximum period of disqualification under this section is five years if the order is made by a court of summary jurisdiction, or 15 years in any other case.

The circumstances in which an offence would be 'in connection with' the management of a company were considered in *R v Goodman*.

¶41-600

> **Case example**
> The defendant was convicted of insider dealing and disqualified from being a
> director for ten years. He appealed on the ground that the court had no power to
> disqualify him for that offence. The court held that an offence would be in
> connection with the management of the company if there was any 'relevant factual
> connection'. Insider dealing was such an offence. The disqualification order was
> upheld. *R v Goodman* [1992] BCC 625.

Persistent breaches of companies legislation

A disqualification order may also be made against a director for being
persistently in default of the statutory provisions under which returns, accounts or
documents must be filed with or disclosed to the registrar of companies (CDDA
1986, s. 3). A 'persistent default' arises where, in the five years ending with the
date of application for the disqualification order, the director has been adjudged
guilty of three or more defaults in relation to those provisions. The maximum
period for disqualification under this section is five years.

Fraud, etc. in winding up

The next ground for disqualifications under the 'general misconduct' provision is
fraud. The rule applies where, in the course of the winding up of a company, it
appears that the person has been guilty of an offence of fraudulent trading under
s. 458 of the *Companies Act* 1985 (*R v Kemp* [1988] QB 645; (1988) 4 BCC 203),
or has been guilty, while an officer or liquidator of the company or receiver or
manager of its property, of any fraud or breach of duty (CDDA 1986, s. 4). A
maximum 15-year disqualification order may be imposed by the court under this
provision.

Offences in relation to returns, etc.

A disqualification order may also be made where a person is convicted of certain
summary offences (CDDA 1986, s. 5). There are offences in relation to failure to
comply with legislation which calls for delivery, filing or disclosure of information
to the registrar of companies. If, during any five-year period ending with the date of
the conviction, three default orders have been made against that person, a
maximum disqualification period of five years may be imposed.

¶41-700   Disqualification for unfitness

Disqualification orders may be made for 'unfitness' in two circumstances. The
first is where the company is insolvent, i.e. where the company is in liquidation and
cannot pay its debts, where an administration order has been made, or where an
administrative receiver has been appointed (CDDA 1986, s. 6(2)). The second is
subsequent to an investigation of the company under the Companies Act (CDDA
1986, s. 8). Both de jure and de facto directors may be liable (*Re Lo-Line Electric
Motors Ltd* [1988] Ch 477; (1988) 4 BCC 415; *Re Cargo Agency Ltd* [1992] BCC

388; *Re Moorgate Metals Ltd* [1995] BCC 143). Further, shadow directors are equally subject to this regime (CDDA 1986, s. 22(4)).

(1) Where the company is insolvent

If a person is or has been a director of a company which has become insolvent and the court is satisfied that his conduct makes him unfit to be concerned in the management of a company, the court 'shall' make a disqualification order (CDDA 1986, s. 6(1)). A duty is thus imposed upon the court to make the order. The minimum or maximum periods of disqualification are two years and 15 years respectively. In *Re Sevenoaks Stationers (Retail) Ltd* [1991] Ch 164; [1990] BCC 765, the court categorised the seriousness of an offence as follows:

- penalty of over ten to a maximum of 15 years for particularly serious cases, e.g. persons being disqualified for a second time;
- penalty of six to ten years for offences of moderate gravity; and
- penalty of two to five years for the least serious offences.

A duty to report potential disqualification cases to the Secretary of State is imposed upon the official receiver, liquidators, administrators and administrative receivers. However, a two-year limitation is imposed for applications to the court for an order, unless this is extended by leave of the court. Applications for a disqualification order under s. 6 may be made by the Secretary of State or, at his direction concerning a director of a company being wound up by the court in England and Wales, by the official receiver.

The courts have developed a summary method for hearing disqualification cases, often referred to as a 'Carecraft' disposal (after the case that first sanctioned the idea: *Re Carecraft Construction Ltd* [1993] BCC 336). The Department of Trade and Industry (DTI) and the respondent director agree:

(1) a statement of agreed facts (there may also be non-agreed facts);

(2) that the director is, e.g., unfit to act; and

(3) the approximate length of the disqualification period.

While the court is not bound by (2) and (3), the director is invariably held to be unfit and the period of disqualification set at or near to that agreed. Carecraft disposals are quicker and cheaper than contested disqualification cases, there is no cross-examination and thus less strain on a respondent. They are mostly used in unfitness cases but there seems no reason why they could not be used in disqualification cases on other grounds.

The above procedure has proved popular and there have been attempts to go one step further and allow a respondent director to make a formal undertaking with the DTI not to act as a director for an agreed period (or even without a time-limit) rather than be disqualified formally by the courts. These undertakings have been allowed by the courts on a few occasions, usually where the respondent's health has been a consideration (see *Re Homes Assured Corporation plc* [1996] BCC 297 and *Secretary of State for Trade and Industry v Cleland* [1997] BCC 473).

¶41-700

According to the Court of Appeal in a case where there were no health considerations or other exceptional circumstances, the DTI could insist on continuing formal proceedings in court to seek a judicial finding of unfitness; the court added that legislative change would be needed to allow binding undertakings instead of formal disqualification (*Re Blackspur Group plc. Secretary of State for Trade and Industry v Davies (No. 2)* [1998] BCC 11). The DTI subsequently announced on 11 February 1998 that it does intend to legislate to permit undertakings in lieu of disqualification orders, but no timetable has been set for this.

In deciding the period of disqualification, courts can consider guidelines given by the Court of Appeal in *Secretary of State for Trade and Industry v Griffiths* [1998] BCC 836.

The courts have clamped down on shadow and de facto directors and also non-executive directors of companies which become insolvent. Developments in director disqualification cases have shown courts to be less tolerant of non-executive, or nominee, directors claiming no part in the management of insolvent companies. Such directors are likely to find it increasingly difficult to escape the personal responsibilities imposed upon them. This is true of wives of executive directors where the wife acts almost as a nominee (e.g. *Re Peppermint Park Ltd* [1998] BCC 23) and 'pure' nominee directors (*Potier v Secretary of State for Trade and Industry* [1999] BCC 390). The practice of inactive nominees being appointed as directors was effectively outlawed when one such director was disqualified for 12 years (*Official Receiver v Vass* [1999] BCC 516). A company was set up at the instigation of an individual who was already disqualified and was using the nominee director to evade the disqualification. The nominee director was a resident of Sark and held nominee directorships of 1,313 UK companies and company secretaryships in a further 513.

The question of whether a company could be subjected to disqualification proceedings under the *Company Directors Disqualification Act* 1986 was considered for the first time (*Official Receiver v Brady* [1999] BCC 258). There were two nominee Jersey companies involved. Each company was a director and they had both manifestly failed. It was clear that companies could be directors of other companies (CDDA 1986, s. 22(4)). It was useful in practice to be able to disqualify companies as well as the individuals behind them; this would enable the unfit directors behind the companies to be attacked. The companies were disqualified from being directors for the maximum period of 15 years.

The courts increasingly frown on executive directors whose level of delegation leads them to rely almost entirely on managers: this does not relieve them of their duty to monitor and supervise the manner in which relevant duties are discharged (*Re Barings plc. Secretary of State for Trade and Industry v Baker (No. 5)* [1999] 1 BCLC 433). A management consultant who had had invested money in and was involved in the management of a company was also a de facto director and could be disqualified (*Secretary of State for Trade and Industry v Jones* [1999] BCC 336).

(2)   Following investigation of the company

The Secretary of State may appoint inspectors to report on a company's affairs under s. 437 of the *Companies Act* 1985. The Secretary of State may obtain access to the books and papers of a company under s. 447 and 448 of the *Companies Act* 1985, or when assisting overseas regulatory authorities under s. 82 of the *Companies Act* 1989. He may also appoint inspectors to investigate and report upon suspected insider dealing in a company's securities (FSA 1986, s. 177). If, on the exercise of these powers, it appears to the Secretary of State expedient in the public interest to make a disqualification order against a director, an application to this effect may be made to the court. The court will make the order if it is satisfied that the director's conduct in relation to the company makes him unfit to be concerned in the management of the company (CDDA 1986, s. 8). The maximum period of disqualification on this ground is 15 years.

Information from a respondent contained in transcripts obtained by investigators under Companies Act powers may be used in disqualification proceedings even though this was compelled evidence. According to the Court of Appeal in *R v Secretary of State for Trade and Industry, ex parte McCormick* [1998] BCC 379, use of such information is not a violation of art. 6(1) of the European Convention for the Protection of Human Rights and Fundamental Freedoms which entitles every one to a 'fair and public hearing', as disqualification proceedings do not involve a criminal charge (if the proceedings were criminal in nature there could be a breach of art. 6(1) because the use of compelled transcripts would be regarded as self-incrimination (*Saunders v UK* [1997] BCC 872), although this decision of the European Court of Human Rights has been the subject of significant criticism in terms of both its outcome and its logic; it will be interesting to see if it is followed by UK courts following the incorporation of the European Convention on Human Rights into UK domestic law).

¶41-750   Matters to which the court is to have regard

The court is directed to have regard to the following matters in establishing a director's unfitness to manage a company (see ¶41-700) (CDDA 1986, s. 9(1), Sch. 1). Those listed in (1)–(5) are applicable in all cases; those in (6)–(10) apply only when the company has become insolvent.

(1) any misfeasance or breach of any fiduciary or other duty by the director in relation to the company;

(2) any misapplication or retention by the director of, or any conduct by the director giving rise to an obligation to account for, any money or other property of the company;

(3) the extent of the director's responsibility for the company entering into a transaction defrauding creditors (within IA 1986, s. 423–425);

(4) the extent of the director's responsibility for any failure by the company to comply with any of the following provisions of the *Companies Act* 1985:

¶41-750

(a) s. 221 (companies to keep accounting records: see ¶70-050);

(b) s. 222 (where and for how long records are to be kept: see ¶70-050);

(c) s. 288 (register of directors and secretaries: see ¶40-200);

(d) s. 352 (obligation to keep and enter up register of members: see ¶23-350);

(e) s. 353 (location of register of members: see¶23-350);

(f) s. 363 (company's duty to make an annual return: see ¶23-450);

(g) s. 399 and 415 (company's duty to register charges it creates: see ¶53-300);

(5) the extent of the director's responsibility for any failure by the directors of the company to comply with s. 226 and 227 of the *Companies Act* 1985 (directors' duty to prepare annual accounts: see ¶70-050) or s. 233 (approval and signature of accounts: see ¶70-350);

(6) the extent of the director's responsibility for the causes of the company becoming insolvent;

(7) the extent of the director's responsibility for any failure by the company to supply any goods or services which have been paid for (in whole or part);

(8) the extent of the director's responsibility for the company entering into any transaction or giving preference, being a transaction or preference:

(a) liable to be set aside under s. 127 or s. 238–240; of the *Insolvency Act* 1986 or

(b) challengeable under s. 242 or s. 243 of the *Insolvency Act* 1986 or under any rule of law in Scotland;

(9) the extent of the director's responsibility for any failure by the directors of the company to comply with IA 1986, s. 98 (duty to call creditors' meetings in creditors' voluntary winding up);

(10) failure by the director to comply with any obligation imposed on him by or under any of the following provisions of the *Insolvency Act* 1986:

(a) s. 22 (company's statement of affairs in administration);

(b) s. 47 (statement of affairs to administrative receiver);

(c) s. 66 (statement of affairs in Scottish receivership);

(d) s. 99 (directors' duty to attend meeting; statement of affairs in creditors' voluntary winding up);

(e) s. 131 (statement of affairs in winding up by the court);

(f) s. 234 (duty of anyone with company property to deliver it up);

(g) s. 235 (duty to co-operate with liquidator, etc.);

Re Dawson Print Group Ltd is a prime example of the way in which these provisions are applied in practice.

> **Case example**
> D was a director of two companies (DPG and Princo) both of which became
> insolvent at the same time. As they were being wound up, D started a third
> company which was trading profitably when the official receiver sought an order
> for the disqualification of D. Hoffmann J commented (at pp. 324–325) on the type
> of conduct necessary to make a director unfit: 'It seems to me that if that sort of
> mismanagement in itself were a ground for making a disqualification order under
> [CDDA 1986, s. 6] the effect of the section would be quite arbitrary ... There
> must, I think, be something about the case, some conduct which, if not dishonest,
> is at any rate in breach of standards of commercial morality, or some really gross
> incompetence which persuades the court that it would be a danger to the public if
> he were to be allowed to continue to be involved in the management of companies
> ...' *Re Dawson Print Group Ltd* (1987) 3 BCC 322.

In *Re Douglas Construction Services Ltd* (1988) 4 BCC 553 at pp. 557–558,
Harman J commented further:

'I have seen enough cases to have some idea of the prevalence of this sort of conduct and
to get some idea of the badges of the man who is simply exploiting limited liability in a
cynical way with a disregard for proper responsibility or, alternatively, exploiting it
because he is so stupid and ignorant that he is quite incapable of appreciating what has
happened and thereby causes large losses by, in a sense, incompetence.

In either of those cases the court should protect, in my view, the public from that man
further abusing the privileges [of limited liability].'

However, the fact that a subsequent business is being run successfully is only
one factor to be taken into consideration (*Re D J Matthews (Joinery Design) Ltd*
(1988) 4 BCC 513). The acceptance of professional advice is indicative of a
responsible attitude to management, but this cannot be relied upon to escape
liability. In *Re Grayan Building Services Ltd* [1995] Ch 241; [1995] BCC 554, the
court stated that 'unfitness' would be made out if the 'conduct [of the directors],
viewed cumulatively, and taking into account extenuating circumstances, fell below
the appropriate standards of probity and competence'. Where directors' conduct fell
below that level, an order under s. 6 of the *Company Directors Disqualification Act*
1986 would be mandatory. The court has a discretion to allow a disqualified person
to continue as a director of another company under such terms as it thinks fit (*Re
Majestic Recording Studios Ltd* (1988) 4 BCC 519).

¶41-800   Other cases of disqualification

Disqualification orders may be made by the court consequent upon a declaration
under s. 213 or 214 of the *Insolvency Act* 1986, that a person shall make
contributions to a company's assets because of his involvement in the company's
fraudulent or wrongful trading. The maximum period of disqualification in such
circumstances is 15 years (CDDA 1986, s. 10). This measure has rarely been
invoked in practice, perhaps because of the relatively few cases on fraudulent
and/or wrongful trading, but for a reported example in which the directors of a

company were disqualified under s. 10 for two and five years respectively see *Re Brian D Pierson (Contractors) Ltd* [1999] BCC 26.

In *Re Hydrodan (Corby) Ltd* [1994] BCC 161, the court concluded that liability under s. 214 of the *Insolvency Act* 1986 for wrongful trading extended to de facto directors. Such directors could then be subject to an order made under s. 10 of the *Company Directors Disqualification Act* 1986.

It is an offence for an undischarged bankrupt to act as a director of a company, or directly or indirectly to take part in or be concerned in the promotion, formation or management of a company except with leave of the court (CDDA 1986, s. 11; see *In re McQuillan* (1989) 5 BCC 137). In *R v Brockley* [1994] BCC 131, s. 11 was construed as a strict liability offence. In other words, a director will be guilty of the offence even if he is unaware that he has not been discharged from his bankruptcy. A prohibition is also applied to persons under an administration order under Pt. VI of the *County Courts Act* 1984 (for failure to pay a judgment debt) in respect of whom the order has been revoked. Such persons are prohibited from acting as a director or liquidator of, or from directly or indirectly taking part, or being concerned in the promotion, formation or management of, a company, except with the leave of the court which made the order (CDDA 1986, s. 12).

¶41-850   Consequences of contravention

Criminal penalties await persons who act in contravention of a disqualification order. The offence may result in imprisonment for not more than two years and/or a fine, or imprisonment for not more than six months and/or a fine, for convictions on indictment or summary convictions respectively (CDDA 1986, s. 13). The Act also enables the court to 'look through' companies who commit the offences, to prosecute persons responsible for the contravention, or with whose consent or as a result of whose neglect the offences were committed (CDDA 1986, s. 14).

A person who is involved in managing a company in contravention of a disqualification order or within the prohibition under s. 11 of the *Company Directors Disqualification Act* 1986 as an undischarged bankrupt (see ¶41-800) may be held liable for all the 'relevant debts' of a company (CDDA 1986, s. 15). Liability extends to persons who act in the management of a company under the instructions of a person so disqualified or prohibited. The 'relevant debts' of a company are those incurred at a time when the person was involved with the management of the company or when that person was willing to act on instructions of the prohibited or disqualified person (CDDA 1986, s. 15(3)).

A register of disqualification orders is maintained by the Secretary of State (CDDA 1986, s. 18).

The Department of Trade and Industry has a 'Rogue Directors Hotline' encouraging members of the public to report persons whom they suspect of acting as a director while disqualified or bankrupt. The hotline is open 24 hours per day and the telephone number is 0845 601 3546.

It is possible to carry out a search of a list of disqualified directors available on the Companies House Internet website for which the address is: 'http://www.companieshouse.gov.uk'.

There is no contravention if the director obtains the court's leave to act as director of a particular company or companies while subject to a disqualification order (CDDA 1986, s. 17). The court may grant interim leave for a disqualified director to act in the period before the application for leave is heard if proper undertakings are given: *Re Amaron Ltd* [1998] BCC 264. In the latter case the judge, who refused the application for leave under s. 17, added that despite the disqualification order the respondent could continue in business without the advantage of limited liability by entering into a partnership with his former co-director and trading from the company's premises; they could even use the company's name (without 'Ltd') for the benefit of any goodwill. In refusing the application for leave under s. 17 the judge also gave the respondent a transitional period of six weeks to sort out matters (without being in contravention of the disqualification order) to avoid prejudice to the business. Note that the Court of Appeal in *Secretary of State for Trade and Industry v Griffiths* [1998] BCC 836 gave useful guidelines on the considerations to be borne in mind in s. 17 applications.

¶41-900   Prohibition on re-use of company names

Directors of companies which have gone into insolvent liquidation are restricted from being involved in other companies with the same or similar name as that of the insolvent company.

Where a company has gone into insolvent liquidation, any director or shadow director of the company (or anyone who so qualified in the 12-month period before the liquidation) may not, without leave of the court:

(1) be a director of any other company that is known by the name of the insolvent company, or a name so similar as to suggest an association with that company, or

(2) in any way, whether directly or indirectly, be concerned or take part in the promotion, formation or management of any such company,

(3) in any way, directly or indirectly, be concerned or take part in the carrying on of a business carried on (otherwise than by a company) under such a prohibited name (IA 1986, s. 216).

The period of disqualification is for five years from when the insolvent company went into liquidation. Contravention of the section exposes the persons concerned to a fine, imprisonment or both. Any person or persons who act in contravention of s. 216 may also be held personally responsible for the debts of the new company incurred while they were involved in its management (IA 1986, s. 217).

According to the Court of Appeal, the offence of being a director of a company with a prohibited name under s. 216 of the *Insolvency Act* 1986 is a strict liability offence, i.e. the fact of doing so constitutes the offence and the prosecution does not have to prove an intention (*R v Cole, Lees & Birch* [1998] BCC 87).

¶41-950   Vacation, removal and retirement from office

A company's articles of association will often provide for vacation of office by directors by incorporation of Table A, reg. 81 (in the *Companies (Tables A to F) Regulations* 1985). This article (see ¶31-050) states that a director's office is vacated where:

(1) he ceases to be a director by virtue of any provision of the *Companies Act* 1985, or he becomes prohibited by law from being a director; or

(2) he becomes bankrupt or makes any arrangement or composition with his creditors generally; or

(3) he becomes of unsound mind, as evidenced by court order or hospital admission;

(4) he resigns his office by notice to the company; or

(5) he has been absent without permission of the directors from meetings of the directors for a period of more than six months and the directors resolve that he shall vacate office.

The company can add to the list of circumstances in which a director must vacate his office.

Resolution to remove director

A company can remove a director before his office was due to expire. This can be done by an ordinary resolution of the company, for which special notice is given (CA 1985, s. 303). A copy of this notice must be sent to the director the company seeks to remove, who is given the opportunity to address the shareholders at the meeting at which the vote is to be taken (CA 1985, s. 304). Accordingly, the decision to remove a director in this way cannot be made by written resolution (CA 1985, Sch. 15A, para. 1(a)). The director can also require the company to circulate any written representations (which must be reasonable in length) that the director may wish to make to the shareholders who received notice of the meeting (CA 1985, s. 304).

The company cannot contract out of the right to remove directors under s. 303. However, it may be impossible to obtain a majority vote under s. 303, if the articles provide for weighted voting rights for particular shareholders on a resolution to remove a director from office, as happened in *Bushell v Faith* [1970] AC 1099 (see ¶30-500). However, as a matter of general law a company may also remove a director from office by special resolution, without the incidents attaching to an ordinary resolution under s. 303.

There are other factors which must be taken into account before a decision to remove a director from office. The company may expose itself to an action for breach of contract. This will arise where the appointment was expressly stated to be for a fixed term, or where the director has a contract of employment with the company. The procedure for removal by ordinary resolution does not deprive the director of any compensation or damages payable in respect of the termination of employment (CA 1985, s. 303(5)).

Retirement from office

The provisions which regulate retirement by rotation are considered in ¶41-400. If a director retires from office because he reached retirement age during the year, he is not taken into account in establishing the number of directors who must retire by rotation (CA 1985, s. 293(6)).

AUTHORITY OF DIRECTORS

Management of the company's
  affairs .... ¶42-300

Acts done on the company's
  behalf .... ¶42-400

¶42-300 Management of the company's affairs

The structure and workings of the board of directors are determined by the articles of association. A wide discretion will usually be conferred upon the directors in the conduct of the necessary administration and procedure. Table A of the *Companies (Tables A to F) Regulations* 1985 (see ¶31-050) provides that 'subject to the provisions of the articles, the directors may regulate their proceedings as they think fit' (Table A, reg. 88). It is usual for directors to confer and reach decisions in meetings, of which a record is kept (Table A, reg. 100). The directors may appoint one of their number to preside over the meeting as chairman, who is to have a casting vote in the event of a deadlock (Table A, reg. 88).

Managing director

The articles may confer power upon the board to appoint a managing director and executive director (see, e.g., Table A, reg. 84). The managing director usually accepts a greater measure of responsibility for the company's overall affairs as a consequence of delegation by the rest of the board. An executive director accepts responsibility for one particular area of the company's activities, such as a sales, marketing or financial director.

Directors to manage company

The shareholders do not retain much control of the day-to-day administration of the company's affairs. They often do not have much influence on the formulation and implementation of policy either. This abdication of power into the hands of the board of directors is often recognised in the articles of association, which are a contract between the company and the shareholders. This is expressed by reg. 70 in the following terms:

'Subject to the provisions of the Act, the memorandum and articles and to any directions given by special resolution, the business of the company shall be managed by the directors who may exercise all the powers of the company.'

The board may appoint agents for whatever functions they determine (Table A, reg. 71). The board may also conditionally or otherwise delegate their authority to committees (Table A, reg. 72).

Shareholders' powers

Certain matters are left to the shareholders in general meeting under the Companies Act, such as amendments to the articles of association or memorandum of association (see ¶30-500, ¶30-450), a resolution for a voluntary winding up (IA 1986, s. 84) and alteration of the capital structure of the company (CA 1985, s. 121 and 135: see ¶30-450). Some issues may also be reserved for determination by the shareholders by the articles of association. For example, under Table A, reg. 82 (see ¶31-050) directors' remuneration is to be determined by ordinary resolution.

Despite the assumption of control of the company's affairs by directors under the articles of association, the courts have acknowledged circumstances in which the shareholders in general meeting must take charge of the reins. Deadlock in the boardroom, inability to fulfil the management role, or the fact that the board has ceased to exist, will vest power in the shareholders, to overcome the incapacity. However, once the board is again in a position to function as envisaged under the articles of association, power is returned to the board. This principle, and the circumstances in which the residual power of the shareholders may be called into play, are illustrated by the case of *Barron v Potter*.

Case example
The articles of association of a company provided that the quorum for directors' meetings should be two. There were only two directors, Mr Potter (the chairman), and Canon Barron, and they lived some distance apart. Canon Barron refused to attend board meetings at which Mr Potter was present. When Canon Barron arrived at Paddington Station for a shareholders' meeting, Mr Potter confronted him, but Canon Barron replied, 'I have nothing to say to you.' Mr Potter replied, 'I formally propose that we add the Reverend Charles Herbert, Mr William George Walter Barnard and Mr John Tolehurst Musgrove as additional directors to the board ... [of the company] ... do you object?' Canon Barron stated that he objected, and that he objected to speaking to Mr Potter at all. Mr Potter then said, 'In my capacity as Chairman, I give my casting vote in their favour, and declare them duly elected.' This appointment was not upheld as valid. A later exchange between the two characters was also not recognised as a valid board meeting. However, a general meeting of shareholders was then convened by Canon Barron, at which additional directors were appointed. This appointment was upheld. The court held that, for practical purposes, the board of directors was non-existent. Thus, there had to be 'some power in the company to do itself that which under other circumstances would be otherwise done'. *Barron v Potter* [1914] 1 Ch 895.

ACTS DONE ON THE COMPANY'S BEHALF

¶42-400   General

Corporate personality is a legal fiction. Companies operate through servants and agents. The directors have been likened to the 'brain and nerve centre' of the company (*H L Bolton Engineering Co Ltd v T J Graham & Sons Ltd* [1957] 1 QB 159). They represent the mind and will of the company, and control what it does. It is possible for the directors to delegate part of their management function to subordinate employees. If an employee were permitted to act independently of instructions from the directors, he would be acting as the company. However, it is usually acts of the directors which are to be viewed as acts of the company itself. Those employees who do not influence the company's activities were described in the above case as 'hands which hold the tools and act in accordance with directions from the centre'. The fact that the company must operate through agents raises two important issues. The first is the extent to which the company can be held responsible for the 'tortious' or criminal acts of its directors (see ¶42-450). The second is how the boundaries of the directors' authority to bind the company are defined (see ¶42-500).

¶42-450   Civil and criminal liability

It is possible for a company to be held liable for a civil wrong ('tort'), if the offending act or omission can be viewed as the 'very action of the company itself' (*Lennard's Carrying Co Ltd v Asiatic Petroleum Co Ltd* [1915] AC 705). Personal liability is attributed to the company on the following basis:

> ' ... where the law requires personal fault as a condition of liability in tort, the fault of the manager will be the personal fault of the company ... the intention of the company can be derived from the intention of its officers and agents. Whether their intention is the company's intention depends on the nature of the matter under consideration, the relative position of the officer or agent and the other relevant facts and circumstances of the case' (Denning LJ in *H L Bolton Engineering Co Ltd v T J Graham & Sons Ltd* [1957] 1 QB 159 at pp. 172–173).

In *Meridian Global Funds Management Asia Ltd v Securities Commission* [1995] BCC 942, the Privy Council ruled that, in deciding whether to attribute the act of a director to the company itself, one had to look at the relevant substantive legislation. A judge would have to be guided by the language and purpose of the legislation. In effect, there was no absolute rule of attribution. Each case would depend on the individual circumstances. The fact that a tortious act was not within the scope of the company's memorandum will not afford a defence to any action founded thereon (*Campbell v Paddington Corporation* [1911] 1 KB 869).

¶42-400

The above form of civil liability is to be distinguished from the 'vicarious' liability of an employer for (say negligent) acts of an employee which are undertaken in the course of his employment. The director is acting as the company. 'He is an embodiment of the company, or as one could say, he hears and speaks through the persona of the company, within his appropriate sphere, and his mind is the mind of the company.' (*Tesco Supermarkets Ltd v Nattrass* [1972] AC 153.)

Where a director authorises employees of a company to commit what amounts to a tort, then the director himself may be personally liable for doing so (*Mancetter Developments Ltd v Garmanson Ltd* (1986) 2 BCC 98,924). He would not be liable for actions of the employees which he did not authorise.

Criminal liability

It is possible for the company to incur criminal liability as a consequence of the acts and state of mind of those persons identifiable as the company itself. This was explained in the following terms by Lord Reid in *Tesco Supermarkets Ltd v Nattrass* (at p. 173D):

'I think that the true view is that the judge must direct the jury that if they find certain facts proved then as a matter of law they must find that the criminal act of the officer, servant or agent including his state of mind, intention, knowledge or belief is the act of the company.'

The culpability of a corporation for such a serious crime as manslaughter was considered in *R v Her Majesty's Coroner for East Kent, ex parte Spooner* (1987) 3 BCC 636. Bingham LJ at p. 642 concluded that a corporation could be guilty of conduct amounting to manslaughter:

'A company may be vicariously liable for the negligent acts and omissions of its servants and agents, but for a company to be criminally liable for manslaughter ... requires that the *mens rea* [criminal intent] and the *actus reus* [criminal act] of manslaughter should be established not against those who acted for or in the name of the company but against those who were to be identified as the embodiment of the company itself.'

¶42-500 Directors' authority to bind the company

Directors who undertake acts on behalf of the company are usually accorded wide powers of management under the articles of association. The directors and secretary exercise these powers as agents of the company. The power of the directors to bind the company is thus determined by agency principles. An agent's power to bind his principal is based upon the concepts of actual, usual and apparent authority.

Actual authority is the power which the principal has expressly conferred upon his agent.

Usual authority is determined by the nature of the agency itself, and is the power which an agent of that type usually has.

Apparent (or ostensible) authority arises where the principal represents to third parties that the agent's authority extends beyond his actual or usual authority. The principal is then 'estopped' from denying the extent of the authority as held out by his own representations. The third party can rely on the apparent authority unless he has such notification as would make a reasonable man suspicious of its actual extent.

Translated into terms of company law, a company officer has the power to bind his company to the extent of his authority, be it actual, usual or ostensible. Actual authority is co-extensive with usual authority unless the third party has notice of a restriction placed by the company on that officer's authority. If the company allows the director to represent to third parties that his authority extends beyond that actually conferred upon him, the company is estopped from avoiding acts within this ostensible authority.

The 'usual' authority of executive directors and the managing director will be broader than that of other members of the board and agents. If a third party is put on enquiry of the fact that a director may be exceeding his actual authority, the company will not be bound by the transaction (*B Liggett (Liverpool) Ltd v Barclays Bank Ltd* [1928] 1 KB 48).

When company bound by unauthorised acts

If the board allows a director to hold himself out as authorised to engage in transactions which are, in fact, beyond his actual authority, the company cannot deny that authority, even if the articles contain no power of delegation (*Freeman & Lockyer v Buckhurst Park Properties (Mangal) Ltd* [1964] 2 QB 480). In this case, Diplock LJ identified four conditions for a company to be bound by an agent acting outside his authority:

(1) there must have been a representation that the agent had authority to bind the company on this type of contract;

(2) that representation must have been made by a person with actual authority to manage the business;

(3) the third party must have relied on the representation and been induced into the contract on its faith; and

(4) the company must have been empowered to enter the type of contract involved.

A director or other agent may bind a company in contract without condition (d) having been satisfied (CA 1985, s. 35: see ¶30-800).

On the other side of the coin, if a third party gives notice of a particular matter to the director of a company, the company is treated as having knowledge of that fact (*J C Houghton & Co v Nothard, Lowe & Wills Ltd* [1928] AC 1).

¶42-500

DIRECTORS' TRANSACTIONS WITH THE COMPANY

¶42-800   General

Involvement of directors in transactions with the company is the subject of stringent statutory regulation. Extensive duties of disclosure are placed upon the company in respect of such matters.

This area can be conveniently divided into the following topics: directors' remuneration (see ¶42-900, ¶43-000), loans to directors (see ¶43-100ff.), substantial property transactions involving directors (see ¶43-450, ¶43-500), directors' fiduciary duties (see ¶43-600), general disclosure requirements (see ¶43-700), and listed companies (see ¶43-800). Also examined are directors' interests in the company's shares, etc. (see ¶43-900, ¶43-950).

¶42-900   Directors' remuneration

A director has no automatic right to remuneration for his services (*Hutton v West Cork Rly Co* (1883) 23 ChD 654). Payment of remuneration to directors is usually governed by the articles of association. For example, Table A, reg. 2 of the *Companies (Tables A to F) Regulations* 1985, provides that:

'The directors shall be entitled to such remuneration as the company may by ordinary resolution determine and, unless the resolution provides otherwise, the remuneration shall be deemed to accrue from day to day.'

A managing director is usually appointed upon such terms as the company and the directors determine, and they may remunerate any such director for his services as they think fit (Table A, reg. 84: see ¶31-050).

If there is a procedure provided in the articles for determination of directors' remuneration, there is no entitlement to remuneration outside that procedure. For this is what the directors have contracted for (*Re New British Iron Co, ex parte Beckwith* [1898] 1 Ch 324). Entitlement to remuneration under the articles thus turns on construction of the relevant term and is, of course, vulnerable to alteration under the general power of a company to amend the articles. Of course, it is open to a director to negotiate a service contract with the company. A right to remuneration will then arise independent of any contract implied into, or contained expressly in, the articles of association.

If a director's entitlement to remuneration is agreed before performance of duties, but subsequently challenged on technical grounds, such as the validity of his appointment or the contract of service, the director can enforce a restitutionary claim against the company. This is a 'quantum meruit' claim, and entitles the director to a reasonable reward for the services he has provided (*Craven-Ellis v Canons Ltd* [1936] 2 KB 403). The basis for this award is factual necessity of the director's services. The company would have to have paid somebody to undertake his duties. To the extent that the company could escape liability for the payment, it would have been unjustly enriched.

Particulars of a proposed compensation payment must be disclosed to the members, and the payment approved in a general meeting (CA 1985, s. 312). If the director receives a payment in contravention of these provisions, he holds the money as constructive trustee, for the benefit of the company (CA 1985, s. 313(2)).

A director who stands to receive compensation for loss of office if the company's shareholders accept an offer for their shares is placed under an obligation to disclose the details of the proposed payment to those shareholders. The shareholders must then approve the payment before any transfer is made in pursuance of the offer (CA 1985, s. 314 and 315).

Certain payments on termination of office are outside the requirements for approval by the shareholders. A 'bona fide payment of damages for breach of contract or by way of pension in respect of past services' is placed expressly outside s. 312–315 by s. 316(3).

A director's right to compensation for loss of office on the occurrence of his removal (by ordinary resolution in general meeting) is expressly preserved by s. 303(5) of the *Companies Act* 1985.

¶43-000   Disclosure of directors' remuneration, etc.

The company must disclose directors' remuneration in the annual accounts. If the company fails to disclose this information, the auditors are required to do so (CA 1985, s. 237(4)).

The disclosure requirements of directors' remuneration under Sch. 6 to the *Companies Act* 1985 in respect of companies' financial years ending on or after 31 March 1997 require each company to disclose:

- the aggregate amount of directors' emoluments (as defined under Sch. 6, para. 1(3));

- the aggregate amount of gains made by directors on share options (listed companies only);

- the aggregate of moneys paid to or receivable by directors under long-term incentive schemes (as defined in para. 1(4)) and the net value of assets other than money and share options received or receivable by directors under such schemes (for non-listed companies, 'assets' does not include shares for this purpose).

¶43-000

Where the aggregate of these disclosures totals £200,000 or more, then so much as is attributable to the highest paid director must be separately disclosed, as must the value of company contributions to a pension scheme in respect of that director.

There must also be disclosed the aggregate value of company contributions to a pension scheme in respect of directors' services; and the number of directors for whom retirement benefits are accruing under money purchase schemes and defined benefit schemes (both as defined). In the case of non-listed companies only, the company must disclose the number of directors who exercised share options and the directors who received shares under long-term incentive schemes.

The aggregate of *excess* retirement benefits of present and past directors (i.e. in excess of the amount paid or receivable on the date when the benefits first became payable or 31 March 1997, whichever is the later) must be respectively shown; the aggregates do not include sums paid or receivable if the funding of the scheme was such that the amounts were or could have been paid without recourse to additional contributions and amounts paid to or receivable by all pensioner members of the scheme on the same basis (CA 1985, Sch. 6, para. 7).

Small companies, as defined, may now disclose the total of the aggregates of directors' emoluments, gains on share options and company contributions to directors' pension schemes instead of giving those aggregates individually. They do not need to disclose the number of directors exercising share options and receiving shares under long-term incentive schemes, details of the highest paid director's emoluments or excess retirement benefits of directors and past directors.

Directors of public companies listed on the London Stock Exchange have far heavier disclosure requirements, imposed by the *Listing Rules*, resulting from recommendations by the Greenbury Committee (July 1995) and Hampel Committee (January 1998) reports. These include disclosure in the annual accounts showing a breakdown of the constituent elements of each individual director's remuneration package. A new rule applies for accounting periods ending on or after 31 December 1998.

LOANS TO DIRECTORS

¶43-100   General

The rules regulating loans to directors govern all credit-related transactions made between a company and its directors or persons who have a like status. The legislation has two main effects. The first of these is to prohibit credit transactions between a company and its directors, subject to exceptions. The second effect is to ensure that disclosure is made of those loans not prohibited by law.

The legislation draws a distinction between 'relevant' and 'non-relevant' companies, and applies a different regulatory code to each category (see ¶43-200, ¶43-250). Before considering these rules, it is necessary to understand the meaning of terms used in the statute, which define the scope of the legislation (see ¶43-150).

¶43-150   Loans, quasi-loans and credit transactions

Oddly enough, nowhere in the Companies Act is there provided a definition of the term 'loan'. However, it is generally understood to mean an advance of money on the understanding that repayment will be made (see *Champagne Perrier-Jouet v H H Finch* [1982] 1 WLR 1359).

The Act extends the ambit of the rules, by including 'quasi-loans' and credit transactions within its scope. A quasi-loan arises where the company assumes liability for debts incurred by the director on the understanding that the director will repay the company (CA 1985, s. 331(3)). A credit transaction is one by which the company either supplies goods or sells land, under a hire-purchase agreement or a conditional sale agreement, or leases or hires land or goods in return for periodical payments, or otherwise disposes of land or supplies goods or services, on the understanding that payment is to be deferred (CA 1985, s. 331(7)).

The value of a loan which falls under these heads is the principal sum advanced. The size of a quasi-loan is the maximum amount that the company is liable to reimburse the director's creditor. A credit transaction is measured by reference to the price which could be obtained for the goods or services provided to the director at the time the transaction was entered into (CA 1985, s. 340). However, if the value of the transaction cannot be assessed, it is deemed to exceed £100,000 (CA 1985, s. 340(7)).

Directors and connected persons

A director is identified as any person who occupies the position of director, by whatever name called, or any person, other than a professional adviser, in accordance with whose instructions the directors are accustomed to act (CA 1985, s. 741). Persons connected with the directors are covered by the legislation. The categories of 'connected persons' extend to family relationships, companies in which the director has an interest, trustees and business associates. A director is connected with a spouse, and with a child or stepchild under 18 years of age, with a company in which he (with interests of other connected persons) controls 20 per cent of the nominal share capital or voting power, with a trustee of a trust in which the director (or anyone connected with him) has or may have a beneficial interest, and with any partner of the director or of somebody connected with the director (CA 1985, s. 346).

¶43-150

¶43-200 Rules applicable to relevant companies

A 'relevant company' is a public company or a company which is part of a group in which there is a public company, a non-relevant company being one which is outside this definition (CA 1985, s. 331(6)).

A relevant company cannot make a loan to a director, guarantee a loan to a director, provide security for such a loan or enter into a credit transaction with him. The prohibition extends to the company's holding company and covers any transactions of a similar nature with persons connected with the director (CA 1985, s. 330(7)). However, there are exceptions to this rule.

Exceptions

An exemption of £5,000 for loans to each director is provided, from all companies within the same group (but not for connected persons) (CA 1985, s. 334 and 339). 'Quasi-loans' are exempted if they are repayable within two months and the amount outstanding does not exceed £5,000 in any case (CA 1985, s. 332). A further exemption is conferred for loans to director which are made to meet expenditure incurred by them for purposes of the company's business, or to enable directors to perform their duties. The approval of the company in general meeting must be obtained (either before the loan or at the first general meeting to follow the loan) and the total value of such loans outstanding cannot exceed £20,000. If approval of the company is not obtained the loan must be repaid within six months (CA 1985, s. 337).

A company can also enter into credit transactions on behalf of directors, or persons connected with them, up to a value of £10,000 per director (CA 1985, s. 335). Also outside the prohibitory rules are money-lending companies, i.e. those companies whose ordinary business includes making loans or quasi-loans, up to £100,000 (CA 1985, s. 338), and credit companies, i.e. those who enter into credit transactions in the ordinary course of their business (CA 1985, s. 335).

Prohibition of certain assignments, etc.

It is not permissible for a relevant company to assume obligations or liabilities by assignment, which would have been prohibited under the Companies Act if originally entered into by that company (CA 1985, s. 330(6)). Further, a third party cannot enter into a transaction with a director which, had the company entered into such transactions, would have been prohibited if the third party obtains a benefit from the company, its holding company or a subsidiary as a result of that transaction (CA 1985, s. 330(7)).

¶43-250 Non-relevant companies

A non-relevant company (see ¶43-200) cannot make a loan, guarantee any loan or provide security to or for a loan to a director or a director of that company's holding company (CA 1985, s. 330). An exemption of £5,000 per director is provided (CA 1985, s. 334). A company cannot accept assignments of loans to directors or enter into an arrangement to circumvent the prohibitions contained in the Act (CA 1985, s. 330(6)). There is an exemption for loans made to meet expenses to be incurred for the purposes of the company's business (CA 1985, s. 337). It is necessary for the loan to be approved at a general meeting before the loan is made, or at the next general meeting, unless it is to be repaid within six months. There is no upper limit on the aggregate value of such sums for non-relevant companies.

¶43-300   Consequences of prohibited loans, etc.

A prohibited loan or credit transaction is voidable at the option of the company. However, this cannot be done if it is not possible to restore the status quo, or if the company has been indemnified against loss it may suffer, or if a third party (who had no notice of the breach of statute) has acquired rights for which valuable consideration was given and which would be affected by avoidance of the transaction. Directors who are in breach of the statute are liable to account for any benefit received. This is irrespective of the company's decision to avoid or affirm the transaction. The rule applies to connected persons who may have benefited, and also to directors who authorised the prohibited transaction.

A director of a relevant company who knowingly participates in or authorises transactions which are prohibited under the Act is liable to criminal sanctions of a fine, imprisonment, or both (CA 1985, s. 342).

¶43-350   Disclosure requirements for loans, etc.

There is no distinction between relevant and non-relevant companies for the purpose of disclosure in financial statements. A company's accounts must disclose transactions with its own directors, or directors of its holding company or with persons connected with such directors. The rules apply to transactions with persons who held office for only part of the financial year. The group accounts of a holding company or, if it is not required to prepare group accounts, its individual accounts must disclose transactions of companies in the group with directors, or persons connected with directors, of that company or of its ultimate holding company (CA 1985, Sch. 6).

These rules of disclosure apply to loans, quasi-loans, guarantees, credit transactions (see ¶43-100 to ¶43-250) and also to any security given by the company in respect of such transactions. Assignments to the company of directors' liabilities which would have been prohibited under the Companies Act must be disclosed. The Act also calls for disclosure of arrangements between a third party, a company and its director prohibited under s. 330(7) of the *Companies Act* 1985.

The details to be disclosed are set out in Sch. 6, para. 22 of the *Companies Act* 1985. There is an overriding requirement that the main terms of the arrangement be set out. The general disclosure requirements, and those specific to credit transactions, guarantees and assignments are set out in the following table. Exemptions from disclosure are provided for credit transactions, guarantees, assignments or arrangements involving the company or its subsidiaries, if no one director (or director of the company's holding company) owes more than £5,000 (including sums owed by persons connected with that director) at any stage in the financial year (CA 1985, Sch. 6, para. 24).

Table: Considerations on directors' loans

	Relevant company or a company with a relevant company in same group	*Exemptions*	*Non-relevant company*	*Exemptions*
Loan	Prohibited	1. £5,000 per director.	Prohibited	1. £5,000 per director.
		2. Loans to holding companies		2. For the purposes of the company, or to perform directors' duties.
		3. For the purposes of the company or to perform directors' duties. Up to £10,000 aggregated loans.		
		4. Loans to group companies.		
		5. Money-lending companies up to £100,000.		
Quasi-Loan	Prohibited	1. For the purposes of the company or to perform directors' duties up to £10,000 aggregated.		
		2. Loans to holding companies.		
		3. Loans to group companies.		
		4. Money-lending companies up to £100,000.		
		5. Up to £5,000 per director.		
Credit Transaction	Prohibited	1. Credit transaction up to £10,000 per director.		
		2. Made in ordinary course of the company's business.		
		3. Transactions for holding companies.		

SUBSTANTIAL PROPERTY TRANSACTIONS INVOLVING DIRECTORS

¶43-450   General

A company cannot enter into arrangements whereby a director or a shadow director of the company or its holding company acquire from or provide to that company one or more non-cash assets of the requisite value, unless the transaction is approved in a general meeting (CA 1985, s. 320) of one company or, if it is a wholly-owned subsidiary, of its holding company (CA 1985, s. 320(1) and 321(1)). A 'non-cash asset' is of the requisite value if at the time of the transaction its value is:

● not less than £2,000, and

● greater than £100,000 or ten per cent of the company's net asset value.

The net asset value is to be determined from the latest accounts. Where no accounts have been prepared the called-up share capital is to be taken as the net asset value.

In *Re Duckwari plc* [1997] BCC 45 it was thought at first instance that the mischief, and only mischief, addressed by s. 320–322 of the *Companies Act* 1985 was an acquisition by a company at an inflated value or disposal by a company at an undervalue, so that if restitution was not possible then compensation would be the difference between the market value of the property at the date of the transaction and the price paid or received, with no compensation for change in value between the date of the transaction and some subsequent date such as the trial. The Court of Appeal (*Duckwari plc v Offerventure Ltd (No. 2)* [1999] BCC 11) considered this analysis to be incorrect: the loss in value of property after it had been transferred had to fall somewhere and should lie with the directors who effected the transaction. Nor was it likely that a director in such a situation could claim relief under s. 727 of the 1985 Act (by showing that he had acted honestly and reasonably and in the circumstances ought fairly to be excused – see ¶41-000) for he would be unlikely to have acted reasonably.

According to the Court of Session (confirming an earlier High Court decision), a contractual right to compensation for loss of office for a director is not a non-cash asset and so is not caught by s. 320 (*Lander v Premier Pict Petroleum Ltd* [1998] BCC 248).

Although s. 321 of the *Companies Act* 1985 expressly exempts substantial property transactions with a director by a liquidator on behalf of a company in compulsory or creditors' voluntary winding up (but not members' voluntary winding up) from the avoiding provisions contained in s. 320, the courts will not imply an exemption concerning such transactions by a receiver (*Demite Ltd v Protec Health Ltd* [1998] BCC 638). Any directors who do wish to purchase

¶43-450   CCH New Law qualifying substantial non-cash assets from a receiver should first obtain approval by the company in general meeting.

Exceptions

The above prohibitions do not apply to intra-group transactions, arrangements entered into the course of a winding up (other than a members' voluntary winding up) or acquisitions of assets from a company by a director in his capacity as a shareholder or a transaction on a recognised investment exchange through an independent broker (CA 1985, s. 321).

¶43-500   Consequences of a prohibited transaction

A transaction prohibited under s. 320 of the *Companies Act* 1985 (see ¶43-450) is voidable at the company's option (CA 1985, s. 322(1)). However, the transaction will stand if:

- it is no longer possible to restore to the company the asset or cash which passed under the transaction; or
- the company has been indemnified against any loss; or
- a third party has acquired rights for value and without notice of the prohibited transaction which would be adversely affected by avoidance thereof; or
- the transaction is affirmed by the company in general meeting within a reasonable time (CA 1985, s. 322(2)).

Director's liability to account to and indemnify company

Any director (or person connected with the director) of a company which entered into a prohibited transaction, or of the holding company thereof who participated in the transaction, is liable to account for any profit made, and to indemnify the company for any loss suffered (CA 1985, s. 322(3)). However, a director is not liable to account for a prohibited transaction if he took reasonable steps to secure the company's approval in a general meeting or was unaware of the circumstances which constitute the contravention of the Act (CA 1985, s. 322(5), (6)).

Where board exceed their powers

There are special rules as regards transactions with directors entered into by a company where the board of directors exceed their authority to bind the company, or authorise others to do so (CA 1985, s. 322A). While such a transaction is deemed to be free of any limitation under the company's constitution in dealings with a third party who is in good faith, such a transaction with a director is voidable (but may be ratified by the company). However, this does not affect the operation of s. 35A of the *Companies Act* 1985 (see ¶30-800) in relation to any other party who deals with the company in good faith, and accordingly where a transaction is void as against a director, but valid as against a third party, the court may, on application, sever the transaction, or set aside all or part of a transaction, on such terms as appear to the court to be just (CA 1985, s. 322A).

¶43-600   Fiduciary duty of a director when contracting with the company

An obvious problem which can arise from contracts between a director and his company is the possibility of a conflict between his interest and duty. A general rule has developed under the common law that a director is prohibited from entering into such contracts (*Aberdeen Railway Co v Blaikie Bros* (1854) 23 LT 315). However, if the director can show that there was no possibility of conflict, by evidence of disclosure and company approval, the transaction will stand (*Movitex Ltd v Bulfield* (1986) 2 BCC 99,403). Although the Companies Act regulates transactions between companies and their directors, these rules should be considered against the background of the common law position (see ¶40-700ff.).

¶43-700   General disclosure requirements

A company must disclose in its accounts all transactions in which its own directors, or in which the directors of its holding company (or persons connected with such directors), have a 'material interest'. Similarly, group accounts of a holding company (or, if it is not required to prepare group accounts, its individual accounts) must contain details of transactions of the holding company or its subsidiaries in which a person who was a director of either company at any time during the year had a material interest (CA 1985, Sch. 6, para. 15(c), 16(c)). Any transaction between a company and one of its directors or any director of its holding company, or between the company and persons connected with such directors, is to be treated as a contract in which the director is interested.

There is no definition of 'material'. However, a director's interest in the contract is not material if the rest of the board consider it is not so (CA 1985, Sch. 6, para. 17(2)). If the board fail to consider the issue, materiality must fall to be considered by reference to the value of the director's interest in relation to the value of the contract as a whole.

¶43-800   Listed companies

Where a company is involved in one of the above transactions, additional obligations may arise if the company is either listed on the London Stock Exchange or quoted on the Alternative Investment Market (AIM), which was introduced in June 1995 and designed for smaller public companies desirous of public finances). The *Listing Rules* of the London Stock Exchange explains the further rules incumbent on listed companies.

¶43-600

DIRECTORS AND SHARES

¶43-900 Directors' disclosure of share, etc. interests

A director who is interested in a company's shares or debentures must notify the company of that interest when it arises (CA 1985, s. 324). The duty extends to interests of the director's spouse and children (CA 1985, s. 328).

Every company must keep a register of directors' interests (including those of a spouse and minor children who are not themselves directors) in its own shares and debentures. The register must also disclose interests of those directors (and their spouses and minor children, if not themselves directors) in shares and debentures of that company's holding company, subsidiary companies or other subsidiaries of the parent, if appropriate (CA 1985, s. 325(1)).

Interests affected

A director is 'interested' in these shares or debentures if he has an interest of any kind in them, whether or not restrictions on his ownership have been imposed (CA 1985, Sch. 13, para. 1). The Act identifies specific types of interests in shares and debentures which require notification and registration, as follows (CA 1985, Sch. 13, para. 2, 3):

(1) an interest in a trust which comprises shares or debentures;

(2) an interest under a contract to purchase shares or debentures or to acquire them for valuable consideration; and

(3) a right or obligation, whether absolute or conditional, to acquire shares or debentures or an interest in them, other than a right or obligation to subscribe shares and debentures.

It would be easy for a director who was so minded to avoid disclosure of his interest in the company, by holding his shares through another company. Accordingly the Act defines circumstances in which a director is to be identified as 'interested' in company shares or debentures in which another company or body corporate is interested, as follows (CA 1985, Sch. 13, para. 4, 5):

(1) If the latter company or its directors are accustomed to act in accordance with the instructions of the director in question.

(2) If the director is entitled to exercise or to control the exercise of one-third or more of the voting power at general meetings of the other company or body corporate. The voting power of any third company or body corporate must be treated as that of the director if he is entitled to exercise or control one-third of the voting power in the third company. Interests of the director's spouse or minor children are not aggregated with those of the director for the purposes of these tests. However, if a spouse or minor child, who is not a

director of the company, alone controls one-third or more of the voting power of the third company this interest is attributed to the director.

The Act specifically provides that a director is not interested in shares or debentures by virtue of his appointment as a proxy at a specified meeting, or of his appointment as the representative of a corporate shareholder or debenture holder, or on account of his reversionary interest in settled shares in respect of which he has no right to the income, or where he acts as trustee for other persons (CA 1985, Sch. 13, para. 3(3), 9, 10).

A power is conferred upon the Secretary of State for Trade and Industry to exempt directors from the disclosure requirements in certain cases (CA 1985, s. 324(3)). The power has been used, inter alia, to provide an exemption where the interest has arisen as a consequence of restrictions imposed upon the transferability of shares under the company's memorandum and articles of association, and where a holding company is incorporated outside Great Britain and the interest is held by a director of a wholly-owned British subsidiary.

Time-limits, etc.

A director must give notice of his interest within five days of it arising or, where he was unaware that it had so arisen, five days from the date of knowledge (CA 1985, Sch. 13, para. 14, 15). For these purposes, an interest is deemed to include:

- becoming interested in the shares or debentures or ceasing to be so;
- contracting to sell the shares or debentures, or an assignment of a right to subscribe the shares or debentures; or
- being granted a right to subscribe the shares or debentures (CA 1985, s. 324(2)).

The company must register this information within three days of the notification (CA 1985, Sch. 13, para. 22).

If a company grants to its directors the right to subscribe shares or debentures, this right must be registered within three days of its creation. Exercise of the right must also be registered within three days of its occurrence (CA 1985, Sch. 13, para. 22).

A director must inform the company of the grant of rights of subscription to his spouse or minor child. The company must then register this information within three days. The exercise of the rights by the spouse or minor child must follow the same procedure (CA 1985, s. 328).

If the shares or debentures are listed on the London Stock Exchange the company must disclose to the Exchange on the following day the details contained in the notice which the director has given to the company under s. 324 or 328 of the *Companies Act* 1985 above (CA 1985, s. 329).

The register of directors' interests must be kept at the same place as the register of members (CA 1985, Sch. 13, para. 25). Any shareholder can inspect the register of directors' interests, and call for copies of it (CA 1985, Sch. 13, para. 25, 26).

¶43-950 Prohibition on directors dealing in share options

It is an offence for the director of a company, his spouse, or his minor children, to purchase options to call for delivery of shares or debentures of any company in the group, if the shares or debentures are listed on a stock exchange (CA 1985, s. 323). Although the statute does not specifically avoid the transaction, the fact of the illegality would render it void.

For insider dealing offences, see ¶45-000ff.

AUDITORS

¶44-300 Nature and qualification of auditors

The regulation of auditors as a profession underwent significant change under the *Companies Act* 1989 which implemented the eighth EU company law directive. Its main purposes were to secure that only persons fully supervised and appropriately qualified are appointed company auditors, and that audits by persons so appointed are carried out properly and with integrity and with the proper degree of independence (CA 1989, s. 24).

The provisions are primarily of significance to the professional accountancy bodies, and are not considered here in detail.

Eligibility for appointment

Previously, a person could be appointed an auditor if he was a member of one of the designated professional accountancy bodies or if he was authorised under the *Companies Act* 1967. Now a person is eligible for appointment as a company auditor only if he is:

- a member of a recognised supervisory body; and

- eligible for appointment under the rules of that body (CA 1989, s. 25).

An individual or a firm may be appointed a company auditor. The appointment of a firm pertains to the partnership, and not to individual partners. Where the partnership ceases, the appointment continues with the succeeding partnership (CA 1989, s. 26). A person authorised under s. 13(1) of the *Companies Act* 1967 is eligible only for appointment as auditor of an unquoted company (CA 1989, s. 34).

Ineligibility

No person may act as auditor if ineligible for appointment. The following persons are expressly ineligible on the ground of lack of independence:

(1) an officer or an employee of the company; or

(2) a partner or employee of such a person, or a partnership of which such a person is a partner;

or if he is ineligible by virtue of (1) or (2) above for appointment as a company auditor of any associated undertaking (as defined) of the company. For this purpose an auditor of a company shall not be regarded as an officer or employee of the company (CA 1989, s. 27(1)). In case these provisions are found in practice to be insufficient to ensure the independence of auditors, the Secretary of State has the power to designate any type of link between the company auditor (or any associate of his) and the company (or any associated undertaking) as ground for ineligibility (CA 1989, s. 27(2)).

Effect of ineligibility

An auditor who becomes ineligible during his term of office must vacate his office and write to the company stating that the reason for vacating the office was ineligibility (CA 1989, s. 28(2)).

Accepting office as an auditor when ineligible, or failing to vacate office on becoming ineligible, is a criminal offence and gives rise to a fine, plus a further daily default fine (CA 1989, s. 28(3), (4)). However, such a person has a defence if he can show that he did not know, and had no reason to believe, that he was or had become, ineligible for appointment (CA 1989, s. 28(5)).

Secretary of State's power to require second audit

In cases of ineligibility, the Secretary of State has specific powers to direct the company to retain another auditor to provide a second audit, or to review the first audit and report. This must be done within 21 days of the direction (CA 1989, s. 29).

Register of auditors

A register of all persons (individuals or firms) eligible for appointment as a company auditor will be kept. Further, individuals holding appropriate qualifications who are responsible for company audit work on behalf of such firms must be registered (CA 1989, s. 35). If a person describes himself as a registered auditor or holds himself out so as to indicate, or be reasonably understood to indicate, that he is a registered auditor while not appearing on the register of auditors, then he is committing an offence. He is liable on summary conviction to imprisonment of up to six months, or to a fine, or both.

¶44-400   Appointment of auditors

The first auditors of a company may be appointed by the directors or, in default, the company in general meeting. The first auditors hold office until the end of the first general meeting at which the accounts are presented (CA 1985, s. 385(3)). Subsequently, auditors are appointed at each general meeting at which accounts are presented. The auditors so appointed hold office until the conclusion of the next general meeting at which accounts are presented (CA 1985, s. 385(2)).

Private company's election not to appoint auditors annually

A private company may elect not to appoint auditors annually (CA 1985, s. 386(1)). If so, the auditors will be deemed reappointed for each succeeding financial year (CA 1985, s. 386(2)). This applies until a resolution is passed to bring their appointment to an end.

Appointment by private company which is not obliged to lay accounts

Where a private company has elected to dispense with the laying of accounts before the company in general meeting, then a separate regime for appointment applies (CA 1985, s. 385A(1)). The first auditors of the company may be appointed by the directors within 28 days of the company's first annual accounts being sent out to members (CA 1985, s. 385A(2)). If notice is given under s. 253(2) of the *Companies Act* 1985 requiring the laying of the accounts at the general meeting, then the first auditors may be appointed at any time before the beginning of that meeting (CA 1985, s. 385A(3)). The auditors appointed hold office until the end of that period or until the conclusion of that meeting respectively. Subsequently, auditors must be appointed by the company at each general meeting within 28 days of the copies of the annual accounts for the previous financial year being sent out or, if a notice under s. 253(2) has been issued requiring the laying of the accounts, then before the conclusion of that meeting.

Appointment by Secretary of State in default of appointment by company

If the directors or shareholders fail to appoint an auditor, the company must notify the Secretary of State within one week. The Secretary of State will then appoint a person to fill the vacancy. Failure to give notice may result in a fine (up to one-fifth of the statutory maximum) on the company and every officer of it in default. For a continued contravention a daily default fine may also be imposed (CA 1985, s. 387).

Filling of casual vacancies

The directors, or the company in general meeting, may appoint an auditor to fill a casual vacancy. However, for as long as the vacancy continues, the surviving or continuing auditor may continue to act (CA 1985, s. 388).

Rights of auditors who are not reappointed, etc.

A resolution at a general meeting requires special notice if it proposes to appoint to office an auditor other than the retiring auditor, or to fill a casual vacancy, or to reappoint a retiring auditor who was appointed to fill a casual vacancy. A person whom it is proposed to appoint, a retiring auditor whom it is not proposed to reappoint, and an auditor whose resignation caused the casual vacancy must be sent a copy of the relevant resolution. A retiring auditor whom it is not proposed to reappoint may make written representations of a reasonable length, which must be circulated to members of the company who receive notice of the meeting. If the company fails to circulate the representations, the retiring auditor can have them read out at the meeting (CA 1985, s. 391A).

¶44-500 Removal of auditors

An auditor can be removed from office at any time by an ordinary resolution (CA 1985, s. 391) of which special notice has been given (CA 1985, s. 391A(1)). However, this cannot be decided by a written resolution (CA 1985, Sch. 15A, para. 1(b)).

The auditor must be sent a copy of the resolution, and of any notices of meetings at which his term of office would otherwise have expired or at which it is proposed to fill the vacancy caused by his removal (CA 1985, s. 391A(2)). He must also be sent communications which relate to such meetings and which any company member is entitled to receive. He can make written representations to the members, or address them directly. However, copies of auditor's representations need not be sent out or read out at meetings if the court is satisfied that the auditor is seeking needless publicity for a defamatory matter.

A company which has passed a resolution to remove its auditor before his term of office expires must notify the registrar of companies within 14 days. Failure to do this exposes the company and every officer in default to a fine with a daily default fine (CA 1985, s. 391(2)).

Removal of auditors not appointed annually

Where a private company has elected not to appoint auditors annually, any member of the company may deposit notice in writing at the company's registered office proposing that the appointment of the company's auditors be brought to an end (CA 1985, s. 393). This right may only be exercised by a member once during the financial year of the company. The directors must convene a general meeting of the company within 28 days of the notice being given, and put forward a resolution enabling members to decide to bring the appointment of the company's auditors to an end. If the members so decide, the auditors shall not be deemed to be reappointed when next they would be. If the notice was deposited within 14 days after the annual accounts were sent to members under s. 238, any deemed re-appointment for the financial year following that to which those accounts relate which has already occurred shall cease to have effect.

A member of a company may convene the meeting himself, but only if the directors do not themselves convene a meeting within 14 days of the notice being deposited. This meeting must be convened within three months from that date. Reasonable expenses incurred by a member convening such a meeting are recoverable by him from the company. In turn, the company may recoup any such sums from such of its directors as were in default from their directors' fees or other remuneration.

¶44-500

¶44-600 Resignation of auditors

An auditor can resign from office by depositing written notice at the company's registered office (CA 1985, s. 392(1)). His resignation is effective as from the date of deposit of the notice, or any date specified in it, if later.

However, an auditor's letter of resignation is only effective if it includes either a statement that there are no circumstances connected with his resignation which he considers should be brought to the notice of members or creditors of the company, or a statement of those circumstances (CA 1985, s. 394). A company must send any notification by an auditor of his resignation from office to the registrar of companies within 14 days (CA 1985, s. 392(3)).

Resigning auditors' rights

If the auditor has specified circumstances connected with his resignation which he feels ought to be brought to the attention of members, these must be circulated to all persons entitled to receive copies of the accounts under s. 238 of the *Companies Act* 1985 (CA 1985, s. 394). In the latter event the auditor can request the company's directors to call an extraordinary general meeting. At this meeting the members can receive and consider such explanation of the circumstances of the auditor's resignation, which he feels ought to be brought to the attention of members and creditors, as he wishes to raise. The auditor can circulate to shareholders, with the notice of the meeting, a written statement of reasonable length, of the circumstances connected with his resignation and also address the meeting. However, copies of the auditor's statement need not be sent out or read out at the meeting if the court is satisfied that he is seeking needless publicity for defamatory matter (CA 1985, s. 392A).

An auditor who has resigned may attend the general meeting at which his office would otherwise have expired, and also any general meeting at which the vacancy caused by his resignation is to be filled. The auditor can receive all notices of such meetings, communications relating to them which any member of the company is entitled to receive, and he can speak at the meetings.

Copies of any written statement of the circumstances connected with the auditor's resignation may be circulated at his request, and he can also address the meeting (CA 1985, s. 392A(3), (8)).

¶44-700 Remuneration and duties of auditors

An auditor's remuneration is to be determined by the directors if they appoint him, by the Secretary of State if he made the appointment, or by the company in general meeting (CA 1985, s. 390A).

Any amount received or receivable by the company's auditors or their associates for audit services must be disclosed by way of a note to its accounts (CA 1985, s. 390A). Companies must disclose auditors' remuneration for non-audit work (CA 1985, s. 390B). The rules only partially apply to companies that qualify as small under CA 1985, s. 247 (see ¶70-900).

Auditors are normally regarded as company officers and so entitled to any lawful protection for officers contained in the company's articles of association (*Mutual Reinsurance Co Ltd v Peat Marwick Mitchell & Co (A Firm), KPMG Peat Marwick* [1996] BCC 1,010, Privy Council).

Auditors could potentially be liable in negligence in their audit of a group company to the holding company (see *Barings plc (in administration) v Coopers & Lybrand* [1997] BCC 498), and the auditors of a number of group companies could potentially owe a duty of care to a company which they did not audit where the business of the companies was inextricably linked (see *Bank of Credit & Commerce International (Overseas) Ltd v Price Waterhouse* [1998] BCC 617, Court of Appeal). In a subsequent development in the latter proceedings on 24 March 1998 Laddie J held that, although there might be a duty of care, that duty was only in relation to the *scope* of the kind of damage from which the auditor had to take care to render the company safe from harm, and the damage claimed was outside the scope of that duty.

Auditors' duties

The auditor's duties under the Companies Acts are considered at ¶70-900. The standard of skill with which the auditor should perform his duties is that which a reasonably competent, careful and cautious auditor would use (*Re Kingston Cotton Mill Co (No. 2)* [1896] 2 Ch 279). The auditor is retained by the company and reports to the shareholders. The purpose of such report is to enable shareholders as a body to exercise informed control of the company, and not to enable individual shareholders to buy shares with a view to profit. Accordingly, the auditor owes no duty of care to a potential investor, whether or not that person already holds shares (*Caparo Industries plc v Dickman* [1990] 2 AC 605; [1990] BCC 164). However, this does not prevent accountants preparing a report for, e.g., a potential purchaser of a company owing a duty of care to the recipient (see *ADT Ltd v BDO Binder Hamlyn* [1996] BCC 808, where a firm of accountants were held liable in respect of a negligent mis-statement relating to the value of a company). No duty of care is owed to existing creditors or potential creditors (*Al Saudi Banque v Clark Pixley* [1990] Ch 313; (1989) 5 BCC 822).

Indemnification of auditors

For a company's power to indemnify auditors against liability for negligence etc., see ¶41-000.

INSIDER DEALING

¶45-000　General

The public marketing of shares in public companies is an important feature of commercial life. The ability to match finance with commerce in this way was a significant factor in the development of the limited liability company. Investment in companies involves an element of risk, and those who purchase shares enter a market place in which only a certain measure of protection is provided. The aim of the protective measures is to ensure that investment decisions are, as far as possible, informed and that those with special access to information cannot exploit this to the detriment of other investors.

Legislation which governs the information to be disclosed in documents which offer shares to the public is considered at ¶54-000ff. This section of the commentary is concerned with the rules which regulate the use of information for profit by those who, as a consequence of their relationship to a company, have access to price-sensitive information in advance of the rest of the market. Historically, there have been three sources of regulation. The first is the general law of equity (see ¶45-100), the second is the statute which applies to 'insider dealing' (see ¶45-200 to ¶45-400), and the third is the rules applied by the regulatory bodies of the relevant share markets (see ¶45-500, ¶45-600). The development of the last two has rendered the first considerably less significant.

¶45-100　Equitable principles and insider dealing

The principle that a fiduciary cannot profit from his position, except in well-defined circumstances, is considered at ¶40-700ff., with regard to directors' duties. If a person has access to price-sensitive information as a consequence of his position in a company, and that position is one which gives rise to fiduciary duties to the company, any profit which is derived from exploitation of the information must be paid over to the company. Directors are always in a fiduciary relationship with their company. Agents of the company (such as auditors, advisers and brokers) will also owe fiduciary duties, which are determined by the extent of their authority. Those who are trusted with confidential information would be expected to account for unauthorised profits derived therefrom. However, the fiduciary duty does not extend to individual shareholders, and there is no general equitable remedy by which indignant shareholders can recover profits from those with privileged information to whom they have sold their shares, or by which the sale can be avoided. Employees who have access to price-sensitive information would also be liable to account to their employer for benefits which arise from resultant share dealings.

It is possible that unauthorised profits from insider dealing may be treated as resulting from a breach of confidence. A breach of confidence will arise where a person with access to confidential information discloses this information to the detriment of the other party, in circumstances which imposed an obligation to respect the confidentiality. It must be reasonable to enforce the condition of confidentiality in view of the circumstances (*Dunford & Elliot Ltd v Johnson Firth & Brown Ltd* [1977] 1 Ll Rep 505). If price-sensitive information about company shares was imparted in confidence, further disclosure of that information, or indeed its use for an unauthorised purpose, may amount to a breach of confidence. It is possible to recover profits from a breach of confidence.

¶45-200   Overview of insider dealing legislation

The UK's insider dealing legislation is contained in the *Criminal Justice Act* 1993, Pt. V, which came into force on 1 March 1994. The legislation implements the EC Directive on Insider Dealing (89/592), which was adopted on 13 November 1989. Market manipulation and dishonest concealment are separate offences under s. 47 of the *Financial Services Act* 1986 (see below) and, depending on the facts, may overlap with insider dealing. Self-regulating organisations (SROs) impose additional prohibitions on insider dealing in their rule books, as do the London Stock Exchange (LSE) by its Model Code and the Takeover Panel by the Takeover Code.

If an insider dealing offence is committed, it is punishable by up to seven years in jail and an unlimited fine. In addition, SROs can also impose unlimited fines on their members and on directors or employees of their members. Contrary to what was originally proposed, there is no new statutory civil remedy as such; however, investors may be able to claim damages against an FSA-authorised firm where the offender is employed by the firm and has caused the firm to contravene its SRO's insider dealing rules.

Offence of insider dealing

The main offence is set out in deceptively simple language in s. 52, which, incorporating some clarifications in square brackets, provides that, unless an exemption applies:

> 'An individual who has [non-public price-sensitive] information as an insider [or recipient of information from an insider] [because it is "from an inside source"] is [normally] guilty of insider dealing if he "deals" [in the prohibited circumstances] in securities [quoted on a regulated market in the European Economic Area: the EU and EFTA (excluding Switzerland)] that are price-affected securities in relation to the information [or in derivatives relating to them] [or procures someone else to do so].'

Additional offence

Unless a defence or exemption applies (see ¶45-300), it is also an offence for someone who has non-public price-sensitive information 'from an inside source' (inside information) to encourage someone else to deal in the prohibited circumstances, or to disclose the information except in the proper performance of his employment or office.

Scope of insider dealing legislation

The insider dealing legislation applies to all EEA-quoted securities even if they are issued not by companies but by governments, local authorities or central banks (and so, for example, including gilts); however, the commentary below is limited to dealings in corporate securities.

The two circumstances in which dealings are prohibited are:

(1) if they take place on a 'regulated market': this classification is different from the classification of exchanges as 'regulated markets' for the purposes of the Investment Services Directive (93/22), though many exchanges are both; and

(2) if they are as, through, or probably with, a 'professional intermediary' acting as such, for example, a stockbroker or a corporate finance house bringing the two parties together.

The insider dealing legislation applies only if the inside information is obtained 'from an inside source', namely from or through being a 'primary insider'; 'primary insiders' include directors, employees and shareholders of any issuer of EEA-quoted securities (whether corporate or public) and, importantly, anyone else who has access to the information by virtue of his employment or office. This 'inside source' requirement must in practice limit 'primary insiders' (as distinct from tippees) to persons connected in some sense with:

(1) the company they deal in, or another company to which the information relates; or

(2) a third party, such as a credit-rating agency which is about to issue a price-sensitive change in ratings or a securities house which is about to issue a dealing recommendation relating to the company or likely to affect the price of its securities.

Individual liability

The offence of insider dealing can be committed only by an individual and not by a company, although companies can presumably be guilty as accessories or as party to a conspiracy. However, if a director or employee with inside information deals on behalf of his company, or tells other directors or employees of the company to deal or discloses the non-public information to them, he will be guilty personally if the facts are sufficient. The fact that companies as such cannot be 'insiders' means that, if only a particular executive knows the inside information and he does not tell anyone else, or procure or encourage anyone else to deal on it, other directors (who do not know the inside information) will be free to deal on behalf of the company of their own accord without either the directors or the company committing any offence.

Misleading statements and practices

Quite apart from the question of insider dealing, it is important to remember that the facts may also give rise to criminal liability under s. 47 of the *Financial Services Act* 1986. This would be the case if the insider makes any statement which he knows to be misleading because of the unstated inside information. Similarly, it would be an offence if the insider 'dishonestly conceals' material information, for example that the company whose securities he is selling has made big losses, although it is not totally clear that it is in fact 'dishonest' to refrain from disclosing something confidential. The Securities and Investments Board (SIB) can bring a civil action to require disgorgement of any profit made by the insider or reimbursement of any loss suffered by the counterparty.

In addition to the prohibitions on insider dealing contained in the insider dealing legislation, SROs, the LSE and the Takeover Panel all impose additional prohibitions in their own rules; these prohibitions are much wider than those in the insider dealing legislation, but contravention of them is not a criminal offence. However, contravention of the SRO prohibition may give rise to civil claims under s. 62 of the Financial Services Act.

¶45-300 Defences to insider dealing charges

The insider dealing legislation contains many defences or exemptions. However, the burden of proof is on the defendant; this is because it would be very difficult for the prosecution to prove a negative. Mere disclosure will not be a criminal offence, even if it is not in the proper performance of the defendant's duties, if the defendant can show that he did not expect any person (not just the recipient of the information) to deal on the inside information in the prohibited circumstances; this is because it would be almost impossible for the prosecution to prove that he did expect such a dealing to result from the disclosure. This defence applies only if the insider did not expect 'any' dealing in the prohibited circumstances to result from the disclosure, unless, if he did expect such a dealing, he did not expect the insider transaction to result in a profit or avoid a loss by reason of the inside information; if he did expect such dealings seeking to benefit from the inside information, the defence would not apply even if the dealing itself is within one of the defences for dealings (see below). Conversely, it is for the prosecution to show that the defendant knew that the information was inside information and that he had it 'from an inside source'.

There is a wide defence for dealings on the basis of inside information which qualifies as 'market information'.

In addition, an insider will also be able to deal if he does so to 'facilitate' a contemplated transaction in which he is involved. In particular, this allows an offeror (or, seemingly, its merchant bank) to buy securities in order to build a platform for a takeover before the announcement of the bid. The defence does not extend to allowing the offeror to buy securities of the target company once the target company has disclosed confidential information to it; the rules of the Takeover Code and the Substantial Acquisition Rules must be complied with in any event. The better view is that the defence does not protect transactions entered into in order to make profits which are to be used to fund the contemplated transaction, such as contracts for differences.

There is also an interesting defence where, although the information has not yet been made public, it has been disclosed to a selected group of people and they deal only with each other. The insider dealing legislation provides what is called the 'restricted circle' defence. The insider will not be guilty if he reasonably believes that the information was disclosed so widely that 'none of those taking part in the dealing would be prejudiced by not having the information'.

The insider also has a defence if he shows that he would have done what he did even if he had not had the information. This will very much depend on the facts of each case. A typical example would be where the insider needs to sell shares in order to meet a pressing financial commitment or where a trustee with inside information deals on the advice of an independent adviser who did not have the information and on whose advice he normally relies.

No expectation of profit, etc.

There is an additional defence if the insider can show that he did not expect to make a profit or avoid a loss by reason of the inside information (or expect anyone else to do so). This is a very limited defence, especially as the term used is 'expect' rather than 'intend'. The defence would apply, for example, to a transaction at a price which differs from the current market price in that it reflects what is likely to have been the price if the information had been made public.

Market operations

Finally, there are some specific defences for market operations.

¶45-400 Investigation of suspected insider dealing

If it appears to the Secretary of State that there are circumstances suggesting that an offence under the insider dealing legislation has been committed, he may appoint inspectors to carry out investigations to establish whether this is the case. The inspectors report the results of their investigations to the Secretary of State (FSA 1986, s. 177).

Failure to co-operate with insider dealing investigation

The inspectors may require information and assistance from persons they consider able to provide this (FSA 1986, s. 177). A failure to comply with a request made under s. 177 may result in an inquiry into the case by the courts in the absence of a reasonable excuse. A person will not be treated as having a reasonable excuse where the alleged or suspected contravention is in relation to a dealing by him or under his instructions, just because he did not know the identity of the other person or because he was prohibited from disclosing information under the law of another jurisdiction. The onus is on the inspectors to prove that the person does not have a reasonable excuse; however, a journalist cannot rely on professional privilege to protect his confidential sources (*Re an Inquiry under the Company Securities (Insider Dealing) Act 1985* [1988] AC 660; (1988) 4 BCC 35).

The court may punish the person as if he had been guilty of contempt of the court, or serve on him one of the notices specified in s. 178(3) of the *Financial Services Act* 1986. These specified notices may cancel his authorisation to carry on an investment business, disqualify him from becoming authorised to carry on investment business, restrict any authorisation in respect of investment business during a specified period to the performance of contracts entered into before the notice comes into force, prohibit entering into transactions of a specified kind or entering into them except in specified circumstances or to a specified extent, prohibit soliciting of business from persons of a specified kind or otherwise than from such persons or prohibit carrying on business in a specified manner or otherwise than in a specified manner.

Inspectors' powers

To assist the inspectors in their investigation, they may require a person who is or may be able to give information concerning the suspected insider dealing to produce documents in relation to the securities concerned, and may examine such person on oath (FSA 1986, s. 177(3), (4)). A warrant to enter and search premises may also be obtained from a justice of the peace to reinforce these powers (FSA 1986, s. 199). Further, a person convicted after an investigation may be ordered to pay the costs thereof.

Under the reforms to financial services regulation, it is proposed that the Financial Services Authority (FSA) as sole regulator will be given wide powers to investigate and prosecute insider dealing and other market abuses. The draft Financial Services and Markets Bill and the FSA's draft Code of Market Conduct both contain substantial powers for the FSA to impose civil sanctions against market abuse (see ¶23-700).

¶45-500   The SRO rules against insider dealing

The self-regulating organisations (SROs) require firms regulated by them to include prohibitions on insider dealing on personal account. The Securities and Investments Board (SIB) principles also prohibit insider dealing; SIB Principle 1 insists on market integrity and fair dealing and SIB Principle 3 requires firms to observe best market practice. The SROs have also created an insider dealing offence on a corporate basis; it may perhaps be called 'corporate insider dealing'. Their rules normally prohibit member firms from dealing for their own account when they 'know' of circumstances which mean that an employee of the firm (or of an affiliate) would have been prohibited from doing so by the insider dealing legislation; the better view is that the defences in the insider dealing legislation can be taken into account. In addition, the firm cannot effect a transaction for a customer whom it 'knows' to be prohibited by the insider dealing legislation from dealing himself.

¶45-600   Other non-statutory prohibitions on insider dealing

Additional prohibitions on insider dealing are imposed by the London Stock Exchange (LSE) and the Takeover Panel. Here again the contraventions need to be proved only on a balance of probabilities as they are not criminal offences.

The LSE's Model Code applies to directors and employees of companies whose securities are quoted on the LSE main market or Alternative Investment Market (AIM) and directors or employees of their subsidiaries with access to inside information. The Model Code prohibits them from dealing when in possession of 'unpublished price-sensitive information' (that is, information which is 'inside information'), even if a defence would have been available under the insider dealing legislation, and also prevents the company giving the required clearance for a dealing by them if the company has unpublished price-sensitive information, even if the director or employee is not aware of it. The Model Code requires directors and employees to try to prevent their family, and investment managers acting for them or for family members, from dealing when the insider has inside information, as well as during close periods.

The Takeover Code provides that no person other than an offeror can deal or recommend dealings in the securities of a target company (or options or cash-settled derivatives, such as contracts for differences, relating to them) between the time an offer is contemplated and the time when it is announced, if he has confidential price-sensitive information (that is, 'inside information') about the offer. This is a prohibition on a corporate or institutional basis, and applies even if there would have been a defence under the insider dealing legislation, and in principle even if the individual effecting the transaction did not know the inside information or the firm was acting as an exempt fund manager or exempt market maker. However, it is understood that in practice the Takeover Panel normally does not regard the Code as prohibiting transactions where the inside information is held behind a Chinese wall and does not influence the transaction.

CAPITAL, DIVIDENDS AND BORROWING

Table of Contents

continued over

continued over

CAPITAL AND DIVIDENDS

NATURE AND TYPES OF SHARE

¶50-000   Nature of a share

Two reasons for the ascendancy of the company as the vehicle for commercial enterprise are the features of limited liability and the ability of investors to purchase a unit of ownership and control. An important feature of share capital is that it is one method of attracting finance into the company. It may be necessary for directors to decide whether additional capital should be raised by means of debt or additional shares in capital, and the nature of those shares or debt. Many factors, particular to each company, will influence such a decision. Those considering whether or not to subscribe its securities will also have to consider the relative merits of each option.

A shareholder's liability to contribute to the company's capital is restricted to the issue value of his shares. A shareholder will also be entitled to receive dividends paid out of the company's profits on a pro rata basis, based on the class rights of his shares and the size of his shareholding. Further control of the company's affairs rests ultimately with the shareholders, who exercise votes in accordance with the class rights and number of shares held. Finally, entitlements on distribution of surplus assets in the event of the winding up of a company are determined by the class rights and size of shareholdings.

The rights and obligations that attach to a particular class of shares may be derived from the memorandum or articles of association. They may also be set out in any contract for allotment of shares made between the proposed subscriber and the company (but see generally ¶30-350). The memorandum of association must state the amount of the capital which the company is authorised to issue, and its division into shares of a fixed amount (CA 1985, s. 2). The issue price must amount at least to the nominal amount (CA 1985, s. 100). If the shares are issued for a sum which exceeds their nominal amount, the excess is termed a 'share premium'. A company may issue capital denominated in more than one currency (*Re Scandinavian Bank Group plc* [1988] Ch 87; (1987) 3 BCC 93).

The Department of Trade and Industry on 7 January 1998 issued a consultative document entitled *The Euro: Redenomination of Share Capital* seeking comments on UK companies redenominating their share capital in light of the introduction of the euro, the single European currency, in January 1999. A specific question posed in the consultation exercise was whether allowing 'no-par value' shares in the UK would do more to facilitate redenomination than other specific suggestions in the consultation paper (such shares are already allowed in some EU member states).

Legal nature of a share

A share is a 'chose in action', in that it is assignable, and the assignee would be entitled to sue upon it to obtain his appropriate share of the net profits (*Singer v Williams* [1921] 1 AC 41). This means ownership of a share carries rights which can be legally enforced, but does not confer ownership in tangible property. The Companies Act expressly provides that shares in a company are personal estate and not real estate (CA 1985, s. 182(1)). This ensures ease of transferability, subject to any rules contained in the articles of association particular to that company.

Authorised capital

A company's memorandum of association will disclose the total nominal share capital that the company is allowed to issue (CA 1985, s. 2(5)). This 'authorised' share capital is the maximum amount a company is permitted to raise by way of share capital. That amount may be increased by a procedure set out in statute or the company's articles.

Paid up capital

The 'paid up' share capital is the amount of issued share capital that has actually been paid up to the company by its shareholders. For the purposes of calculation, paid up share capital does not include any sums still owed by shareholders in respect of their shares, or any premium to be paid over and above the nominal amount of those shares.

Called up capital

The 'called up' share capital is the total sum the company has requested from members, and will be a greater sum than the paid up share capital in the event that subscribers still owe the company moneys for their shares.

Types of Shares

¶50-050 General

A company may have different classes of shares, which confer different rights on their owners. The significance of different classes of shares therefore lies in the rights accruing to each class to vote, to receive dividends and to receive capital in the event of a winding up. Where a company issues shares the rights of which are not stated in the memorandum or the articles, it must keep a public record of the rights which attach to each class of shares, and lodge with the registrar within one month a statement setting out those rights (CA 1985, s. 128(1)). Similar notification obligations apply if those rights are varied (CA 1985, s. 128(3)) or if the company assigns a new name to a particular class of shares (CA 1985, s. 128(4)).

The different classes of shares are infinitely varied, as the rights accorded to each are determined by agreement between the company and the subscribers. However, it is possible to identify common classes of shares (see ¶50-075 to ¶50-150).

¶50-075 Ordinary shares

There is no statutory definition of an ordinary share for company (as opposed to tax) law purposes, but these are the most common form of share in existence. This class carries both the ultimate risk (in that holders of other classes of shares, in particular preference shares, will recoup their initial investment first in the event of the company being wound up) and the greatest opportunity for capital growth. It is possible that ordinary shares will themselves be divided into classes, with different voting rights.

Ordinary shares can be of different class and nominal amount and may have rights of participation in profits relegated behind those of other ordinary shareholders, in which case they are commonly termed 'deferred shares'. A company has absolute freedom to create as many types and classes of ordinary shares as it chooses, within the confines of the articles of association and memorandum. Whether a potential subscriber is prepared to accept shares with the terms offered is ultimately a commercial decision.

¶50-100 Preference shares

Preference shares confer on their owners preferential rights over the ordinary shareholders. The nature of the preference is a question of construction of the terms of the share issue. They usually carry a right to an annual dividend, expressed as a percentage of the nominal amount of the shares. The right to this dividend arises only if a dividend is declared or resolved to be paid. The preference can also extend to the repayment of capital contributed on a winding up. However, preferential shares do not usually carry a vote unless dividend payments are in arrears. Within this class of shares, different categories of preference share may be issued by the company. The commonest terms are as follows.

Participating preference shares

Holders of participating preference shares have the right to participate, with holders of ordinary shares, in profits which remain after preference shareholders have their preferred rights satisfied. This entitlement may also extend to rights over surplus assets on a winding up. However, the right to participate in surplus profits, or in assets on a winding up, must be express, i.e. there is no presumption of a right to participate above the fixed rate of return and nominal amount of the preference shares (*Re Isle of Thanet Electric Supply Co Ltd* [1950] Ch 161).

Cumulative preference shares

If a company has failed to pay a fixed dividend by reference to a particular year or years, holders of cumulative preference shares must be paid any arrears of fixed dividend in respect of previous years and the current year before holders of other classes of shares can participate in a distribution for that or future years. Preference shares are assumed to be cumulative unless expressly described to the contrary (*Webb v Earle* (1875) LR 20 Eq 556).

¶50-125 Convertible cumulative redeemable participating preferred ordinary shares (CCRPPOS)

With the increasing popularity of management buy-outs, the ingenuity of lawyers has been directed towards producing a class of shares which, in income terms, yields a fixed cumulative preferential dividend and/or participates in profits, but is principally designed to determine an ultimate division of a company's equity dependent upon its results in its formative years. These are convertible cumulative redeemable participating preferred ordinary shares (CCRPPOS); the precise formulae are many and varied, but the principle is that the proportion of CCRPPOS which is convertible will be in an inverse ratio to the company's success (as defined in the particular formula). For example, management might hold one class of ordinary shares (say 30 per cent of the initial equity) and institutional investors another (say 70 per cent of the initial equity). Institutional investors would additionally hold CCRPPOS which, if the company attained the highest foreseen result in terms of profits or otherwise, would be redeemed at par, but, at the other end of the scale, would convert into ordinary shares. In the former case, the managers would keep their 30 per cent of the equity; in the latter, they would be diluted down to, say, 15 per cent. This device is called a 'ratchet' (in this case, a 15/30 ratchet).

¶50-150 Deferred shares

A company will sometimes issue deferred shares to those who manage or founded the enterprise. The purpose of such shares is to secure a return for such persons out of the profits of the company, which is paid after holders of the other classes of shares have received their dividend. These have now largely been superseded by CCRPPOS.

ALTERATION OF CLASS RIGHTS

¶50-250 General

As previously explained, the significance of different classes of shares lies in the respective rights conferred upon the owners. It was felt necessary to extend the circumstances in which such rights can be amended or abrogated altogether. The relevant statutory rules were introduced in the *Companies Act* 1980. The rights of a class of shareholders may be affected by alteration of the number or rights of another class. However, the courts do not regard this as a variation of the rights of the former class of shareholders (*White v Bristol Aeroplane Co Ltd* [1953] Ch 65), although objections to such a strategy could be founded upon its being unfairly prejudicial to a minority group of shareholders under s. 459 of the *Companies Act* 1985 (see ¶62-550ff.), or upon the use of power for an improper purpose, depending on the particular circumstances. The House of Lords case *House of Fraser plc v ACGE Investments Ltd* (1987) 3 BCC 201 illustrated the way in which the fulfilment of class rights does not necessarily constitute a variation of those rights.

Case example

The appellants held preference shares in the respondent company. The company passed a special resolution at a general meeting to reduce its capital which involved paying off preference share capital. The preference shareholders were not present at that meeting. They argued that because the resolution 'commuted' or 'affected' their rights in accordance with the articles, their prior approval was required. The court held that the company was permitted to make the capital reduction. The preference shareholders' rights had been fulfilled because the resolution gave the shareholders the priority of payment that they were entitled to. No variation of class rights had occurred because that contemplated a situation where some rights still attached to the shares after the variation took place. In this case, the proposed reduction of capital precipitated a complete end to the shareholding. *House of Fraser plc v ACGE Investments Ltd* [1987] AC 387; (1987) 3 BCC 201.

The alteration of a provision in the company's articles of association which regulates the procedure for variation of class rights, or the introduction of such a provision, is to be treated as a variation of class rights (CA 1985, s. 125). The legislation introduces two distinct regulatory codes. The first applies to the alteration of the rights themselves (CA 1985, s. 125–127: see ¶50-300), the second guarantees public registration of the distinguishing features of the different classes of shares (CA 1985, s. 128: see ¶50-050).

¶50-300   Procedure for altering class rights

The statute stipulates the procedure which must be followed for an alteration of class rights. Distinctions are drawn between rights conferred by the memorandum or otherwise, companies which have a procedure for alteration of class rights set out in their constitution and those which do not, and alterations which affect the authority to issue shares and to make a capital reduction and those which concern other matters.

Such distinctions are set out in the following table.

Table: Statutory regulation of the variation of class rights

Rights conferred by	Procedure for alteration contained in	Alteration concerned with	Procedure
(1) Memorandum	Neither articles nor memorandum	Any shareholder right	Agreement of all shareholders.
	Memorandum or articles	Shareholders rights other than authority to issue shares or make a capital reduction	Compliance with the articles.
		Authority to issue shares or make reduction in capital	Agreement of holders of $3/4$ nominal amount of the shares, or extraordinary resolution pased at a separate general meeting of that class. Other requirements of memorandum or articles.

Rights conferred by	Procedure for alteration contained in	Alteration concerned with	Procedure
(2) Other than the memorandum	Memorandum or articles	Shareholders' rights other than authority to issue shares or make a capital reduction	Compliance with the articles.
		Authority to issue shares or make reduction in capital	Agreement of holders of 3/4 in nominal amount of the shares, or extraordinary resolution passed at a separate general meeting of that class. Other requirements of memorandum or articles.
	Other than articles	Any shareholder right	Agreement of holders of 3/4 nominal shares, or extraordinary resolution passed at a separate general meeting of that class. Other requirements, howsoever imposed.

Rights conferred by memorandum

Where the shareholder rights are conferred by the memorandum it is necessary to consider whether a procedure for alteration is provided anywhere in the company's constitution. If not, it is necessary to obtain unanimous agreement of the shareholders to the proposed alteration (CA 1985, s. 125). If the procedure for alteration is set out in the memorandum or articles, it is necessary to consider the effect of the proposed alteration. If the proposal is connected with 'the giving, variation, revocation or renewal of an authority for [the issue of share capital] or with a reduction of share capital' the rights cannot be varied unless the following conditions are satisfied:

(1) the holders of three-quarters in nominal amount of the issued shares of that class consent in writing to the variation; or

(2) an extraordinary resolution passed at a separate general meeting of the holders of that class sanctions the variation; and further

(3) any requirement in the memorandum or articles in relation to the variation of the rights of that class is complied with to the extent that it is not sanctioned as above.

For all alterations of shareholder rights, it is necessary to comply with the procedure set out in the articles (CA 1985, s. 125).

Rights conferred otherwise than by the memorandum

Where the company's constitution sets out the procedure for effecting the variation of class rights it is necessary to comply with the same procedures as above if the alteration concerns the authority to issue shares or make a reduction in capital. For all other types of variation it is necessary to comply with the procedure set out in the articles. However, where no provision for variation of class rights is made in the articles, it is necessary to satisfy the above conditions for any proposed alteration.

The general provisions in the 1985 Act which regulate length of notice for calling meetings (CA 1985, s. 369) and circulation to members of resolutions (CA 1985, s. 376) are expressly applied to the variation procedure, as are the terms of any relevant articles (CA 1985, s. 125(6)). The rules as to conducting meetings (CA 1985, s. 370) are also expressly included but with a modification of the necessary quorum (for an adjourned meeting, one person holding the shares in question or his proxy, otherwise two persons or their proxies holding one-third of the nominal amount of the shares) and the right to call for a poll (which can be done by any holder of that class of shares).

The right of a minority of the shareholders of a particular class to object to a proposed variation in their rights is conferred by s. 127 of the *Companies Act* 1985. Holders of 15 per cent of the issued nominal share capital of the relevant class (excluding those who voted in favour of the change) have 21 days in which to apply to the court for cancellation of the variation. If this is done the variation is ineffective unless and until confirmed by the court. The company must supply to the registrar a copy of the court order within 15 days of its having been made (CA 1985, s. 127(5)).

SHARE ISSUES

¶50-400   General

A share issue is the basic way in which a company raises long-term finance. The statutory rules that define valid consideration for shares are examined at ¶50-850ff. A company can also issue shares in exchange for non-cash assets, subject to the rules set out in the Companies Act. Before an issue of shares can be made to the public for cash, the company must be registered as a public company (see ¶20-150). Regulations which govern the making of an offer must also be satisfied (see generally ¶54-000ff.).

Legally, a share issue will involve a contractual agreement between the company and each subscriber. Thus it is necessary to consider how basic contractual principles are applied to the process. The Companies Act closely regulates a company's ability to make the issue and the procedure by which the issue is made. These two components of the share issue process are separately dealt with in this section. The special rules which apply to shares of persons who subscribed the memorandum are then reviewed.

¶50-450   Common-law rules

An issue of shares involves an 'invitation to treat' (the advertisement by the company of its shares for subscription), an offer (the application to the company for shares by interested parties) and an acceptance of that offer (the allotment of shares to individual applicants). This is followed by registration of the allottees in the company's register of members and the issue of share certificates. Money is due from allottees once the allotment is made. This is usually done by letter (the letter of allotment). Thus the subscription price of the shares is due once the letter is posted by the company (*Household Fire Insurance Co v Grant* (1879) 4 ExD 216). Once an allotment is completed, the company is unable to rescind the contract except by following the statutory procedure for a reduction of capital.

It is possible for the company to enter into a conditional contract for the allotment of shares, by which the offeror has a right to call for allotment of a specified number and class of shares. This arrangement is termed a 'share option' agreement, and the relevant time limit for exercise of the option is usually set out in the contract. Alternatively, a company may (and as part of a rights issue normally does) allot shares provisionally, such allotment being effectively defeasible in the absence of payment by the due date.

The letter of allotment issued by a company may permit the transfer of the right to call for shares and to be entered into the register of shareholders thereby conferred. The document is then termed a 'renounceable letter of allotment'.

¶50-500   Misrepresentation

If an allottee is induced to enter into a contract for the subscription of shares by a material misrepresentation of fact, made by an agent of the vendor company, the usual contractual remedies are available to him. The subscriber of the shares may apply to the court for rescission of the contract. However, the court may award damages in lieu of rescission (*Misrepresentation Act* 1967, s. 2).

The allottee will lose the right of rescission if it is no longer possible to restore both parties to the status quo (e.g. because the company has commenced winding up), or if the allottee affirms the contract after having learned of the misrepresentation (e.g. by the exercise of votes), or if the allottee has delayed in asking for rescission.

If the remedy of rescission is unavailable to an allottee who was induced to subscribe shares by a misrepresentation, an action for damages will lie. Originally, this could not be brought against the company itself (*Houldsworth v City of Glasgow Bank and Liquidators* (1880) 5 App Cas 317; *Misrepresentation Act*

1967, s. 2(1)). Accordingly, the allottee had to seek to recover his loss (measured as the difference between the subscription price for the shares and their actual value) from any person who fraudulently or negligently made the misrepresentation. However, this restriction was removed in 1989 (CA 1985, s. 111A), and accordingly an action may now be brought against the company itself.

It would also be possible to found a criminal charge against those responsible for the misrepresentations under s. 15 of the *Theft Act* 1968, or the *Financial Services Act* 1986. It is also a criminal offence for a person to make a statement which he knows to be, or recklessly to make a statement which is, misleading, false or deceptive (FSA 1986, s. 47). This applies whether or not the statement is made dishonestly.

Finally, any person who acquires securities in a company as a result of an untrue or misleading statement in that company's prospectus will be able to claim compensation for any loss suffered (see the *Public Offers of Securities Regulations* 1995 (SI 1995/1537), reg. 14).

Statutory Rules of Share Issues

¶50-550   General

The provisions of the *Companies Act* 1985 which regulate the share issue procedure are considered at ¶50-575 to ¶50-700 and are summarised in the following table.

Table: Statutory rules for making a share issue

Procedure	Matters arising	Companies Act reference
Authorised share capital	It may be necessary to increase the authorised share capital.	s. 121
Need for authority of existing shareholders to make the share issue	Directors cannot: • allot shares; • grant options to subscribe shares; or • issue securities convertible into shares; without the authority of existing shareholders.	s. 80

Procedure	Matters arising	Companies Act reference
Issue pre-emption rights	Directors cannot allot equity securities for a cash consideration without the offer being made first to the relevant shareholders.	s. 89
Return as to allotment	A return must be made to the registrar of companies within one month of the allotment.	s. 88
Issue of share certificates	Share certificates must be ready for delivery for all the shares allotted within two months of the allotment.	s. 185
Disclosure of share issue	The allotment of shares and specified details thereof must be disclosed in notes to the company's balance sheet for the year of issue.	Sch. 4, para. 35 and 39

¶50-575 Authorised share capital

The maximum number of shares of any class which a company is permitted to issue is set out in the capital clause of the memorandum of association. However, the shareholders in a general meeting can increase the authorised share capital (CA 1985, s. 121). There must be a power to increase the authorised share capital in the articles of association. If such an increase is made, a copy of the necessary resolution with the appropriate notice (form 123) must be sent to the registrar of companies within 15 days of its adoption.

¶50-600 Authority to issue shares

Directors are not permitted to allot shares, to grant options to subscribe shares, or to issue any other securities which carry a contractual right of conversion into ordinary shares, without the authority of the shareholders. Such authority can be specific to a particular share issue or a general power contained in the articles of association or an ordinary resolution. If the power is a general one, the articles or resolution must:

- specify the maximum number of shares which can be allotted under that permission; and
- confer the power for a period which does not exceed five years.

The general power can be cancelled or altered by an ordinary resolution of the shareholders, despite the fact that this will effect an alteration of the articles (for which a special resolution is usually required). A copy of any resolution by which the power of directors to allot shares is granted, changed or cancelled must be sent to the registrar of companies within 15 days of its adoption. Whilst the power is extant, a copy of the resolution must also be attached to copies of the memorandum and articles.

Election by private company as to duration of authority

A private company can decide by elective resolution (see ¶60-800) to give authority to directors to allot a maximum number of shares, either:

- for an indefinite period; or
- for a fixed period, in which case it must state the date on which the period would expire (CA 1985, s. 80A).

Such authority may be revoked or varied by the company in general meeting, and an authority given for a fixed period may be renewed or further renewed by the company in general meeting. When an election which has been made for an indefinite period, or for a fixed period of more than five years, ceases, there are two possible results. If the election had been made more than five years previously, then the authority ceases to have effect; if otherwise, it runs for a five-year period from the date of election (CA 1985, s. 80A(7)).

Penalty

Shares which are allotted without the requisite authority are not void. However, the directors responsible are guilty of a criminal offence (CA 1985, s. 80(9)).

¶50-625   Pre-emption rights

An important provision requires holders of 'relevant shares' to be given first refusal of further allotments of 'equity securities' which are to be issued for cash. The offer for allotment of new shares to existing shareholders must be made in the ratio of their current holding, so as to provide them with the opportunity of maintaining their proportionate interest in, and control of, the company.

These 'issue pre-emption' rights are conferred upon holders of 'relevant shares' and of 'relevant employee shares' (CA 1985, s. 89). A relevant share is any share in a company, other than those which have rights to dividends and capital limited to a specified amount, and those which are held or are due to be held under an employee share scheme (CA 1985, s. 94). 'Relevant employee shares' are defined as any shares which would be 'relevant shares' except for the fact that they are held as part of an employees' share scheme (CA 1985, s. 94). Holders of relevant shares or relevant employee shares are given issue pre-emption rights in respect of 'equity securities'. Equity securities are any relevant shares other than subscribers' shares or bonus shares. They include both options to subscribe relevant shares and securities which carry a right of conversion into relevant shares.

Disapplication of pre-emption rights

Directors can be given the power to allot equity securities without regard to the pre-emption rules. This can be conferred either by a specific authority in relation to one share issue, by special resolution, or under a general authority to allot without regard to the pre-emptive rights under the articles of association. If the authority is to be granted for a specific share issue, the special resolution must be recommended by the directors. The directors must set out in a written statement which is circulated with the notice of the meeting (or in the case of a written resolution, to each member before he signs the resolution: CA 1985, Sch. 15A, para. 3), details of the directors' reasons for recommending the share issue, the sum to be paid for the equity securities and a justification of that amount (CA 1985, s. 95).

A general power for directors to allot relevant securities without regard to the pre-emption rules can be added to a general authority under the articles (CA 1985, s. 80). This power is coterminous with the general authority to make allotments. When the general power expires, it must be renewed by special resolution, for a period equivalent to or shorter than the general authority to allot shares.

More than one class of relevant shares

If the company has more than one class of relevant shares, a proposed allotment of any one class must be offered first to holders of that class. Any balance must then be offered pro rata to holders of the other relevant securities in a second pre-emptive offer. The balance can then be offered to holders of the same class, or other persons.

Consequences of contravening pre-emption provisions

An allotment of equity securities made without regard to the pre-emptive rules cannot be avoided. However, the directors and other company officers responsible for the allotment are jointly and severally liable to compensate any person to whom an offer should have been made (CA 1985, s. 92).

¶50-650 Return of allotment

A return of allotment must be submitted to the registrar of companies within one month of a share allotment (CA 1985, s. 88).

¶50-675 Issue of share certificates

A share certificate must be ready for delivery to allottees within two months of the allotment. This is subject to the terms of the share issue, which may provide otherwise (CA 1985, s. 185). An allottee who does not receive his share certificate within the statutory or contractual period can call for the company to issue his certificate. If this is not done within ten days, the allottee can apply to the court for an order that the company issue the certificate (CA 1985, s. 185(6)). Certificates are usually sealed, as this is prima facie evidence of title (CA 1985, s. 186). However, shares traded in listed companies are now the subject of a new electronic share transfer system called 'CREST' (see further ¶51-300).

¶50-700 Disclosure of allotment in accounts

A company which has made an allotment of shares in a financial period must disclose the following details in the balance sheet for that period end (CA 1985, Sch. 4, para. 39):

- the reason for making the allotment;
- the class of shares allotted; and
- the number, nominal amount and capital received in respect of each class of shares allotted.

¶50-750   Subscriber shares

Persons who subscribe shares in the memorandum have an unconditional right to be entered into the register of members when the certificate of incorporation is issued by the registrar of companies. However, by agreement, shares need not actually be issued to subscribers.

PAYMENT FOR SHARES

General	¶50-850	Calls on shares	¶50-950
Share premiums	¶50-900	Forms of payment for shares	¶51-000

¶50-850   General

Payment for shares raises two separate questions. The first is the value for which a share can be issued (see below); the second is the consideration which can be taken by the company in exchange for shares (see ¶50-900 to ¶51-000).

The value for which a share is issued

Each share issued by a company will have a monetary nominal amount. A prohibition is placed upon the issue of shares by companies for a consideration which is less than the nominal amount of the share (CA 1985, s. 100). If this rule is broken, the allottee of the share is liable to make up the difference between the nominal amount and the issue price, with interest at five per cent which runs from the date of allotment (CA 1985, s. 100 and 107).

Underwriting an issue

It is possible for a company to guarantee that all the shares offered for subscription will be taken up by means of an underwriting contract. By this agreement, the underwriter agrees to take those shares which are not otherwise subscribed. In exchange for his promise the underwriter is paid a commission, which is usually a fixed percentage of the total offer price of the shares. The company must have power under its articles to pay such commission; if it does, and the issue is within the scope of an authority to allot and (if necessary) disapplication of the statutory issue pre-emption rules (see ¶50-625), the payment is lawful. Thus it is possible that a company will receive less than the nominal amount of shares issued, because commission is paid out of the subscription moneys.

It is unlawful for a company to pay a commission greater than any limit set in the articles of association, or of ten per cent of the total cash subscribed (CA 1985,

s. 97). It is permissible for a company to pay a commission (termed 'brokerage') to persons who introduce to the company potential applicants for an allotment of shares (CA 1985, s. 98).

¶50-900   Share premiums

If the sum paid or value of assets contributed for shares exceeds the nominal amount of the shares, this difference is termed a 'premium'. The premium is disclosed separately from the share capital in the company's balance sheet. This reserve, called the 'share premium account', can then be used only for specific purposes (CA 1985, s. 130):

- to fund a bonus issue of shares; or
- payment of preliminary expenses, i.e. the costs incurred in actually incorporating the company; or
- payment of the costs of making the share issue; or
- payment of premiums due on redemption of the company's redeemable loan stock.

Public companies

Shareholders are not always required to pay the premium on allotment. However, public companies must receive the premium on or before the allotment, unless the shares are issued to trustees of an employee share scheme (CA 1985, s. 101(1), 117(4)). If a public company does not receive the premium on allotment, the allottee is liable for this amount plus interest at five per cent, calculated from the allotment date (CA 1985, s. 101(4)), 107).

¶50-950   Calls on shares

It is possible for a company to take payment for shares in instalments. In such a case, it is usual for a deposit to be paid on the application for shares, with the balance falling due on allotment.

A company may allot shares for which not all the consideration has been received. The shares are then termed 'partly paid'. The balance can be requested from the shareholders at any time, unless the shareholders decide by special resolution that the money is not to be called up except on the winding up of the company (CA 1985, s. 120).

Public companies

A public company can only issue partly paid shares if at least one-quarter of the nominal amount is paid up before allotment (CA 1985, s. 101(1)). If this rule is contravened, the allottee is liable for the shortfall, plus interest at five per cent from the date of the allotment (CA 1985, s. 101(4), 107).

Provision for different amounts to be paid on shares

The company's articles may provide that calls on different classes of partly paid shares can be made at different times (e.g. *Companies (Tables A to F) Regulations* 1985, Table A, reg. 17: see ¶31-050). This is expressly permitted by s. 119 of the *Companies Act* 1985. If the articles do not so provide, the calls must be made equally on holders of all classes of such shares.

Lien, forfeiture, etc.

The articles usually give the company a lien over partly paid shares in respect of which a call has been made (e.g. Table A, reg. 8: see ¶31-050). This is an exception to the prohibition on a public company placing a charge over its own shares (CA 1985, s. 150). As an alternative to a lien, the company may seek to recover call money which is due by forfeiture (CA 1985, s. 143(3)(d)) or an action on the debt (CA 1985, s. 14). In the latter case, the limitation period is 12 years (*Limitation Act* 1980, s. 8). If shares are forfeited the shareholder loses the capital he originally subscribed. The articles may provide that the shareholder is still liable for outstanding contributions even after the forfeiture of his shares (e.g. Table A, reg. 21: see ¶31-050). If not, forfeiture by the company and forgiveness of the outstanding sum due thereon is outside the prohibition on a company acquiring its own shares (CA 1985, s. 143). It is also possible for the company to accept a surrender of the shares on which a call has been made, provided that the articles allow this (CA 1985, s. 143). In this case the rules on forgiveness of the outstanding sum still apply.

On a forfeiture or surrender of shares, the company becomes the owner and must attempt to reissue them in order to make up the outstanding capital. The liability of the prior owner is reduced to the extent of any consideration received on the reissue.

Reduction of share capital

A company which has outstanding contributions due on its shares may, by special resolution confirmed by the court, agree to cancel or reduce the liability (CA 1985, s. 135). However, the articles must confer a power to do this (e.g. Table A, reg. 34: see ¶31-050).

Shares shown as asset in balance sheet

Where shares remain surrendered or forfeited at the balance sheet date, they are to be treated as investments for disclosure purposes in the case of public companies and a transfer equal to the value of the shares must be made from distributable profits to an undistributable reserve termed the 'reserve for own shares' (CA 1985, s. 148(4)). Further, a public company is prohibited from exercising voting rights attaching to the shares (CA 1985, s. 146).

Public companies failing to sell forfeited shares

If a public company fails to sell shares it has forfeited, or which have been surrendered, within three years of the event, these shares are to be cancelled (CA 1985, s. 146). The company's share capital is therefore reduced, which may necessitate re-registration as a private company (CA 1985, s. 146; see ¶22-600).

Directors' report

The directors' report of a company (which must accompany its annual accounts) must disclose (CA 1985, Sch. 7, para. 7):

(1) the number and nominal amount of shares acquired by forfeiture or surrender or in respect of which a lien has been exercised due to unpaid calls in the financial year, and the percentage of the paid-up share capital of the company which those shares represent;

(2) the number and the nominal amount of such shares which were disposed of by the company during the period covered by the accounts, the consideration received and the percentage of the total paid-up share capital of the company these shares represented;

(3) the number and the nominal amount of such shares cancelled during the year, and the percentage of the total paid-up share capital of the company represented by those shares;

(4) the maximum number and the nominal amount of such shares held during the year, and the percentage of the total paid-up share capital of the company represented by that maximum; and

(5) the amounts for which any liens were imposed.

¶51-000 Forms of payment for shares

It is not uncommon for shares to be issued for a non-cash consideration. For example, on the incorporation of a business the assets and undertaking are exchanged by the proprietor for shares in the company. The *Companies Act* 1980 implemented the provisions of the second EU company law directive, which regulate the forms of contribution given for share capital. The rules comprise outright prohibitions and provision for valuation of non-cash assets.

Prohibitions

A company is permitted to issue shares for a non-cash consideration (CA 1985, s. 99). The Act defines 'cash consideration' as (CA 1985, s. 738):

- cash including foreign currency;
- cheques which the directors have no reason to believe will be dishonoured;
- the release of a liability to pay a liquidated sum; and
- an undertaking to pay cash to the company in the future.

However, public companies cannot accept an undertaking to perform services in return for the issue of shares (CA 1985, s. 99).

Subscribers of the memorandum of a public company must always pay cash for their shares (CA 1985, s. 106). A public company is prohibited from allotting shares in exchange for any undertaking which could be performed more than five years from the day of allotment (CA 1985, s. 102).

Valuation rules

Special rules as to valuation and disclosure govern the allotment of shares by public companies for a non-cash consideration. These provisions call for valuation of the assets and disclosure of the result.

A non-cash consideration must be valued by an independent person appointed by the company, and the report must be completed within the six months which precede the share issue. A copy of the report must then be provided to the proposed allottee (CA 1985, s. 103). Once the allotment has been made, a copy of the report is to be sent to the registrar for registration along with the return of allotment (CA 1985, s. 111). However, the public company does not have to satisfy these rules where the non-cash consideration is shares in another company for which an offer is made to all the shareholders of that company, or a proposed merger of the issuing company with another company (CA 1985, s. 103(3)–(5)).

A valuation report must be made by an independent person, who would qualify to be the company's auditor. However, the independent person may delegate some or all of his task to someone who appears to have the requisite knowledge and experience (CA 1985, s. 108) – classically a surveyor in the case of freehold or leasehold property. The person making the valuation report owes a duty of care to the shareholders but, unless he is specifically appointed as a specialist, he must exercise only the care of a reasonably competent accountant in general practice (*Whiteoak v Walker* (1988) 4 BCC 122).

Contents of valuation report

The valuation report should set out:

(1) the nominal amount of the shares to be issued in consideration of the related non-cash assets and whether those shares are to be fully or partly paid;

(2) any premium on those shares;

(3) a description of the consideration;

(4) the method and date of valuation, that the method of valuation was reasonable, and that no material change in the assets' value had occurred since the valuation date;

(5) the extent to which the nominal amount of the shares and any premium is paid up by either the consideration or in cash;

(6) any involvement of persons other than the maker of the report in the valuation process, along with that other person's name, and his knowledge

and experience to carry out the valuation: the maker of the report should also state that it was reasonable for the other person to make the valuation;

(7) a description of the consideration valued by that other person, and the method and date of valuation; and

(8) that the value of the consideration plus cash to be received by the company is not less than the total amount which will be treated as paid up by the company.

TRANSFER OF SHARES

¶51-100   General

The way in which a person disposes of his ownership of shares to another is by transfer. The procedure by which this is done differs according to whether or not the transfer is by way of sale on the London Stock Exchange. The *Stock Transfer Act* 1963 calls for execution of a document in one of the forms contained in a Schedule to that Act. The Schedule contains stock transfer forms for transactions other than by way of sale on the London Stock Exchange, and transfer forms for the London Stock Exchange transactions for the transfer of fully paid shares (*Stock Transfer Act* 1963, s. 1), but note that the transfer of securities on the London Stock Exchange may now be subject to the electronic CREST system (see ¶51-300). The Act does not apply to transfers of partly paid shares, for which a transfer procedure is usually set out in the articles of the issuing company. It is possible for a company to issue share warrants, which effectively enable a transfer of the shares represented by the warrants by delivery (CA 1985, s. 188). The articles must specifically permit the issue of warrants, and no such provision is contained in Table A.

Equitable interests in shares

Where a person has an equitable interest in shares but is not their legal holder (e.g. an equitable chargee), he is vulnerable to a third party who buys the shares in good faith for value and without notice of that equitable interest.

Stop notices

Such a person may protect his interest by applying to the court for a 'stop notice' (see the *Charging Orders Act* 1979, s. 5 and the *Civil Procedure Rules* 1998 (SI 1998/3132), r. 50 and Sch. 1, O. 50, r. 11–15, re-enacting the *Rules of the Supreme Court* 1965 (SI 1965/1776), O. 50, r. 11–15). The notice prevents the company from registering a share transfer for a period of 14 days from when that person is notified by the company of such proposed transfer. The issuer of the notice may then apply for an injunction within that 14-day period to restrain the company from registering such a transfer.

¶51-150   Transfers other than by stock exchange sale

A share transfer must be by a 'proper instrument of transfer' (CA 1985, s. 183(1)). A partially completed stock transfer form has been considered 'proper' by the court because it sufficiently recorded the nature of the transaction *Nisbet v Shepherd* [1994] BCC 91).

The transferor completes the stock transfer form, which he also signs. If he is parting with the whole of his holding of shares of that class, the form and the related share certificate(s) are passed on to the transferee, who pays stamp duty (if the shares are sold) at 0.5 per cent of the consideration, and returns the stock transfer form and certificate to the company. The transferee is then registered in the register of shareholders, and a new certificate is issued to him.

If the transferor is not parting with all his shares of a particular class, the form and sufficient share certificates to cover the shares sold are sent to the company. The company will then verify that he has produced a certificate which shows that he is the owner of the shares he purports to transfer. The company returns a certificate to the transferor which certifies his ownership of his retained shares. The stock transfer form is sent on to the transferee for payment of stamp duty (which is calculated at 0.5 per cent of the consideration which is given for the shares), and this is subsequently returned to the company so that his ownership can be entered on the register of members and a certificate issued to him.

The directors do not have to give a reason for refusing to register a transfer of shares, but if they do there is no rule of law that they are confined to the reasons given (per the Privy Council in *Village Cay Marina Ltd v Acland* [1998] BCC 417).

Registration of transfers

Changes in the share register must be made with the approval of the directors of the company (*South London Greyhound Racecourses Ltd v Wake* [1931] 1 Ch 496), or of all of the shareholders (*Re Zinotty Properties Ltd* [1984] 1 WLR 1249; (1984) 1 BCC 99,139).

Refusal of registration of transfer

It is possible that the articles permit the directors to refuse a registration of shares. The court will not interfere with the exercise of this discretion unless it is shown that it was not exercised bona fide in the interest of the company (*Re Smith and Fawcett Ltd* [1942] Ch 304). However, the proposed transferee must be informed of a refusal to register a transfer within two months of its being lodged with the company (CA 1985, s. 183). If the company has not refused to register the transferee, a new share certificate must be ready for delivery to him within two months of the lodgement of the transfer. If this does not occur, the transferee can request the company to issue the certificate, and then after ten days obtain a court order to enforce this right (CA 1985, s. 185).

¶51-200   Transfers by stock exchange sale

Currently, a sale of listed shares is undertaken by the completion of a 'sold transfer form'. This transfers the shares to a nominee holder (SEPON Ltd) which holds the shares until the end of that dealing period. If the vendor is not selling all of the shares of a particular class that he holds, the share certificate and sold form are sent first to the Stock Exchange Certification Office. The certificate is then returned to the company, which issues a new certificate for the balance of shares held. The Certification Office indicates on the sold form that the vendor is the owner of the shares he intends to sell.

However, if the vendor is parting with all his shares, the certificate is sent to the Stock Exchange Settlement Department, and then to the issuing company. In either case, SEPON Ltd is registered as the owner of the shares to be transferred.

The purchaser of shares is allocated shares from the pool held by SEPON Ltd. A 'bought' form is sent to the company, on which the purchaser's name appears. The company then registers him as the holder, and issues a new certificate. Once registration is completed, the share certificate is returned to the Stock Exchange Settlement Department, and then on to the purchaser. This method of transfer is in the process of being superseded by the CREST settlement system (see ¶51-300).

¶51-250   Forged transfers

A forged share transfer is a nullity and accordingly does not pass title to the shares. However, payment of money on the basis of a forged certificate does give rise to a right to compensation from the company. The company may recover, in turn, from the transferee under the forged certificate (*Sheffield Corporation v Barclay* [1905] AC 392).

¶51-300   CREST

Under the *Uncertificated Securities Regulations* 1995 (SI 1995/3272), the legal structure for a paperless and electronic means of share transfer was brought into being. The paperless settlement system, known as CREST, went live on 15 July 1996, replacing the previous TALISMAN system, and leaving CREST as the primary means of share transfer on the London Stock Exchange.

CREST offers simultaneous settlement of securities and funds transfer. At settlement the buyer's payments bank assumes an unconditional and irrevocable obligation to pay the seller's payments bank, the obligation being discharged at the end of the payments day. At the point of settlement a book entry transfer is made within CREST giving the buyer a statutory defined equitable interest in the securities which should be registered by the registrar for the securities within two hours of settlement to give the purchaser full legal title.

The use of CREST is voluntary (there is no change to the rule that legal ownership of a company's securities is constituted by entries in the register maintained by the company or on its behalf by a registrar and this remains true for CREST). Stock held in CREST is fully dematerialised: it exists only in electronic form, no certificates exist anywhere for that stock and for security reasons transfers of the stock can only be transferred by electronic instructions from CREST (it does not actually hold any of the underlying securities, but rather it provides a means for the owners of the securities to hold them securely in electronic form).

Investors have a choice of how to hold the shares:

- to hold share certificates in their own name, with CREST providing the facilities for the holders to sell the shares or for buyers to receive certificates if they wish to;

- to hold shares through a nominee account operated through a bank or stockbroker, which is likely to be held electronically in CREST but does not have to be; and

- to become a 'sponsored member' of CREST (i.e. the shares are held electronically in the name of the individual investor but the operation opf the electronic interface with CREST is carried out by a bank or stockbroker appointed by the investor).

Within two years of the introduction of CREST, stock equivalent to about 80 per cent of the value of all UK listed companies was held electronically in the system. The settlement system has involved considerable development, often following consultation with users, and now includes rules of internal regulation, the so-called CREST 'White Book'. A whole host of descriptive material is available from CRESTCo Limited, a co-operative company owned by financial institutions, which built and operates the settlement system. Trading costs have been reduced by use of the system since they are based on the number of *trades*, not the number (or value) of shares actually traded. As use of the system is voluntary, private shareholders who trade infrequently may refuse to dematerialise their share certificates – if they subsequently trade through CREST, the charges may be higher because the certificate will have to be dematerialised and the rematerialised once the settlement has taken place.

The CREST regulations attribute liability to the CREST operator if a holder of securities suffers a loss as a result of forged instructions sent through the system.

NOTIFICATION OF INTERESTS IN SHARES

¶51-400 General

All public companies (whether or not their shares are listed or otherwise publicly traded) are required to maintain a register of interests in shares (CA 1985, s. 211). The register must contain:

- information received as a consequence of a person's duty to disclose a substantial interest in the shares under s. 198 of the *Companies Act* 1985 (see ¶51-450); and

- information received as a consequence of a notice issued by the company under s. 212 of the *Companies Act* 1985 (see ¶51-500).

The purpose of the register is to enable the public to know the 'real' owners of the shares concerned (*Re Geers Gross plc* [1987] 1 WLR 837; (1987) 3 BCC 528). Listed or quoted companies must therefore notify the London Stock Exchange of all such information received by them.

¶51-450 Shareholders' duty to disclose substantial interests in shares

A person must notify a public company within two business days of the obligation arising if one of the following circumstances applies (CA 1985, s. 198, 199(2), 202(1)):

- he acquires a three per cent interest in the company's 'relevant share capital'; or

- he ceases to hold a three per cent interest in the company's relevant share capital; or

- the level of his interest in the company crosses an integral percentile, but it is still above the three per cent level.

In the case of the following interests (as defined by CA 1985, s. 199(2A)), the relevant threshold notification is ten per cent (the Act provides for a situation where the same person's interest falls into both categories):

- an interest held by a person authorised to manage investments belonging to another; or

- an interest arising from the operation of a unit trust scheme; or

- an interest to be disregarded by virtue of s. 209(10) of the *Companies Act* 1985 (non-listed public companies); or

- an interest of another which a person is taken to have either by virtue of s. 203 of the *Companies Act* 1985 (family and corporate interests: see below) or s. 205 (agreements to acquire interests), but which falls into one of the above three categories.

The Secretary of State may alter the notifiable percentage (CA 1985, s. 210A).

Only issued shares which carry a right to vote in all circumstances at a general meeting are 'relevant share capital' (CA 1985, s. 198(2)).

Notifiable interests in shares

An 'interest' in shares is defined very widely in the Act (CA 1985, s. 208):

- an interest in shares includes a reference to any interest of any kind whatsoever in shares (but excludes an interest in unissued shares, e.g. an option to subscribe shares or a holding of loan stock carrying a right of conversion into shares);
- a person may have an interest in shares where another person's interest is attributable to him;
- restraints or restrictions to which the exercise of any right attached to the interest is, or may be, subject are to be disregarded; and
- it is immaterial that the shares in which a person has an interest are unidentifiable.

Family and corporate interests, etc.

A person is taken to be interested in any shares if his spouse or children are so interested, or if an interest is held by way of a body corporate which he controls (CA 1985, s. 203). Where an interest in shares is held on trust, a beneficiary of the trust is taken to have an interest in the shares. If shares are held on trust under English law, a bare trustee or custodian trustee is not regarded as having an interest in them, nor is anyone with an interest in a discretionary trust. Where a person is a party to a 'concert party' agreement (a wide definition which is not limited to a formal agreement: CA 1985, s. 204), each party's interest is attributable to the other parties (but the latter point does not apply to directors' interests: see ¶43-900). The Act describes other situations in which a person is deemed interested in shares (CA 1985, s. 208), as well as cases which are to be disregarded (CA 1985, s. 209). Sections 208 and 209 can be amended by the Secretary of State (CA 1985, s. 210A).

Particulars

Notification must be made in writing and specify the share capital to which it relates. It must state the number of shares in which the person making the notification is interested immediately after the time the obligation to make the notification arose. Where the person making the notification no longer has an interest subject to notification requirements, he must state that he no longer has such an interest. The notification should also include, so far as known to the person making the notification, the identity of each registered holder of the shares to which the notification relates and the number of shares held by each of them (CA 1985, s. 202(3)). He must keep the company informed of any change in particulars or any particulars of which he becomes aware at a later date (CA 1985, s. 202(4)).

Sanctions

Failure to fulfil the obligations to notify a substantial interest in shares constitutes an offence carrying up to two years' imprisonment and an unlimited fine (CA 1985, s. 210). In addition, the Secretary of State may, by a 'freezing order' under s. 454–457 of the *Companies Act* 1985, impose restrictions on shares in which the offender is or was interested (CA 1985, s. 210(5)).

City Code on Takeovers and Mergers

One situation in which a company might need to know the identity of the owners of its shares is when a takeover bid has been announced or the offer has actually been made. In such a situation, the City Code on Takeovers and Mergers is applicable. Rule 8.3 imposes a disclosure requirement in relation to dealings in any class of 'relevant securities' in the target company (or, indeed, the offeror) by anyone who holds or controls at least one per cent of that class. The City Code outlines exactly what particular interests must be disclosed, and such disclosure must be made public through the London Stock Exchange, the Takeover Panel and the press.

¶51-500   Public companies' powers to investigate share interests

A public company may investigate interests in its shares (CA 1985, s. 212). This may be at its own instigation or at the request of members holding not less than ten per cent of the paid up capital of the company which carries the right of voting at general meetings (CA 1985, s. 214). A company can serve a written notice (a Section 212 Notice) on a person whom the company knows, or has reasonable cause to believe, either to be interested in any of the shares comprised in the 'relevant share capital' or to have been so interested at any time during the previous three years.

The recipient of a Section 212 Notice must confirm or deny that he has, or had, such an interest and, if so, give particulars of his own past or present interest. Where he has, or has had, such an interest, and where another interest in shares subsisted during the three-year period, the person must give (so far as lies within his knowledge) such particulars with respect to that other interest as may be required by the notice. Where a person's interest ceased within the last three years, he must give (so far as lies within his knowledge) particulars of the identity of the person who held the interest immediately after him (CA 1985, s. 212(2)).

The references to 'interests in shares' are construed by reference to s. 203–205 and s. 208 of the *Companies Act* 1985 (see ¶51-450). The exemptions contained in s. 209 of the *Companies Act* 1985 (see ¶51-450) do not apply, and therefore even bare trustees have a disclosable interest: this is essential for starting on the trail to an ultimate owner.

Although not intended to protect a company against takeovers, Section 212 Notices are often used as a first line of defence against a feared predator; discovering his identity before he is ready to pounce or freezing the holdings he is building up often give the first round in the battle to the target company.

It is in this light that the answers to the questions posed in a Section 212 Notice must be considered. A company is entitled to ask for whatever particulars it thinks fit under s. 212(2)(b) of the *Companies Act* 1985, provided that they are 'with respect to that other interest' (*Re TR Technology Investment Trust plc* (1988) 4 BCC 244). Non-UK persons or companies must also reply to Section 212 Notices *Re F H Lloyd Holdings plc* (1985) 1 BCC 99,402).

A reply to a Section 212 Notice must be given in writing within a reasonable time (CA 1985, s. 212(4)). It would only be in exceptional circumstances that a recipient would be allowed more than two clear days (*Lonrho plc v Edelman* (1989) 5 BCC 68). However, this case considered a Section 212 Notice served on a foreign company, and therefore one day may be deemed a reasonable period within the UK.

Offence

If a person makes a statement purporting to be in reply to a Section 212 Notice which he knows to be false, or recklessly makes a statement which is false, then he commits an offence.

Freezing orders

Further, failure to comply with a Section 212 Notice will allow the company to apply to the court for a 'freezing order' under s. 454–457 of the *Companies Act* 1985.

The court has a discretion to make an order for restrictions under s. 454–457 of the *Companies Act* 1985 (*Lonrho plc v Bond* (1989) 5 BCC 193). Under such a freezing order:

- any transfer of shares or, in the case of unissued shares, any transfer of the right to call for their issue and any issue of them, is void;

- no voting rights are exercisable in respect of the shares;

- no further shares shall be issued in right of them, or in pursuance of any offer made to their holder; and

- except in a liquidation, no payment shall be made of any sums due from the company on the shares, whether in respect of capital or otherwise (CA 1985, s. 454).

A freezing order may be made for an interim period only, and on any conditions that the court may consider appropriate (CA 1985, s. 216(1A)). The court is additionally empowered to protect the rights of innocent third parties by ordering that certain acts will not constitute a breach of the restrictions under s. 454–457 of the *Companies Act* 1985 (CA 1985, s. 216(1B)).

Any agreement to transfer or issue shares, or to transfer any right to call for the issue of other shares in right of them, or to receive any payment on them, is void (CA 1985, s. 454(2), (3)). Relaxation or removal of the restrictions is possible by application to the court (CA 1985, s. 456).

Stock Exchange listing rules

The London Stock Exchange permits listed companies to provide in their articles a right to remove voting and dividend rights attaching to shares held by persons who refuse to comply with a Section 212 Notice. Chapter 13 of the *Listing Rules* of the London Stock Exchange (App. 1, para. 13) sets out the particular sanctions that may be imposed. In any event, they may not take effect until at least 14 days after service of the notice.

Where the relevant shareholding is less than 0.25 per cent of any class of shares, prohibitions may only extend to voting rights and attendance at meetings.

If the relevant shareholding exceeds 0.25 per cent, payment of dividends may be withheld. Further, restrictions on the transfer of shares may be imposed unless the purchaser is a 'bona fide unconnected third party' (i.e. where the sale is made on a stock exchange).

Where the company is informed that the shares have been sold to such a third party, the sanctions must be lifted within seven days. Similar provisions apply if the requirements contained in the Section 212 Notice are met.

MAINTENANCE OF CAPITAL AND DIVIDENDS

Minimum share capital	¶51-600	Redeemable shares	¶51-950
Serious loss of capital	¶51-650	Financial assistance for share	
Dividends	¶51-700	purchases	¶52-000
Reduction of capital	¶51-750	Acquisition of non-cash	
Purchase by a company of its		assets	¶52-150
own shares	¶51-800		

¶51-600 Minimum share capital

Before a public company can do business or borrow money it must obtain a certificate from the registrar of companies (CA 1985, s. 117(1)). To acquire this certificate an application is made to the registrar, along with a statutory declaration. The declaration must:

(1) confirm that the nominal share capital of the company is not less than the 'authorised minimum' prescribed by statute (currently £50,000: CA 1985, s. 118);

(2) specify the paid-up share capital at the date of application;

(3) specify the preliminary expenses of the company (actual or estimated) and the persons by whom any of those expenses have been paid or are payable; and

(4) specify any amount or benefit, paid or given, or intended to be paid or given, to any promoter of the company, and the consideration for the payment or benefit.

The registrar cannot issue the certificate to do business unless the nominal amount of the allotted share capital is at least equal to the authorised minimum (CA 1985, s. 117(2)). As a public company cannot allot shares unless 25 per cent of the nominal amount, together with the whole of any premium on the shares, has been paid (CA 1985, s. 101(1)), the minimum called-up share capital of a public company is £12,500. Importantly, if a company's authorised nominal share capital is £50,000, 12,500 fully paid-up shares of £1 each will not meet the s. 101 requirement because every individual share must be paid up to one-quarter of its value and the whole of any premium on it. Fifty thousand £1 shares paid up to 25 pence each will, however, satisfy s. 101. Shares allotted under an employee share scheme are not included in establishing the nominal amount of the allotted share capital of a company unless these shares are paid up as to 25 per cent of their nominal amount.

Private companies

No rules as to minimum capital subscriptions are applied to private companies.

¶51-650 Serious loss of capital

If a public company has net assets (i.e. 'the aggregate of assets less the aggregate of liabilities') with a value of less than 50 per cent of its called-up share capital, a 'serious loss of capital' has occurred (CA 1985, s. 142(1)). When this state of affairs first comes to the directors' knowledge, an extraordinary general meeting must be convened.

The meeting is to be called within 28 days of the directors' discovery. The meeting must actually be held within 56 days of this date. Failure to convene a meeting will expose directors who are aware of the loss of capital to a fine (CA 1985, s. 142(2)). At the meeting, the company considers what, if any, steps should be taken to deal with the situation.

¶51-700 Dividends

The payment of dividend is how shareholders participate in the profits of the company. The procedure for determining the amount of a dividend payment is usually set out in the articles of association. For example, Table A of the *Companies (Tables A to F) Regulations* 1985 provides both the procedure by which the level of dividends is to be decided (as regards a final dividend, by recommendation of the directors and approval of the shareholders) and how that entitlement to dividends is determined (on the basis of paid-up share capital) (reg. 102–108: see ¶31-050).

A final dividend (recommended by the directors and formally 'declared' in general meeting) constitutes a debt of the company to the relevant shareholders. Articles of association normally give power to the directors to 'resolve to pay' interim dividends; any such resolution may be rescinded before it is acted upon. If the articles empower the directors to 'declare' interim dividends, then such declaration operates in the same manner as one in general meeting. A dividend may consist of assets rather than cash, but articles of association normally require such a 'distribution in specie' to be specifically authorised by shareholders.

'Profits available for distribution'

The size of dividend payments is also subject to statutory rules, which differ as between private and public companies. Any company can make a distribution provided that it has 'profits available for the purpose' (CA 1985, s. 263(1)). This term is defined as its 'accumulated, realised profits so far as not previously utilised by distribution or capitalisation, less its accumulated, realised losses, so far as not previously written off in a reduction or reorganisation of capital'. Losses to be taken into account are of both a capital and income nature.

'Distributions'

A distribution is defined as any distribution of the company's assets to shareholders, other than:

(1) the issue of bonus shares;

(2) the redemption or purchase of a company's shares out of capital (including the proceeds of a fresh issue of shares) or out of unrealised profits (in either case in accordance with CA 1985, s. 159–181);

(3) the reduction of share capital by the extinction or reduction of a liability in respect of amounts not paid up on partly-paid shares or by paying off paid-up share capital; or

(4) the distribution of assets on a winding up (CA 1985, s. 263(2)).

Public companies

A public company has further restrictions placed upon its powers to make 'distributions'. The net assets as at the date of the distribution must exceed the company's called-up share capital and 'undistributable reserves'. Further, the distribution must not reduce the net assets below the aggregate of the called-up share capital and undistributable reserves (CA 1985, s. 264).

'Undistributable reserves'

The undistributable reserves of a public company for the above purposes are:

(1) the share premium account;

(2) capital redemption reserve;

(3) the surplus of accumulated unrealised profits not previously capitalised over accumulated unrealised losses not previously written off in a reduction or reorganisation of capital; and

(4) any reserve which the company is prohibited from distributing for other reasons, such as by special legislation applicable to companies of that type, or the terms of the company's constitution.

The effect of the additional restrictions on public companies is that they cannot distribute unrealised profits, and must make good any unrealised losses before making a distribution.

Relevant accounts

Determination of the ability of a company to make a distribution must be based upon the 'relevant accounts', i.e. the last annual audited accounts, or interim accounts where the annual accounts would not permit the proposed distribution (CA 1985, s. 270). If a distribution is planned during the company's first accounting reference period (i.e. before the publication of the first set of annual accounts), 'initial' accounts must be used.

Special rules are applied to the use of the relevant accounts. The interim or initial accounts of a private company must add all previous distributions, which were made on the basis of those same accounts, on to the proposed distribution. This is to prevent a single prohibited distribution being achieved by a series of smaller qualifying distributions. The use of annual accounts of private and public companies, and of interim and initial accounts of public companies, must observe the following additional rules:

(1) They are to be 'properly prepared', i.e. comply with the Companies Act requirements as to form, contents and signature.

(2) They must provide a 'true and fair view'.

(3) Annual accounts should carry an auditors' report, and initial financial statements should carry an auditors' opinion as to whether they have been 'properly prepared'. Interim accounts need not carry an opinion.

(4) Where a private company has elected to dispense with laying accounts before the general meeting, it must send a copy of its accounts to members together with the auditors' report.

(5) If the auditors have given a qualified report on the 'relevant accounts' they should confirm that the subject matter of the qualification is not material as regards the legality of the proposed distribution. A copy of this statement should be laid before members in a general meeting (see CA 1985, s. 271(4)), and must be lodged with the registrar of companies pursuant to s. 242 of the *Companies Act* 1985.

(6) A public company cannot treat uncalled capital as an asset (CA 1985, s. 264(4)).

¶51-700

¶51-750   Reduction of capital

A company may reduce the capital value of its shares as recorded in the balance sheet, provided that a power to do so is contained in the company's articles of association (CA 1985, s. 135).

The purpose of a reduction of share capital is to return contributions to shareholders, to cancel the liability of shareholders to meet calls on their shares, or to take into account reductions in the value of the shares themselves or the underlying assets of the company. If the reason for the reduction is a loss in value, preference shareholders should be the last to have their capital reduced (*Re Floating Dock Co of St Thomas Ltd* [1895] 1 Ch 691). If the reduction is to effect a return of surplus capital, priority goes to any class with superior rights to a return of capital on a winding up (*Scottish Insurance Corp Ltd v Wilsons & Clyde Coal Co Ltd* [1949] AC 462).

The reduction in share capital must first be authorised by a special resolution. The company must then have the resolution confirmed by the court. Any expression of the unanimous will of all the shareholders acting together outside a special resolution will not be accepted by the court as an alternative to the statutory procedure (*Re Barry Artist Ltd* [1985] 1 WLR 1305, though this decision pre-dated the statutory regime for written resolutions by private companies: see ¶60-750).

The company must have a greater share capital than the amount by which it is to be reduced at the date of the resolution (*Re Transfesa Terminals Ltd* (1987) 3 BCC 647). This does not prevent a public company from momentarily reducing its capital below the authorised minimum (see ¶51-600) before an increase to above that minimum (*Re M B Group plc* (1989) 5 BCC 684).

Class rights

Conflicts may arise where a company attempts to reduce its capital by cancelling a certain class of shares to which are attached particular rights. In *Re Saltdean Estate Co Ltd* [1968] 1 WLR 1844, the company attempted to reduce its capital by cancelling preference shares. The court did not view this as an alteration of class rights requiring separate consent from the preference shareholders, and consequently approved the petition. Conversely, the court arrived at a different conclusion in *Re Northern Engineering Industries plc* [1994] BCC 618. In that case, the articles stated that a reduction of capital paid up on the shares in question was to be deemed a variation. Hence, separate class consent was required.

Creditors' list, etc.

The court has a discretion to settle a list of creditors who are entitled to object to any reduction of capital. The company must make full disclosure of its creditors, and it is an offence for company officers to conceal the identity of creditors (CA 1985, s. 141). The court will publish notices which fix a date before which creditors can apply to be included in this list. If a listed creditor objects to the reduction, the court can dispense with his objection if the company sets aside a sum sufficient to meet the whole of his claim (where the liability is admitted), or a sum adjudicated sufficient by the court (where the claim is disputed, contingent or unascertained). An order confirming the reduction can then be made, on such terms and conditions as the court thinks fit.

The court can (but normally does not) require that the words 'and reduced' be added to the end of the company's name, and publication of information (such as the reason for the reduction), as conditions of the reduction.

Registration of order and minute of reduction

On confirmation of the reduction by the court, a copy of the order, with a minute approved by the court which sets out the details of the new capital structure, must be sent to the registrar of companies. The registrar then issues a certificate, which is conclusive as to the satisfaction of the Companies Act rules on reductions of capital. The minute submitted with the order is then deemed to have been substituted for the capital clause in the company's memorandum (CA 1985, s. 138).

Public company reducing capital below authorised minimum

If a proposed reduction in share capital would reduce a public company's allotted capital below the statutory minimum of £50,000, it must (save as above) be re-registered as a private company. This can be done by the re-registration procedure set out in s. 53 of the *Companies Act* 1985, or together with the application for confirmation of the reduction to the court (CA 1985, s. 139).

Members' liability on reduced shares

If a creditor who would have been entitled to object to the reduction is accidentally omitted from the list of creditors, and the company is later unable to meet his claim, all persons registered as shareholders at the date of registration of the court order can be made to pay capital returned to them in satisfaction of his claim (CA 1985, s. 140).

Purchase by a Company of Its Own Shares

¶51-800 General

Before the coming into force of the *Companies Act* 1981, companies were prohibited from purchasing their own shares. It is convenient to consider the rules which govern such share repurchases in four stages. Private companies are considered first (see ¶51-825), then public companies (see ¶51-850). The rules which apply to payment for share repurchases are then reviewed (see ¶51-875), and finally liabilities which may arise in respect of repurchases (see ¶51-900).

Shares repurchased in the manner described at ¶51-825ff.) are treated as cancelled in the same way as shares which are redeemed (CA 1985, s. 160(4), 162(2)).

The Department of Trade and Industry on 7 May 1998 issued a consultation paper entitled *Share Buybacks* seeking comments on whether the *Companies Act* 1985 should be amended to allow companies to buy back their shares, hold them *in treasury* and resell them later. This would provide greater flexibility than the existing procedure under s. 162, under which a company may purchase its own shares but must then treat them as cancelled and diminish its capital accordingly. The latter procedure appears outdated, especially in comparison with European countries and the US.

¶51-825 Share repurchases by private companies

The following conditions must be fulfilled before a private company can make a share repurchase:

- the articles of association must authorise the repurchase (CA 1985, s. 162(1));
- the shares to be repurchased must be fully paid up (CA 1985, s. 159(3), 162(2));
- the consideration from the company must actually be paid when the sale occurs;
- there must be irredeemable shares in issue, held by at least two persons, after the repurchase has taken place (CA 1985, s. 162(3)); and
- there must be shareholder approval of the proposed contract for repurchase (CA 1985, s. 164(1), (2)).

Repurchases out of capital, etc.

A private company can fund the share repurchase out of profits available for the purpose of a distribution (CA 1985, s. 160) (see ¶51-700), from the proceeds of a fresh issue of shares (CA 1985, s. 160) or out of capital (CA 1985, s. 171(1)). However, a statutory limit is placed upon the payment which can be drawn out of capital. This is termed the 'permissible capital payment' (CA 1985, s. 171(3)). The permissible capital payment is the purchase price of the shares to the company, less the distributable reserve and proceeds from fresh share issues. The accounts on the basis of which the permissible capital payment is calculated must be prepared as at a date within the three months preceding the date on which the directors make the statutory declaration required by s. 173(3) of the *Companies Act* 1985, to the effect that the company will be solvent both immediately after the payment and for the subsequent year.

The declaration must also have attached an auditors' opinion on its reasonableness. The payment out of capital must then be made between five and seven weeks after the date of the special resolution.

Special resolution

If the company proposes to make a share repurchase from capital, a special resolution must be passed to this effect, within one week of the statutory declaration by the directors (CA 1985, s. 173(2), 174(1)). The votes attached to shares which the company proposes to repurchase are not included in calculation of the majority. The shareholders must be afforded the opportunity to inspect both the directors' declaration and the auditors' report at the meeting.

Publicity for repurchases out of capital

Within one week of the special resolution, the company must advertise the repurchase out of capital, and the facility for making objections thereto, in the *London Gazette* (or *Edinburgh Gazette* if the company is registered in Scotland). The company must also supply these details to an 'appropriate national newspaper', or to each creditor. The company must supply a copy of the declaration and the auditors' report to the registrar of companies before the date of publication of details of the repurchase in the *Gazette* and national newspaper (CA 1985, s. 175).

Objections by members and creditors

Shareholders and creditors can object to the repurchase out of capital within five weeks of the special resolution (CA 1985, s. 176(1)). An application must be made to the court for cancellation of the special resolution. However, this facility is not open to persons who originally voted in favour of the repurchase.

The court will either confirm or cancel the resolution on such terms as it thinks fit. The court is accorded wide powers to make orders and give appropriate directions, in order to achieve a satisfactory arrangement (CA 1985, s. 177).

Disclosure of share repurchases

A private company which has made a share repurchase must send a return to the registrar of companies within 28 days of delivery of the shares to the company (CA 1985, s. 169(1)). The company must keep copies of contracts for the repurchase of shares, contingent contracts, and variations thereto, at its registered office (CA 1985, s. 169(4)). Details of the share repurchase must also be published in the directors' report. Note that in *Acatos & Hutcheson plc v Watson* [1995] BCC 446, the court approved an agreement whereby company A purchased the issued share capital of company B despite the fact that B owned shares in A. Because A was not directly purchasing its own shares, the court concluded that the agreement did not fall foul of the above statutory rules.

¶51-850   Share repurchases by public companies

The repurchase of shares by a public company is, essentially, subject to the same regulatory code as applies to private companies (see ¶51-825). However, extra restrictions are imposed upon public companies. First, there is a prohibition upon repurchases out of capital. The rules which govern minimum allotted share capital of public companies must also continue to be satisfied after the repurchase (see ¶51-600).

The publicity requirements for share repurchases by public companies are more onerous than for private companies. A repurchase may be a market purchase or an off-market purchase. The former is made 'on a recognised investment exchange' (CA 1985, s. 163), except where the shares are not subject to a 'marketing arrangement' on that exchange. Shares are subject to such an arrangement where they are either listed, or there are unrestricted facilities to deal in those securities, on the exchange in question. Shares listed on the London Stock Exchange or quoted on the Alternative Investment Market (AIM) would therefore be subject to an on-market, as opposed to an off-market, purchase. Authority for such a transaction is conferred by an ordinary resolution, but can only be granted for a maximum period of 18 months. The authority must specify the maximum number of shares which can be repurchased, the maximum and minimum prices, and can either relate to a specific class of shares or be of a general nature. This authority can be varied, revoked or renewed by a subsequent ordinary resolution. A copy of any resolution having such an effect must be sent to the registrar of companies within 15 days of its having been passed.

Off-market purchases, etc.

An off-market purchase relates to securities in companies that are not listed on a recognised investment exchange, or which are not subject to a marketing arrangement as described above (CA 1985, s. 163(1)). The rules which govern off-market repurchases are the same as for private companies (see ¶51-825), except that a date must be specified for expiration of the authority. Contingent repurchase contracts (which give rise to obligations upon the occurrence of a specified eventuality) are subject to the same regulatory regime as off-market repurchases (CA 1985, s. 165(2)).

Assignment or release of company's right to repurchase

Assignment of rights by a company under a contract for repurchase are prohibited (CA 1985, s. 167) for both market and off-market transactions. A release of a company's rights conferred under a contract for repurchase or a contingent contract is permitted with the authority of a special resolution (CA 1985, s. 167).

Stock Exchange listing rules

In respect of listed companies, the listing rules of the London Stock Exchange (see the *Listing Rules*, ch. 15) specify additional requirements in this context. Various obligations are set out that relate to notification by a company when purchasing its own shares. Different rules apply depending on whether the securities are equity or non-equity.

¶51-875 Payment for shares on a repurchase

Rules are set out for maintenance of capital on a share repurchase. This is achieved by mandatory transfers to undistributable reserves, in the following circumstances:

(1) repurchase of shares wholly out of distributable profits: a transfer to the capital redemption reserve must be made equivalent to the nominal amount of the shares repurchased (CA 1985, s. 170(1));

(2) repurchase of shares wholly out of the proceeds of a new issue of shares: a transfer to the capital redemption reserve must be made of any amount by which the nominal amount of the shares redeemed exceeds the proceeds from the new issue (CA 1985, s. 170(2)); and

(3) repurchase of shares out of capital: a transfer to the capital redemption reserve must be made of the amount by which the nominal amount of the shares repurchased exceeds the payment out of capital (CA 1985, s. 171(4)).

If a repurchase is funded out of both a new issue of shares and a payment out of capital, a transfer to the capital redemption reserve must be made of the amount by which the nominal amount of the shares repurchased exceeds the proceeds of the issue plus the capital payment (CA 1985, s. 171(6)).

Payments to be made out of distributable profits

The following items can only be paid for out of distributable profits (CA 1985, s. 168):

(1) acquisition of rights for a share repurchase under a contingent purchase contract;

(2) variations of contracts to make off-market or contingent purchase contracts; and

(3) release of a company's obligations under a contract for an off-market share repurchase or contingent repurchase contract.

¶51-900 Liabilities in respect of repurchases

If a company is wound up within a year of repurchasing shares out of capital, any director who signed the statutory declaration and any shareholder whose shares were repurchased may be liable to contribute to the assets of the company (IA 1986, s. 76). The shareholders may have to return the consideration received on the repurchase. The directors are jointly and severally liable with the shareholders for this amount, but can be exempted if reasonable grounds for forming the opinion in the statutory declaration can be shown. A director or shareholder who has contributed to the assets of the company under these rules can apply to the court for an order that any other person who is liable under the sections should reimburse him with such an amount as the court considers just and equitable (IA 1986, s. 76). A director who is responsible for a statutory declaration, and who did not have reasonable grounds for the opinion expressed therein, may be liable to a fine or imprisonment or both (CA 1985, s. 173(6)).

Effect of failure to repurchase

Where a company has agreed to repurchase shares, but fails to do so, the shareholder cannot sue the company for damages (CA 1985, s. 178(1), (2)). Although an order for specific performance may be available to the shareholder, the court can refuse to award this if the company has insufficient distributable profits to meet the commitment (CA 1985, s. 178(3)).

If a company is wound up after having agreed to repurchase shares, the shareholder can enforce his contract provided that all other debts and liabilities have been paid, and rights attaching to shares with priority have been satisfied (CA 1985, s. 178(4), (6)). However, the contract for repurchase is unenforceable if this was to take place after the winding up commenced, or if the company was unable to make a lawful distribution equal to the repurchase price between the date specified for repurchase and commencement of the winding up (CA 1985, s. 178(5)).

¶51-950   Redeemable shares

A company is permitted to issue redeemable shares, provided the articles of association permit this (CA 1985, s. 159–161). However, before such an issue can be made, there must be non-redeemable shares already in issue (CA 1985, s. 159(2)).

Only fully paid up redeemable shares can be redeemed and payment must be made on the redemption (CA 1985, s. 159(3)). The redemption can be funded from distributable profits or the proceeds of a new issue. Private companies can also make payments out of capital for the redemption, provided that the articles of association permit this (CA 1985, s. 160, 171). Once redeemed, shares are to be treated as cancelled (CA 1985, s. 160(4)).

Financing, etc. of redemption

Any premium which falls due on redemption must be paid out of distributable profits (CA 1985, s. 160(1)). However, if the shares were originally issued at a premium, a proportion of the proceeds of any new issue made to finance the redemption can be used to fund the redemption premium (CA 1985, s. 160(2)). The proportion is the lower of the premiums originally received on the issue of the shares to be redeemed and the balance on the company's share premium account after the new issue. If any premium paid on redemption is funded by a new issue, the company's share premium account must be reduced by this amount (CA 1985, s. 160(2)). The authorised share capital is not affected by a redemption (CA 1985, s. 160(4)).

Application of share repurchase provisions

The provisions which regulate redemption out of capital, the reserve accounting which must be followed, the effect of winding up on obligations to redeem, and potential liabilities of past shareholders and directors, are as for share repurchases (see ¶51-825ff.).

Effect of failure to redeem

Failure by a company to honour redemption terms will not expose it to an action for damages (CA 1985, s. 178(1), (2)).

Financial Assistance for Share Purchases

¶52-000   General

A public company is expressly prohibited from providing financial assistance for the purchase of its shares, subject to a few specific exceptions (see ¶52-025) (CA 1985, s. 151). The prohibition also extends to assistance from subsidiary companies. However, a holding company is not prohibited from providing financial assistance for the purchase of shares of a subsidiary. In *Arab Bank plc v Mercantile Holdings Ltd* [1994] Ch 71; [1993] BCC 816, the court concluded that an agreement whereby a subsidiary incorporated in Gibraltar financially assisted the English parent company to acquire its own shares did not fall foul of the following statutory rules.

Auditors who fail to warn clients that transactions might contravene the prohibition of financial assistance by a company for purchase of its shares may be liable to negligence (*Coulthard v Neville Russell (a Firm)* [1998] BCC 359).

Following more than one consultation exercise, the Department of Trade and Industry announced in April 1997 that it intended to introduce legislation, when parliamentary time permits, to simplify the Companies Act procedure for financial assistance by a company to purchase its shares. As at September 1998 this had not materialised.

Private companies

A private company, or a subsidiary of a private company (which is itself a private company), can provide financial assistance for the purchase of its shares. However, the approval of the company by a special resolution is necessary, and the directors must make a declaration of solvency (CA 1985, s. 155). The declaration is made on a standard form. See further ¶52-050.

'Financial assistance', etc.

The rules which govern financial assistance regulate direct and indirect assistance given before, during or after the share purchase (CA 1985, s. 151). The term 'financial assistance' covers (CA 1985, s. 152):

- a gift;
- a guarantee, security or indemnity;
- a release or waiver;
- a loan;
- an agreement by which the person giving assistance has to fulfil an obligation under the agreement before the obligations of the other party are fulfilled;
- a novation or assignment of rights which arise under a loan or an agreement as above; and
- any other financial assistance which materially reduces the company's net assets.

In *Parlett v Guppys (Bridport) Ltd* [1996] BCC 299, an agreement was made whereby the plaintiff, who controlled four companies, transferred his shareholding in one of the companies in return for a salary of approximately £100,000 plus a bonus and pension. The court held that this did not amount to unlawful financial assistance because no material reduction of the companies' assets had taken place. In assessing the extent of the reduction, the court restricted its consideration to amounts currently payable and additionally took into account the companies' other assets.

For the consequences of contravening the financial assistance prohibition, see ¶52-075.

¶52-025   Financial assistance by public companies

The prohibition imposed on public companies financially assisting the purchase of their shares (see ¶52-000) does not apply where any one of the following circumstances apply (CA 1985, s. 153):

(1) the principal purpose of the company's act (either before or after acquisition of the shares by the individual concerned):

    (a) was not to provide assistance for the acquisition; or

    (b) was only part of a larger purpose (see *Brady v Brady* (1988) 4 BCC 390 below); and

    (c) in either case, the assistance was given in good faith in the interests of the company;

(2) the financial assistance is provided by means of:

    (a) a lawful distribution by dividend or on winding up the company;

    (b) an allotment of bonus shares;

(c) a reduction of capital under s. 137 of the *Companies Act* 1985;

(d) a redemption or repurchase of shares;

(e) an arrangement or compromise with creditors or members (under either CA 1985, s. 425 or IA 1986, s. 1–6); or

(f) an arrangement entered into by the company's liquidator under s. 110 of the *Companies Act* 1985, for accepting shares as consideration for the sale of property;

(3) money is loaned in the ordinary course of the company's business;

(4) assistance is provided in good faith in the interests of the company for the purposes of an employee share scheme; or

(5) the money is loaned in good faith by the company to employees, other than directors, with a view to enabling those persons to acquire shares.

In cases (3)–(5) provision of assistance is permitted only if either:

(a) the company's net assets are not reduced as a consequence of the assistance; or

(b) the assistance is made out of 'distributable profits'.

Without prejudice to case (4), assistance may be provided to enable or facilitate transactions in shares for their own benefit between persons who are employees or former employees of the company or another company in the same group or their close relatives (as defined).

The application of the rules can be seen in *Brady v Brady* (1988) 4 BCC 390.

Case example

A family business was run through a holding company, B Limited, and a number of subsidiaries. Members of the family fell out and deadlock followed. To prevent the possible winding up of the companies under s. 459 of the *Companies Act* 1985, the parties agreed to a complete reconstruction of the group which would split the two core businesses. The assets of the business were divided equally but the main company remained. Later, one party wished to argue that the assets had not been divided fairly and refused to perform his part of the contract. The other party petitioned for specific performance; however, the first party maintained that a disposal of the assets which had been effected as part of the reconstruction was ultra vires and that unlawful financial assistance had been given for a purchase of shares which had also been so effected.

In allowing the appeal on the basis that the financial assistance would have been lawful if the procedure in s. 155ff. of the *Companies Act* 1985 (see below) had been followed, the House of Lords took a narrow view of the 'larger purpose' test, effectively holding that, where financial assistance was given for the purpose of an acquisition, the test was not satisfied. 'Larger purpose' did not just mean 'more important reason' (Lord Oliver at p. 779; 408). *Brady v Brady* [1989] AC 755; (1988) 4 BCC 390 at p. 408.

¶52-050   Financial assistance by private companies

Private companies are given greater freedom than public companies to provide financial assistance for the purchase of their own shares or those of a holding company. However, the additional freedom is available only where the private company is not owned by a public company. A private company can provide assistance provided that either its net assets are not reduced as a consequence, or assistance can be provided out of distributable profits.

Conditions for financial assistance relaxation

Before financial assistance is permitted under the Act, the following conditions must be fulfilled:

(1) The assistance must be approved by a special or written resolution, unless the company proposing to give the assistance is a wholly-owned subsidiary (CA 1985, s. 155(4)).

(2) The directors must make a statutory declaration as set out in s. 156 of the *Companies Act* 1985. The resolution must be passed within one week of the directors' declaration. The auditors must report on the directors' declaration. Further the directors' declaration and auditors' report must be available to shareholders who approved the financial assistance (in the case of a written resolution, prior to the signature thereof – CA 1985, Sch. 15A). The registrar must be sent a copy of the directors' declaration and the auditors' report.

(3) The assistance must not be given earlier than four weeks after the passing of the special resolution (unless every shareholder entitled to vote voted in favour of the assistance) or later than eight weeks after the directors have made the statutory declaration.

Application for cancellation of special resolution

Minority shareholders can apply to have the special resolution (under (1) above) cancelled (CA 1985, s. 157(2)). The facility for objection is open to either:

(a) holders of not less than ten per cent of the company's nominal share capital (or ten per cent of any class of that share capital); or

(b) at least ten per cent of the company's shareholders in number, if the company is not limited by shares.

Members of the company who voted in favour of the special resolution cannot be included in the numbers who make up the ten per cent minority. The dissentient minority has 28 days to apply for cancellation of the special resolution.

The court may either cancel the special resolution (in which case the special resolution ceases to be effective), or affirm the resolution on such terms as it thinks fit. Once an application by a minority has been made to the court, the company must give the registrar of companies notice of this fact. The company is also required to supply the registrar with a copy of any court order made in response to the application.

¶52-075   Liability for contravening financial assistance rules

A company which provides financial assistance for the purchase of its shares outside the statutory procedure is liable to a fine, and any officer in default is liable to a fine, imprisonment, or both (CA 1985, s. 151(3)).

A director who expresses an opinion in the statutory declaration without reasonable grounds for doing so is liable to a fine, imprisonment or both (s. 156(7)).

Failure to submit copies of the statutory declaration, the auditors' report, applications to the court by minority shareholders (if appropriate) or court orders made as a consequence will expose the company and company officers to the possibility of a fine (s. 156(6)).

¶52-150   Acquisition of non-cash assets

Special rules regulate acquisitions of non-cash assets by public companies. The rules (contained in CA 1985, s. 104) apply to acquisitions from:

(1) subscribers to the memorandum of association of a new public company; or

(2) members of a company which has converted its status from a private to a public company.

The prohibition

The acquisition of non-cash assets from persons in classes (1) and (2) above is prohibited if:

(1) the acquisition is within two years of issue of the certificate of authority to conduct business (under CA 1985, s. 117) or within two years of the re-registration of a private company as a public company (the 'initial period'); and

(2) the consideration given for the asset exceeds ten per cent of the nominal amount of the company's issued share capital.

Exceptions

The prohibition above does not apply where one of the following exceptions applies (CA 1985, s. 104(4), (5)):

(1) Both the assets and any non-cash consideration given by the company were valued by an independent person, who submits a report on the value to the company within six months prior to the agreement date. The relevant time for valuing the assets is the date on which the agreement is reached. The contents of the report must be the same as for those made prior to the acquisition of assets for an issue of shares (see ¶51-000). Copies of the resolution and report must be circulated to all members who are entitled to notice (CA 1985, s. 104(4)(d)). If the proposed agreement is with a person who is not a member of the company, then copies should be sent to that person. The acquisition must then be approved by an ordinary resolution of

the shareholders. Further, copies of the report and the resolution must be submitted to the registrar of companies.

(2) The assets to be acquired are of a kind handled in the normal course of that company's business.

(3) The acquisition is supervised by the court.

Liability for contravening the statutory rules

If a public company acquires a non-cash asset in contravention of the above rules, the company is entitled to recover any consideration it has given to the subscriber or member, and the agreement is avoided in so far as it has not been carried out. However, if the agreement involves an allotment of shares in the company, the allotment is not avoided, and the allottee remains liable for the aggregate nominal amount of the shares received (plus premium, if appropriate) (CA 1985, s. 105). Further, the company and any officer of the company who has contravened s. 104 is liable to a fine (s. 114).

BORROWING

¶52-500   General

Borrowing is an important source of finance for companies. The loan may be long-term (such as debenture stock) or short-term (such as bank overdrafts). Each form of borrowing involves separate costs and considerations. The lender is also likely to request security for his loan. That security usually takes the form of either a fixed or floating charge on the company's property (see ¶53-150). The security sought by the lender may be requested from the shareholders of smaller companies (who are usually also directors) which restricts the advantages of limited liability. This might be in the form of a personal guarantee. The guarantors have a right of recovery against the company if called upon to honour their guarantee. They may also request contributions from co-guarantors in respect of any demand made upon them.

¶52-600   Borrowing powers

The authority for a company to borrow money may be contained in the company's constitution. For example, limits on the borrowing powers of directors are sometimes found in the articles of association, with a requirement that borrowing above the limit be put before the company in general meeting. In the absence of any express permission in the articles or memorandum, every trading company has an implied power to borrow. A public company cannot borrow until a certificate to commence business has been issued by the registrar of companies (see ¶51-600). A company with an express power has an implied power to give security for repayment of the loan subject to any express restrictions on the exercise of this power (e.g. approval of the company in general meeting). See generally ¶30-650ff.

¶52-700 Forms of security

Commonly, a company will obtain long-term finance by granting a charge over its assets in return for the loan. In the event of the company becoming insolvent, the lender will then rank as a secured rather than an unsecured creditor. The terms contained in such loan agreements usually give the lender a power of sale over the assets charged in the event of default. If the charge is created under seal, this power is conferred by statute, as is the right to appoint a receiver (*Law of Property Act 1925*, s. 101).

Legal and equitable charges

A distinction must be made between legal and equitable charges. By a legal charge, the borrower actually transfers his legal interest in the charged property to the lender until such time as a stipulated event takes place (usually the repayment of the loan). An equitable charge will arise where either the formalities necessary to effect a valid legal charge are not met, or where no legal interest subsists in the charged property.

This distinction is important for the determination of priorities, where the borrower either disposes of the charged assets to a third party subsequent to the grant of the charge, or executes further charges on the assets to a different lender. Generally, a legal charge takes priority over an equitable charge over the same property. Successive legal charges rank in the order of their creation.

Application of these rules to company charges is considered at ¶53-200ff.

DEBENTURES

¶52-800 General

Company borrowing takes various forms. The most common form of long-term corporate borrowing is by debenture.

A debenture is commonly a deed under seal, which sets out the terms of the loan. It is usual for a debenture to acknowledge the fact of the company's indebtedness, and to set out the amount of the loan, the annual rate of interest payable by the company on the principal sum, the date of redemption of the loan, the property (if any) over which the debenture holders have a charge and the circumstances in which the debenture holders will have recourse to the charged property.

Meaning of 'debenture'

Despite the widespread use of debentures and the many statutory references to them, the legislation does not provide an exhaustive definition of the term. A debenture 'includes debenture stock, bonds and any other securities of a company, whether constituting a charge on the assets of the company or not' (CA 1985, s. 744).

Types of debenture

A company may issue debentures which are payable to the registered holder, and also debentures which are payable to bearer. In the latter case, the debenture is transferable by delivery.

It is possible for the company to issue irredeemable debentures or debentures which carry rights of conversion to fully paid ordinary shares at a later date.

If the debenture does not create any charge on particular assets, the holders will rank with general creditors for repayment of their loan in the event of the winding-up of the company. If the debenture is not charged on any of the company's assets, the holder has only contractual rights thereunder.

An alternative form of borrowing is by debenture stock. In such a case, the sum borrowed is secured under one document, and each stock holder is entitled to repayment of a fraction of that loan.

Right to demand copies of accounts and reports

Holders of debentures have the right to call for a copy of the company's accounts, director's report and auditor's report (CA 1985, s. 239).

¶52-850   Trust deeds for securing debentures

If debentures are issued to a large number of persons, or the distribution of debenture stock under the one deed is widespread, it is common to appoint trustees to act on behalf of the holders. The trustees then represent the debenture holders in all dealings with the borrowing company, and have the property which is identified under the deed as security for the loan mortgaged in their favour. The trust deed would then specify the terms of the loan, and the circumstances in which the trustees may enforce the rights of debenture holders.

The trustees safeguard the interests of the debenture holders, and are usually empowered to call meetings and to receive specified information from the company to this end. Remuneration of the trustees is provided for in the trust deed. Any debenture holder can obtain a copy of the deed for a small fee.

¶52-900   Interest on debentures

Debentures carry a right to interest at a specified rate. The receipt of interest on debentures is not dependent on the profits of the company. The holder stands as a creditor in respect of the interest due to him. In this respect, the debenture is a safer medium for investment than shares. However, the rate of interest is usually unalterable, and accordingly the debenture holder cannot participate in any capital growth of the company. Further, in times of inflation, the debenture holder will experience a diminution in the value of this right to receive the fixed annual sum from the company.

In contrast to debentures, dividends paid to shareholders may only be paid out of available realised profits. An attraction of debenture finance for companies is the fact that interest paid thereunder is deductible from profits for corporation tax purposes.

¶52-950   Redemption and reissue of debentures

Debentures may carry a right to a premium on redemption. This premium can be paid out of any share premium account (CA 1985, s. 130).

Companies are specifically empowered to reissue redeemable debentures (CA 1985, s. 194). This power is subject to any prohibition (express or implied) contained in the company's articles of association. Section 194 also prohibits reissue if the company is contractually bound not to do so, or if it has represented in some other way that the debentures are to be cancelled on redemption. The reissue of redeemed debentures (or replacement thereof with different debentures) will not be classified as an issue of new debentures which may be in breach of the company's borrowing powers.

On a reissue of the redeemed debentures, the holders are deemed to have the same priorities as before the redemption. Debentures issued to secure an overdraft are not deemed to have been redeemed by reason only of the bank account going into credit.

There is nothing to prevent the issue of debentures at a discount (unlike shares, which are subject to s. 100 of the *Companies Act* 1985: see ¶50-850).

¶53-000   Register of debenture holders

There is no requirement for companies to maintain a register of debenture holders. However, if the company should decide to do so, the register must be kept at either the registered office or the office of the company at which the register is compiled or the office of the person who makes up the register. If the register is not kept at the registered office, the company must inform the registrar of its location (CA 1985, s. 190).

Right to inspect and copy register

If a register of debenture holders is maintained it must be open to inspection by shareholders and debenture holders free of charge, and by members of the public for a fee not exceeding £2.50 per hour (CA 1985, s. 191). Any person may require a copy of the register for a fee, which starts at £2.50 for the first 100 entries on the register.

¶53-050 Borrowing from the public

A company may decide to issue debt securities to the public in the same way as equity securities. The rules for public offers of securities listed on a recognised investment exchange are contained in s. 142–157 of the *Financial Services Act* 1986 (Pt. IV). If the securities are listed on the London Stock Exchange, further reference should be made to the *Listing Rules*. Public offers of securities not so listed are generally regulated by the *Public Offers of Securities Regulations* 1995 (SI 1995/1537: see generally ¶54-000ff.).

The rules as to minimum subscriptions and prohibitions of allotments without full subscriptions, applied to public share sales, do not apply to the issue of debt securities. Further, underwriting arrangements do not have to be disclosed and no overall limit is placed on the commission paid or agreed to be paid in consideration for subscribing debt securities (unlike shares, which are subject to restrictions: see ¶50-850).

FIXED AND FLOATING CHARGES

¶53-150 General

The grant of security for a loan by giving the creditor a right to recover his capital sum from specific assets is termed a 'fixed charge'. Fixed charges on the same assets will rank in order of date of creation.

Companies may also borrow money on the security of a corpus of assets, such as stock in trade or trade debtors. The charge is then over the assets within the stated category. This arrangement is known as a 'floating charge'. The floating charge is not secured on specific, ascertainable assets, but rather upon a category or pool of assets. The company may therefore deal with these assets in the ordinary course of its business unless and until the charge is enforced. The floating charge is a mechanism for the grant of security which is open only to companies. See further ¶53-300.

¶53-200 Floating charges

A floating charge is defined as 'a charge which, as created, was a floating charge' (IA 1986, s. 251). The funds from the realisation of assets covered by the charge must go to the company's preferential creditors before being used to repay the creditors with the floating charge (IA 1986, s. 40).

The classic description of a floating charge was given in *Illingworth v Houldsworth* [1904] AC 345 as follows (per Lord Macnaghten at p. 358):

'a floating charge ... is ambulatory and shifting in its nature, hovering over and so to speak floating with the property which it is intended to affect until some event occurs or some act is done which causes it to settle and fasten on the subject of the charge within its reach and grasp.'

Floating charges are commonly granted over current assets such as stock in trade and book debts. The floating charge is not a legal charge as it does not fix on a specific item of mortgageable or registrable property. It is possible for a company to grant both fixed charges over specific assets and floating charges over all its assets and undertaking, although a deed will normally be entered into to establish the related priorities. The holder of a floating charge has no right to the possession of the assets covered by the charge until the occurrence of one of the events specified in the charge allows the security to be enforced. At that point the charge is said to 'crystallise'. The way in which the security is enforced is either by appointment of an administrative receiver who conducts the business of the company to realise the assets and recover the capital sum, or by the trustee for the debenture holders taking possession of the assets.

As a further description of the distinction between a fixed and a floating charge the Court of Appeal in *Royal Trust Bank v National Westminster Bank plc* [1996] BCC 613 stated that it depends on whether the company is free to deal with the charged property in the ordinary course of business free from the lender bank's security; if so, the charge is a floating charge. However in *Re Cosslett (Contractors) Ltd* [1997] BCC 724 the Court of Appeal thought that the question was not whether the chargor had complete freedom to carry on business as it chose but whether the chargee was in control of the charged assets.

Crystallisation of floating charges

The events which trigger the operation of the floating charge, so as to attach the equitable charge to the classes of assets mortgaged under the loan agreement without any further act by the lender, are not clearly defined.

The events which will definitely crystallise the charge are:

(1) the winding up of the company (*Re Colonial Trusts Corporation, ex parte Bradshaw* (1879) 15 ChD 465);

(2) the appointment of a receiver (*Re Panama, New Zealand and Australian Royal Mail Co* (1870) 5 Ch App 318); and

(3) the cessation of business as a going concern (*Governments Stock & Other Securities Investment Co Ltd v Manila Railway Co Ltd* [1897] AC 81).

In *Re Brightlife Ltd* [1987] Ch 200; (1986) 2 BCC 99,359, the court considered that a charge could crystallise by agreement of the parties (such agreement being in the terms of the charge or by the chargee giving notice to the chargor) rather than by operation of law, and it was not open to the courts to restrict that freedom without legislative authority.

There is some uncertainty as to whether the occurrence of other events (such as the grant of subsequent charges on the same assets), which are described in the loan agreement as crystallising the charge, can have this effect without the intervention of the debenture holder. There is authority for the view that this can be achieved if the event which triggers crystallisation is appointment of a receiver under an earlier or later charge, and the latter event was expressly identified as the trigger by the debenture (*Re Woodroffes Musical Instruments Ltd* [1986] Ch 366).

It would appear that it is possible to effect an automatic crystallisation on the occurrence of events other than the appointment of a receiver under a separate charge as in, for example,*Re Manurewa Transport Ltd* [1971] NZLR 909.

Fixed charges over circulating assets

It is possible for a debenture to create an equitable fixed charge over 'circulating' assets such as book debts by restriction of the creditor company's ability to dispose of them (*Siebe Gorman & Co Ltd v Barclays Bank Ltd* [1979] 2 Ll Rep 142). Further, if not inconsistent with the provisions of the debenture, the company and debenture holder may agree to treat future as well as current book debts as fixed charges (*Re New Bullas Trading Ltd* [1994] BCC 36).

Priorities

As a floating charge is not a legal charge over the assets covered by the security, a subsequent legal charge over the same assets would take priority over it.

Debentures by which a floating charge is created commonly prohibit creation of subsequent charges on the same assets ('negative pledge' clauses). This strategy will not protect the debenture holder against certain legal claims on the assets covered by the floating charge which may arise prior to attachment of the floating charge (e.g. by operation of rights of set-off, rights of distraint under a lease or execution of judgment debts). Preferred creditors under s. 386 and Sch. 6 of the *Insolvency Act* 1986 take priority over a floating charge in the event of the winding up of the company.

A legal charge takes priority over a floating charge despite the prohibition of creation of subsequent fixed charges in the floating charge debenture if, at the time of the creation of the former, the creditor who acquires this fixed charge was unaware of either the floating charge or the prohibition it contained.

However, a prohibition will protect the first creditor with a floating charge against claims under subsequent floating charges over the same assets, even if the subsequent creditors have no notice of the prohibition. It is possible to grant a fixed charge on terms that it is subject to an earlier floating charge.

Retention of title clauses

Often, a trade creditor of a company will insert a 'retention of title' clause into a contract for the sale of goods. By providing that the goods are still the property of the vendor until the purchaser has paid for them, the creditor gains secured status. Under certain circumstances, this may have the effect of creating a fixed or floating charge over those goods. If other charges are already in existence, questions will arise as to which charges take priority if the company goes into liquidation.

The priority of the various forms of charges is affected by the registration rules considered at ¶53-300ff.

REGISTRATION OF COMPANY CHARGES

¶53-300 General

Two separate registration regimes are applied to companies. The first is maintained by the registrar of companies (see below); the second is the register maintained by the company itself (see ¶53-450). The details which must be registered are considered below, and the effects of non-registration are considered at ¶53-350.

Charges which have to be registered

Registration of the following charges (which includes mortgages) must be made with the registrar of companies (CA 1985, s. 396(1)):

(1) a charge for the purpose of securing any issue of debentures;

(2) a charge on the uncalled share capital of the company;

(3) a charge created or evidenced by an instrument which, if executed by an individual, would require registration as a bill of sale;

(4) a charge on land (wherever situated) or any interest in land, but not including a charge for any rent or other periodical sum issuing out of the land;

(5) a charge on the book debts of the company;

(6) a floating charge on the company's undertaking or property;

(7) a floating charge on calls made but not paid;

(8) a charge on a ship or aircraft, or any share in a ship; and

(9) a charge on goodwill, on a patent or licence under a patent, on a trade mark or on a copyright or a licence under a copyright.

Generally, the registrar of companies must be notified within 21 days of the charge's creation (CA 1985, s. 395(1)).

Particulars which must be registered

The particulars of the charge which must be registered are as follows (CA 1985, s. 401(1)):

(1) In the case of a charge to the benefit of which the holders of a series of debentures are entitled, the particulars specified in s. 397(1) of the *Companies Act* 1985, i.e.:

   (a) the total amount secured by the whole series;

   (b) the dates of the resolutions authorising the issue of the series and the date of the covering deed (if any) by which the security is created or defined;

   (c) a general description of the property charged; and

   (d) the names of the trustees (if any) for the debenture holders.

(2) In the case of any other charge:

   (a) if it is a charge created by the company, the date of its creation, and if it is a charge which was existing on property acquired by the company, the date of the acquisition of the property; and

   (b) the amount secured by the charge; and

   (c) short particulars of the property charged; and

   (d) the persons entitled to the charge.

The documents which must be delivered to the registrar are the prescribed form which sets out the particulars required in s. 397(1) (as above) plus the deed itself or a copy of one of the debentures if there is no deed. If debentures were issued in a series, it is necessary to send to the registrar the date and amount of each issue.

Verification of charges on property outside UK

In the case of charged property situated outside the UK, registration with the registrar is called for if the charge is created within the UK (CA 1985, s. 398(3)). If the charge is created outside the UK it is necessary to provide the registrar with a copy of the instrument creating the charge within 21 days of the date on which the instrument or a copy thereof, could in due course of post (and if dispatched with due diligence) have been received in the UK (CA 1985, s. 398(1), (2)).

Charges on property in England and Wales created elsewhere

Charges by companies incorporated outside Great Britain (see ¶20-600) which attach to property in England and Wales must be registered with the registrar of companies (CA 1985, s. 409).

Charges existing on property acquired

It is also necessary to register charges within s. 396(1) of the *Companies Act* 1985 (above) which attach to assets acquired by the company, even though the company did not create the charge (CA 1985, s. 400). Registration must then occur within 21 days from the date of acquisition.

¶53-350   Effect of non-registration with the registrar

Registration acts as constructive notice of the existence of a charge to all persons affected thereby (*Wilson v Kelland* [1910] 2 Ch 306). However, registration is only constructive notice of the charge, and not of its terms. Accordingly notice of prohibitions on creation of subsequent charges is not given by registration.

Failure to register a charge within 21 days of its creation (i.e. the date the agreement creating the charge is concluded) renders the charge void as against a liquidator, administrator or creditor of the company (CA 1985, s. 395(1)). However, the obligation to repay the underlying debt remains (CA 1985, s. 395(2)), though ranking only as an unsecured debt in the event of the company's liquidation. The money secured by the charge becomes immediately repayable upon the charge becoming void (CA 1985, s. 395(2)).

The importance of the charge becoming void is that the lender loses his security. Thus, for example, preferential creditors, floating charges and fixed equitable charges would rank higher in priority in the event of a liquidation than the lender with a fixed charge who had failed to register.

The registrar is unable to register a charge if either the particulars prescribed under s. 395 of the *Companies Act* 1985 (above), or the instrument creating the charge, are not submitted to him within 21 days (subject to late registration: see ¶53-400). Once the registrar's certificate of registration has been issued, the charge must be taken to have been properly registered, irrespective of whether this was the case, as the registrar's certificate is 'conclusive evidence' that the requirements as to registration have been satisfied (CA 1985, s. 401(2)). Accordingly the charge is valid from the date of registration, and on the terms as disclosed on the registrar's certificate (*R v Registrar of Companies, ex parte Esal (Commodities) Ltd* (1985) 1 BCC 99,501).

¶53-400   Rectification of register of charges

It is possible to rectify the register of charges maintained by the registrar of companies (CA 1985, s. 404). This may be done to correct mistakes or allow late registration.

It is necessary for an application to be made to the court, which may grant the rectification if satisfied that the error was accidental, or due to inadvertence or to some other sufficient cause, or is not of a nature to prejudice the position of the creditors or shareholders of the company, or that on other grounds it is just and equitable to grant relief.

The court will usually only grant the application on terms that rights in the charged property acquired subsequent to expiry of the 21-day time limit for registration but before the late registration are not to be prejudiced by that registration (*Watson v Duff, Morgan and Vermont (Holdings) Ltd* [1974] 1 WLR

450). This protection is not extended to later charges created within 21 days after the first charge.

¶53-450 The company's register

Companies must maintain a register of charges at their registered office (CA 1985, s. 407(1)), or, in the case of oversea companies (CA 1985, s. 409), at their principal place of business in England and Wales (see ¶20-600). The charges which must be registered are those set out in CA 1985, s. 396(1) (see ¶53-300). The details which must be recorded are (CA 1985, s. 407(2)):

- a brief description of the property charged,
- the amount of the charge, and
- persons entitled to the charge.

Effect of omitting entries

Failure to maintain the register does not invalidate the security created by the charge but exposes directors and company officers who knowingly and wilfully authorise or permit the omission to a fine (CA 1985, s. 407(3)).

Right to inspect register of charges, etc.

The register (and copies of the instruments which have to be sent to the registrar) must be available during normal business hours (CA 1985, s. 408(1)). The register must also be available for inspection by other persons on payment of a fee not exceeding five pence (CA 1985, s. 408(2)). Refusal to permit inspection may result in a fine on company officers responsible and the right can be enforced by application to the court (CA 1985, s. 408(3), (4)).

¶53-500 Discharge of registrable charge

The procedure for discharge of a charge is not very satisfactory. Section 403 of the *Companies Act* 1985 calls for filing with the registrar of companies of a statutory declaration verifying that the debt for which the charge was given has been paid or satisfied in whole or in part (form 403a) or that the charged property or undertaking has been released from the charge or ceased to form part of the company's property or undertaking (form 403b). The registrar then *may* enter on the register a memorandum of satisfaction in whole or in part (in which event he must copy this to the company), or of the fact that the property has been released or no longer forms part of the company's property. As it is the company, and not the charge-holder, who submits the relevant form, the system is dependent upon the honesty of the person who fills out the statutory declaration. It is noticeable that the legislation does not make the registrar's memorandum of satisfaction conclusive evidence of discharge of the charge.

PUBLIC ISSUES

¶54-000   General

When securities are offered to the public in the UK for the first time, it is normally necessary for the offeror to publish a prospectus containing prescribed disclosures about the issuer and the securities. The disclosures are normally those required by the London Stock Exchange (LSE) if the securities are subject to an application for listing on the LSE and those required by the *Public Offers of Securities Regulations* 1995 (SI 1995/1537) (the prospectus regulations) if they are not.

The 'listing particulars' regime for the admission of securities to listing on the LSE of securities (LSE securities) is contained in s. 142–157 of the *Financial Services Act* 1986 (Pt. IV). The 'prospectus' regime contained in the *Companies Act* 1985, for securities which were neither listed nor subject to an application for listing on the LSE, continued in force until 1995 and was supposed to be replaced in due course by the regime in s. 158–171 of the *Financial Services Act* 1986 (Pt. V). It has now been superseded instead by the prospectus regulations, which normally apply to 'first time' UK public offers even if the securities are subject to an application for listing on the LSE. However, in the latter case the prospectus must be approved by the LSE and the prescribed disclosures are those required by the LSE under Pt. IV above (as amended by the prospectus regulations) rather than those required by the prospectus regulations themselves.

If there is no 'first time' UK public offer (either because there is no UK public offer at all or because the securities have already been the subject of a UK public offer), or the securities are not subject to the prospectus directive, it is still necessary, unless an exemption applies, to publish and file 'listing particulars' before securities subject to the listing directives can be admitted to listing on the LSE.

Accordingly, except in the case of securities already listed on the LSE under Pt. IV of the *Financial Services Act* 1986 above, the prospectus regulations apply whenever securities subject to them are offered to the public in the UK for the first time (in what may be called, in the American phrase, an initial public offering: IPO).

Registration and publication of prospectus

The prospectus regulations (see above) require all offerors of securities to publish and file a prospectus containing the detailed disclosures set out in Sch. 1 to the regulations (and all other material information) before they can make an IPO in the UK (SI 1995/1537, reg. 4, 8(1)). As a result of helpful exemptions, many 'restricted' offers of non-LSE securities to UK offerees do not need a prospectus, although they will normally be subject to the general regulatory regime of the *Financial Services Act* 1986. In the UK context, IPOs of non-LSE securities normally occur on the LSE's Alternative Investment Market (AIM) for young and growing companies; indeed, the prospectus regulations came into force on the day that dealings started on AIM.

STOCK EXCHANGE LISTINGS

¶54-100   Admission requirements

Sections 142–157 of the *Financial Services Act* 1986 (Pt. IV) require the publication and filing with the registrar of companies of a document approved by the London Stock Exchange (LSE) and containing the disclosures required by the listing rules; where there is an initial public offering (IPO: see ¶54-000) of LSE securities, the document is called a 'prospectus' and, in other cases, 'listing particulars'.

Schedule 11A to the *Financial Services Act* 1986 (inserted by the prospectus regulations: see ¶54-000), explains when securities are treated as offered to the public in the UK, so that the offer is an IPO requiring a prospectus if this is the first time that the securities concerned (rather than merely other securities of the same class) are offered to the public in the UK.

General duty of disclosure in listing particulars

Prospectuses and other listing particulars of LSE securities must normally contain all such information as investors and their professional advisers would reasonably require to make an informed assessment of the assets and liabilities, financial position, profits and losses and prospects of the issuer of the securities and would reasonably expect to find in listing particulars (FSA 1986, s. 146(1)).

The 1986 Act allows the nature and extent of this information to be determined by the circumstances: for example the nature of the issuer and the prospective market and, in particular, existing public information (FSA 1986, s. 146(3)). The Act requires the persons 'responsible' for preparing the listing particulars to make reasonable enquiries to ascertain any such information not within their personal knowledge, but the disclosure obligation is restricted to information which they actually know or ought to know (FSA 1986, s. 146(2)).

Derogations and exemptions from disclosure

The LSE has a general right to grant derogations from the listing particulars requirements in particular cases if authorised by the listing rules (FSA 1986, s. 156(2)).

In addition, the LSE may authorise the omission from listing particulars generally of particular 'financial condition' information otherwise required by s. 146 above (FSA 1986, s. 148(1)), but only on particular grounds:

(1) that its disclosure would be contrary to the public interest (as to which a certificate from the Treasury will be conclusive: s. 148(3)) of the *Financial Services Act* 1986; or

(2) that its disclosure would be seriously detrimental to the issuer (though the LSE cannot allow anything to be omitted on this ground if its omission would mislead a prospective investor as to any essential facts); or

(3) in the case of debt securities of any class prescribed by the listing rules, because its disclosure would be unnecessary for persons of the kind who may be expected normally to buy or deal in the securities concerned – this is intended to help preserve the speed and informality of the Eurobond market.

Supplementary listing particulars

It may be necessary for the issuer to publish a supplementary prospectus or listing particulars (for example, during the course of an offer) in certain circumstances (FSA 1986, s. 147). They will be required if, after the preparation of listing particulars for submission to the LSE and before the commencement of dealings following admission, there is a significant change affecting any matter required to be contained in those particulars (for example, the financial condition of the issuer). They will also be required if a significant new matter arises which would have had to have been included in the original listing particulars if it had arisen before they were prepared.

¶54-150   Compensation payable by persons 'responsible'

The *Financial Services Act* 1986 imposes civil liabilities on the persons 'responsible' for listing particulars if they contain false or misleading statements or omit any matter required to be included by the Act or the listing rules and the statement or omission results in loss (FSA 1986, s. 150(1)). The Act thus contains a civil sanction for mere non-disclosure of prescribed information. The issuer of the securities will be similarly liable if he fails to publish supplementary listing particulars when he is required to do so, as will anyone else who is responsible for listing particulars if he fails to notify the issuer of the significant change or new matter requiring supplementary listing particulars to be issued (FSA 1986, s. 150(3)). If the facts are sufficient, the issuer or offeror may also be guilty of an offence under s. 47 of the *Financial Services Act* 1986 (misleading statements), which would enable the Securities and Investments Board (SIB) to bring a civil action for compensation and disgorgement of profits under s. 61 of the *Financial Services Act* 1986.

Compensation for false or misleading particulars

Subject to certain defences, compensation will be payable to any person who suffers loss because the securities are as a result worth less than (effectively) they were represented to be (FSA 1986, s. 150(1)). Although s. 150 is not totally clear, the better view is that compensation is payable unless a statutory defence is available, even if the investor did not invest in reliance on the listing particulars and, indeed, even if he did not see them or he bought the securities in the secondary market; however, no compensation will be payable to a person who bought with knowledge of the default (FSA 1986, s. 151(5)).

Exemptions from liability to pay compensation

The 1986 Act provides the reasonable defences that would be expected: for example that the person 'responsible' published a correction (FSA 1986, s. 151(3)), or reasonably believed that the statement was true and not misleading or that nothing that should have been disclosed was omitted (FSA 1986, s. 151(1)). However, in this latter case, ignorance of the facts will not itself be an excuse unless he has made all reasonable enquiries to ascertain the true position. In addition, he must have continued in that belief not just until admission to listing but until the securities were acquired, or must have had no time to publish a correction or bring it to the attention of prospective investors, or (which may help limit liability to purchasers in the market) the securities must have been acquired after a material lapse of time, provided, in this last case, that he had continued in his belief at least until the commencement of dealings (FSA 1986, s. 151(1)).

There are similar defences for reasonable reliance on an expert's statements provided that the expert consented to their inclusion in the form and context in which they were included (FSA 1986, s. 151(2)). In the case of a failure to publish supplementary listing particulars, there will be no liability if the issuer or other person 'responsible' reasonably believed that there was no need for them (FSA 1986, s. 151(6)).

Persons responsible for particulars

The persons who are deemed to be responsible for all or part of listing particulars or supplementary listing particulars are the issuer, every director or person who authorised himself to be named as a director of the issuer, every person who expressly accepts responsibility (for example, under the listing rules) and every other person who authorised their contents (FSA 1986, s. 152). Where the listing particulars are a prospectus relating to an IPO, references to the 'issuer' include references to the 'offeror' (FSA 1986, s.154A(b)), except that directors of the offeror are not responsible as such.

Liabilities

The 1986 Act provides that its 'listing particulars' liability does not exclude other liabilities, for example in deceit or misrepresentation (FSA 1986, s. 150(4)); accordingly, there are still many different varieties of potential prospectus liabilities. However, the Act does exclude liability for non-disclosure of matters which do not have to be disclosed in listing particulars by the person or persons responsible for them (FSA 1986, s. 150(6)).

A recent case has held that even purchasers in the market may be entitled to sue directors of an issuer for negligence on a prospectus if the facts showed that it had the additional, intended, purpose of informing and encouraging purchasers in the market and the purchaser established that he had reasonably relied on the negligent misrepresentation and reasonably believed that the representor had intended him to act on it (*Possfund Custodian Trustee Ltd v Diamond* [1996] 1 WLR 1351).

OFFERS OF UNLISTED SECURITIES

¶54-250   The prospectus

When non-London Stock Exchange (LSE) securities are offered to the public in the UK for the first time (and even if other securities of the same class have previously been offered to the public in the UK), it is normally necessary for the offeror to publish and file a prospectus containing prescribed disclosures and to refer to the prospectus in all marketing materials. Unless an exemption applies, the prospectus requirements apply to offers even of existing securities (by a shareholder), except where the particular securities themselves have been offered to the public in the UK on an earlier occasion.

The prospectus regime which applies to these initial public offerings (IPOs) is contained in the *Public Offers of Securities Regulations* 1995 (SI 1995/1537) (the prospectus regulations), reg. 3–16 (Pt. II). Similar compensation provisions for non-disclosure apply to prospectuses registered under the prospectus regulations as to listing particulars (including prospectuses) registered under Pt. IV of the *Financial Services Act* 1986 (see ¶54-400). However, there are many important exemptions from the prospectus requirements in the case of qualifying restricted offers, on the basis that the offer is not an offer to the public in the UK for the purposes of the prospectus regulations. Whether or not there is a need for a prospectus, the general regulatory regime of the *Financial Services Act* 1986 will normally apply.

Registration and publication of prospectus

Where the prospectus regulations apply, a prospectus containing specified information about the issuer and the securities must normally be filed in a public register in the UK, and copies must be made available at a UK address (SI 1995/1537, reg. 4). There is no requirement actually to send the prospectus to the offerees; however, that would certainly be best practice and would normally need to be done for commercial reasons.

Convertible securities and guaranteed debentures

Where the securities are convertible into, or otherwise give a right to acquire, securities issued by a different issuer or are guaranteed, the prescribed financial information must also be given in respect of the issuer of the underlying securities and the guarantor (SI 1995/1537, Sch. 1, para. 50, 51). The information must be presented in as comprehensible a form as possible (SI 1995/1537, reg. 8(3)).

Advertisements, etc. in connection with offers of securities

In addition, any marketing materials relating to the offer, for example a newspaper advertisement, must state that a prospectus is or will be published and give an address in the UK from which it can be obtained (SI 1995/1537, reg. 12).

Contraventions

If a *Financial Services Act* 1986-authorised firm fails to comply with these requirements the failure is treated as a contravention of self-regulating organisation (SRO) or Securities and Investments Board (SIB) rules (SI 1995/1537, reg. 16(1)); the firm can therefore be sued under s. 62 of the *Financial Services Act* 1986 by a qualifying investor (who must normally be an individual) for any loss suffered as a result. Non-compliance by anyone else is a criminal offence, and any investor who suffers loss as a result can normally sue for compensation (SI 1995/1537, reg. 16(2), (4)).

General duty of disclosure in prospectus

The prospectus must normally contain the detailed disclosures about the issuer and the securities being offered which are set out in the prospectus regulations (SI 1995/1537, Sch. 1). In addition, as in the case of Pt. IV prospectuses and listing particulars (see ¶54-100), there is a specific obligation to provide all information which investors would need in order to make an 'informed assessment' of the issuer's assets and liabilities and its profits and losses, of the financial condition of the issuer and of its prospects, and of the rights attaching to the securities (SI 1995/1537, reg. 9(1)), with consequent civil liability for any failure to do so.

Supplementary prospectus

A supplementary prospectus must be issued (and registered) if there is a significant change affecting the required disclosures or a significant new matter arises which would have had to be disclosed or a significant inaccuracy is discovered in any information contained in the prospectus (whether or not a required disclosure); in all these cases, 'significant' means important for the purpose of making that informed assessment (SI 1995/1537, reg. 10). Strangely, there is no requirement to send the supplementary prospectus to the original offerees or advertise its publication.

¶54-300 Exemptions from prospectus requirements where offer to the public

The prospectus (see ¶54-250) does not need to include the prescribed detailed information about the issuer's assets and liabilities, financial condition and profits and losses (or its principal activities and its directors) if the omission is authorised in specified circumstances by a person or body designated by the Treasury (*Public Offers of Securities Regulations* 1995 (SI 1995/1537, reg. 8(4)). Those circumstances are that the securities being offered are shares; that the shares are to be dealt in on an 'approved exchange'; that the shares are being offered on a pre-emptive basis (for example, by a rights issue) to some or all of the existing holders of shares; and that up-to-date information equivalent to the omitted prescribed information is already available under that exchange's rules.

An 'approved exchange' is a recognised investment exchange under the *Financial Services Act* 1986 which has been specifically approved by the Treasury for this purpose. The Treasury has 'approved' the Alternative Investment Market (AIM) for this purpose.

In addition, the Treasury can designate a UK regulator (and has so designated the London Stock Exchange (LSE)) who can authorise public offers of shares to be made without a registered prospectus at all if they are of the same class as shares which have already been admitted to dealings on an approved exchange (typically, AIM); the number or value of the offered shares is less than ten per cent of the number or value of the shares already quoted; and up-to-date information equivalent to the detailed disclosures required by the prospectus regulations (SI 1995/1537, Sch. 1) is already available under that exchange's rules (SI 1995/1537, reg. 8(5)). The offered shares seemingly do not need to be quoted themselves.

Authorised omissions

The LSE can also authorise the omission from a prospectus of information relating to the issuer in specified circumstances (SI 1995/1537, reg. 11(3)) even though the securities are non-LSE securities and the LSE does not have to approve the prospectus. The specified circumstances are either that the publication of the information would be 'seriously detrimental' to the issuer and its omission would not be likely to mislead investors, or that the information is of only minor importance.

'Bring-down' prospectuses

There is also an important exemption under which a full prospectus is not needed even if the securities (whether or not shares) are being offered to the public in the UK for the first time and the 'approved exchange' exemptions do not apply. The exemption applies only to offers for subscription and will apply if, within the 12 months preceding the date when the new securities are first offered to the public in

¶54-300

the UK, the same issuer has published a full prospectus in relation to other securities issued by the issuer, whether or not of the same class. Instead of a full prospectus, the issuer must either publish that earlier full prospectus (and any supplementary prospectus) or merely refer to it (or them) in its offer document and, in either case, must publish disclosures about any changes to the information contained in that earlier prospectus (and supplementary prospectus) which are likely to influence the value of the securities (SI 1995/1537, reg. 8(6)). This 'bring-down' prospectus is a helpful development in UK prospectus law.

¶54-350 Exemptions from prospectus requirements where no offer to the public

The prospectus regulations (*Public Offers of Securities Regulations* 1995 (SI 1995/1537)) contain important private placement exemptions; where they apply, the offer is not a 'public offer' and therefore no prospectus is required, although the general regulatory regime of the *Financial Services Act* 1986 may still apply. The main exemptions are as follows:

(1) Offers to qualifying securities professionals (who buy or sell securities, as principal or agent, or act as investment manager, rather than merely advise on securities or arrange transactions). As a result, offers to stockbrokers, investment banks, investment managers and most commercial banks will be exempted on this basis; the offer can be accepted by them for the account of clients but seemingly cannot be passed on to a client to accept personally. Offers to listed investment trusts, including venture capital trusts, and life assurance companies will also be exempted.

(2) Offers to no more than 50 persons (SI 1995/1537, reg. 7(2)(b)). This is the first time that UK prospectus law has specifically provided a private placement exemption for a specified number of offerees (in the UK). The relevant number is the number of people in the UK who receive the offer and are not in another applicable exemption (see below); the number who actually accept the offer is irrelevant. The prospectus regulations contain aggregation provisions to prevent the splitting up of offers to get within the exemption. In order to see whether the 50-person limit is reached for a particular offer, it is accordingly necessary to include all offerees in the UK who have previously received any offer from the same offeror in respect of the same class of securities, if the previous offer was open (rather than merely first made) during the 12 months before the proposed offer is first made and was exempted from the prospectus regulations by this '50 persons' exemption (SI 1995/1537, reg. 7(6)).

(3) Offers to a restricted circle of experienced investors (in the UK) whom the offeror reasonably believes to be sufficiently knowledgeable to understand the risks involved in accepting the offer (SI 1995/1537, reg. 7(2)(d)); any information supplied by the offeror is to be disregarded for this purpose,

apart from information about the issuer (SI 1995/1537, reg. 7(7)). As there is no statutory test, it would be prudent not to rely on this exemption unless the position is clear.

(4) Offers where the minimum purchase price which may be paid under the offer by each offeree is not less than ECU 40,000 or an equivalent amount (SI 1995/1537, reg. 7(2)(i)); this is the first time that UK prospectus law has provided an exemption for what may be called 'non-retail' offerings.

(5) Offers made in connection with a 'takeover offer' (SI 1995/1537, reg. 7(2)(k) and (10)). For this purpose, a 'takeover offer' is a qualifying offer to acquire all the shares, or all the shares of a particular class, not owned by the offeror or a qualifying partial offer. Accordingly, no prospectus normally needs to be issued in relation to securities offered as consideration in a bid.

(6) Offers by a UK private company to members or employees of the company, and qualifying family members, or to holders of its debt securities (SI 1995/1537, reg. 7(2)(f), (8)). The exemption covers offers to restricted classes of family members of the shareholders or employees (but not of the holders of debt securities), including, helpfully, family trusts. However, it does not cover holders of debt securities with an original maturity of less than one year, as they are not 'securities' for the purpose of the prospectus regulations (SI 1995/1537, reg. 2(1)). This exemption (which mirrors that in the *Companies Act* 1985) shows that even private companies can make public offers within the prospectus regulations, provided that the offer is not a 'public offer' within the old *Companies Act* 1985 definition.

(7) Offers where the securities being offered are non-transferable (SI 1995/1537, reg. 7(2)(u)).

(8) Offers where the total consideration payable is limited to ECU 40,000 (SI 1995/1537, reg. 7(2)(h)). This is a maximum limit on the whole offer (to UK offerees) rather than the minimum threshold for each application or acceptance as referred to in (4) above.

(9) Offers restricted to qualifying employees of the issuer or its group, or specified classes of their family members, not, however, including family trusts, (SI 1995/1537, reg. 7(2)(o), (12)).

¶54-400   Compensation payable by persons 'responsible'

The prospectus regulations introduce for public offers of non-London Stock Exchange (LSE) securities a compensation regime similar to that relating to securities listed on the LSE under Pt. IV. They provide that, if a prospectus (or supplementary prospectus) for non-LSE securities does not comply with the applicable disclosure requirements or contains any untrue or misleading statement, the person or persons 'responsible' for the prospectus or supplementary prospectus must normally compensate investors who suffer loss as a result (*Public Offers of*

Securities Regulations 1995 (SI 1995/1537, reg. 14(1)). If the facts are sufficient, the offeror may also be guilty of an offence under FSA 1986, s. 47 (misleading statements), which would enable the Securities and Investments Board (SIB) to bring a civil action for compensation and disgorgement of profits under FSA 1986, s. 61.

Persons responsible for prospectus

The persons 'responsible' for the prospectus are listed in the prospectus regulations (SI 1995/1537, reg. 13). They include the issuer and its directors (unless the offer is one of existing securities, and the issuer has not authorised it), anyone who is named in the prospectus with his consent as a director or proposed director of the issuer and, if the offeror is not the issuer, the offeror and its directors.

The persons 'responsible' also include everyone who has authorised the contents of the prospectus or supplementary prospectus (or, as the case may be, part of it) or who has accepted responsibility for it and is described in it as having done so; where a person has authorised the contents only of part of the prospectus or supplementary prospectus, he is 'responsible' only for that part. Even if a firm which sponsors an offer is technically not an offeror, which is unlikely, it will normally be a person 'responsible' on the basis that it authorised the contents of the prospectus; however, its directors will normally not be persons 'responsible' unless, perhaps, they personally authorised the contents of the prospectus. Professionals such as lawyers who advise on the contents of a prospectus or supplementary prospectus only in a professional capacity are expressly stated not to be 'responsible' for it (SI 1995/1537, reg. 13(4)).

The prospectus must state the names of the persons 'responsible' for it (SI 1995/1537, Sch. 1, para. 9).

Exemptions from liability to pay compensation

The prospectus regulations contain detailed exemptions from the liability of persons 'responsible' to pay compensation, which mirror those under s. 142–157 of the *Financial Services Act* 1986 (Pt. IV) (SI 1995/1537, reg. 15). As would be expected, they depend on the lack of knowledge of the person 'responsible', his taking of reasonable steps to issue a correction, his reasonable belief that no supplementary prospectus was necessary or the knowledge of the person suffering the loss as to the true position. The burden of proving that an exemption applies is on the person 'responsible'.

In addition, a director of the issuer is not responsible for a prospectus or supplementary prospectus if it is published without his knowledge or consent and he makes this public as soon as he finds out (SI 1995/1537, reg. 13(2)). Strangely, there is no similar exemption for directors of the offeror.

'Offerors'

The prospectus regulations impose compensation liability on the 'offeror', and indeed make the 'offeror' the person who has to publish the prospectus (SI

1995/1537, reg. 4(1)). It defines the 'offeror' of securities as the person who 'as principal' makes an offer which, if accepted, would give rise to a contract for the issue or sale of the securities or who invites such an offer (reg. 5); this definition applies also in the case of the 'offeror' of listed securities, where the term is similarly important in the case of compensation liability. It is irrelevant whether the securities subject to the offer are to be issued or sold by the offeror or by another person with whom he has made arrangements for their issue or sale (reg. 5(a)).

Where the offer is made by the issuer himself or by the owner of existing securities, it is quite clear that the 'offeror' is the issuer or owner. Where there is an 'offer for sale' by an issuing house or other 'sponsor' of securities to be issued by the issuer to the sponsor and then sold on to the investor, it is, again, clear that it is the sponsor which is the 'offeror'; the securities are technically to be 'sold' under an offer made by the sponsor and issued directly by the issuer under arrangements made with the sponsor (albeit at the request of the issuer).

However, it is not totally clear who the 'offeror' is where the sponsor makes the offer to investors on behalf of the issuer or shareholder but does not himself buy the securities on the way; the typical case (applying to both new and existing securities) is where the securities are 'placed' by a sponsor acting as 'placing agent' (assuming that the placing is technically an offer to the public) or securities are floated on the Alternative Investment Market (AIM) by way of a public offer made by a sponsor. The 'obvious' view is that the offeror is the issuer or shareholder, since he issues or owns the securities and the sponsor is acting as his 'agent', not 'as principal'. As the shareholder is liable as an 'offeror', it is accordingly 'responsible' for the whole prospectus and not just the portion (perhaps about itself) which it has authorised; all the directors are therefore also responsible and there is no clear exemption for them as in the case of the directors of the issuer.

¶54-500 Continuing Companies Act restrictions on 'public offers'

Two key provisions in the *Companies Act* 1985 still continue to apply to public offers of non-London Stock Exchange securities. The first is the prohibition on allotments if the minimum amount which must be raised by the prospectus to fund certain prescribed matters is not achieved (CA 1985, s. 83). Accordingly, if the stated minimum amount is not raised within the 40-day period specified in s. 83, the offer period cannot be extended and the offer must be aborted. The second is the prohibition on public offers by UK private companies (CA 1985, s. 81). The prohibition applies to the offer of shares or debt securities to the public; it does not apply to the other securities covered by the prospectus regulations, unless they can be regarded as an indirect offer of the shares or debt securities. Because the prospectus regulations do not affect this prohibition, the definition of 'offer to the public' remains that in s. 59 and 60 of the *Companies Act* 1985 which are retained in force for this purpose. The Companies Act definition is much wider than that in the prospectus regulations; for example, it includes most offers which are treated as not being 'offers to the public in the UK' for the purposes of the prospectus regulations. An offer by a UK private company may therefore be prohibited by the Companies Act even though it could have been made without a prospectus under the prospectus regulations.

SHAREHOLDERS
• MINORITY
PROTECTION

Table of Contents

continued over

SHAREHOLDERS

¶60-000   Definition of a member

The separation of ownership and control of a company is one of the fundamental consequences of corporate personality. This division results in a need for identification of shareholder rights, and specific procedures through which enforcement of those rights can be guaranteed.

The form of application submitted by persons who wish to subscribe shares will contain an agreement to become a member. If a person purchases shares from another, the agreement of the purchaser to acquire shares is usually contained in the stock transfer form which is submitted to the company (this is implied by the request for registration of the transfer). It is also necessary for the shareholder's name to appear on the register of members. Thus, holders of renounceable letters of allotment and share warrants are not members of the company. However, it is possible for the articles of association to confer membership rights on holders of share warrants (CA 1985, s. 355(5)).

It is possible for a person whose name appears on the share register to call for removal of his name, because he has not agreed to become a member (*Re Compania de Electricidad de la Provincia de Buenos Aires Ltd* [1980] 1 Ch 146; CA 1985, s. 359). Where a person subscribes shares in a company, an agreement to become a member arises notwithstanding the absence of a bilateral contract between that person and the company (*Re Nuneaton Borough Association Football Club Ltd* (1989) 5 BCC 377).

The memorandum and articles of association of a company constitute a contract between the company and each of its members (see ¶30-000). The capacity to become a shareholder is governed by normal contractual principles. Hence, a minor may become a member, but the contract is voidable. If the contract for allotment is avoided, the shares are treated as if they had never been issued. If a contract for sale is avoided the vendor continues to be a member of the company.

¶60-100   Register of members

All companies must maintain a register of members (CA 1985, s. 352). The following particulars must be recorded in the register in relation to each member:

(1) his name and address;

(2) the date on which a person was registered as a member; and

(3) the date on which any person ceased to be a member.

The following additional details are required for companies which have a share capital:

(4) a statement of the shares held by each member, distinguishing each share by number (if the share has a number: most private companies dispense with this formality) and the class of share (if the company has more than one class); and

(5) the amount paid, or agreed to be treated as paid, on the shares of each member.

The name which appears on the register is taken to be the owner of the shares, and no notice of any trust can be entered on the register (CA 1985, s. 360). The register must be maintained at the company's registered office, or at the place where the register is made up. However, in the latter case, the company must notify the registrar of companies of where the register is kept, and any change in that place. If a company is registered in England or Wales, the register cannot be kept outside England or Wales. Similarly, if the company is registered in Scotland, the register cannot be maintained outside Scotland (CA 1985, s. 353).

If a company has more than 50 members, it must maintain an index to the register of members, which will facilitate identification of the interests of each member (CA 1985, s. 354).

The register must be available to all members for inspection. Other persons must also be given access to the register, but may be charged a fee (CA 1985, s. 356). The register is prima facie evidence of the details recorded therein (CA 1985, s. 361).

The facility for rectification is set out in s. 359 of the *Companies Act* 1985 in the following circumstances, if:

(1) the name of any person is, without sufficient cause, entered in or omitted from the register; or

(2) default is made, or unnecessary delay takes place, in entering on the register the fact of any person having ceased to be a member.

An application to the court for rectification can be made by any person aggrieved by the current state of the register, any member of the company, or the company itself. The court may then refuse the application, or order rectification of the register. The court may also order the company to pay damages to the applicant.

GENERAL MEETINGS

¶60-150   General

Members of a company exercise their control over company affairs through company general meetings. In view of the importance of general meetings the Companies Act regulates both the frequency with which they occur, and the procedure to be followed in the conduct of such a meeting.

Types of meeting

The Companies Act identifies various types of company meetings, and the circumstances in which they should be called (see ¶60-200 to ¶60-300).

¶60-200   Annual general meeting

Prior to the *Companies Act* 1989, all companies were required to hold an annual general meeting (AGM). A private company may now elect (by elective resolution in accordance with s. 379A of the *Companies Act* 1985) to dispense with an AGM. Subject thereto, an AGM should be held in each calendar year, not later than 15 months after the preceding AGM. But a new company need not hold an AGM in the year of its incorporation, or in the following year, provided that the first AGM is held within 18 months of the date of incorporation (CA 1985, s. 366).

It is usually at the AGM that the company's audited accounts are presented to members in accordance with s. 241 of the *Companies Act* 1985, recommendations as to dividends are made, and auditors' fees and directors fees are proposed for approval prior to payment.

If an election to dispense with the AGM is in force, this has only prospective effect and does not affect any liability already incurred by reason of default in holding an AGM; and any member of the company may, by notice to the company given no later than three months before the end of a calendar year, require the holding of an AGM in that year. If the election ceases to have effect when there is less than three months of the year remaining, then the company is not obliged to hold an AGM in that year (CA 1985, s. 366A(5)).

¶60-250   Extraordinary general meeting

An extraordinary general meeting (EGM) is any meeting of shareholders other than the AGM. A company's articles of association usually provide for the calling of EGMs at the discretion of the directors, or at the request of the members (e.g. Table A, reg. 37 of the *Companies (Tables A to F) Regulations* 1985: see ¶31-050).

There is also a statutory right for members to call for an EGM (CA 1985, s. 368). Holders of ten per cent of the paid-up share capital of the company can request a meeting by deposit of a requisition at the company's registered office. The requisition must state the objects of the meeting. The company's directors must proceed to convene the general meeting within 21 days from the deposit of the requisition. If they fail to do so, the requisitionists themselves (or any of them representing more than a half of the total voting rights of them all) can convene the meeting.

Until the 1988 Scottish case of *McGuinness, Petitioners* (1988) 4 BCC 161 applied common sense, there was no statutory requirement as to the length of notice of a meeting convened by the directors following a requisition. Now, they are deemed not to have duly convened such a meeting if they convene it on more than 28 days' notice (CA 1985, s. 368(8)).

The Court of Appeal in *Ross v Telford* considered whether a company in deadlock could convene a meeting under s. 371 of the *Companies Act* 1985 to remove the deadlock.

> **Case example (1)**
> Husband and wife R and T controlled a number of companies. They were directors and equal shareholders in 'PLB' and the two directors of 'L', in which latter company R and PLB were equal shareholders. The quorum for board and general meetings was two. R and T went through an acrimonious divorce and the companies became deadlocked. In the divorce the judge ordered that the net proceeds from the sale of PLB or L be divided equally between R and T. R caused L to commence proceedings against its bank in relation to the payment of cheques drawn on L's account allegedly forged by T. R did not have the authority of L's board to commence the proceedings and applied to the court under s. 371 for an order that a meeting of L be called and that one member present could constitute the meeting. The judge instead ordered that a meeting be held to consider a resolution to appoint a representative of R's solicitors as a third director of L for a year and that a representative of the solicitors might attend the meeting to vote on behalf of PLB. This was at the judge's own suggestion to break the deadlock. The Court of Appeal decided that s. 371 was not intended to enable the court to break a deadlock between equal shareholders and the judge had not had jurisdiction to regulate the affairs of PLB in the way he did. *Ross v Telford* [1997] BCC 945.

Power of court to order meeting

A residual power to convene an extraordinary general meeting is provided for any director of the company, or any member of the company who would be entitled to vote at the meeting. This facility arises where for any reason it is impractical to call a meeting of a company, and is achieved by application to the court (CA 1985, s. 371). The court may also call for an extraordinary general meeting of its own motion.

Section 371 may be used by members who wish to convene a quorate meeting, but are prevented from doing so by an intransigent company member. These circumstances arose in *Re Opera Photographic Ltd*.

Case example (2)
The company's share capital was owned by two members, both of whom were directors. A owned 51 per cent and B owned 49 per cent. The two parties fell out, and subsequently A attempted to convene a meeting for the purpose of removing B as director. B refused to attend, which resulted in the meeting not having the requisite quorum of two. The court granted an order under s. 371 of the *Companies Act* 1985 to convene the meeting. Because A owned the majority of the share capital, he had a statutory right to remove B as a director. Further, the quorum provisions in the articles could not be used by B as a power of veto. *Re Opera Photographic Ltd* [1989] 1 WLR 634; (1989) 5 BCC 601.

¶60-300   Class meetings

The Companies Act sometimes calls for a vote of all the shareholders of a particular class. Class meetings are those meetings at which votes are taken on issues which only concern shareholders of that class. Shareholders of other classes are not entitled to attend or vote at such meetings (*Carruth v Imperial Chemical Industries Ltd* [1937] AC 707).

When a written resolution is agreed by all holders of shares, or a class of shares, no meeting need be convened (see ¶60-750).

CONDUCT OF MEETINGS

General . . . . ¶60-400
Length of notice for calling
   meetings . . . . ¶60-450
Contents of notices . . . . ¶60-500

Organisation and conduct of the
   meeting . . . . ¶60-550
Resolutions and voting . . . . ¶60-600

¶60-400   General

The organisation of a meeting of shareholders necessitates consideration of the notice which should be given (see ¶60-450), the contents of such notice (see ¶60-500), the size of the majority vote required (see ¶60-600), and the conduct of the meeting itself (see ¶60-550).

¶60-450   Length of notice for calling meetings

Shareholders must be given at least 21 days' notice of the annual general meeting and of any meeting at which a special resolution is to be proposed, and at least 14 days' notice of any other meeting (CA 1985, s. 369(1)). Subject thereto, the rules as to notice of meetings are regulated by the company's articles. If the articles fail to deal with the issue of notice the provisions of Table A as regards service (see ¶31-050) are incorporated by s. 370(2) of the *Companies Act* 1985.

Agreement to short notice

The period of notice can be dispensed with, provided that the agreement of all the shareholders is obtained in the case of an annual general meeting, and that the consent of 95 per cent of the persons entitled to attend and vote (in the case of a company limited by shares, holders of not less than 95 per cent of the nominal amount of the shares giving a right to attend and vote) agree in the case of extraordinary general meetings (CA 1985, s. 369(3)). The company may, by an elective resolution in accordance with s. 379A of the *Companies Act* 1985, reduce the threshold to a percentage not lower than 90 per cent (CA 1985, s. 369(4)).

Manner in which notice should be served, etc.

The manner in which notice should be served on shareholders is usually provided in the articles. It is usual for the articles to provide for notice periods to exclude the days of deemed service and of the meeting itself, and to state that accidental failure to inform all members of a meeting will not invalidate the proceedings at that meeting (e.g. Table A, reg. 39 of the *Companies (Tables A to F) Regulations* 1985: see ¶31-050). However, deliberate failure to inform shareholders that a meeting is to be held will entitle members who fail to attend as a consequence to have resolutions passed at that meeting invalidated (*Musselwhite v C H Musselwhite & Son Ltd* [1962] Ch 964).

Resolutions requiring special notice

The Companies Act calls for special notice to be given to the company for particular resolutions (e.g. removing a director by an ordinary resolution: see ¶41-950). Special notice must be given to the company 28 days before the meeting (see ¶60-450). The company must then circulate notice of the resolution to shareholders. However, if, after the notice has been given, the meeting is convened for a date which results in less than 28 days' notice having been given, the notice is deemed to have been properly given (CA 1985, s. 379(3)).

Circulation of members' resolutions

A body of shareholders with five per cent of the total voting rights, or who are more than 100 strong with an average of £100 paid up per member, can request the company to circulate to all shareholders notice of any resolution which they wish to have moved at an annual general meeting. Such a request must be made not less than six weeks before the meeting (CA 1985, s. 377(1)(a)). The shareholders who request circulation of notice of the resolution will be liable for any reasonable expenses incurred, unless the company agrees to meet those costs (CA 1985, s. 376(1)).

¶60-500   Contents of notices

It is necessary to disclose an intention to propose extraordinary or special resolutions in any notice calling the meeting (CA 1985, s. 378). Apart from this, the contents of notices circulated to shareholders are usually determined by the articles

¶60-500

of association. For example, Table A requires that the time and place of the meeting and the general nature of the business to be transacted be disclosed in the notice (Table A, reg. 38 of the *Companies (Tables A to F) Regulations* 1985: see ¶31-050). It is possible for a special or extraordinary resolution to be amended after its circulation but before the vote is taken, provided that the alteration does not change the substance of the resolution (*Re Moorgate Mercantile Holdings Ltd* [1980] 1 WLR 227).

It is sometimes necessary to provide more details of a proposed strategy than can be set out in a notice to shareholders. Notices of meetings are often accompanied by circulars, which must provide a full and balanced account of the issues to be voted upon.

Circulation of members' statements

A requisition may be made by a body of shareholders which is at least 100 strong (and by whom an average of £100 per member has been paid up) or which holds five per cent of the total voting power (CA 1985, s. 376) that a company should circulate a statement of not more than 1,000 words on the matters referred to in any proposed resolution or business to be transacted at a general meeting of that company unless the court is satisfied on application that this right is being abused to secure needless publicity for defamatory matter (CA 1985, s. 377(3)). A copy of the statement must be delivered to the registered office within one week before the annual general meeting. The expense of circulating the notice must be borne by those shareholders who requested it, unless the company resolves otherwise.

¶60-550   Organisation and conduct of the meeting

Before the meeting can be validly commenced, there must be a sufficient number of shareholders in attendance. The necessary quorum is determined by the company's articles of association (e.g. under Table A, reg. 40 of the *Companies (Tables A to F) Regulations* 1985, a quorum of ' . . . two persons entitled to vote upon the business to be transacted, each being a member or a proxy for a member or a duly authorised representative of a corporation', is stipulated). If the articles provide for a quorum of two, this is not satisfied by only one person in attendance in more than one capacity. If the articles do not specify the necessary quorum, it will be two (CA 1985, s. 370). In respect of single-member private companies, the requisite quorum is one (CA 1985, s. 370A).

Resolutions passed at inquorate meetings

Resolutions passed at an inquorate meeting are invalid. The validity of business transacted by a quorate meeting which later becomes inquorate is to be determined by construction of the articles of association. Table A articles prescribed by the *Companies Act* 1948 specify that a quorum is required when the meeting proceeds to business. The 1985 Table A articles are different in that no business can be transacted at a meeting unless a quorum is present (reg. 40: see ¶31-050).

Appointment of chairman

The appointment of a chairman of a meeting of shareholders is also governed by the articles of association. However, the Companies Act does provide for appointment of a chairman if the articles fail to do so (CA 1985, s. 370).

Minutes of meetings

A company is required to keep a record of proceedings at general meetings, which are evidence of the business transacted, if signed by the chairman (CA 1985, s. 382). Members of the company are to be given access to the minutes at the company's registered office (CA 1985, s. 383(1)). Copies of the minutes can also be obtained by members for a small fee (CA 1985, s. 383(3)). Certain resolutions will also have to be filed with the registrar of companies, within 15 days of being passed. Most of these resolutions are set out in s. 380 of the *Companies Act* 1985.

Adjournment of meetings

It may become necessary to adjourn a meeting. The articles of association will usually stipulate the circumstances in which an adjournment should take place, persons with the power to make the adjournment, and the procedure for doing so. It is common for the articles to grant a power of adjournment only with the members' consent (e.g. Table A, reg. 45 of the *Companies (Tables A to F) Regulations* 1985: see ¶31-050). The chair of a meeting has a common law power to adjourn it, and must exercise this power properly and reasonably (*Byng v London Life Association Ltd* [1990] Ch 170; (1989) 5 BCC 227).

An adjourned meeting may only consider those issues left undecided at the original meeting. Accordingly, it is not permissible to discuss a new resolution if outside the scope of the business of the first meeting (*Robert Batcheller & Sons Ltd v Batcheller* [1945] Ch 169).

¶60-600 Resolutions and voting

Decisions to be taken at general meetings will necessitate one of three types of resolution being passed. These are:

(1) *an ordinary resolution*: passed by a simple majority of members who vote on the issue;

(2) *an extraordinary resolution*: passed by a three-quarters majority of such members as (being entitled to do so) vote in person, or, where proxies are allowed, by proxy at a general meeting of which notice specifying the intention to propose the resolution as an extraordinary resolution has been duly given (CA 1985, s. 378(1)); and

(3) *a special resolution*: passed by such a majority as is required for the passing of an extraordinary resolution and at a general meeting of which not less than 21 days' notice, specifying the intention to propose the resolution as a special resolution, has been given (CA 1985, s. 378(2), (3)) – the 21-day period of notice may be reduced if members holding not less than 95 per

cent of the nominal amount of the shares consent to such a reduction (CA 1985, s. 378(3)).

The articles of association may provide that a particular type of resolution is necessary for a vote on a particular issue. The Companies Act also specifies that special or extraordinary resolutions are required in particular circumstances. In the absence of any requirement for a special or extraordinary resolution, a vote can be passed on an ordinary resolution.

Informal agreement

If, however, the members unanimously consent to something on which a vote ought to be taken, the fact that no meeting was called and no resolution passed will not invalidate the decision reached (*Re Duomatic Ltd* [1969] 2 Ch 365). The decision is therefore binding, unless the company is actually prohibited from making decisions in this way. This was illustrated in the case of *Re Express Engineering Works Ltd*.

> **Case example (1)**
> All the shareholders of the company also held office as directors. The articles of association expressly prohibited a director from voting on contracts if that director had any interest in the contract. All the shareholders approved a contract for sale of property to the company from a syndicate in which they were interested. The vote was taken at a board meeting. However, the company was bound by the contract for every member of the company assented to the purchase. The directors' meeting could equally well be considered a general meeting of the company. *Re Express Engineering Works Ltd* [1920] 1 Ch 466.

A further example of an informal unanimous agreement amongst shareholders, which was upheld as having the force of a special resolution, is provided in *Cane v Jones*.

> **Case example (2)**
> The articles of a company provided that the chairman of directors' meetings and shareholders' meetings was to have a casting vote. However, by a later agreement, all the shareholders decided that the chairman should lose his casting vote. This agreement was upheld by the court. The agreement was to have the same effect as a special resolution which altered the articles. The court took the view that all the corporators, acting together, could do anything which was intra vires the company, and that the procedure for alteration of the articles under s. 9 of the *Companies Act* 1985 merely lays down a procedure whereby some only of the shareholders can validly alter the articles. *Cane v Jones* [1980] 1 WLR 1451.

Examples of when this type of informal resolution may not be used instead of a resolution in general meeting usually relate to statutory requirements, such as authorising a substantial property transaction with a director or connected person under s. 320 of the *Companies Act* 1985 (*Demite Ltd v Protec Health Ltd* [1998] BCC 638) or approving a contract for acquisition of a company's own shares under, e.g. s. 164 of the 1985 Act (*Re R W Peak (Kings Lynn) Ltd* [1998] BCC 596).

Votes of members

Voting by shareholders is usually governed by a company's articles of association. For example, Table A of the *Companies (Tables A to F) Regulations* 1985 provides that, subject to any rights or restrictions attached to any shares, on a show of hands every member who (being an individual) is present in person or (being a corporation) is present by a duly authorised representative, not being himself a member entitled to vote, shall have one vote and on a poll every member shall have one vote for every share of which he is the holder (reg. 54). However, in the absence of express provisions in the articles, s. 370 of the *Companies Act* 1985 provides that each member is to have one vote in respect of each share or each £10 of stock held by him.

Proxies

If a shareholder who is entitled to attend and vote is unable to attend a meeting, he may send a proxy to vote in his place (CA 1985, s. 372). Further, a proxy has the right to speak at the meeting if the company is a private company. Notice of the appointment of a proxy will also be governed by the articles.

Method of voting

Votes may be taken by a show of hands or by a poll. In the former case, each shareholder has only one vote, irrespective of the size of his shareholding. Proxies are not entitled to vote unless the articles provide otherwise (CA 1985, s. 372). The declaration of the chairman as to the result of the vote is usually conclusive (e.g. Table A, reg. 47 of the *Companies (Tables A to F) Regulations* 1985: see ¶31-050).

Right to call for a poll

The articles usually confer upon members the right to call for a poll and specify the procedure for the conduct of the poll. A company's articles cannot exclude the right to call for a poll if the request is made by specified persons. A poll can be requested by any five shareholders who are entitled to vote at the meeting, or by any member with one-tenth of the voting rights of all members entitled to vote at that meeting, or by members holding shares on which the sum paid up is not less than one-tenth of the total amount paid up on all voting shares (CA 1985, s. 373(1)). A proxy can instigate or join in the demand for a poll (CA 1985, s. 373(2)). The right to call for a poll is also conferred upon classes of shareholders whose rights are to be altered in accordance with s. 125 of the *Companies Act* 1985 (see ¶50-300) and upon any member who votes on a redemption or repurchase of shares out of capital under s. 174 of the *Companies Act* 1985 (see ¶51-825ff.).

¶60-600

WRITTEN RESOLUTIONS AND THE ELECTIVE REGIME

¶60-700   General

The Companies Acts have often been criticised for not providing effectively for the practical running of small companies. Provisions for the deregulation of private companies introduced by the *Companies Act* 1989 took the form of two new concepts: the written resolution (see ¶60-750) and the elective regime (see ¶60-800).

¶60-750   Written resolutions

A private company may do anything which can be done:

- by resolution of the company in general meeting; or
- by resolution of a meeting of any class of members of the company,

by a written resolution. No meeting need take place, nor is any previous notice required; however, the resolution must be signed by all members of the company who are entitled to attend and vote at the general (or class) meeting concerned (CA 1985, s. 381A). A written resolution may be passed in lieu of a special, extraordinary or elective resolution (see ¶60-600, ¶60-800). This statutory scheme may conflict with the company's constitution, e.g. if reg. 53 of Table A, which sets out a less onerous written resolution procedure, is incorporated into the company's articles. The statutory scheme has effect notwithstanding any provision in the company's memorandum or articles, but does not prejudice any power conferred by such provision (CA 1985, s. 381C(1)).

The mechanics of a written resolution must be considered. A document which accurately states the terms of the resolution is sent to each member of the company, who agrees to the resolution by signing the document. However, the signatures need not be on the same document. The date of the last signature is the date of the resolution. Once agreed to, the resolution has effect as if passed by the company in general meeting, or at a meeting of the relevant class of shareholders (CA 1985, s. 381A(2)–(4)).

The aim of the provision is to allow private companies to avoid the bureaucracy of a meeting when it is not needed. There is no question of prejudice against a minority of members, as any one of them may decline to sign, in which case the resolution will fail. Where a company director or secretary either knows of an attempt to seek agreement by written resolution, or knows the terms of such a resolution, he must ensure that either a copy of the resolution is sent to the company's auditors, or that they are notified of the resolution's contents (CA 1985, s. 381C). Failure to do so will result in the company officers becoming liable to a fine. However, if it appears that:

- it was not practicable for the company officer to fulfil the above obligations; or

- the officer reasonably believed that a copy of the resolution had been sent to the auditors,

then that officer will have a proper defence. Importantly, a written resolution is still valid notwithstanding the above requirements (CA 1985, s. 381B(4)).

Recording of written resolutions

Once a written resolution has been agreed, it must be recorded in the same way as the minutes of a general meeting of the company. If this purports to be signed by a director of the company or the company secretary, it is evidence of the passing of the resolution; there is then a presumption that the requirements of the Companies Act have been fulfilled (CA 1985, s. 382A).

Exceptions, etc.

There are exceptions and adaptations to the procedure for a written resolution as outlined above (CA 1985, Sch. 15A). A written resolution cannot be used to remove a director or an auditor before the expiration of their respective periods of office. Special procedural requirements for the passing of a written resolution must be followed for the disapplication of pre-emption rights (see ¶50-625), the provision of financial assistance for the purchase of a company's own shares or those of its holding company (see ¶51-800), seeking an authority for an off-market purchase or contingent purchase contract of a company's own shares (see ¶51-850, ¶51-875), approval of a payment out of capital (see ¶51-825, ¶51-875), approval of a director's service contract (CA 1985, s. 319) and the funding of a director's expenditure in performing his duties (see ¶43-200).

¶60-800   Elective regime

A private company may elect by the unanimous agreement of its members to dispense with certain requirements of the *Companies Act* 1985. Such a resolution is called an 'elective resolution'. An elective resolution is not effective unless (CA 1985, s. 379A(2)):

(1) at least 21 days' notice in writing is given of the meeting, stating that an elective resolution is to be proposed and stating the terms of the resolution; however, an elective resolution is still binding even if less than 21 days' notice are given, providing that all members entitled to attend and vote at the meeting so agree; and

(2) the resolution is agreed to at the meeting in person or by proxy by all the members entitled to attend and vote at the meeting.

An elective resolution may also be made by the passing of a written resolution (see ¶60-750).

¶60-800

A private company may, by elective resolution, decide to lengthen the period in which directors may allot securities without prior approval (see ¶50-625). It may also elect to dispense with:

(1) the laying of accounts and reports before a general meeting (see ¶70-450); or

(2) the holding of an annual general meeting (or to sanction short notice of a company meeting) (see ¶60-200 and ¶60-450 respectively); or

(3) the annual appointment of auditors (see ¶44-400).

The elective resolution will cease to have effect if the company revokes it by passing an ordinary resolution to that effect, or if the company is re-registered as a public company (CA 1985, s. 379A(3), (4)).

¶60-900 Exercise of voting rights

Shares are the property of their owner, and votes which attach to the shares are, similarly, the property of persons entitled to exercise them. However, this will be subject to any arrangement whereby the owner holds the shares on trust, in which case the beneficiary may have the right to decide how those voting rights are to be exercised.

Shareholders (including shareholders who are also directors) are therefore free to exercise their voting power in their best interests, even though this may result in other shareholders suffering loss as a consequence (see *North-West Transportation Co Ltd v Beatty* (1887) 12 App Cas 589). However, against the background of this principle, there are situations in which a shareholder may find a fetter placed upon enjoyment of his rights. One is where exercise of the rights amounts to unfairly prejudicial conduct under s. 459 of the *Companies Act* 1985 or a fraud on the minority, as an exception to the rule in *Foss v Harbottle* (1843) 2 Hare 461. These matters are considered at ¶62-550ff.

It is also possible for a shareholder to contract that votes will be exercised in a particular fashion. Such contracts can be enforced (*Puddephatt v Leith* [1916] 1 Ch 200). However, such agreements are not automatically binding upon subsequent holders of the shares.

MINORITY PROTECTION

¶61-700   General

'Majority rule' acknowledges that a company is governed by the will of the majority of the shareholders. There is, therefore, no point in permitting minority shareholders to commence litigation in respect of an issue to which the majority can subsequently grant their approval. However, this principle could not stifle an objection that the act complained of was ultra vires or illegal, if such an act could not be retrospectively ratified by the majority (see ¶30-750, ¶62-300).

A second constraint on the minority is that a company which has suffered harm is the proper 'person' to commence proceedings in respect of that harm. This may be through directors acting under a general power of management (*John Shaw & Sons (Salford) Ltd v Shaw* [1935] 2 KB 113) or at the request of the company in general meeting through powers conferred by the articles of association (e.g. Table A, reg. 70 of the *Companies (Tables A to F) Regulations* 1985: see ¶31-050). This is a result of the separate legal personality of the company.

In view of these difficulties, it is necessary to consider how minority shareholders can overcome these bars to enforcing a remedy on the company's behalf. Where a shareholder's personal rights have been infringed, an action may be brought to enforce those rights. Such rights will often be derived from the company's articles of association, and may include voting at meetings or the opportunity to inspect various registers. 'Personal' rights are unaffected by the rule in *Foss v Harbottle* (see ¶61-800).

¶61-800   The rule in Foss v Harbottle

The rule in *Foss v Harbottle* is an inescapable consequence of the fact that a company has an independent legal personality, separate from its shareholders. The rule states that only a company can sue in respect of wrongs done to it. This principle embraces both the restriction founded on majority rule, and the individual shareholder's lack of capacity to enforce company rights. An illustration of how the rule operates is provided by the case itself.

> **Case example**
> Two shareholders in a company complained to the court that the company's assets were improperly applied. The acts complained of were of two kinds. The first category was within the company's powers and accordingly capable of ratification.

¶61-700

The second category was ultra vires, and accordingly not capable of subsequent ratification. They requested the court to hold the director and others accountable for the loss, and also to appoint a receiver.

Wigram V-C identified the company itself as the party which had suffered harm. However, the company was not represented as a plaintiff. The shareholders attempted to sue on behalf of and represent the company itself. Dealing first with intra vires acts, Wigram V-C explained that, if reasons of an 'urgent' character were shown, it may be appropriate for individual members of a corporation to seek vindication of the corporation's rights. However, outside of such special circumstances, the fact that 'the governing body of proprietors assembled at the special general meeting may so bind even a reluctant minority . . .' to the act complained of was decisive to show that an application to the court by the minority shareholders could not be sustained whilst that governing body retained its functions.

However, an act which was ultra vires the company may admit of no confirmation whilst any dissenting voice is raised against it. *Foss v Harbottle* (1843) 2 Hare 461.

The courts have identified exceptions to the rule in *Foss v Harbottle*, which are considered at ¶62-150ff. However, a minority shareholder who wishes to bring an action must first select the appropriate procedure, as outlined at ¶61-900ff.

The rule itself is relatively straightforward to understand. Complexities arise in the different forms of action (see ¶61-900) and in the inconsistencies by the courts in the exceptions to the rule (see ¶62-150). The Law Commission's report *Shareholder Remedies* (Law Com No. 246, Cm 3769, October 1997) recommends abolition of the rule and its exceptions, at least in part, and replacement with a new statutory derivative action available only against breaches of duty by directors (including breaches of skill and care) and cases where a director has allowed a conflict between his duties and personal interest. The court's leave would be needed to commence litigation and the court would operate an active case-management function of all shareholder proceedings (e.g. they could not be compromised or discontinued without the court's leave).

THE DIFFERENT FORMS OF ACTION

¶61-900   General

When a shareholder applies to the court in respect of harm done to a company, the form of the application can be of three kinds. The shareholder will act in his personal capacity if he has suffered a wrong himself. This is a personal action (see ¶61-950). If a shareholder seeks to represent himself and the other shareholders who have suffered harm, a representative action is appropriate (see ¶62-000). However, if a minority of the shareholders seek to vindicate the company's rights, they must do so by means of a derivative action (see ¶62-050).

¶61-950   Personal action

A personal action is brought by somebody who has been wronged, and wishes to recover on his own behalf. Such an action may be used by a shareholder to restrain a company from undertaking an ultra vires act. It is also appropriate for vindication of the contractual rights which are conferred upon a shareholder under the articles of association. A personal action is therefore brought by the shareholder against the company. This is illustrated by the case of *Pender v Lushington*.

> **Case example (1)**
> Mr Pender sought to have a resolution passed at a meeting of shareholders. An amendment to the resolution was proposed to which Mr Pender objected. However, his votes were ignored by the chairman when the shareholders voted on the amendment, and the proposal was carried. Mr Pender brought an action to prevent the company acting on the amended resolution. The court held that Mr Pender was entitled to have his votes counted. For this was a right of property, and he could institute legal proceedings to compel observance thereof. *Pender v Lushington* (1877) 6 ChD 70.

If, however, a shareholder objects to a breach of the articles which amounts to a technical irregularity in the company's procedures, it is unlikely that the court would interfere. Accordingly, in the above case example, had Mr Pender's votes been irrelevant to the outcome of the vote, his application would have been refused.

A personal action is accordingly brought by a shareholder *against the company* to remedy a wrong (or potential wrong). He cannot bring a personal action against a wrongdoing director for loss to the company even though he believes that he has suffered loss, for the cause of action is then in the company and a *derivative* action might be needed for the company to proceed against the wrongdoer because he has control. The Court of Appeal case of *Stein v Blake* illustrates this point.

> **Case example (2)**
> X and Y were equal shareholders in a group of companies. X alleged that Y had misappropriated assets of the companies, which then went into liquidation, and transferred them to other companies controlled by Y. X claimed to have suffered loss and commenced a personal action against Y. He was not allowed to do so: the only loss alleged by X was reflected in the loss sustained by the companies in whom lay the right of action. X could not sue Y to recover the diminution in value of his shares and if the companies, via the liquidator, sued Y, then the damages would go into the companies' assets thereby increasing the share value again. The reason why X attempted to bring his action personally was that the restoration of the companies' assets in their liquidation would first be used to pay off creditors before any return of capital to members. *Stein v Blake* [1998] BCC 316.

¶61-950

¶62-000 Representative actions

A representative action is appropriate where a shareholder brings an action on behalf of both himself and other persons to enforce their collective personal rights. The relief sought will therefore be beneficial to all those persons represented by the plaintiff. Any judgment obtained in respect of a representative action binds all persons so represented. The function of this procedure is obviously to prevent duplicity of actions in respect of the same issue. Detailed rules as to commencement and conduct of representative actions are contained in the *Civil Procedure Rules* 1998 (SI 1998/3132), r. 50 and Sch. 1, O. 15, r. 12 (re-enacting the *Rules of the Supreme Court* 1965 (SI 1965/1776), O. 15, r. 12).

¶62-050 Derivative actions

A derivative action by minority shareholders can be used to enforce the rights of the company against majority shareholders. Where the derivative action is founded upon fraud on the minority, the plaintiff must additionally prove that the majority doing the wrong are in control of the company. However, a derivative action cannot be brought by a shareholder who participated in the wrongdoing.

Although derivative actions are technically a type of representative action, the company is named as a co-defendant (*Civil Procedure Rules* 1998 (SI 1998/3132), r. 50 and Sch. 1, O. 15, r. 12 (re-enacting RSC, O. 15, r. 12)). If the action is successful, any order will be in favour of the company and not the minority member who brought the action on a derivative basis. The individual claimant or applicant does not, therefore, directly benefit if the action is successful. The company must be joined in the action, and must indemnify the shareholder who acted on its behalf if the litigation was successful, or if it was a reasonable and prudent course to take in the circumstances. For the detailed procedural rules on derivative actions see the *Civil Procedure Rules* 1998 (SI 1998/3132), r. 50 and Sch. 1, O. 15, r. 12A (re-enacting Rules of the Supreme Court, O. 15, r. 12A).

If the company asks the court to strike out a derivative action, before commencement of proceedings, the action will be allowed to continue only if allegations in the statement of claim justify a derivative action, and a prima facie case is proved (*Prudential Assurance Co Ltd v Newman Industries Ltd (No. 2)* [1982] Ch 204. If, however, the facts are not disputed, a derivative action can proceed if the plaintiff has an arguable case in law (*Estmanco (Kilner House) Ltd v Greater London Council* [1982] 1 WLR 2). This could equally be raised as a preliminary issue (*Smith v Croft (No. 2)*).

> **Case example**
> Three shareholders of a company brought an action claiming that a series of payments to the executive directors and associated companies were excessive, ultra vires, and hence constituted a fraud on the minority. The defendant directors sought to strike out this action on the grounds that it was frivolous. The judge held that the action should be so struck out, concluding that, on the issue of whether the payments were excessive, the shareholders were more likely to fail than succeed.

In this case, it was appropriate to have regard to the will of the independent majority of shareholders, i.e. those members who were neither petitioners nor defendants in the case. The rule in *Foss v Harbottle* would be applied and the derivative action struck out at this preliminary stage. *Smith v Croft (No. 2)* [1988] Ch 114; (1987) 3 BCC 207.

EXCEPTIONS TO THE RULE IN FOSS V HARBOTTLE

¶62-150   General

It is clear that the rule in *Foss v Harbottle* (see ¶61-800) may operate greatly to the disadvantage of minority shareholders. If, however, the rule is exploited by a majority to the obvious prejudice of minority shareholders, the courts may refuse to apply it. The circumstances in which the court will not apply the rules are often confused with those in which application of the rule would be inappropriate. However, for all practical purposes, it is possible to list the circumstances in which *Foss v Harbottle* will not preclude an objection by minority shareholders to an act of the majority, as follows:

(1) the activity objected to is ultra vires or illegal (*Foss v Harbottle*, above: see ¶62-300);

(2) the activity undertaken must be sanctioned by a special resolution (*Baillie v Oriental Telephone & Electric Co Ltd* [1915] 1 Ch 503: see ¶62-350);

(3) the activity is an infringement of personal rights of shareholders (*Pender v Lushington* (1877) 6 ChD 70: see ¶62-400);

(4) the activity amounts to a fraud on a minority shareholder (*Menier v Hooper's Telegraph Works Ltd* (1874) LR 9 Ch App 350: see ¶62-450); or

(5) the activity is unfairly prejudicial to minority shareholders (see ¶62-550ff.).

¶62-300   Ultra vires or illegal acts

A shareholder can sue in person to restrain the company committing an illegal or ultra vires act. Such an action can be personal (see ¶61-950) or representative (see ¶62-000).

A company may sue its directors for recovery of property or compensation where that loss has been incurred as a result of an ultra vires act. In this case, the action (if brought by shareholders) must be derivative (see ¶62-050). However,

¶62-150

with the reform of the ultra vires doctrine in the *Companies Act* 1989, the rights of a shareholder have been altered. He may still bring an action to restrain the doing of an act which is beyond the capacity of the company, but only if the act to be done is not in fulfilment of a legal obligation arising from a previous act of the company. Further, an act which is beyond the power of the board of directors may now be sanctioned by a special resolution and accordingly fall under ¶62-350.

See generally ¶30-750ff.

¶62-350　The activity undertaken must be sanctioned by a special resolution

If the majority shareholders propose to force an issue which should have been sanctioned by a special resolution (e.g. an alteration of the articles: see ¶30-500), a shareholder may apply to the court to restrain the proposed action. For the company cannot, by an ordinary resolution, ratify this breach.

The shareholder would sue by a representative action (see ¶62-000). However, if the breach was actually committed, the shareholder could sue in his personal capacity on the basis of his contractual rights under the articles of association (¶61-950).

This rule operates to ensure that resolutions which require a special or extraordinary resolution are not passed by a bare majority.

¶62-400　The activity infringes shareholders' personal rights

This is the situation considered in *Pender v Lushington* (see ¶61-950). Because shareholder rights are property, it is possible to commence a personal action to compel observance of these rights. However, the courts will only uphold such objections where the consequences of not doing so are potentially significant.

¶62-450　The activity amounts to fraud on the minority

It is difficult to define what the courts will consider to be a fraud on the minority. Some guidelines are provided from the authorities.

First, the majority shareholders must pass resolutions 'bona fide for the benefit of the company as a whole' (*Allen v Gold Reefs of West Africa Ltd* [1900] 1 Ch 656). This requirement has been applied to situations by considering whether the resolution discriminates between the majority shareholders and the minority shareholders so as to give the former an advantage of which the latter was deprived (*Greenhalgh v Arderne Cinemas Ltd* [1951] Ch 286). Many of the cases concern situations in which the majority have lined their pockets at the expense of the minority (*Menier v Hooper's Telegraph Works* (1874) 9 Ch App 350).

However, it is possible that the court will interfere to prevent majority shareholders benefiting from a situation in which the minority have no opportunity to participate, even though the minority suffer no actual loss. It is possible that the rule will permit a derivative action by minority shareholders to recover a loss sustained by the company as a consequence of a controlling director's negligent act, where the director has profited thereby (*Daniels v Daniels* [1978] Ch 406).

The second requirement for application of this exception is that the majority should have control. It would appear that a clear voting majority is necessary (*Prudential Assurance Co Ltd v Newman Industries Ltd (No. 2)* [1982] Ch 204).

STATUTORY PROTECTION AGAINST UNFAIRLY PREJUDICIAL CONDUCT

¶62-550   General

There are legislative measures for the protection of minority shareholder interests from acts of the majority. The relief is provided under two provisions.

The first provision affords the extreme remedy of winding up the company on just and equitable grounds (IA 1986, s. 122(1)(g), considered at ¶62-800). To qualify for this remedy on grounds of misconduct by the majority, a petitioner must show acts of a serious character, which harm his interests as a shareholder.

An alternative course of action is to apply to the court for relief under s. 459 of the *Companies Act* 1985. The petitioner must prove that the company's affairs are being conducted in a manner unfairly prejudicial to his interests or that he has been unfairly prejudiced by some act or omission of the company. The court has wide powers to remedy the conduct.

It is necessary to consider the meaning of 'unfairly prejudicial conduct' (see ¶62-600), the forms of relief available (see ¶62-650), and the factors that determine the value of shares should the court compel the majority to purchase the minority's shareholding (or vice versa) (see ¶62-700).

A binding arbitration clause in, e.g., a company formation agreement, will mean that arbitration must be pursued before a petition under s. 459 of the *Companies Act* 1985 will be heard (*Re Vocam Europe Ltd* [1998] BCC 396).

The statutory remedy against unfair prejudice has undoubtedly been of considerable success. The disadvantage of the remedy has been in the cost of proceedings, for in order to establish unfairly prejudicial conduct petitioners have often researched through the company's history over many years to rake up whatever conduct might assist their case. This has resulted in notorious high costs of s. 459 actions, sometimes with several days in court merely going through the evidence. Thus the Law Commission's report *Shareholder Remedies* (Law Com No. 246, Cm 3769, October 1997) has recommended that the remedy should continue substantially unchanged (and in particular that there should be no statutory definition of 'unfairly prejudicial conduct') but that methods be employed to reduce

¶62-550

the length of s. 459 trials, e.g. by the greater use of case management powers by the courts and a statutory presumption of unfair prejudice where there is exclusion of a member from management in a quasi-partnership company.

In the House of Lords decision of *O'Neill v Phillips* [1999] BCC 600 Lord Hoffmann stressed the importance of avoiding the protracted litigation involved in s. 459 petitions and encouraged potential respondents to a petition to make a fair offer to buy out the potential petitioner's shares. Such an offer would have to be at a fair value, if not agreed by the parties then to be determined by a competent expert acting as an expert, the parties should each have the same right of access to information about the company in considering the offer and, if litigation has already being going on for some time, the offer should include payment of the other party's costs.

¶62-600 'Unfairly prejudicial conduct'

Some guidance as to the meaning of 'unfairly prejudicial conduct' can be obtained from cases both before and after the enactment of s. 459 of the *Companies Act* 1985.

Negligent or inept management of the company will only amount to unfairly prejudicial conduct (*Re Five Minute Car Wash Service Ltd* [1966] 1 WLR 745) if that conduct puts at risk the value of the minority shareholder's interest (*Re R A Noble and Sons (Clothing) Ltd* [1983] BCLC 273). Further, in the absence of bad faith, disagreements as to company policy will not afford grounds for a petition (*Re Jermyn Street Turkish Baths Ltd* [1970] 1 WLR 1194).

Actionable conduct under s. 459 must harm a shareholder's interest in his capacity as shareholder. The range of 'interests' which can potentially be protected under s. 459 are wide. In *Re Posgate and Denby (Agencies) Ltd* (1986) 2 BCC 99,352, a member brought a s. 459 petition attempting to prevent the directors from disposing of a substantial business asset. Equity shares with no voting rights constituted the shareholder's 'interest'. However, the petition was struck out on the grounds that there was no reason to think that the board would not exercise its powers properly. Conversely, in *Re J E Cade & Son Ltd* [1991] BCC 360, a s. 459 petition failed because the petitioner was attempting to protect a freehold interest in a property which was completely distinct from his shareholding interest in the company.

An application may be made to restrain anticipated acts of prejudice. In *Re Kenyon Swansea Ltd* (1987) 3 BCC 259, the petitioner applied to the court to prevent the majority shareholder from voting in the future on a special resolution which would have effectively excluded him from management. The court held that an order may be necessary if the petitioner's interests were to be endangered by an act likely to be proposed in the future. However, the act of the majority can be other than the exercise of voting power. This principle is illustrated by *Scottish Co-operative Wholesale Society Ltd v Meyer*.

> **Case example (1)**
> The petitioner in this case was a subsidiary whose major shareholder was its parent company. In the course of business, the parent supplied various raw materials to its subsidiary. After a quarrel between the minority shareholders of the subsidiary and the parent company, the parent refused to supply necessary raw materials except at vastly inflated prices. The anticipated prejudice was liquidation of the subsidiary to the detriment of the minority shareholders. The Court of Session recognised a duty on the parent to conduct its affairs with the subsidiary fairly, so that the interests of the minority were not harmed. *Scottish Co-operative Wholesale Society Ltd v Meyer* [1959] AC 324.

Section 459 petitions are most often used when a minority shareholder in a quasi-partnership company is excluded from management. The factors which will lead a court to conclude that the company is a quasi-partnership were discussed in *Ebrahimi v Westbourne Galleries Ltd* (considered at ¶62-800). 'Exclusion from management' cases often highlight the connection between s. 459 petitions and winding-up applications under s. 122(1)(g) of the *Insolvency Act* 1986, but note *Practice Direction: Applications under the Companies Act and the Insurance Companies Act 1982* [1999] BCC 741 which at para. 9 urges practitioners not to claim for both unless it is absolutely necessary. Despite this Practice Direction (which was first introduced in 1990) the Court of Appeal has allowed both to be asked for in the appropriate circumstances (*Re Copeland & Craddock Ltd* [1997] BCC 294), and it is increasingly the case that both claims are set out in the statement of case.

In order to succeed under s. 459, the petitioner must prove that his exclusion from management was unfairly prejudicial. The test to be applied is objective (see *Re R A Noble and Sons (Clothing) Ltd* [1983] BCLC 273), i.e. the question to be posed is whether a reasonable bystander would view the relevant conduct as unfairly prejudicial.

Re Ghyll Beck Driving Range Ltd is a case that illustrates the ways in which a member of a company may be excluded from management in an unfairly prejudicial way.

> **Case example (2)**
> Four individuals set up a golf driving range business. Each agreed to contribute £25,000 as an initial investment. By the time the company commenced trading, it was unclear whether two of the parties had invested the promised sums. The petitioner brought a successful action compelling the other three parties to purchase his shares at a price representing 25 per cent of the going concern. The court concluded that the petitioner had been excluded from the management for the following reasons:
>
> - an argument with one of the three respondents had resulted in the petitioner being ostracised;
>
> - two respondents had dishonestly evaded making the investment that they had promised to make;

- one respondent had manufactured evidence regarding a scheme for directors to withdraw their loans from the company;
- the petitioner had received less interest on his loan than the other parties; and
- although the petitioner had received notice of directors' meetings, these 'meetings' were in fact a sham designed to remove him as a director.

All the evidence taken together was clearly suggestive of exclusion from management. *Re Ghyll Beck Driving Range Ltd* [1993] BCLC 1126.

The courts may not grant relief if the applicant has either been guilty of serious misconduct himself, has delayed in making an application despite knowing about the prejudicial conduct (*Re R A Noble & Sons (Clothing) Ltd* [1983] BCLC 273), or if the application appears to the court to be merely an attempt by the petitioner to get his own way in the running of the business (*Re Bellador Silk Ltd* [1965] 1 All ER 667). However there is no overriding requirement in a s. 459 action to come to court with 'clean hands' (*Re London School of Electronics Ltd* [1986] Ch 211; (1985) 1 BCC 99,394). In this respect, contrast a petition under s. 122(1)(g) of the *Insolvency Act* 1986 where there probably is such a requirement (see further ¶62-800).

Most unfairly prejudicial conduct petitions are brought concerning small, private companies, often quasi-partnership companies where the relationship between the members has broken down or a member is excluded from management and his 'legitimate expectations' are not met. However the House of Lords has held that because there had been no agreement with the company and the minority had not been made any promise enforceable in contract or in equity the minority could not have any 'legitimate expectations' (*O'Neill v Phillips* [1999] BCC 600). Petitions in relation to public companies are rare (see *Re Blue Arrow plc* (1987) 3 BCC 618), given that in particular legitimate expectations are unlikely to arise (see *Re Astec (BSR) plc* [1999] BCC 59).

Although the wording of s. 459 does not actually restrict unfairly prejudicial conduct petitions to minorities, and petitions have been brought by a majority, these will not succeed where the majority wishes to buy out the minority and alleges that the latter has not fulfilled its functions diligently since this is unlikely to be 'unfairly' prejudicial to the majority *Re Legal Costs Negotiators Ltd* [1999] BCC 547.

¶62-650 Forms of relief

The court is empowered to give such relief as it thinks fit in cases of unfairly prejudicial conduct (CA 1985, s. 461). A list of orders available to the court is set out in s. 461(2) of the *Companies Act* 1985. However, this list is not exhaustive. The suitability of any one form of relief will obviously depend on the circumstances of the conduct. The statutory list is as follows:

(1) an order regulating the conduct of the company's affairs in the future;

(2) an order requiring the company to refrain from a particular act, or to undertake to do an act in the future;

(3) authorisation of the commencement of proceedings in the company's name, by such persons and on such terms as the court thinks fit; or

(4) an order which calls for purchase of the petitioner's shares by the majority or vice versa, or by the company itself.

The legislation also provides for the alteration of the memorandum or articles of association in order to comply with the court order.

The remedy under s. 461 is discretionary. In *Re Full Cup International Trading Ltd. Antoniades v Wong* [1998] BCC 58, although unfairly prejudicial conduct was established the court could find no relief that would do justice to the case (other than winding up, which had not been asked for), a result with which the Court of Appeal agreed.

A person who is not a member of the company, but to whom shares are transferred or transmitted by operation of law (e.g. the personal representative of a deceased member) may petition the court under s. 459 of the *Companies Act* 1985 (CA 1985, s. 459(2)). However, an informal agreement for an eventual transfer is not sufficient for this purpose (*Re a Company No. 003160 of 1986* (1986) 2 BCC 99,276). The court may refuse a request in a s. 459 petition that the majority buy out the minority if the majority have already offered to do so and the minority rejected that offer. However, according to the Court of Appeal, the offer must have been a serious one, including an offer to pay the minority's costs to date (*Re Pectel Ltd* [1998] BCC 405). In the House of Lords in that case it was also held that s. 459 did not provide for a shareholder who had not been excluded to demand that his shares should be purchased at a fair value merely because trust and confidence had broken down (*O'Neill v Phillips* [1999] BCC 600). Lord Hoffmann mentioned his regret at the introduction (by himself) in earlier s. 459 cases of allowing relief where 'legitimate expectations' had not been met (and see ¶62-600). He also considered that an unfairly prejudicial conduct petition should not be allowed to be used to permit a disgruntled member to exit the company at will where there was no fault by the member(s) of a quasi-partnership company.

¶62-700   Valuation of shares

A difficulty which arises in the application of s. 461 of the *Companies Act* 1985 is the value to be placed on the shares if the court makes a share purchase order. The principal questions which have to be resolved are the date at which the valuation should be made, and the basis for making the valuation.

The question of timing of the valuation was considered in *Re a Company No. 002567 of 1982* (1983) 1 BCC 98,930. The finding was that the valuation date was a question of fairness, which was to be determined by the court. A valuation at a date before the award by the court (which would have favoured the petitioner) was not allowed, because he had chosen to turn down an offer from the other shareholders for sale of his shares at an early date. The petitioner had refused because he was keen to see the company wound up. Consequently, Vilene J considered it would be wrong to let him benefit from the earlier date. However, in circumstances in which the petitioner was not culpable, a date earlier than the award may be the correct one to apply. This observation has been approved in *Re O C Transport Services Ltd* (1984) 1 BCC 99,068, in which a valuation as at the date of the unfairly prejudicial act was applied. In *Re a Company No. 002612 of 1984* (1986) 2 BCC 99,495 the Court of Appeal considered that, on the facts of the case, the appropriate valuation date was when the petition was presented, rather than the date of the court order some 12 months later (even though the respondent claimed that this result might bankrupt him).

The formula for share valuation is also founded upon the principle of 'fairness' (*Re Bird Precision Bellows Ltd* [1986] Ch 658; (1985) 1 BCC 99,467). What is 'fair' must depend on the facts of each case. Shares in a company which is run on a quasi-partnership basis will be valued pro rata to the total value of all the shares, with no discount applied. If the petitioner deserves to be excluded by virtue of his conduct, he will be treated as having elected to sever his connection with the company. An open market basis for valuation is then appropriate. A fair discount may be applied, taking into account the size of the shareholding.

On occasion, the court's powers will conflict with a company's articles. This happened in *Re Abbey Leisure Ltd*.

Case example

A company was incorporated to undertake a single project. When that task was completed, the majority attempted to embark on a second project. These shareholders offerd to buy the petitioner's shares in accordance with a mechanism set out in the articles of association. The court concluded that this procedure might unfairly prejudice the minority petitioner's interests, and ordered that the petition be heard in full. *Re Abbey Leisure Ltd* [1990] BCC 60.

¶62-800 Just and equitable winding up

'Winding up' is the process of concluding a company's affairs before its existence is brought to an end by dissolution. Section 122(1)(g) of the *Insolvency Act* 1986 provides a mechanism whereby a company can be wound up on the ground that it is 'just and equitable' to do so. Any 'contributory', i.e. any person liable to contribute to the company's assets in the event of it being wound up, may petition the court under this section. Holders of partly paid shares are therefore contributories. Holders of fully paid shares will be if they have a 'tangible interest' (e.g. if the company is solvent, assets will be distributed to these shareholders after the creditors are paid off).

This procedure has commonly been used in situations in which it is no longer practical to perpetuate the existence of small 'quasi-partnership' type companies. This is most likely to occur because of a breakdown in the relationship of those responsible for running the company. A good example of the circumstances in which the court will grant the petitioner's request is provided by *Ebrahimi v Westbourne Galleries Ltd.*

Case example

A company was formed in 1958 to take over the business of two partners. The partners became directors of the company and all of the profits were paid out to them as remuneration. The son of one of the directors was later appointed to the board. The other director was subsequently removed from office by the majority power now wielded by the father and son. He therefore petitioned for a winding up on just and equitable grounds. The petition was granted.

The approach of the court to applications for a just and equitable winding up was outlined by Lord Wilberforce in the following terms (at p. 379E–G): 'It would be impossible, and wholly undesirable, to define the circumstances in which these considerations may arise. Certainly the fact that a company is a small one, or a private company, is not enough. There are very many of these where the association is a purely commercial one, of which it can safely be said that the basis of association is adequately and exhaustively laid down in the articles. The superimposition of equitable considerations requires something more, which typically may include one, or probably more, of . . . (i) an association formed or continued on the basis of a personal relationship, involving mutual confidence – this element will often be found where a pre-existing partnership has been converted into a limited company; (ii) an agreement, or understanding, that all, or some (for there may be "sleeping" members), of the shareholders shall participate in the conduct of the business; (iii) restriction on the transfer of the members' interest in the company – so that if confidence is lost, or one member is removed from management, he cannot take out his stake and go elsewhere.' *Ebrahimi v Westbourne Galleries Ltd* [1973] AC 360.

Because of the equitable basis of the jurisdiction afforded under s. 122(1)(g) of the *Insolvency Act* 1986, the court will consider the petitioner's conduct as well as that of the other shareholders. In effect, the petitioner must come to the court with 'clean hands' (but contrast a situation where the petitioner brings an action under s. 459 of the *Companies Act* 1985: see further ¶62-550ff.). The court will not order a winding up if there is an alternative remedy which the petitioner is unreasonably refusing to pursue as an option (IA 1986, s. 125(2)).

The courts have granted petitions to wind up companies on just and equitable grounds for reasons other than deadlock or breakdown in a quasi-partnership company:

(1) Formation of the company for a fraudulent or illegal purpose (*Re Thomas Edward Brinsmead & Sons* [1897] 1 Ch 406).

(2) Oppression of the minority shareholders by a majority. The acts of oppression must be of a serious character and not isolated acts of misconduct (*Re Diamond Fuel Co* (1879) 13 ChD 400).

(3) Exhaustion or impossibility of the purpose for which the company was formed. If a company is formed for specific purposes, which are either no longer capable of attainment, or which have been achieved, the court will

grant a petition for just and equitable winding up (*Re Kitson & Co Ltd* [1946] 1 All ER 435).

The fact that the court must consider whether the petitioner is acting unreasonably in seeking the winding-up order where some other remedy is available indicates that the grant of a petition for winding up is a remedy of last resort. The facility for companies to purchase their own shares (see ¶51-800ff.) and the availability of the statutory remedy for unfair prejudice of minority shareholders (see ¶62-550ff.) have reduced the significance of the rules for just and equitable winding up.

In a modern example of the exercise of jurisdiction to wind up on the just and equitable ground, in *Bell Group Finance (Pty) Ltd (in liq.) v Bell Group (UK) Holdings Ltd* [1996] BCC 505 the court considered it just and equitable that a company be wound up so that the liquidator could consider whether there was any advantage to creditors in the liquidation where assets with a book value of £353m had nil realisable value and an investigation seemed to be called for. It was no ground to dismiss the petition merely because the DTI had a right to petition for winding up on the just and equitable ground in the public interest under s. 124A of the *Insolvency Act* 1986.

INVESTIGATIONS OF COMPANIES AND THEIR SECURITIES

¶63-500   Powers of the Secretary of State

Although the conduct of the internal affairs of a company is primarily a matter for the parties involved, public interest factors may play a role. Where fraud or other misconduct is suspected, where shareholders have been denied reasonable information, or where a minority has its interests jeopardised by the acts of majority shareholders, there may be recourse to an investigation of the company by the Department of Trade and Industry (see ¶63-600ff.). The importance and frequency of such appointments have increased, especially in the increasingly regulated field of financial services. Media interest also gives these reports a high profile, and they avoid the costs of a legal action that would otherwise fall upon a complainant.

¶63-600 Investigation of a company's affairs

The Secretary of State for Trade and Industry has a power to appoint inspectors to investigate a company's affairs. This can be instigated by the company itself (CA 1985, s. 431(1), (2)(c)), by shareholders with ten per cent of the issued share capital or who are at least 200 in number (CA 1985, s. 431(2)(a)), the Secretary of State himself (CA 1985, s. 432(2)) or the court (CA 1985, s. 432(1)). The report is to the Secretary of State and may be declared confidential (CA 1985, s. 432(2A)).

Applications by the shareholders or the company must be supported by sufficient evidence to show good reason for the investigation.

Circumstances when inspectors may be appointed

The Secretary of State may appoint inspectors where there is evidence that:

(1) the company's affairs are being conducted to defraud creditors, or for a fraudulent or illegal purpose, or in a way that will unfairly prejudice its members; or

(2) an act or omission by the company has had, or will have, a prejudicial effect, or that the company was formed for a fraudulent purpose; or

(3) persons connected with the formation or management of the company have been guilty of fraud, misfeasance or misconduct towards the company or its shareholders; or

(4) the shareholders have been deprived of information which they might reasonably expect to have been given.

The Secretary of State has a discretion to decide which complaints to pursue. Only between a third and a quarter of all such requests are investigated. Other bodies such as the Serious Fraud Office, the Securities and Investments Board or the London Stock Exchange may be better able to undertake a particular investigation.

There has been much judicial consideration whether information obtained in an investigation under Pt. XIV of the *Companies Act* 1985 may be used in proceedings against the person who gave the information. Section 434(5) provides that answers to inspectors' questions may be used in evidence against the person giving them, but the European Court of Human Rights in *Saunders v UK* [1997] BCC 872 decided that the use, in later criminal proceedings, of self-incriminating statements given to Companies Act inspectors was a violation of art. 6(1) of the European Convention for the Protection of Human Rights and Fundamental Freedoms and that s. 434(5) provided no defence to this. See ¶23-850 and ¶41-700.

Inspectors' powers, etc.

The inspectors appointed to investigate a company's affairs are generally leading lawyers or accountants. Inspectors are accorded wide powers. Past and present officers and agents of the company, together with any other persons who are or may be in possession of information useful to the inspector, may be required:

(1) to produce any relevant documents in their custody or power;

(2) to attend before the inspectors; and

(3) otherwise to give all assistance to the inspectors in connection with the investigation (CA 1985, s. 434).

Nature of proceedings before inspectors

Proceedings before inspectors are not quasi-judicial, but the inspectors have a duty of fairness (*Re Pergamon Press Ltd* [1971] Ch 388; *Maxwell v Department of Trade and Industry* [1974] 1 QB 523).

Inspectors' reports

On completion of their investigation, the inspectors submit a copy of their report to the Secretary of State. However, if matters come to light in the course of the inspectors' investigation which suggest that a criminal offence has been committed, and such matters have been referred to the appropriate investigating and prosecuting body, the Secretary of State may direct the inspectors either to desist from their investigation, or to take only specified further steps. In very long investigations, the investigators may submit an interim report.

Copies of the report

Once a finalised report has been sent to the Secretary of State, it may then also be sent to the company, its members, any person whose conduct is referred to, the company's auditors, the persons who requested the investigation, and any other persons who may have had their financial interests affected (CA 1985, s. 437(3)(b)). If the report is by order of the court, a copy must be supplied to the court. Frequently such reports are published (CA 1985, s. 437); however, inspectors may be appointed by the Secretary of State on terms that any report which they may make is not for publication. In such a case, the report need not be made available to the other persons mentioned above.

Winding up on public interest grounds

The Secretary of State may petition for the winding up of a company on which a report has been made. The court may grant such a petition if it thinks it just and equitable (IA 1986, s. 124A). The Secretary of State may also commence proceedings in the company's name (CA 1985, s. 438), and may also petition to the court for relief against unfair prejudice (CA 1985, s. 460(1)(b) and see ¶62-550ff.). The expenses of investigating a company are borne by the Secretary of State in the first instance, but he may recover these expenses from persons found liable (CA 1985, s. 439).

¶63-700   Investigation of share transactions

As outlined at ¶51-500, a public company has a right to investigate and ascertain who is the ultimate owner of its shares. If the issue is of wider public interest, inspectors may be appointed by the Secretary of State for Trade and Industry to investigate a company's ownership.

The Secretary of State may appoint inspectors to investigate and report on the membership of a company, to determine the true persons who are or have been financially interested in the success or failure (real or apparent) of the company or able to control or materially to influence its policy (CA 1985, s. 442–444). He may make such an appointment where it appears that 'there is good reason to do so' or if there is an application for such an investigation by shareholders with ten per cent of the issued share capital or who are at least 200 in number. In the latter case the Secretary of State must appoint inspectors (unless the application is vexatious). However, he may require applicants to give security, or he may exclude from the ambit of the investigation any matter which he believes it unreasonable to be the subject thereof.

The Secretary of State may decline to appoint inspectors in favour of an investigation by his own officers (CA 1985, s. 444).

Investigations of share dealings

Inspectors may also be appointed to examine the circumstances in which the statutory rules which prohibit, or require disclosure of, certain securities transactions have been infringed. The inspectors are given wide investigatory powers to uncover breaches of these provisions, similar to those conferred by s. 434 of the *Companies Act* 1985 for the conduct of investigations (see ¶63-600) (CA 1985, s. 446).

¶63-800   Power to require production of documents

A third method of investigation is sometimes called a 'confidential investigation' because it is carried out by departmental officials rather than appointed inspectors. This type of investigation is pursuant to the power granted to the Secretary of State for Trade and Industry to compel production of specified documents (CA 1985, s. 447). Failure to comply with such an order may expose the company or any officer on whom the order has been imposed to a fine (CA 1985, s. 447(6)). 'Documents' include information recorded in any form (CA 1985, s. 447(9)). This allows legible copies to be made of data held on computer and other methods of storage.

Entry, search and seizure

If there are reasonable grounds for believing that there are, on any premises, documents which should have been produced pursuant to any investigation under Pt. XIV of the *Companies Act* 1985, then a magistrate may authorise the entry and search of the premises and seizure of the documents (CA 1985, s. 448).

Provision for security of information obtained

Information or documents obtained under s. 447 or 448 of the *Companies Act* 1985 above must not be disclosed by the DTI without the consent of the company concerned, except in certain specified circumstances (CA 1985, s. 449). Supplementary provisions deal with the position where legal professional privilege or banking confidentiality is claimed (CA 1985, s. 452).

ACCOUNTS AND AUDIT

Table of Contents

continued over

242

ACCOUNTS

¶70-000   General

Properly kept accounts which reflect the current financial position of a company are essential for efficient management and control. Company law imposes various requirements on companies to maintain accounting records and draw up annual audited accounts. Such information can then be used by both shareholders and prospective investors to gauge the company's overall solvency.

The fourth and seventh EC company law directives harmonised the treatment of individual and group accounts throughout the European Community, and were implemented in the UK by the Companies Acts 1981 and 1989 respectively. This relatively new statutory regime is outlined below.

Consideration is also given to the extra-statutory rules prescribed by the Accounting Standards Board (see ¶70-600). This body is responsible for the implementation and revocation of various financial reporting standards which provide a framework of accounting principles.

The rules regarding auditing of accounts are outlined, together with the circumstances in which audit exemptions may be granted, at ¶70-875 to ¶70-925.

¶70-050   Accounting records

All companies must keep accounting records (CA 1985, s. 221). These records must be sufficient to show and explain the company's transactions, and be such as to:

(1) disclose with reasonable accuracy, at any time, the financial position of the company at that time; and

(2) enable the directors to ensure that any balance sheet and profit and loss account prepared under s. 221–262A of the *Companies Act* 1985 (Pt. VII) comply with the Act's requirements.

The requirement that the records be sufficient to disclose the financial position is less demanding than the need for disclosure of a 'true and fair view' which s. 226(2) of the *Companies Act* 1985 requires the balance sheet and profit and loss account to give, since the latter standard requires consideration of factors which may be outside the accounting records.

Further guidance on accounting records is as follows (CA 1985, s. 221(2), (3)).

(1) The accounting records must in particular contain:

    (a) entries from day to day of all sums of money received and expended by the company, and the matters in respect of which the receipt and payment takes place; and

    (b) a record of the assets and liabilities of the company (s. 221(2)).

(2) If the company's business involves dealing in goods the accounting records must contain:

    (a) statements of stock held by the company at the end of each financial year of the company;

    (b) all statements of stocktakings from which any such statement of stock as is mentioned in paragraph (a) has been or is to be prepared; and

    (c) except in the case of goods sold by way of ordinary retail trade, statements of all goods sold and purchased, showing the goods and the buyers and sellers in sufficient detail to enable all these to be identified (s. 221(3)).

The company must, therefore, maintain sufficient records to be able to ascertain with reasonable accuracy the cash position, tangible assets and liabilities and pre-tax results of the company at any time. Accounting records may be maintained in non-legible form, provided the recording is capable of reproduction in a legible form. The requirement is satisfied if information is organised and labelled in such a way that retrieval is possible. 'Statements of stock' are simply a summary of records which support the year-end stock figure. The statements of stock are to be derived from 'statements of stocktaking', which are stock lists themselves, or summaries of these lists.

A parent company may have a subsidiary undertaking (see ¶70-100) which is not subject to the same obligations to maintain accounting records as its parent. In this case, the parent company must take all reasonable steps to ensure that the undertaking keeps such accounting records as to enable the accounts of the parent company to be prepared in accordance with the Act.

The records are to be maintained at the company's registered office, or at any other place which the directors think fit. If, however, the company maintains its records outside Great Britain, accounts and returns must be sent to and kept at a place in Great Britain. These accounts and returns must:

(1) disclose with reasonable accuracy the financial position of the business in question at intervals of not more than six months; and

(2) enable the directors to ensure that the company's balance sheet and profit and loss account comply with the requirements of s. 222(3) of the *Companies Act* 1985.

Company officers must be given access to the accounting records, and the records are to be kept for three years in the case of private companies, and six years by public companies (s. 222(5)).

Failure to comply with the requirement to maintain and keep accounting records is an offence. The statutory penalties are imprisonment, or a fine, or both, but these will not be imposed if the officer acted honestly and the default was excusable in the circumstances (s. 221, 222).

¶70-100   Parent and subsidiary undertakings

Directors must prepare annual accounts and, if a parent company, group accounts (CA 1985, s. 226, 227). Before the enactment of the *Companies Act* 1989, there was one definition of subsidiary which was used for all the purposes of the Companies Acts. A new definition of subsidiary has been introduced for non-accounting purposes (see ¶20-575), and a different definition for accounting purposes. The latter definition is derived from the seventh EC company law directive on group accounts.

In contrast to the words 'subsidiary company' and 'holding company' as defined in s. 736 of the *Companies Act* 1985, the accounting rules use the terminology 'subsidary undertakings' and 'parent undertakings'. The striking difference is that the word 'undertaking' can include not only a body corporate, but a partnership or an unincorporated association carrying on a trade or business, with or without a view to profit (s. 259). This widening of the definition was introduced to counteract various abuses of off-balance sheet financing which had occurred under the previous rules.

¶70-150   'Parent undertaking'

It is important to examine the rules whereby an entity will be a parent or subsidiary undertaking. A parent company is a parent undertaking which is also a company. An undertaking is a parent undertaking in relation to another undertaking (a subsidiary undertaking) if (CA 1985, s. 258(2)):

(1) it holds a majority of the voting rights in the undertaking; or

(2) it is a member of the undertaking and has the right to appoint or remove a majority of its board of directors; or

(3) it has the right to exercise a dominant influence over the undertaking by virtue of:

(a) provisions contained in the undertaking's memorandum or articles, or

(b) a control contract; or

(4) it is a member of the undertaking and controls alone, pursuant to an agreement with other shareholders or members, a majority of the voting rights in the undertaking; or

(5) it has a participating interest in the undertaking over which it actually exercises a dominant influence, or both undertakings are managed on a unified basis.

These definitions – which operate indirectly as well as directly (CA 1985, s. 258(5)) – are expanded upon in s. 259 and 260 of and Sch. 10A to the *Companies Act* 1985.

Right to exercise a dominant influence

These tests are based on the concept of control, and replace the emphasis on the ownership of share capital. Most striking is the introduction of the concept of the 'right to exercise a dominant influence'. This is defined further in Sch. 10A. However an undertaking cannot be a parent undertaking merely as a result of its right to exercise a dominant influence. Various structural requirements are built into the definition to ensure that, for example, a bank, which may direct how the undertaking formulates its operating and financial policies, does not unwittingly become a parent undertaking for the purposes of the Act. Also of importance is the definition of a 'control contract' in para. 4(2) of Sch. 10A to the *Companies Act* 1985: i.e. a contract in writing conferring a right to exercise a dominant influence which:

(1) is of a kind authorised by the memorandum or articles of the undertaking in relation to which the right is exercisable; and

(2) is permitted by the law under which that undertaking is established.

The latter point is material because control contracts are more common in other member states of the EU, in particular Germany.

Participating interests

The concept of a 'participating interest' is a structural test which extends the consolidation of undertakings beyond purely control grounds. A 'participating interest' is an interest held by an undertaking in the shares of another undertaking on a long-term basis for the purpose of securing a contribution to its activities by the exercise of control or influence arising from or relating to that interest (CA 1985, s. 260). A holding of 20 per cent or more of the shares of an undertaking is presumed to be a participating interest unless the contrary is shown.

Off-balance sheet financing, etc.

Undertakings must now closely examine their relationships with other undertakings, and in particular any off-balance sheet financing, to ensure compliance with the statutory requirements. They should also have regard to s. 227(6) of the *Companies Act* 1985, which provides a test of substance rather than form in the preparation of accounts.

ACCOUNTING REFERENCE PERIODS AND DATES

¶70-200   General

Accounts must be prepared 'for each financial year of the company'. A financial year is determined by reference to an 'accounting reference period' (ARP). That period is in turn determined by the 'accounting reference date' (ARD), i.e. the date on which each ARP ends.

For companies incorporated before 1 April 1996, a nine-month period from the date of incorporation is allowed within which the registrar must be notified of the company's nominated ARD. Failure to provide such notification will result in a deemed ARD. For companies incorporated before 1 April 1990, that date will be 31 March. For other companies, the date will be the last day of the month in which the anniversary of its formation falls. In either case, the length of the first accounting reference period must be between six and 18 months, commencing with the date of incorporation and ending with the first ARD.

For all companies incorporated on or after 1 April 1996, the ARD will be the last day of the month in which the company was first incorporated.

Unless a company subsequently alters its ARD in accordance with the procedures outlined below, successive ARDs will be of 12 months' duration.

¶70-225   Alteration of accounting reference dates

A facility for altering a company's accounting reference period (ARD), and hence its accounting reference period (ARP), is provided by s. 225 of the *Companies Act* 1985. A company must give notice to the registrar specifying the new ARD for its present and future ARPs. The company's immediately preceding ARP may also be changed providing that the time for laying the accounts and reports for that period has not expired.

Once the ARD is altered, each ARP will end on that new date. In any event, the new ARP cannot be of more than 18 months' duration, unless the company is subject to an administration order by virtue of the *Insolvency Act* 1986 (see below).

Notice under s. 225 of the *Companies Act* 1985 can be given at any time. Further, an ARP can be reduced to any duration, i.e. it is possible for a company to have a reference period of only one day if it so chooses.

The notice of alteration of the accounting reference date sent to the registrar must state whether the effect of the change is to shorten or extend the current or previous accounting reference period. The company cannot extend its accounting reference period (even prospectively) more than twice in any five-year period, unless this is done to make accounting reference periods of a company coterminous with those of its parent or subsidiary undertaking, or the Secretary of State grants an exemption.

A special regime exists for the alteration of the accounting reference periods of companies subject to an administration order under Pt. II of the *Insolvency Act* 1986. The accounting reference period may be altered retrospectively as well as prospectively, may be extended to exceed 18 months, and an extension may be made at any time notwithstanding the five-year rule mentioned above.

A 'financial year' must end within seven days either side of successive accounting reference periods; this is to enable companies (e.g. retailers) to draw up accounts to the end of a week. In relation to a subsidiary undertaking which is not a company, the 'financial year' is any period in respect of which a profit and loss account of the undertaking is required to be made, irrespective of whether that period is a year. The requirement to make up accounts for this period may derive from its own constitution or by the law under which it is established (CA 1985, s. 223(4)).

¶70-300   Preparation of the accounts

Every company must produce a balance sheet which gives a true and fair view of the state of affairs of the company as at the end of the financial year. A profit and loss account must also be prepared which provides a true and fair view of the profit and loss of the company (CA 1985, s. 226).

A parent company must also prepare group accounts. Group accounts comprise a consolidated balance sheet and a consolidated profit and loss account which must give a true and fair view of the undertakings included in the consolidation as a whole, so far as concerns members of the company (CA 1985, s. 227).

In respect of both individual and consolidated accounts, the company must provide additional information in the accounts, or in a note thereto, where mere compliance with the *Companies Act* 1985 would not give a true and fair view of the company's finances (s. 226(4), 227(5)). Further, the company may depart from the Act's requirements so far as necessary to give a true and fair impression of the company's finances (s. 226(5), 227(6)). The particulars of any such departure, the reasons for it and its effect must be given in a note to the accounts.

Exemption from need to prepare group accounts

A parent company need not prepare group accounts if it is itself a subsidiary undertaking and its immediate parent undertaking is established under the law of a member state of the EU, and:

(1) the company is a wholly-owned subsidiary of that parent undertaking; or

(2) where that parent undertaking owns more than 50 per cent of the shares of the company, and a notice requesting the preparation of group accounts has not been served on the company by a shareholder holding in aggregate:

   (a) more than half of the remaining shares in the company, or

   (b) five per cent of the total shares of the company (CA 1985, s. 228(1)).

These provisions were introduced in 1989 to relax the burdensome requirement of consolidation in inappropriate circumstances. The shares held by directors to comply with any share qualification are disregarded for determining whether a company is 'wholly owned'. Prior to the *Companies Act* 1989, the parent company had to be incorporated in Great Britain. Further conditions are prescribed in relation to companies established under the laws of other member states of the EU (CA 1985, s. 228(2)). However a company listed on any stock exchange within the EU cannot take advantage of the exemption (CA 1985, s. 228(3)).

Further exclusions

Group accounts need not deal with a subsidiary undertaking if:

(1) its inclusion is not material for the purpose of giving a true and fair view (but two or more undertakings may be excluded only if they are not material taken together);

(2) severe long-term restrictions substantially hinder the exercise of rights of the parent company over the assets or management of that undertaking;

(3) the information necessary for the preparation of group accounts cannot be obtained without disproportionate expense or undue delay; or

(4) the interest of the parent company is held exclusively with a view to subsequent resale and the undertaking has not previously been included in consolidated group accounts prepared by the parent company (CA 1985, s. 229(3)).

Where the activities of one or more subsidiary undertakings are so different from those of other undertakings that their inclusion would be incompatible with the obligation to give a true and fair view, they need not be included (CA 1985, s. 229(4)). This does not apply merely because the undertakings provide different services, or one is commercial while the other is industrial. If all the subsidiary undertakings satisfy the exemptions contained in s. 229 above, then no group accounts need be prepared by the parent company.

Individual accounts, etc.

A parent company must still prepare individual accounts even if it also prepares group accounts under the Act. However the profit and loss account may be omitted from the accounts in certain circumstances (CA 1985, s. 230). An obligation is imposed upon public companies to prepare full interim accounts (s. 272) and initial accounts (s. 273) to establish whether distributions can be made in certain circumstances.

¶70-350 The accounts for a financial year

A company's accounts for a financial year are the profit and loss account, the balance sheet, a directors' report and auditors' report, and group accounts if the company has any subsidiary undertakings.

It is necessary for the company's annual accounts to have the directors' approval (CA 1985, s. 233). This approval is signified by one director's signature on the balance sheet. The name of the director signing must be stated on every copy of the balance sheet. If, however, approval is given in circumstances where the annual accounts do not comply with the Companies Act, then all the directors who are party to the approval and know of such non-compliance, or approve the accounts recklessly, are guilty of an offence and liable to a fine. All directors of the company are party to the approval unless a person who is a director can show that he took all reasonable steps to prevent them being approved (s. 233(5)). Ordinarily, this would mean voting against the resolution approving the annual accounts at the board meeting.

Directors' and auditors' reports

The directors must make a report each financial year which:

(1) contains a fair review of the development of the business of the company and its subsidiary undertakings during the financial year and of their position at the end of it; and

(2) stating the amount (if any) which they recommend should be paid as dividend (CA 1985, s. 234).

Other specific items which the directors' report should disclose are considered at ¶70-700.

The balance sheet, the profit and loss account and group accounts (if appropriate) must be reported on by the company's auditors (see ¶70-900).

¶70-400   Delivery of accounts to the registrar

The Companies Act calls for the delivery of annual accounts to the registrar of companies. This duty is placed upon the directors (CA 1985, s. 242). The accounts of a public company and a private company must be filed within seven and ten months respectively from the end of the related accounting reference periods (s. 244). An extension of the deadline for filing accounts may be granted by the Secretary of State. A company which carries on business outside the UK, the Channel Islands and the Isle of Man may claim a three-month extension of the time limit. Companies qualifying as either 'small' or 'medium' are subject to a less onerous disclosure regime (s. 246: see ¶70-750).

Where a parent company has an overseas or unincorporated subsidiary undertaking excluded from consolidated accounts requirements pursuant to s. 229(4) of the *Companies Act* 1985, it must deliver to the registrar the subsidiary undertaking's individual accounts or, if the latter is a parent undertaking, its latest group accounts. The accounts of the subsidiary undertaking must be made up to date within a year of the end of the parent company's financial year. The auditors' report (if any) must be attached to these accounts. No accounts need be prepared to satisfy this requirement if they would not otherwise be prepared, nor need a document not otherwise published or available for public inspection be attached (CA 1985, s. 243).

Failure to submit accounts to the registrar pursuant to s. 242 above exposes each of the directors of the company to prosecution and, upon conviction, a fine of up to £5,000. Continued contravention will result in a further daily fine of up to £500 (CA 1985, Sch. 24). A statutory defence arises where a director takes all reasonable steps to secure timely delivery of the accounts (CA 1985, s. 242(4)). Where directors fail to deliver accounts, the court may, on application by any member or creditor of the company, make an order compelling the directors to deliver those accounts (s. 242(3)).

The company will also be liable to a civil penalty for the late filing of accounts (CA 1985, s. 242A). The amount of penalty depends on how late the accounts are delivered. Submission of an unsigned balance sheet or directors' report to the registrar may result in a fine levied on both the company and every officer who is in default (s. 233(6), 234A(4)).

Unlimited companies

An unlimited company does not have to file accounts with the registrar, but this exemption is only available if, at no time during the relevant accounting reference period:

(1) has the unlimited company been, to its knowledge, a subsidiary undertaking of an undertaking which was then limited;

(2) have there been, to its knowledge, rights (exercisable by or on behalf of two or more undertakings which were then limited) which, if exercisable by one of them, would have made the company its subsidiary undertaking; or

(3) has the unlimited company been a parent company of an undertaking which was then limited.

Other unlimited companies, such as banking and insurance companies or promoters of trading stamp schemes, must file accounts (CA 1985, s. 254(3)).

¶70-450 Laying of accounts before the company

Public companies and private companies must lay their accounts before shareholders at a general meeting within seven months and ten months respectively of the end of the related accounting period (CA 1985, s. 241, 244). Usually the annual general meeting is the appropriate occasion. A three-month extension of the time limit may be claimed by companies which have interests, or trade, outside the UK, the Channel Islands and the Isle of Man (CA 1985, s. 244). An extension may be granted to other companies on application.

Failure to lay accounts exposes the directors to liability for fines (see CA 1985, s. 241(2) and ¶70-400).

Copies of the accounts, together with the directors' and auditors' reports, must be sent to the shareholders, the company's debenture holders, and any other persons entitled to receive notice of the general meeting not less than 21 days before the meeting at which they are to be laid. That 21-day period may be reduced if all the members entitled to be sent accounts so agree (CA 1985, s. 238(4)). Failure to meet the above obligations is an offence rendering the company and every officer in default liable to a fine (s. 238(5)).

Private companies may decide to dispense with the laying of accounts before a general meeting by the elective resolution procedure (see CA 1985, s. 252 and ¶60-800).

In addition to s. 238 above, members and debenture holders are accorded a right to receive, upon demand, copies of the company's latest annual accounts (together with the accompanying directors' and auditors' reports) free of charge (CA 1985, s. 239). New share and debenture holders thus have the opportunity to examine the company's financial position. Failure to provide these documents within seven days of the request will render the company and every officer who is in default liable to a fine (s. 239(3)).

¶70-500   Revision of defective accounts and reports

The need to be able to remedy defective accounts and reports was considered by the Dearing Committee which reported in November 1988. Most of the proposals of that committee were enacted in the *Companies Act* 1989, in the form of a regime for the rectification of defective accounts.

The directors of a company may voluntarily prepare revised annual accounts, or a revised report, if it appears to them that the original version did not comply with the Companies Act (CA 1985, s. 245(1)). If copies of the previously prepared documents have already been delivered to the registrar or laid before the company in general meeting, then the revisions must only:

- correct those respects in which the previous accounts or report did not comply with the Act; and
- make consequential alterations.

The revision procedure is established by the *Companies (Revision of Defective Accounts and Report) Regulations* 1990 (SI 1990/2570, as amended). Such revision may take place by either replacing the accounts and reports, or appending a note to the original documents which contain details of the revisions to be made. There is an overriding requirement that the revised accounts must represent the company's financial situation in a true and fair light as at the date of the original accounts. The regulations also provide for the approval and signature of revised accounts, miscellaneous issues regarding the auditors' report, the effects of revision, and the publication, laying, and delivery of revised accounts.

Once accounts have been sent to the registrar or laid before the company in general meeting, the Secretary of State may issue a notice to the company if it appears to him that there is, or may be, a question as to whether its accounts comply with the Act (CA 1985, s. 245A). The directors must be given at least a month to explain the accounts or prepare revised accounts. Failure on the part of the directors, either to give a satisfactory explanation or to prepare revised annual accounts, gives the Secretary of State power to apply to the court under s. 245B of the *Companies Act* 1985.

By virtue of s. 245C of the Companies Act, the Secretary of State has authorised the Financial Reporting Review Panel to examine companies' accounts and, if necessary, apply to the court under s. 245B.

The court may declare that the annual accounts of a company do not comply with the Companies Acts, and may make an order requiring the directors to prepare revised accounts. The court may give directions with respect to:

(1) the auditing of the accounts;

(2) the revision of any directors' report or summary financial statement (see ¶70-700, ¶70-825);

(3) the taking of steps by the directors to bring the making of the order to the notice of persons likely to rely on previous accounts; and

(4) such other matters as the court thinks fit (CA 1985, s. 245B(3)).

Those directors who were a party to the approval of the defective accounts may be liable for the costs of and incidental to the application, and any reasonable expenses incurred by the company in connection with, or in consequence of, the preparation of the revised accounts. To avoid liability a director must show that he took all reasonable steps to prevent their being approved (CA 1985, s. 245B(4)).

The accounts of a company are a matter for public concern, and accordingly notice of an application for revision, together with a statement of the matters at issue, must be sent by the applicant to the registrar for registration (CA 1985, s. 245B(2)). Once the proceedings are concluded or withdrawn, this must also be registered (s. 245B(6)).

ANNUAL ACCOUNTS: FORM AND CONTENT

¶70-550 General

The form and content of the financial statement of a company are prescribed by Sch. 4 to the *Companies Act* 1985. Schedule 4 is divided into seven parts, and those parts of more general application are considered at ¶70-575 to ¶70-650). Special provisions which apply to investment companies (as defined under CA 1985, s. 266) are set out in para. 71–73 of Sch. 4 to the *Companies Act* 1985 (Pt. V): these are not considered further.

General principles in relation to group accounts are considered at ¶70-675. Miscellaneous matters about related undertakings which must be disclosed in the notes to the accounts are outlined at ¶70-675. The rules are self-explanatory.

The provisions for the disclosure of particulars of emoluments and loans made to directors, and details of other transactions and agreements entered into with them, are considered at ¶43-000ff.

The contents of the directors' report, the ability to submit abbreviated accounts and disclosure by dormant companies are considered at ¶70-700 to ¶70-825, together with the facility for public listed companies to provide summary financial statements.

A different set of disclosure rules for banking and insurance companies is set out in Sch. 9 and 9A to the Companies Act. These are not considered further.

¶70-575   Rules and formats

A company is given the choice of two balance sheet formats and four profit and loss account formats and the accompanying notes. The accounts must disclose figures for each heading with the corresponding figure for the previous year.

Once a particular format is selected, the company must apply the same format in future years, unless the directors can identify special reasons for a change (CA 1985, Sch. 4, para. 2). If the format should change, particulars of the change and the reasons for it must be disclosed in notes to the accounts. Further, the comparative figures for the previous year must be adjusted to make the results comparable. Particulars of the adjustment and the reason for it must be disclosed.

The formats present a minimum standard for the level of disclosure. If a company has no amount to be disclosed under a particular heading in both the current and previous year, the heading can be omitted. The company is free to make more detailed disclosure if it chooses. The headings contained in the formats are not exhaustive, but a company cannot treat any of the following as assets in its balance sheet:

- preliminary expenses;
- expenses of, and commission on, any issue of shares or debentures; or
- costs of research.

The headings in each format which are assigned the same Arabic number may be aggregated if the individual items are not material to an assessment of the state of affairs and results of the company, or if the aggregation facilitates assessment of the company's financial position and results. If the amounts under each heading are not material, no further disclosure is required. If the aggregation is undertaken in order to assist in assessment of the company's financial position and results, further disclosure of the individual items is required in notes to the accounts.

In addition to headings under each format, the following details must also be disclosed by all companies:

- profit or loss on ordinary activities before taxation;

- actual or proposed transfers to reserves; and

- actual and proposed dividends.

¶70-600   Accounting principles and rules

In addition to the various requirements specifically stipulated in the Companies Acts, additional reference should also be made to the Financial Reporting Council (FRC). This body has two subsidiaries: the Accounting Standards Board (ASB) and the Financial Reporting Review Panel (FRRP).

The ASB drafts 'financial reporting standards'(which supersede 'statements of standard accounting practice' drafted by the old Accounting Standards Committee). These contain guidelines which assist in the preparation of company accounts.

The FRRP analyses accounts to ensure compliance with the Companies Acts (see ¶70-500). In addition, the Urgent Issues Task Force (UITF), which falls under the aegis of the ASB, reports on problematic accounting issues.

The *Companies Act* 1989 introduces a direct requirement. There must be a statement in a note to the accounts as to whether the accounts have been prepared in accordance with the applicable accounting standards. The details of any material departure from those standards and the company's reason for it must be given (CA 1985, s. 226(5) and Sch. 4, para. 36A).

The amounts to be included under each heading in the accounts are to be determined in accordance with the principles set out in para. 10–14 of Sch. 4 to the *Companies Act* 1985. The Schedule identifies five fundamental principles which must be applied. Company directors can depart from these principles if there are special reasons to do so. However the accounts must disclose particulars of the departure, the reasons for it and its effect. The fundamental principles are as follows:

(1) *The going concern principle.* For the purpose of valuing the company's assets, the company is presumed to be carrying on business as a going concern. If the going concern principle is departed from, sums realisable on the break-up of the company constitute the appropriate valuation basis.

(2) *The consistency principle.* The company must apply consistent accounting policies within the same accounts and from year to year.

(3) *The prudence concept.* Only profits actually realised at the balance sheet date should be taken into account. Liabilities and losses should be anticipated. This includes sums which become apparent between the balance sheet date and the date the directors sign the accounts.

(4) *The accruals concept.* Income and expenditure are recorded in the financial statements as they arise, not when received or paid.

(5) *Separate determination of the value of assets and liabilities.* In the determination of the aggregate value of any category of asset or liability, each individual component is accounted for separately. This precludes set-off, so that there must be separate disclosure of surpluses against deficits. An exception to this rule is provided for tangible assets, raw materials and consumables (CA 1985, Sch. 4, para. 25). Items in respect of which a legal right of set-off is available are outside the requirements and thus can be disclosed as a net figure.

The Act contains rules which set out how amounts to be provided under each heading should be determined. The determination may be based upon historical cost accounting or upon 'alternative' accounting rules. The former basis carries figures at the historical transaction cost. The latter basis seeks to reflect the results and financial position of the company more accurately, by taking into account the effect of changing price levels. However accounts prepared on the 'alternative' basis must disclose the basis of valuation used. These accounts should also disclose, by note, either comparable amounts determined according to the historical cost rules, or the difference between the historical figure and the figure carried in the accounts on the 'alternative basis'.

¶70-625   Notes to the annual accounts

Companies are required to disclose accounting policies in the notes to the accounts. It is also necessary to supplement information on particular balance sheet and profit and loss items in accordance with the details set out in para. 35–58 of Sch. 4 to the *Companies Act* 1985 (Pt. III).

¶70-650   Parent companies and subsidiary undertakings

Where the company is a parent or subsidiary undertaking, further disclosure requirements are imposed by para. 59A of Sch. 4 to the *Companies Act* 1985. Any guarantee or financial commitment made by the company on behalf of:

- a parent undertaking;
- a fellow subsidiary undertaking; or
- a subsidiary undertaking of the company,

must be clearly and separately disclosed in the accounts so that each guarantee made may be easily distinguished.

¶70-675   Group accounts

Generally, group accounts must comply so far as practicable with the provisions of s. 390A(3) of and Sch. 4 to the *Companies Act* 1985 (amount of auditors' remuneration) as if the undertakings included in the consolidation ('the group') constituted a single company (CA 1985, Sch. 4A, para. 1).

The consolidated balance sheet and profit and loss account combine the separate financial statements of companies in the same group. However adjustment may be made in accordance with the provisions of Sch. 4A, and in accordance with generally accepted accounting principles and practices.

Where the financial year of a subsidiary company does not end at the same time as its parent's financial year, the group accounts must be made up from:

- the last accounts of the subsidiary undertaking, if its financial year ended no more than three months before that of a parent company; or, if not,

- interim accounts prepared by the subsidiary undertaking as at the end of a parent company's financial year (CA 1985, Sch. 4A, para. 2(2)).

Where assets and liabilities to be included in group accounts have been valued or otherwise determined by undertakings according to accounting rules differing from those used for the group accounts, the values or amounts should be adjusted in order to accord with the rules used for the group accounts (Sch. 4A, para. 3(1)). The directors may decide that there are special reasons for not making the adjustment (i.e. if they are not material for the purpose of giving a true and fair view) (Sch. 4A, para. 3(2), (3)). Particulars of any departure, the reasons for it and its effect must be given in a note to the accounts. Further, where there are differences between the accounting rules used by a parent company to prepare its group accounts and its individual accounts, this must be disclosed and reasons given (Sch. 4A, para. 4).

Elimination of group transactions

In certain circumstances, transactions between undertakings in the same group should be eliminated in the preparation of the group accounts (CA 1985, Sch. 4A, para. 6).

Acquisition and merger accounting

Acquisition or merger accounting applies where an undertaking becomes a subsidiary undertaking of the parent company. Previously, where certain criteria were satisfied, merger accounting was mandatory. This is now optional. Merger accounting is restricted to where the acquisition is substantially on a share-for-share basis, and may be restricted further by the application of accounting standards (CA 1985, Sch. 4A, para. 10).

Joint ventures, etc.

The accounts of joint ventures may be consolidated into a parent company's accounts (CA 1985, Sch. 4A, para. 19–22).

Disclosure of information: related undertakings

Where the company is not required to prepare group accounts, the information specified in para. 1–13 of Sch. 5 to the *Companies Act* 1985 (Pt. I) must be given.

The information specified in para. 14–32 of Sch. 5 (Pt. II) must be given if the company is required to prepare group accounts. Both Parts call for particulars of any subsidiary undertakings and other shareholdings, details of parent companies, and particulars of arrangements attracting merger relief. Certain exceptions exist if the company is established outside the UK (CA 1985, s. 231(3)), and also if compliance with Sch. 5 would produce information of excessive length (s. 231(5)).

¶70-700   The directors' report

Companies must publish a directors' report for each financial year. The matters to be dealt with in this report are set out fully in s. 234 of and Sch. 7 to the *Companies Act* 1985. There are some important points to note. First, the directors must provide a 'fair review of the development of the business of the company and its subsidiaries during the financial year and of their position at the end of it'. However the level of detail of this review is not stipulated. Secondly, 'likely future developments in the business of the company and its subsidiaries' must be indicated (CA 1985, Sch. 7, para. 6(b)). Forecasts of profitability are not expressly called for and, if made, may bring the directors within the rules which regulate profit forecasts.

Also amongst the details called for in the directors' report are 'particulars of any important events affecting the company of any of its subsidiaries which have occurred since the end of the financial year' (CA 1985, Sch. 7, para. 6(a)). The subject of 'post balance sheet events' is covered in SSAP 17. The disclosure called for under the SSAP is more detailed than the requirements under Sch. 7. However the SSAP states that the information should appear in the notes to the accounts, not in the directors' report. It is common for the directors' report to provide sufficient details of post balance sheet events to satisfy the SSAP, and for a note to the accounts to refer the reader to this report.

Directors' reports of public companies and private companies which do not qualify as small or medium-sized and are members of a group of which the parent company is public must now disclose in the directors' report the company's payment policy and practice. The report must disclose whether it is the company's policy to follow any code or standard on payment practice to some or all of its suppliers and, if so, the name of that code or standard and where information about and copies of it can be obtained. Discrimination between suppliers must also be reported. Payment *practice* is disclosable for financial years ending on or after 25 March 1997. Relevant companies must disclose their practice on payment to suppliers by stating the figure, expressed in days, which bears the same proportion to the number of days in the year as the amount owed to trade creditors at the year end bears to the amounts invoiced by suppliers in the year, i.e. the proportion X:Y where–

X = the aggregate of amounts owed to trade creditors at the year end, and

Y = the aggregate of amounts invoiced to the company by suppliers in the year.

¶70-725   Cash flow statements

The cash flow statement prescribed by FRS 1 is commonly featured in companies' annual financial statements. Its purpose is to illustrate a company's various cash flows so that its liquidity may be evaluated by third parties. Its predecessor, the statement of source and application of funds (SSAP 10), is no longer used.

¶70-750   Small and medium-sized companies and groups

The *Companies Act* 1989 introduced provisions whereby certain companies are exempted from the requirements to comply with relevant accounting standards and are permitted to file abbreviated accounts with the registrar of companies (CA 1985, s. 246, Sch. 8).

The company must not be:

● a public company; or

● a banking or insurance company; or

● an authorised person under the *Financial Services Act* 1986,

nor must it be a member of an ineligible group. A group is ineligible if any of its members is:

● a public company, or a body corporate which (not being a company) has power under its constitution to offer its shares or debentures to the public and may lawfully exercise that power;

● an authorised institution under the *Banking Act* 1987;

● an insurance company to which Pt. II of the *Insurance Companies Act* 1982 applies; or

● an authorised person under the *Financial Services Act* 1986.

A private company may also dispense with the obligation to lay accounts before its general meeting (see ¶70-450).

The format of the abbreviated accounts is determined by the size of the company or group. The criteria used to determine size are turnover, balance sheet total (i.e. the aggregate of the amounts shown on the balance sheet), and the number of employees. Three categories of company and group respectively are identified under the Act for accounting purposes: small companies and groups, medium-sized companies and groups, and others. If a company or group is outside the two qualifying sizes, it is unable to file abbreviated accounts. The relevant formats for abbreviated accounts are set out in Sch. 8 to the *Companies Act* 1985.

The form and content of accounts prepared by small companies prescribed by s. 246 of and Sch. 8 to the *Companies Act* 1985 is easier to understand since the substitution of new versions from 1 March 1997. Schedule 8 is now free-standing (compared with the previous version which operated by way of a large number of derogations from the disclosure requirements for all companies contained in Sch. 4). A new Sch. 8A was also inserted from the above date, providing the form and content of abbreviated accounts of small companies to be delivered to the registrar of companies. Both of these new schedules apply to annual accounts approved by a company's board on or after that date.

Under new s. 247B a special auditors' report (stating that the requirements for exemption from filing full accounts are satisfied) must still be filed with the abbreviated accounts. Although a copy of the auditors' report under s. 235 of the *Companies Act* 1985 (that the accounts were properly prepared and give a true and fair view) still need not be delivered separately, the whole text of it now only needs to be copied if the s. 235 report was qualified (together with further material necessary to understand the qualification) or if the report contained a statement under either s. 237(2) that the accounts, records or returns were inadequate or did not agree, or under s. 237(3) that there was a failure to obtain information and explanations.

Qualification of company as small or medium-sized

A *small company* is one which, for the relevant and preceding financial years (or first financial year), satisfies two or more of the following conditions:

- the amount of its turnover for the year does not exceed £2.8m;

- its balance sheet total does not exceed £1.4m; and

- the average number of persons employed by the company (determined on a weekly basis) does not exceed 50.

A *medium-sized company* is one which, for the relevant financial year, satisfies two or more of the following conditions:

- the amount of its turnover for the year does not exceed £11.2m;

- its balance sheet total does not exceed £5.6m; and

- the average number of persons employed by the company (determined on a weekly basis) does not exceed 250.

The method for calculation of balance sheet totals, the average number of employees and the annual turnover is set out in s. 247 of the *Companies Act* 1985. Additional guidance on the calculation of the relevant figures for groups of companies is given in s. 249.

Special auditors' report

A special auditors' report is filed with the abbreviated accounts which states that, in the opinion of the auditors, the requirements for the exemption are satisfied. A copy of the auditors' report prepared under s. 235 of the *Companies Act* 1985 need not be delivered separately, but the whole text of it must be reproduced with the special report, together with any further material necessary to understand any qualification of the accounts (CA 1985, Sch. 8, para. 24).

¶70-750

¶70-775   Dormant companies

Dormant companies (see ¶20-625) may exempt themselves from the need to appoint auditors by special resolution in accordance with s. 250 of the *Companies Act* 1985. If the company has been dormant since formation, the only requirement is a special resolution. Alternatively, such a resolution may be passed at a general meeting if accounts have been sent out pursuant to s. 238, and the following conditions are met:

- the company has been dormant since the end of the last financial year;

- group accounts are not required; and

- the company is 'small' for the purposes of s. 246.

If a company qualifies for the exemption from appointment of auditors, the accounts laid before members at general meetings and filed with the registrar of companies need not contain an auditors' report. However the directors must state that the company is dormant on the balance sheet (CA 1985, s. 250(4)).

¶70-800   Non-statutory accounts

Statutory accounts are any balance sheet or profit or loss account of a company or a group of companies which must be sent to the registrar.

If a company publishes financial statements other than as a part of 'statutory accounts', the statements are termed 'non-statutory accounts' (CA 1985, s. 240). Non-statutory accounts used to be known as 'abridged accounts'. Such accounts must carry a statement to the effect that they are not statutory accounts, and should not include the auditors' report on the statutory accounts. The non-statutory accounts must carry a statement indicating:

- that they are not statutory accounts;

- whether statutory accounts for that year have been sent to the registrar;

- whether the auditors/reporting accountants have reported on those accounts; and

- if there was such a report, whether the accounts had been deemed properly prepared.

These provisions apply to financial statements such as preliminary announcements by listed companies. The half-yearly reports required from listed companies by the London Stock Exchange qualified as abridged accounts under the previous provisions and are non-statutory accounts. However the contents of the half-yearly report are prescribed in the London Stock Exchange's listing rules. The report must carry a full audit report or a statement to the effect that the accounts have not been audited (*Listing Rules*, Ch. 12, para. 54).

¶70-825   Summary financial statements

A listed public company may, in certain circumstances, send a summary financial statement to shareholders instead of the statutory accounts (CA 1985, s. 251). The provisions relating to the publication of non-statutory accounts do not apply.

Every summary financial statement must state that it is only a summary of the information and also whether the auditors, in their opinion, consider it to be consistent with the statutory accounts and the directors' report. A statement must be included as to whether the auditors' report was qualified or unqualified. Further information must be given to allow any qualification of the accounts to be understood. The summary financial statement must refer to any comment by the auditors on the standard of the company's accounting records. If a statement has been made on the accounting records, then this must be set out in full in the financial summary (CA 1985, s. 251(4)).

Regulations made by the Secretary of State govern the circumstances in which summary financial statements can be prepared, the people who are entitled to receive a copy, and the form and content of the statement (see the *Companies (Summary Financial Statement) Regulations* 1995 (SI 1995/2092)).

AUDIT

¶70-875   General

The auditors' report must be filed along with the company accounts and the directors' report with the registrar of companies (CA 1985, s. 242). The scope, content and meaning of the auditors' report are considered at ¶70-900. The statutory rules which regulate the appointment and removal of auditors are considered at ¶44-400 to ¶44-500.

¶70-900   The auditors' report

The auditors' report must state whether, in the auditors' opinion, the accounts have been properly prepared in accordance with the Companies Act and whether a true and fair view is given (CA 1985, s. 235):

(1) by the individual balance sheet, of the state of affairs of the company as at the end of the financial year;

(2) by the individual profit and loss account, of the profit and loss of the company for the period under report; and

¶70-825

(3) by group accounts, of the state of affairs as at the end of the financial year, and the profit and loss for the financial year, of the undertakings included in the consolidation as a whole, so far as concerns members of the company.

The directors' report must be consistent with the information in the accounts, and the auditor must consider whether this is so (CA 1985, s. 235(3)). Further duties are imposed on auditors by s. 237. The auditor must carry out such investigations as will enable him to form an opinion as to whether:

(1) proper accounting records have been kept by the company and proper returns adequate for their audit have been received from branches not visited by them; and

(2) the company's balance sheet and (if not consolidated) its profit and loss account are in agreement with the accounting records and returns.

Statutory disclosure requirements as to transactions with directors and directors' emoluments must also be checked by the auditor (see ¶43-000 to ¶43-450). If the above statutory rules on accounts and disclosure are not satisfied, the auditor must state this fact in the report.

If a small company wishes to file abbreviated accounts with the registrar of companies, the auditors' report (that the accounts were properly prepared and give a true and fair view) now needs only be copied in the auditors' special report if the former report was qualified (together with further material necessary to understand the qualification) or if the report contained a statement under either s. 237(2) that the accounts, records or returns were inadequate or did not agree, or under s. 237(3) that there was a failure to obtain information and explanations.

Audit exemption

Audit exemption has been considerably extended for financial years ending on or after 15 June 1997. Total exemption is now conferred on companies which qualify as 'small' under s. 247 of the *Companies Act* 1985, have annual turnover not exceeding £350,000 and a balance sheet total not exceeding £1.4m. This relaxation is estimated to have increased the approximate number of companies which could enjoy total exemption from 250,000 to 450,000, i.e. to almost half of all private companies. Partial exemption subject to an 'accountant's report' now only exists for charitable companies. The latter enjoy total exemption if they qualify as small, have gross income (as opposed to 'turnover') below £90,000 and balance sheet total limit as above. Charitable companies are subject to partial exemption if they qualify as small, have gross income between £90,000 and £250,000 and a balance sheet total not exceeding £1.4m.

Rights to information

The auditor is given a right of access at all times to the company's books, accounts and vouchers and is entitled to require from the company's officers such information and explanations as he considers necessary for performance of his duties. Failure to obtain all the information and explanations necessary for the audit must be stated in the audit report. It is a criminal offence for a company officer knowingly or recklessly to make a statement to an auditor which is misleading, false or deceptive in any material particular. The penalty for conviction on indictment is an unlimited fine, up to two years' imprisonment or both.

Right to attend company meetings, etc.

The auditor has a statutory right to attend general meetings of the company and he must also be sent notices of general meetings called by the company. Auditors also have the right to be heard at general meetings on matters which concern them as auditors (CA 1985, s. 390).

Subsidiary undertakings

A subsidiary undertaking which is a body corporate, and its auditor, must provide any information and explanations to the auditor of a parent company which the latter may reasonably require (CA 1985, s. 389A(3)). Failure to comply with this provision by the company or the auditor without reasonable excuse will make the company, directors and auditors guilty of an offence and liable to a fine.

If a parent company has a subsidiary undertaking which is not a body corporate incorporated in Great Britain, the parent company must, if so required by its auditors, take all such steps as are reasonably open to it to obtain the information and explanations (CA 1985, s. 389A(4)).

Private companies

A private company may decide by elective resolution to dispense with the annual appointment of auditors. In effect, they are deemed reappointed for the succeeding financial year (see ¶44-400).

Dormant companies

A dormant company may be exempted from appointing auditors. It is necessary for the company to pass a special resolution to this effect (see ¶70-775).

Other reports

Auditors are called upon to report in circumstances other than the laying and filing of accounts. The most important of these are on the circulation of a prospectus; the re-registration of a private company as public (see ¶22-500); an allotment of shares by public companies for a non-cash consideration (see ¶51-000), the availability of distributable profits (see ¶51-700); the grant of financial assistance for a share acquisition by a private company (see ¶52-050); and the purchase of shares out of capital by a private company (see ¶51-825).

¶70-925   Audit exemption

Many small companies are now exempted from the obligation to procure an auditors' report (*Companies Act 1985 (Audit Exemption) Regulations* 1994 (SI 1994/1935)). Where a company qualifies as 'small' by reference to s. 246 of the

Companies Act 1985, its annual turnover is less than £90,000 and its balance sheet total does not exceed £1.4m, it will be totally exempt. Companies in this category, but which have annual turnovers of between £90,000 and £350,000, must obtain an 'accountant's report' as opposed to a full audit.

Certain types of company are precluded from these exemptions, i.e. public companies and banking and insurance groups. The regulations additionally provide that the above exemptions may not be used where members holding at least ten per cent of the company's issued share capital withhold consent.

CORPORATE REORGANISATION

Table of Contents

continued over

¶80-000   Reconstructions and amalgamations

It is not uncommon for a company, or a group of companies, to undergo changes in corporate structure. The change may be due to the take-over by one company of another, the transfer of the whole or part of a company's undertaking to a new company, the merger of two or more companies into a new company, or a split of one company into two or more companies (a demerger).

These corporate transformations may be termed 'reconstructions' and 'amalgamations'. The terms are not defined in the *Companies Act* 1985, but descriptions have been provided by case law. A reconstruction is a transfer by a company of its assets to a new company, or an alteration to the capital structure of a company or group of companies. An amalgamation is the uniting of two or more companies under common control. Each form of reconstruction or amalgamation may involve difficult issues of taxation, employment law, competition law and accounting disclosure.

Transformations of corporate structure also raise many different issues and considerations of company law. The first of these is the machinery by which the change is to be effected. The *Companies Act* 1985 provides a framework for undertaking both internal reconstructions and also amalgamations of separate corporate entities. There are regulatory provisions to consider, both statutory and extra-statutory.

Management buy-outs are an increasingly common feature of commercial life, and often involve considerations of factors not common to other forms of reconstruction (see further ¶80-800).

STATUTORY SCHEMES FOR RECONSTRUCTION

Reconstruction or
amalgamation under s. 110 of
Insolvency Act .... ¶80-100

Compromises and
arrangements under
s. 425–427A of Companies
Act .... ¶80-150

Mergers and divisions of
public companies .... ¶80-200

¶80-100   Reconstruction or amalgamation under s. 110 of Insolvency Act

If a company is put into members' or creditors' voluntary winding up (see ¶92-200 and ¶92-250, respectively), all or part of its business or property may be transferred to another company for cash, shares or other interests in the transferee company. The liquidator of the transferor company would then, with the appropriate sanction (see below), distribute those interests to shareholders of that company in the course of the liquidation. Alternatively the liquidator may enter into an arrangement whereby the shareholders of the transferor company participate in the profits of the transferee company, or receive any other benefit from that company, instead of cash, shares or other assets. This procedure can be used to effect a demerger by the use of two 'transferee' companies, or to amalgamate two or more companies into an existing company or into a new holding company formed for that purpose.

Procedure to be followed

The necessary procedure to be followed is set out in s. 110 of the *Insolvency Act* 1986:

(1) Details of the scheme must be circulated to shareholders and a general meeting called, if the company is not already in liquidation. If the directors are to derive any special benefit from the scheme, this must be disclosed (*Tiessen v Henderson* [1899] 1 Ch 861).

(2) Appointment of the liquidator and authorisation of the sale by special resolution in the case of a members' winding up (a written resolution procedure may be adopted where the company is private), and by the court or the liquidation committee in the case of a creditors' voluntary winding up.

(3) The assets must be transferred by agreement between the liquidator and the transferee company or companies, but with sufficient funds retained to pay off the transferor company's liabilities.

Dissent from arrangement under s. 110, etc.

A facility for objection to the scheme (known as 'appraisal rights') is provided for shareholders who did not vote in favour of the scheme (IA 1986, s. 111(2)). The dissent must be addressed to the liquidator, and left at the company's registered office not more than seven days after the resolution was passed. The shareholder may request that the liquidator either not go ahead with the proposed resolution, or that his shares be purchased at an agreed price. This price may be determined by arbitration (IA 1986, s. 111(4)). If the liquidator agrees to purchase the dissentient's shares, the money must be raised in such a manner as is determined by special resolution (IA 1986, s. 111(3)).

If an order for winding up of the transferor company is made by the court within one year of the commencement of the voluntary winding up, the sanction of the court is required for the special resolution by which the sale of the assets was made (IA 1986, s. 110(6)). It is possible for creditors of the transferor company to take interests in the transferee company instead of repayment of their debt (*Re City and County Investment Co* (1879) 13 ChD 475). It may be possible for the creditors to dissent from any such arrangement at any time within 12 months.

¶80-150   Compromises and arrangements under s. 425–427A of Companies Act

The forms of compromise and arrangement undertaken under s. 425–427A of the *Companies Act* 1985 differ from those under s. 110 of the *Insolvency Act* 1986 (see

¶80-100, ¶90-650). It is not necessary to wind up the company, but the court must sanction the proposals. The scheme provides a method whereby a compromise or arrangement can be made between a company and its creditors (or any class thereof), its members (or any class thereof) or both its creditors and members. 'Compromise' and 'arrangement' implies mutual benefit, and not abandonment of rights (*Re NFU Development Trust Ltd* [1972] 1 WLR 1548). A special regime of reconstruction applies in certain circumstances to public companies (CA 1985, s. 427A: see ¶80-200).

To effect a scheme under s. 425:

(1) an application to the court must be made by any member, creditor or (if the company is being wound up) the liquidator, for an order that a meeting or meetings of appropriate classes of creditors and/or members be called;

(2) the terms of the scheme are submitted to the court with the application;

(3) if the court considers the proposals suitable, it will order that the appropriate meetings be held: the scheme will be considered at these meetings;

(4) it is necessary for the proposed scheme to obtain the support of a majority in number of the class of shareholders and/or creditors affected representing three-quarters of those present and voting at the meeting: a 'class' is those persons whose rights are not so dissimilar as to make it impossible for them to consult together with a view to their common interest (*Sovereign Life Assurance Co v Dodd* [1892] 2 QB 573);

(5) disclosure of the effect of the compromise upon directors' interests is called for: this includes compensation for loss of office which may result;

(6) if the scheme receives the appropriate support, application is made to the court to sanction the scheme; and

(7) once it is approved, all members of the class concerned are bound by its terms.

Where the proposed scheme involves the transfer of the whole or part of the undertaking of one company to another, the court is given the power under s. 427 of the *Companies Act* 1985 to make any of the following orders, when asked to sanction a compromise or arrangement under s. 425:

(1) the transfer of the whole or part of the undertaking, liabilities and property from the transferor company to the transferee company;

(2) the allotment of shares, debentures or similar interests by the transferee company;

(3) continuation of legal proceedings by or against the transferee company which originated with the transferor company;

(4) dissolution for the transferor company without winding up;

(5) provision for persons who dissent from the scheme; and

(6) any incidental orders which the court considers necessary to carry out the scheme fully and effectively.

The sanction of the court for the proposed arrangements will be granted if the resolutions are supported by the appropriate majority and if an intelligent and honest man might reasonably approve the proposals (*Re National Bank Ltd* [1966] 1 WLR 819).

¶80-200   Mergers and divisions of public companies

A special regime is prescribed under s. 427A of and Sch. 15B to the *Companies Act* 1985, for transactions known as 'mergers and divisions'. Under these provisions, introduced by the *Companies (Mergers and Divisions) Regulations* 1987 (SI 1987/1991), such transactions must satisfy additional criteria before being allowed to proceed under s. 425 of the *Companies Act* 1985 (see ¶80-150). The provisions are derived from the third and sixth EU company law directives, and control types of merger activity more commonly found in other member states than in the UK.

Mergers and divisions are compromises or arrangements proposed between a public company and its creditors or members, or any class of each, for the purpose of, or in connection with, a scheme for reconstruction for any company or companies, or the amalgamation of any two or more companies, but only if the schemes fall within three specified cases (s. 427A(1)).

Case 1: where the undertaking, property and liabilities of a public company are to be transferred to another public company, other than one formed for the purpose of, or in connection with, the scheme.

Case 2: where the undertaking, property and liabilities of each of two or more public companies concerned in the scheme, including the company in respect of which the compromise or arrangement in question is proposed, are to be transferred to a company (whether or not a public company) formed for the purpose of, or in connection with, the scheme.

Case 3: where the undertaking, property and liabilities of the company are to be divided among and transferred to two or more companies, each of which is either a public company or a company formed for the purposes of, or in connection with, the scheme.

If a merger or division falls into any of the three cases set out in s. 427A, then the court may not sanction a compromise or arrangement under s. 425 unless:

- a three-quarters majority of the shareholders of the transferee company agree (cf. s. 425); and

- directors' and experts' reports containing specified information, and relevant company accounts, have been made available to the shareholders (CA 1985, Sch. 15B, para. 1, 3).

The procedure contained in Sch. 15B must also be followed by the companies.

TAKEOVER OFFERS UNDER COMPANIES ACT 1985

¶80-300　General

A company which seeks to acquire all the shares of a target company whose shares are widely held will make an offer for that company's shares. However, the change in ownership may not meet with the approval of all the target company's shareholders. To prevent a dissentient minority from frustrating a takeover bid, the Companies Act gives a right to the offeror to buy out minority shareholders.

A takeover offer is an offer to acquire all the shares, or all the shares of any class or classes, in a company other than shares which at the date of the offer are already held by the offeror. The offer must be on terms which are the same in relation to all the shares of a class to which the offer relates (CA 1985, s. 428(1)). It may include shares which are subsequently allotted before a date determined in accordance with the terms of the offer as well as those which have been allotted on the date of the offer (CA 1985, s. 428(2)). The regime extends not only to shares but also to convertible loan stock and subscription rights, such as employee options.

In order to provide for more complex takeover offers, the provisions allow the compulsory acquisition of shares where the criteria are satisfied by joint offerors whose holdings are accumulated (CA 1985, s. 430D). Detailed provisions are also included for 'associates' (CA 1985, s. 430E). Shares acquired during the offer period other than pursuant to the offer for not more than the offer consideration (original or revised) are treated as acquired pursuant to the offer; otherwise they are excluded from the class to which the offer relates (CA 1985, s. 429(8)).

¶80-350　Compulsory acquisitions by offeror

A power is conferred for compulsory acquisitions of the shares of a minority not greater than ten per cent who do not accept a takeover offer for their class of shares by an offeror (CA 1985, s. 429).

If a takeover offer is accepted (by either transfer or agreement to transfer) by the holders of nine-tenths in value of the shares to which the offer relates, a power is conferred under s. 429 for the compulsory acquisition of the remainder. If the threshold is reached within four months of the offer, the offeror has a further two months to give notice to the dissentients that he wishes to acquire their shares (CA 1985, s. 429(3)). Once notice is given, the offeror company is entitled (and bound) to take the dissentients' shares on the same terms as those offered to other shareholders. If an offeror fails to make the nine-tenths threshold by reason only that the owners of some shares are untraceable, the court may, if just and necessary, authorise the offeror to issue notices compulsorily to acquire the dissentient shares (CA 1985, s. 430C(5)).

Application to the court

A dissentient can object to proposals by application to the court within six weeks of the notice. A court may then order that the offeror shall not be entitled and bound to acquire the shares, or it may specify terms of acquisition different from those of the offer (CA 1985, s. 430C). Although the statutory provisions were altered in 1987, there was an established body of case law which is unlikely to have lost its relevance. In particular, there is a heavy burden on the dissenter to show why a compulsory acquisition should not be approved (*Re Sussex Brick Co Ltd* [1961] Ch 289).

Effect of notice under s. 429

If the shareholders who have not accepted the offer do not apply to the court under s. 430C within the six-week period, the offeror must send a copy of the s. 429 notice to the offeree company, and pay or transfer to the company the consideration for the shares (CA 1985, s. 430(5)). Where the offer gave the holder of any shares a choice of consideration, the notice must give particulars of the choice and state that the holder of shares may elect within six weeks for the type of consideration, and must also state which consideration would be taken as applying if he does not make a choice (CA 1985, s. 430(3)). Where the chosen consideration is no longer available, then in certain circumstances an equivalent amount of cash must be paid (CA 1985, s. 430(4)). When the consideration is paid to the offeree company, it is owed to the shareholders who have not accepted the take-over offer, and the company accordingly holds the consideration on trust for those persons (CA 1985, s. 430(9)).

¶80-400   Compulsory acquisitions from offerees

If less than ten per cent of shareholders have not accepted a take-over offer for shares (or a class of shares), a shareholder may within the period for acceptance of the offer require the offeror to acquire those shares (CA 1985, s. 430A(1), (2)).

An offeror who has attained the threshold must within one month give any non-accepting shareholder notice of his rights to require the offeror to acquire his shares. The notice must allow at least three months for the exercise of these rights. If the option for the compulsory acquisition is not exercised within the three-month period, it lapses (CA 1985, s. 430A(4)). Where the offeror has already given notice for the compulsory acquisition of the shares under s. 429 of the *Companies Act* 1985 (see ¶80-350), notice need not be given by him of the shareholders' rights.

Effect of requirement under s. 430A

Similar rules relating to the choice of consideration apply to the right of a minority shareholder to be bought out by the offeror as to the compulsory acquisition of shares by the offeror (see ¶80-350) (CA 1985, s. 430B). The terms of the compulsory acquisition will be the terms of the offer, or such other terms as may be mutually agreed (CA 1985, s. 430B(2)). If either the shareholder or the offeror disagrees with the terms on which the offeror is entitled and bound to acquire the shares, either may apply to the court which can set the terms as it thinks fit (CA 1985, s. 430C(3)).

THE CITY CODE ON TAKEOVERS AND MERGERS

General . . . . ¶80-500   Scope of the City Code . . . . . ¶80-550

¶80-500   General

The City Code on Takeovers and Mergers ('the code') seeks to facilitate the acquisition of a target company's shares by takeover or merger before and after a bid is announced. It applies to all listed and unlisted public companies, and certain private companies which have had shares listed on the London Stock Exchange within the previous ten years, and which are resident in the UK or the Channel Isles; it also affords some protection for shareholders involved in the bid. The City Code on Takeovers and Mergers was last fully revised and reissued in December 1996; substantial amendments were made in July 1998. The Code is accompanied by the rules governing the 'substantial acquisition of shares'.

¶80-550   Scope of the City Code

The code sets out General Principles and is enforced by the Panel on Takeovers and Mergers ('the panel'). The panel is essentially a self-regulating body with a sophisticated administrative and appeals procedure. However, decisions of the panel are subject to judicial review (*R v Panel on Take-overs and Mergers, ex parte Datafin plc* [1987] QB 815; (1987) 3 BCC 10). The broad objectives of the code are:

- equality of treatment of shareholders in the target company by the offeror;
- equality and sufficiency of disclosure for all shareholders of the target company before and during the takeover;
- careful and responsible consideration of the terms of the offer by the offeror company;
- prevention of the creation of false markets;
- acceptance or rejection of the offer by shareholders of the target without interference of selfish advice by their board of directors; and
- proper organisation of persons acting in concert to ensure they can all fulfil their obligations under the offer.

The code provides detailed rules for the conduct of takeovers. The acquirer of 30 per cent of the shares of a company within the code must make an offer to all the holders of voting shares. The price at which the offer is to be made is the highest at which the target company's shares have been dealt in by the offeror within the 12 months preceding the acquisition of the 30 per cent stake. This rule recognises the fact that control of a company with a widely dispersed shareholding may be obtained with less than 50 per cent of the voting power.

The Substantial Acquisitions Rules are concerned with the speed of acquisition and disclosure requirements where shares (and rights over shares) are required which confer 15 per cent to 30 per cent of the voting power in a public company whose shares are dealt with on either the London Stock Exchange or the Alternative Investment Market. These rules are enforced by the Panel.

Essentially, acquisition of ten per cent of the voting rights of a company cannot be obtained in any seven-day period, if, as a consequence, the purchaser would hold more than 15 per cent but less than 30 per cent of the rights. There are exceptions to this basic rule.

MERGER CONTROL

¶80-650   General

Whereas the *Companies Act* 1985 controls the relationship between parties in a reconstruction or an amalgamation, the *Fair Trading Act* 1973 (FTA 1973) regulates the wider economic and political consequences of certain amalgamations. The underlying philosophy is to restrict the economic power of large business combinations if these will act 'against the public interest', and thereby to promote fairer competition. See further ¶80-700.

Since 1990, mergers having a 'Community dimension' have fallen within the exclusive jurisdiction of the European Commission under Council Regulation 4064/89 (OJ 1990 L257/13) ('the Merger Control Regulation'). Accordingly, subject to limited exceptions, a merger situation qualifying for investigation under the *Fair Trading Act* 1973 which also falls within the scope of the Merger Control Regulation is reviewable only by the European Commission's Merger Task Force. See further ¶80-900.

In the UK, the power for overt political control is contained in s. 11–13 of the *Industry Act* 1975. Under this Act, the Secretary of State may prohibit the transfer or acquisition of an undertaking if there is a serious and immediate probability that control of an 'important manufacturing undertaking' will pass to a person resident outside the UK and the transfer would be contrary to the national interest. However, this provision has never been used.

UK MERGER CONTROL

¶80-700   Definition of a merger

A 'merger' for the purposes of the *Fair Trading Act* 1973 is any form of transaction whereby two or more businesses, which previously carried on independently of one another, fall under some form of common ownership or common control. In general, only mergers:

- where the gross value of the assets taken over exceeds £70m, or

- which result in the merged businesses having a 25 per cent (or larger) share of goods or services of any description in the UK as a whole or a substantial part of the UK,

qualify for investigation. A special regime applies to mergers in the water industry. Under s. 32 of the *Water Industry Act* 1991 the Secretary of State has a duty to refer to the Competition Commission mergers or proposed mergers involving two or more 'water enterprises' when the gross value of the assets taken over exceeds £30m. Newspaper mergers falling within the special provisions of s. 57–62 of the *Fair Trading Act* can only be effected with the consent of the Secretary of State, normally after an investigation of its impact upon the public interest by the Competition Commission.

The Competition Commission replaced the Monopolies and Mergers Commission (MMC) on 1 April 1999. Section 45 of the *Competition Act* 1998 provided for the MMC to be dissolved and for its functions to be transferred to the Competition Commission. Qualifying mergers may only be referred to the Competition Commission by the Secretary of State for Trade and Industry; although the Secretary of State is advised by the Office of Fair Trading (OFT), he is not bound by its opinion.

A reference may be made in anticipation of a merger actually occurring, or within four months after it has taken place. Only a limited number of mergers are referred to the Competition Commission, and the Secretary of State retains a broad discretion in deciding whether or not to refer. Political considerations play their part, and different Secretaries of State have adopted different policies. At present this is limited primarily to competition grounds; however, references have been made for other 'public interest' reasons. The current administration has stated its intention of divesting itself of political discretion in merger cases.

¶80-725   Investigation and report

Once a reference is made, the Competition Commission must:

- determine whether the reference is within the scope of the *Fair Trading Act* 1973; and

- if satisfied that the reference is valid, investigate the circumstances and report whether the merger situation operates, or may be expected to operate, against the public interest (FTA 1973, s. 69).

Matters considered by the Competition Commission

The Competition Commission must take account of all relevant factors and must inter alia have regard to the need for:

(1) maintaining and promoting effective competition between persons supplying goods and services in the UK;

(2) promoting the interests of consumers, purchasers, and other users of goods and services in the UK in respect of prices, quality and variety;

(3) promoting through competition the reduction of costs and development and use of new techniques and new products, and of facilitating the entry of new competitors into the existing market;

(4) maintaining and promoting the balance of distribution of industry and employment in the UK; and

(5) maintaining and promoting competitive activity outside the UK on the part of producers of goods and suppliers of services in the UK (FTA 1973, s. 84).

¶80-750   Reports

A report must be made within four months (occasionally up to six months) to the Secretary of State who must consider it. The report is also sent to the OFT, and laid before Parliament. If the report concludes that there is nothing adverse to the public interest, then the merger will be allowed to proceed. If it concludes that there is something adverse, then the Secretary of State has some discretion. He may:

- allow the merger to proceed; or

- require the OFT to consult the parties concerned to obtain undertakings for the purpose of remedying defects outlined in the report (FTA 1973, s. 88); or

- prohibit the merger or unscramble one which has already taken place, or allow the merger to proceed with certain restrictions (FTA 1973, s. 73, Sch. 8).

Parties to merger references have challenged the former MMC's decisions in the courts by way of judicial review; however, all of these challenges have hitherto been unsuccessful (e.g. *R v Monopolies and Mergers Commission, ex parte Air Europe Ltd* (1988) 4 BCC 182).

¶80-775   Prior notification

Persons proposing a merger have always been able to contact the OFT for a confidential opinion on whether a proposed merger was likely to be referred; however, this obviously constituted an informal statement and could not bind the regulatory authorities.

Proposed mergers which may qualify for investigation may be officially notified on a voluntary basis to the OFT, provided that the proposed merger has been made public (FTA 1973, s. 75A–75F). Accordingly, where a proposed merger has not been made public, the procedure for voluntary notification is unavailable to the parties, but the system of confidential guidance continues to be available. The general rule is that, if the period for considering the notice expires without any reference being made to the Competition Commission, no such reference can be made (FTA 1973, s. 75A(3)). The Secretary of State, together with the OFT, has a period of 20 working days to consider a pre-notification of the merger (*Merger (Prenotification) Regulations* 1990 (SI 1990/501)). This runs from the first day after the merger notice and the fee payable to the OFT have been received. The period may also be extended by another 15 working days.

The OFT may reject a proposed merger notification if it appears that the arrangements are, or would result in, a concentration with a Community dimension such as would be subject to the Merger Control Regulation. A merger notification may also be rejected if materially false information has been given, or if information requested has not been provided or if it is suspected that there is no genuine intention to carry the notified arrangements into effect. Nor is a reference outside the time period prohibited if any material information, which was or ought to have been known to the person who gave the merger notice or any connected person, was not disclosed. If one of the parties merges with a third party before the notified merger takes place, or if the merger has not taken place within six months of the expiry of the period for considering the proposed merger, then the restrictions against a reference being made outside the time limits do not apply. The merger notice may also be withdrawn by the parties (FTA 1973, s. 75C), but this does not affect the Secretary of State's right to refer it to the Competition Commission.

¶80-800   Undertakings as alternative to merger reference

The role of 'undertakings' should be considered. While it is possible for the Secretary of State to require the OFT to obtain undertakings from parties after an adverse report of the Competition Commission (as outlined above), the *Companies Act* 1989 introduced the concept of an undertaking as an alternative to a merger reference. Accordingly, the Secretary of State may, in certain circumstances, obviate the need for a Competition Commission report and, in doing so, make for more speedy merger control. Such undertakings may be taken if the Secretary of State considers that they will remedy or prevent the adverse effect to the public interest which the OFT has outlined in its advice (FTA 1973, s. 75G).

Until 1995, the Secretary of State's powers were confined to structural actions, namely undertakings to effect the division, separation or sale of parts of the resulting entity or group. However, the *Deregulation and Contracting Out Act* 1994 extended the scope of the Secretary of State's powers to accept undertakings concerning the future behaviour of the merged entity. The DTI has indicated that divestments will continue to be favoured in most cases, unless the competition concerns raised by a particular merger are clear cut and capable of remedy by a behavioural undertaking.

Enforcement of undertakings, etc.

Undertakings are initially published in draft form and third parties are given a period to comment before the Secretary of State decides whether to accept the proposed undertakings in lieu of a reference. Once the undertakings are accepted, their implementation is subject to review, and any person may bring civil proceedings in respect of any failure, or apprehended failure, to comply with the undertakings (FTA 1973, s. 93A).

Undertakings may also be taken by the Competition Commission before it makes its report when deciding whether the merger situation is adverse to the 'public interest' (*R v Monopolies and Mergers Commission, ex parte Air Europe Ltd* (1988) 4 BCC 182).

¶80-825   Effect of merger reference

Once a reference has been made, a party to the reference or an associate of his are temporarily restricted from share dealing (FTA 1973, s. 75(4A)). Prior to the *Companies Act* 1989, the restriction was informally enforced by undertakings taken by the OFT from the parties; however, in the Elders IXL/Scottish & Newcastle Breweries reference, the informal process failed.

¶80-850   Time when enterprises cease to be distinct

In certain circumstances, the Secretary of State and the MMC may treat successive transactions leading to the control of an enterprise as having occurred simultaneously on the date on which the latest of them occurred for the purposes of a merger reference, provided that they have all occurred within a two-year period (FTA 1973, s. 66).

EU MERGER CONTROL

¶80-900   General

The EU merger control regime gives the European Commission the exclusive competence to regulate cross-border concentrations that have a so-called 'Community dimension' and that create or strengthen a dominant market position which would significantly impede competition in the common market.

The Community dimension is determined according to quantitative thresholds that have been fixed at sufficiently high levels (see below) to ensure that the Commission deals only with the very largest mergers and acquisitions. When Council Regulation 4064/89 (OJ 1990 L257/13) ('the Merger Control Regulation') was originally adopted it was recognised that these thresholds, based on levels of international and EU turnover, represented a political compromise between the national competition authorities of the larger member states on the one hand and the Commission on the other.

Since 1990, when the Merger Control Regulation took effect, the Commission has been seeking to extend its competence over cross-border mergers and acquisitions through lowering the thresholds for notification of concentrations. However, following the first review of the operation of the regulation, the Council of Ministers would not agree to the extent of the reduction in the thresholds sought by the Commission. Amendments introduced with effect from 1 March 1998 by Regulation 1310/97 (see below) continue the compromise between the Commission's desire to enhance the efficacy of 'one stop shop' merger control under the Merger Control Regulation and the role of the national competition authorities in controlling cross-border mergers. The operation of the thresholds set out below is to be reviewed by the Commission in a report to the Council before 1 July 2000.

Other changes dealing with procedural aspects of the regime were also introduced in Regulation 1310/97 to avoid the problems of multiple notifications at national level and to make notification to the Commission easier.

¶80-925   Concentrations

A concentration, as defined in the Merger Control Regulation, is deemed to arise where two or more previously independent undertakings merge, or where one or more undertakings acquire control (directly or indirectly) of the whole or part of another undertaking or undertakings. Control arises where it is possible to exercise 'decisive influence' on an undertaking. For the purposes of the Merger Control Regulation, the ability to exercise decisive influence may be exercised through the ownership of assets, voting or other rights, contracts 'or any other means'. Accordingly, the acquisition of a minority interest may give rise to the acquisition of control as for example where the holder of the interest can exercise a power of veto.

In 1998 the Commission adopted interpretative notices on the notions of concentration and participating undertaking.

The scope of the Merger Control Regulation was extended by Regulation 1310/97 to cover all full-function joint ventures (i.e. long-term economically independent undertakings) having a Community dimension. The Commission's interpretative notice on full-function joint ventures identifies the criteria used by the Commission in determining if joint ventures fall within the scope of the regulation.

¶80-950   Community dimension

Concentrations with a Community dimension are mergers, acquisitions or certain types of joint ventures in which:

(1) the combined aggregate world-wide turnover of all the companies involved exceeds ECU 5 billion (approximately £4.1 billion): for banks and insurance companies the threshold is based on one tenth of the companies' total assets; and

(2) the aggregate Community-wide turnover of at least two of the companies involved exceeds ECU 250m (approximately £209m); provided that

(3) each of the companies involved does not realise more than two thirds of its aggregate Community turnover within one and the same member state.

The first threshold of world-wide turnover is intended to limit Community competence to companies with considerable aggregate economic and financial powers. The second threshold aims at ensuring that only undertakings with a significant level of activity in the Community are covered and the third threshold is designed to exclude operations which occur primarily in a single member state.

As a result of amendments introduced by Regulation 1310/97 with effect from 1 March 1998, concentrations which do not meet the above criteria will still have a Community dimension, and hence will be notifiable, if:

(1) the combined aggregate worldwide turnover of all the undertakings concerned is more than ECU 2.5 billion;

(2) in each of at least three member states the combined aggregate turnover of all the undertakings concerned is more than ECU 100m and in each of those states the aggregate turnover of at least two of the undertakings concerned is more than ECU 25m; and

(3) the aggregate Community-wide turnover of at least two of the undertakings is more than ECU 100m.

As with the main thresholds, these thresholds will apply only if at least one of the undertakings concerned achieves more than one-third of its aggregate Community-wide turnover outside one member state.

¶80-975   Jurisdiction: the 'one stop shop' principle

Where a Community dimension exists, the Commission or the Merger Task Force will have exclusive jurisdiction to assess the merger. This is the 'one stop shop' principle and the parties to the merger need not approach the national competition authorities in the member states that may otherwise have been affected by the merger. Given that there are now 11 differing sets of merger control throughout the 15 member states of the EU, this one stop shop is a very considerable benefit in cross-border mergers. By contrast, concentrations which do not have a Community dimension are subject only to individual member state control, and clearance may have to be obtained from a wide number of national competition authorities with different régimes in different member states.

¶81-000   Powers of member states

The jurisdictional allocation is complemented by the provisions of art. 9 and 22 of the regulation. Article 9 enables the European Commission, at the request of a member state, to refer cases back to a member state which raise competition issues limited to a distinct market within that territory. The UK has successfully invoked this provision on several occasions including in relation to mergers affecting the cement and pharmaceutical wholesaling industries. Article 22 ('the Dutch clause') allows a member state to request the Commission to apply the Merger Control Regulation to concentrations below the thresholds which create or strengthen dominance within that member state's territory.

In addition, art. 21 allows member states to take appropriate measures to protect legitimate interests (public security, plurality of the media, prudential rules and 'any other public interest') which are not taken into consideration in the Commission's assessment. Unlike the exceptions in art. 9 and 22, a successful application under art. 21 does not affect the Commission's own review, but allows parallel action to be taken by a member state. For example, a bid by a French water company to buy a UK counterpart was examined by the former MMC in parallel with the Commission's investigation due to the special regulatory regime for mergers between water companies in the UK. However, the former MMC's investigation was restricted to the regulatory issues raised by the merger.

¶81-025   Notification

The Merger Control Regulation sets up a system of mandatory prior notification for all concentrations with a Community dimension. Notifying parties must fill out the Form CO, the Commission's standard questionnaire, and submit it to the Commission within one week after the conclusion of the agreement, the announcement of a public bid or the acquisition of a controlling interest, whichever is the earlier. Substantial penalties may be imposed for failure to notify a concentration, or for the provision of incorrect, incomplete or misleading information in the Form CO itself or upon request for further information. However, there is provision for certain information requested by Form CO to be dispensed with where the Commission considers that such information is not necessary for the examination of the case.

¶81-050   Timetable

There are two phases of examination the duration of which is determined by legal deadlines. After an initial one-month phase, the Competition Commissioner must decide whether the concentration falls within the scope of the Merger Control Regulation, and if so whether or not the case raises serious doubts as to its compatibility with the common market. Where the Commission finds that the concentration does raise serious doubts as to its compatibility with the common market, it must initiate an in-depth investigation. Four months after such initiation, the whole Commission must take the final decision on the concentration. The periods of examination commence on the first working day after the effective date of notification, or in the case of second-phase proceedings on the date on which proceedings are initiated.

¶81-075   Appraisal of concentrations

Notified concentrations are assessed from the point of view of their effect on the structure of competition in the common market. The fundamental concept is whether the merger would create a 'dominant position' – the creation or strengthening of such a position will be declared incompatible with the common market if it significantly impedes effective competition (whether in the EC as a whole or in a substantial part thereof). Dominance is measured by reference to the relevant product and geographic markets which are affected by the concentration. Affected markets are defined as those in which the parties have either horizontal or vertical overlapping activities and in which, as a result of the concentration, market shares of 15 per cent (for horizontal overlaps) and 25 per cent (for vertical overlaps) would be attained. Such markets will be subject to more detailed examination by the Commission in determining whether the concentration will create or strengthen a dominant position in any or all of them. However, in practice, as stated in the Form CO, the Commission is unlikely to find dominance in markets where combined market shares are below 25 per cent.

The appraisal process takes into account various aspects of competition, including the structure of the markets concerned, actual and potential competition (both inside and outside the Community), the market position of the parties, freedom of choice for third parties, barriers to entry, the interest of consumers, and technical and economic progress. Accordingly, the Commission will never condemn a concentration on the basis of high market shares alone; and equally it has cleared mergers despite the existence of very high post-merger market shares.

¶81-100   Suspension

The concentration may not be effected before it has been notified and its implementation is suspended until the Commission takes a final decision. However, the parties can apply at any time for the suspension requirement to be lifted. In deciding whether to lift the suspension, the Commission will consider its impact on the undertakings involved or upon third parties, and the threat to competition posed by the concentration.

¶81-125   Undertakings

It has been the Commission's practice to accept commitments in the first phase of its investigation to avoid the initiation of second-phase proceedings in cases where the competition concern is clear-cut and limited compared with the whole deal and can easily be remedied, and where compliance is easily monitored.

Regulation 1310/97 now gives the Commission power to use formal undertakings where appropriate. The Commission is given express powers under the Merger Control Regulation to negotiate and enforce undertakings in second-phase proceedings, which must be submitted to the Commission not more than three months after the date on which proceedings were initiated. Undertakings are usually structural in nature, as in the divestiture of assets or shares, the termination of capital, personal or contractual links between competitors, or the cancellation of exclusive distribution contracts. Less commonly the Commission will accept behavioural commitments by the parties to the concentration. The Commission's authorisation of the concentration is based on the fulfilment of these commitments.

¶81-150   Decisions

Where a concentration is declared incompatible with the common market the parties are prohibited from implementing the concentration at the risk of substantial fines. Where a concentration has already been implemented, the Commission may require divestiture or other appropriate remedial action. If the Commission considers that a concentration would, if modified, fulfil the criteria for compatibility, the decision declaring the concentration compatible may be accompanied by conditions to ensure that the agreed modifications are implemented.

¶81-175   Review by the European Court of Justice

Decisions of the Commission under the Merger Control Regulation that have binding legal effects can be appealed to the Court of First Instance of the European

Communities, attached to the European Court of Justice. Thus decisions to declare a concentration compatible or incompatible, to apply conditions to a declaration of compatibility, to extend the suspension period, or to impose penalties or fines are all capable of review by the court. By contrast, interim steps such as a decision to institute second-phase proceedings cannot be attacked in this way.

MANAGEMENT BUY-OUTS AND BUY-INS

¶81-300   General

A management buy-out involves the purchase of the whole or a part of an enterprise by employees of that enterprise. The relaxation of the rules on financial assistance for share purchases introduced by the *Companies Act* 1981 (see ¶52-025) have assisted in the organisation of management buy-outs.

The machinery for effecting a demerger of a company under the Companies Act is of obvious significance for such buy-outs. Tax exemptions for the reconstruction, and reliefs for persons who have invested money in the purchase, have helped ease the financial burden of buy-outs.

¶81-350   Events affording opportunities for management buy-outs

It is possible to identify particular events which have afforded opportunities for management buy-outs. These are rationalisations of corporate structure, purchase from a liquidator or receiver, the sale of a privately owned business and business start-ups.

In particular, the concept has evolved that, by selling to management, various advantages could be obtained for a vendor group. First, the individuals concerned would know the business intimately with the result that they might find it relatively easy to obtain financial backers ready to support an experienced team. Secondly, as individuals fully acquainted with the business in question, they would be better able to assess the prospects of that business and therefore more likely to pay a fuller price to acquire the business than would an entrepreneur wishing to acquire a division in a 'forced sale' by a conglomerate.

¶81-400   Management buy-ins, leveraged buy-outs, etc.

The term 'management buy-out' is used to describe a transaction whereby a new company, established by the management of an existing company or business, raises equity and debt finance and then acquires a company or business in which the management were formerly employed.

A 'management buy-in' is the same transaction, but it is a different management team which forms the new company. Quite frequently, there will be members of both existing and new management in the management team, and so the elements of both a management buy-out and buy-in are present.

A 'leveraged buy-out' describes a situation where the new company is not necessarily established by management, and is financed largely by debt which is serviced out of cash flow generated by the acquired company or business. Usually, if only to ensure motivation of key management, management will be involved in a leveraged buy-out. However, whether one is dealing with a management buy-out or leveraged buy-out, the values involved are usually such that management does not end up having a majority stake.

¶81-450   The ratchet

The problem in a management buy-out is to ensure that there is an equitable division of any rewards that are finally made, and in particular to try to obtain for institutional investors a good rate of return on their investment and to ensure that, assuming that they are rapidly paid off, the management receives a fair and growing share of the cake. The mechanism by which this is achieved is often referred to as 'the ratchet' when, contingent upon attaining certain targets, the number of equity shares to which the management become entitled is increased or, if targets are missed, decreased (see generally ¶50-250).

¶81-500   Conflicts of interest

A particular pitfall in the case of a public company which is being taken over by its management is that of conflict of interest. The management have fiduciary duties to their existing employers and, if they are directors, may have duties towards the existing body of shareholders; and there is an assumption that, if somebody is prepared to buy out a company, he must believe that, by exercising his skills, he can make the business more valuable. Where he is already a member of the management team, the question of why he is not already exercising his utmost abilities in this direction may be asked. This may be too simplistic an analysis of the situation, but it is important to recognise the potential for conflicts and the need so far as possible to reconcile these duties and responsibilities.

INSOLVENCY

Table of Contents

continued over

continued over

RECEIVERSHIP

¶90-000   General

A receiver is appointed to safeguard the interests of debenture holders (see ¶52-800ff.), in enforcing the security for their loan. The appointment of a receiver is only one of the remedies available to the debenture holders, who also have recourse to avenues of recovery open to creditors generally. It is often necessary to consult the debenture deed to establish whether a receiver can be appointed and, if he has been appointed, the powers that he actually has. Receivers may also be appointed by the court. The *Insolvency Act* 1986 has also introduced a codification of the appointment and powers of a receiver under a floating charge or by a floating charge and other securities (an 'administrative' receiver).

The registrar of companies must be informed of the appointment of a receiver within seven days. The registrar records the appointment in the register of charges (CA 1985, s. 405). Further,

'every invoice, order for goods or business letter issued by or on behalf of the company ... being a document on or in which company's name appears, shall contain a statement that a receiver or manager has been appointed' (IA 1986, s. 39).

Default exposes the company and its officers to a fine.

¶90-050   The office of receiver

The nature of office depends on the type of receivership that arises. Receivers may either be appointed by the court, or under statutory powers (in particular those granted by the *Law of Property Act* 1925) or under the *Insolvency Act* 1986 (i.e. as an administrative receiver: see generally ¶90-350).

No formal qualification is required of company receivers. However, bodies corporate and undischarged bankrupts are liable to a fine (and also imprisonment in the latter case) if they act in the capacity of a receiver of a company (IA 1986, s. 30, 31), and their appointment is void.

An administrative receiver must qualify as an 'insolvency practitioner' under the *Insolvency Act* 1986. This requires the administrative receiver to be authorised as such by a recognised professional body or the Secretary of State (IA 1986, s. 388(1), 390(2)).

An administrative receiver must give a bond in the form of a security for the performance of his functions, the security to meet prescribed requirements in relation to the company involved. He is not qualified to act unless this is done (IA 1986, s. 390(3)).

A person is also not qualified to act as an administrative receiver if, at the time of taking office, he has been adjudged bankrupt (or, in Scotland, a sequestration of his estate has been awarded) and he has not been discharged, or if he is subject to a disqualification order made under the *Company Directors Disqualification Act 1986* ('CDDA 1986'), or if he is a mental patient (IA 1986, s. 390(4)). The role of administrative receivers is considered further below. If a disqualification order is made against a person by the court, he cannot be a receiver or manager of a company's property without leave of the court (CDDA 1986, s. 1).

The appointment of a person as the receiver or manager of a company's property under a debenture is ineffective unless accepted by him before the end of the next business day following receipt of notice of his appointment, and is deemed to occur at the time the instrument of appointment is received by him (IA 1986, s. 33). Once a receiver is validly appointed, it is his duty to deal with the company's assets in accordance with the terms of the debenture (see further ¶90-150). Whether the company is insolvent or not, the receiver's primary objective will be to protect the debenture holder's interest.

¶90-100   Appointment by the court

If the assets upon which a loan is secured are put at risk, the debenture holders may apply to the court for the appointment of a receiver. This is under s. 37(1) of the *Supreme Court Act* 1981, whereby the court may make an appointment if it is just and convenient to do so.

The shareholders may also apply to the court for appointment of a receiver if the company's assets are jeopardised: for example, as a consequence of a deadlock in the management or of a refusal by the directors to act (*Trade Auxiliary Co v Vickers* (1873) LR 16 Eq 303). It is also possible that the court will agree to the appointment of a receiver in the course of an action by shareholders for relief against unfairly prejudicial conduct (see ¶62-550ff.) (*Re a Company No. 00596 of 1986* (1986) 2 BCC 99,063).

Once the receiver is appointed, the company loses all power to trade other than at his direction.

Appointment of a receiver will be granted by the court on the application of the debenture holders if repayment of the principal or payments of interest fall into arrears.

The court will also appoint a receiver if the charge crystallises on a winding-up resolution or a winding-up order, or if the assets secured by the charge are placed in jeopardy.

Once appointed, the receiver is an officer of the court, and must comply with the terms of his appointment. Appointment of a receiver does not terminate the company's existing contracts. However, he may be entitled to repudiate those contracts made prior to his appointment where damages would be an adequate remedy. The company may then become exposed to a claim for damages.

The receiver has a discretion to continue existing contracts, and will not incur personal liability on such contracts. However, he will be liable on any new contracts he makes for the company, though he may be indemnified in respect of liabilities incurred on such contracts out of the company's assets. The remuneration for his services can be taken out of the proceeds realised from sales of assets under his charge.

An application can additionally be made to the court to appoint a receiver in order to enforce a judgment of the court (see the *Civil Procedure Rules* 1998 (SI 1998/3132) r. 50 and Sch. 1, O. 51, re-enacting the *Rules of the Supreme Court* 1965 (SI 1965/1776), O. 51). In deciding whether to grant such an application, the court should consider the amount claimed by the judgment creditor, what reasonable amount the receiver may obtain and the costs that would be incurred by the receiver's appointment.

A court-appointed receiver's remuneration is authorised by the court and may be fixed by reference to professional scales or rates or assessed by a costs judge (previously a taxing master) (*Civil Procedure Rules* 1998 (SI 1998/3132) r. 50 and Sch. 1, O. 30, r. 3, re-enacting *Rules of the Supreme Court* 1965 (SI 1965/1776), O. 30, r. 3). The difficulties facing the court in this process were high-lighted in *Mirror Group Newspapers plc v Maxwell* [1998] BCC 324 where Ferris J referred the matter of assessing the remuneration of the receivers of the very complex estate of the late entrepreneur Robert Maxwell to a taxing master. The interesting assessment of the Chief Taxing Master is reported at [1999] BCC 684.

It is unusual for the appointment of a receiver of a company's assets to be made by application to the court. This is because any relatively modern debenture deed will itself provide for the appointment of a receiver by the debenture holders in all the circumstances upon which a successful application to the court could be made.

¶90-150 Appointment by debenture holders

Appointment of a receiver by debenture holders is regulated by the terms of the debenture deed. The relationship between the receiver and the company will also have to be ascertained from the terms of the deed. If the deed does not identify the receiver as the agent of the company, he will be the agent of the debenture holders by whom he was appointed (*Re Vimbos Ltd* [1900] 1 Ch 470). The debenture deed will usually identify the receiver as the agent of the company. However, this agency is unorthodox as the company is unable to dismiss or instruct the agent, and the agent may be personally liable for contracts made after his appointment.

Powers of receivers

The powers of the receiver are similarly determined by the debenture deed. These powers are usually set out in some detail. However, various powers will also be implied, if incidental to the receiver's ability to realise the assets charged and return the proceeds to the debenture holders. The power to take control of the assets must be implied into the terms of any receivership. If the receiver is granted a power to carry on the business this will widen the scope of the implied powers. A receiver appointed by debenture holders may repudiate contracts of the company concluded prior to his appointment provided that this is in line with the terms and objectives of his appointment (*Airlines Airspares Ltd v Handley Page Ltd* [1970] Ch 193). Expenses incurred by the receiver in carrying on the company's business may be taken out of the property over which the charge was given. This right will take precedence over those of the debenture holders.

Validity of appointment

It is necessary for a receiver to satisfy himself that he is validly appointed. He must ensure that all conditions precedent to his appointment are fulfilled and the persons by whom he was appointed had the authority to do so. The receiver must further establish whether the appointment could be invalidated due to defective drafting in the debenture deed, or because of a failure to comply with the stipulated procedure (e.g. an insufficient number of debenture holders have agreed to the appointment). The receiver must also ensure that he has complied with the rules as to acceptance of appointment (before the end of the business day next following that on which the instrument of appointment is received by him (IA 1986, s. 33)).

Failure to accept office renders the appointment invalid. An invalid appointment could jeopardise the validity of contracts made on the company's behalf and also preclude access to the courts for applications on the company's behalf. However, the acts of an administrative receiver are valid despite any defect in his appointment (IA 1986, s. 232). This provision does not cover other receivers (e.g. those appointed by the court).

It will also be necessary for the receiver to ensure that the charge under which he was appointed is validly registered (see ¶53-300ff.). If this is not the case, a liquidator subsequently appointed may call for the assets of the company in the receiver's hands.

Application for directions

If a receiver is in any doubt as to the scope of his powers in a trust deed, he may apply to the court for directions. The authorities provide that applications to the court cannot be made to establish the validity of the appointment, but only to determine issues for a validly-appointed receiver.

¶90-200   The receiver and directors

Appointment is effective as from the time it is received by the receiver, provided that he accepts the appointment before the end of the next business day (see ¶90-150).

The appointment of a receiver may supersede the directors' powers to manage the business. Whether this is the case will depend upon the terms of the receiver's appointment. If the terms of the appointment are as receiver and manager this will usurp the directors from their control of the company. However, such an appointment does not eliminate the need for directors to fulfil their statutory duties, such as the preparation of accounts (*Smiths Ltd v Middleton* [1979] 3 All ER 842).

A more limited appointment will confer less power upon the receiver to take on the directors' role. A receiver appointed by the court (see ¶90-100) does not obtain management powers. However, an appointment under a debenture (see ¶90-150) may confer such powers.

The division of powers between the directors and the receiver can never be such as to enable the directors to jeopardise the assets which are the basis of the debenture holders' security. However, within this parameter, they are afforded the power to pursue claims in the interests of other creditors so far as such claims do not jeopardise the interests of the debenture holders. (*Newhart Developments Ltd v Co-operative Commercial Bank Ltd* [1978] QB 814).

DUTIES OF A RECEIVER

¶90-250   General

The principal duties of a receiver are to fulfil his obligations under the debenture deed. Beyond this, the duties can be divided into statutory (see ¶90-275) and non-statutory (see ¶90-300).

¶90-275   Statutory duties

A duty to inform the registrar of companies of a receiver's appointment is imposed on the person who is responsible for the appointment of the receiver (CA 1985, s. 405(1)). The appointment will then be recorded in the register of charges. The receiver himself is responsible for notifying the registrar when he ceases to act. The registrar will then enter this fact in the register of charges (CA 1985, s. 405(2)). The receiver (unless an administrative receiver) must lodge abstracts of receipts and payments with the registrar every six months. The final abstract must disclose the totals of receipts and payments since the date of appointment (IA 1986, s. 38).

A receiver must disclose the fact of his appointment on every invoice, order for goods or business letter issued by or on behalf of the company (IA 1986, s. 39).

¶90-300   Non-statutory duties

A receiver owes a general duty to both the debenture holders by whom he is appointed (*Standard Chartered Bank v Walker* [1982] 1 WLR 1410) and to the company (*Re B Johnson & Co (Builders) Ltd* [1955] Ch 634).

Whether a receiver owes a duty of care in negligence is unclear. In *Knight v Lawrence* [1991] BCC 411 the court concluded that the receiver owed a duty of care to the borrowers under the debenture. Failure by the receiver to issue certain rent-review notices for properties subject to the debenture resulted in the borrowers incurring foreseeable loss. That in turn constituted a breach of the duty owed. In *Downsview Nominees Ltd v First City Corporation Ltd* [1993] AC 295; [1993] BCC 46 the Privy Council held that no general duty of care was owed by a receiver to the mortgagor when dealing with the company's assets. Despite this the court did impose on the receiver a more general duty to act in 'good faith', imposed by equity, when dealing with the company's assets. That duty was extended by the Court of Appeal to include an equitable duty to take reasonable care and act with due diligence which went beyond a duty of good faith. The equitable duty applied to receivers as well as mortgagees and applied to the conduct of the mortagor's business as well as to exercise of the power of sale (*Medforth v Blake* [1999] BCC 771). However in *AIB Finance Ltd v Alsop* [1998] BCC 780 the Court of Appeal considered that a duty to maintain goodwill only arises when a mortgagee takes possession or, as in this case, when the bank became entitled to take possession.

A receiver must therefore use the powers granted to him in good faith to fulfil his obligations under the trust deed, and is accountable for his conduct of the receivership.

Specific duties can be identified in relation to the exercise of the power of sale. The receiver must act in good faith (*Kennedy v De Trafford* [1897] AC 180). The need to exercise such a standard of care with which a reasonable man would behave in the realisation of his own property can be imported into the duties of a receiver from the correlative duties imposed upon mortgagees in the exercise of their power of sale (*Cuckmere Brick Co Ltd v Mutual Finance Ltd* [1971] Ch 949).

Notwithstanding the receiver's general duties, documents generated during the receivership are owned according to the purpose for which they were created. The fact that they relate to the company's affairs is immaterial (*Gomba Holdings UK Ltd v Minories Finance Ltd* [1988] 1 WLR 1231; (1989) 5 BCC 27).

ADMINISTRATIVE RECEIVERS

¶90-350   General

The *Insolvency Act* 1986 sought to set out the powers and obligations of receivers and managers appointed under floating charges, and to impose additional duties upon such receivers to keep unsecured creditors informed as to the progress and likely outcome of receiverships.

¶90-350

Definition

The Act identifies 'administrative receivers' as:

(1) a receiver or manager of the whole (or substantially the whole) of a company's property appointed by or on behalf of the holders of any debentures of the company secured by a charge which, as created, was a floating charge, or by such a charge and one or more other securities; or

(2) a person who would be such a receiver or manager but for the appointment of some other person as the receiver of part of the company's property (IA 1986, s. 29(2)).

¶90-375 Appointment, etc. of administrative receivers

On the appointment of an administrative receiver, a notice must be sent to the company and to the company's creditors (IA 1986, s. 46(1)).

Statement of affairs

A statement of affairs must be submitted to the receiver by some or all of the following persons (IA 1986, s. 47(3)):

(1) company officers;

(2) any persons involved in the company's formation during a period of one year preceding the date of appointment of the receiver;

(3) company employees who, in the opinion of the receiver, are able to provide the required information; and

(4) any officers or employees of a company which is itself an officer of the company to which an administrative receiver has been appointed.

The contents of the statement of affairs are prescribed by s. 47(2) of the *Insolvency Act* 1986.

Report by administrative receiver

Within three months of his appointment the administrative receiver must submit a report to the registrar, to any trustees for secured creditors and to the secured creditors themselves. A copy of the report must also go to all unsecured creditors. The administrative receiver's report is to set out (IA 1986, s. 48):

● the events leading up to his appointment;

● actual or proposed disposals of the company's property and actual or proposed carrying on of business by him;

● amounts of principal and interest due to debenture holders by whom he was appointed; and

● the likely surplus available for other creditors.

Committee of creditors, etc.

A facility for creditors' meetings is then provided, with a power for creditors to establish a committee to which the administrative receiver must provide all information in respect of the carrying out of his duties as may be reasonably required (IA 1986, s. 49).

As the administrative receiver is taking over the company's assets in order to secure the best interests of the debenture holders, he may decide that the most satisfactory course of action is continuation of the company's business. Appointment of the administrative receiver will suspend the powers of the directors. However, the administrative receiver may enter new contracts, borrow fresh money and attempt to revitalise the business.

¶90-400   Powers of administrative receivers

The powers conferred upon administrative receivers in the debenture are deemed to include those set out in Sch. 1 to the *Insolvency Act* 1986, except in so far as these are inconsistent with the express terms of the debenture (IA 1986, s. 42). These powers are:

- to take possession of, collect and get in the company's property and, for that purpose, to take such proceedings as may seem to him expedient;
- to sell or otherwise dispose of the company's property by public auction or private contract (or, in Scotland, to sell, feu, hire out or otherwise dispose of the company's property by public roup or private bargain);
- to raise or borrow money and grant security therefor over the company's property;
- to appoint a solicitor or accountant or other professionally qualified person to assist him in the performance of his functions;
- to bring or defend any action or other legal proceedings in the name and on behalf of the company;
- to refer to arbitration any question affecting the company;
- to effect and maintain insurances in respect of the company's business and property;
- to use the company's seal;
- to do all acts and to execute in the name and on behalf of the company any deed, receipt or other document;
- to draw, accept, make and endorse any bill of exchange or promissory note in the name and on behalf of the company;
- to appoint any agent to do any business which he is unable to do himself or which can more conveniently be done by an agent and power to employ and dismiss employees;

- to do all such things (including the carrying out of works) as may be necessary for the realisation of the company's property;
- to make any payment which is necessary or incidental to the performance of his functions;
- to carry on the company's business;
- to establish subsidiaries of the company;
- to transfer to subsidiaries of the company the whole or any part of the company's business and property;
- to grant or accept a surrender of a lease or tenancy of any of the company's property, and to take a lease or tenancy of any property required or convenient for the company's business;
- to make any arrangement or compromise on the company's behalf;
- to call up any uncalled capital of the company;
- to rank and claim in the bankruptcy, insolvency, sequestration or liquidation of any person indebted to the company and to receive dividends, and to accede to trust deeds for the creditors of any such person;
- to present or defend a petition for the company's winding up;
- to change the situation of the company's registered office; and
- to do all other things incidental to the exercise of the foregoing powers.

The above powers may be amplified by the debenture (IA 1986, s. 42(1)). A person dealing with an administrative receiver in good faith and for value does not have to enquire as to whether the latter is acting within his powers.

Power to dispose of charged property, etc.

The court can authorise disposal of property by an administrative receiver, despite the existence of a fixed charge or security over that property, if satisfied that the sale is likely to promote a more advantageous realisation of the company's assets than would otherwise occur (IA 1986, s. 43). However, the sums so realised must be applied first towards discharge of the charge. This does not include the charge in respect of which the administrative receiver was appointed, or any security which ranks behind the same.

¶90-425 Status of administrative receiver

An administrative receiver is deemed the company's agent and is personally liable on contracts he enters into in carrying out his functions, subject to an indemnity from the company's assets (IA 1986, s. 44). An administrative receiver will also be liable for any sum payable on any employment contract adopted by him, provided that:

- the liability is a sum by way of wages, salary, or payment into an occupational pension scheme;

- the amounts are incurred whilst the administrative receiver is in office; and

- the sums relate to services performed after the administrative receiver has taken up office (IA 1986, s. 44(2A)).

The statutory indemnity does not extend to acts of the receiver outside the scope of his authority.

An administrative receiver can be removed from office by court order (but not otherwise), or may resign. On termination of his office, he must inform the registrar of companies within 14 days (IA 1986, s. 45).

An administrative receiver has a duty to report misconduct of directors which may result in a disqualification order being made (CDDA 1986, s. 7).

VOLUNTARY ARRANGEMENTS

¶90-650   The proposal

A procedure is contained in s. 1–7 (Pt. I) of the *Insolvency Act* 1986 by which a company may agree to a composition in satisfaction of its debts or a scheme of arrangement of its affairs. This is termed a 'voluntary arrangement'. The purpose of a voluntary arrangement is to allow the company to work its way out of financial difficulties.

The function of the voluntary arrangement is comparable with the compromise and arrangement measures in s. 425–427 of the *Companies Act* 1985 (see ¶80-150). Under the latter provisions, the company transfers its business and assets to a new company, shares in the transferee company are issued to the members of the transferor company and the new company accepts responsibility for the old company's debts. Under the voluntary arrangement, the company assigns its assets to the supervisor who looks after creditors' rights.

The proposal must provide for the appointment of a qualified insolvency practitioner ('the nominee') who may act as trustee or supervisor in the scheme of arrangement. The proposal may be made by the directors of a company, provided that no administration order is in force (see ¶91-000ff.) and that the company is not being wound up. The liquidator of a company in liquidation, or the administrator of a company for which an administration order has been made, may also propose a voluntary arrangement.

Where the nominee is not the company's liquidator or administrator, he must submit a report to the court within 28 days of notification to him of the proposal (IA 1986, s. 2(2)). The report must state whether, in nominee's opinion, meetings of the company's members and creditors should be called at which the proposals could be considered.

'Creditors of the company' is defined as 'every creditor of the company of whose claim and address the person summoning the meeting is aware' (IA 1986, s. 3(3)). If, in the opinion of the nominee, such meetings should take place (i.e. the proposals are worthwhile), the report submitted to the court should specify the date, time and place proposed. The nominee will then summon the meeting, unless the court directs to the contrary (s. 3(1)). A duty is placed upon the proposer of the voluntary arrangement to supply to the nominee a document which sets out the terms of the proposed voluntary arrangement and a statement of the company's affairs (s. 2(3)).

If the nominee is the company's liquidator or administrator, he is under a duty to summon meetings of the company and its creditors at which the proposal may be considered (IA 1986, s. 3(2)).

¶90-700 Consideration and implementation of proposal

The meeting called under s. 3 of the *Insolvency Act* 1986 (see ¶90-650) may decide to modify the proposals (s. 4(2)). The modification may be to replace the nominee, but cannot alter the proposal so as to take it outside a composition in satisfaction of debts or a scheme or arrangement supervised by a nominee (s. 4(2)). Such modifications as are made must be approved by both creditors and members (s. 5(1)). The proposals will be voted upon at the meetings.

Limitations on proposals and modifications

A proposal or modification which affects the rights of any secured creditor to enforce his security cannot be adopted without the prior approval of that creditor (IA 1986, s. 4(3)). The meeting cannot approve any proposal or modification by which a preferential debt is to lose its priority, or suffer a greater abatement than other preferential debts, without the prior approval of the preferential creditor concerned (s. 4(4)).

Report to the court, etc.

The result of the meeting is reported to the court and also to such persons as may be prescribed (IA 1986, s. 4(6)).

Effect of approval

If the proposals are approved at the meetings, the composition or scheme takes effect as if made by the company at the creditors' meeting, and binds every person who had notice of the meeting, and was entitled to vote (IA 1986, s. 5(2)). The binding effect of an individual voluntary arrangement (IVA) has been considered by the Court of Appeal. The appeal was against an order determining that the effect of an IVA was not such as to release solvent co-debtors of the debtor in the IVA under the rule that the release of one of two or more joint debtors had the effect of releasing the other. The appeal was dismissed on the grounds that the words of release in the IVA would not take effect until the individuals' obligations under the IVA had been fulfilled. This would also apply to company voluntary arrangements (*Johnson v Davies* [1999] BCC 275). Once the proposal is approved, the court may stay proceedings in any winding up, discharge an administration order or make such orders as it thinks fit to assist in implementation of the scheme or arrangement (s. 5(3)). However, such orders cannot be made within 28 days of the report of the result of the meetings to the court (s. 5(4)).

Challenge of decisions

There is a facility for challenging the vote at these meetings, on the grounds that the voluntary arrangement unfairly prejudices the interests of a creditor, member or 'contributory' (see ¶91-700) of the company, or that there has been a material irregularity at, or in relation to, the meetings. The challenge may be made by (IA 1986, s. 6(2)):

(1) any person entitled to vote at the meetings;

(2) the nominee (or any person who has replaced him); or

(3) the liquidator or administrator or the company, if appropriate.

The application must be made within 28 days of the report of the result of the meetings to the court (IA 1986, s. 6(3)). If an application has been made, the court cannot order a stay of proceedings in a winding up or discharge an administration order under s. 5(3) above (IA 1986, s. 5(4)).

Powers of court, etc.

The court is empowered to revoke or suspend the decision taken by the meetings, and direct further meetings to consider any revised proposals which the original proposer may make. The court may also make such supplemental directions as it considers appropriate (IA 1986, s. 6(4)).

Effect of irregularity

Apart from the facility for objection provided by s. 6 of the *Insolvency Act* 1986 above, approval of a voluntary arrangement at meetings of members and creditors cannot be invalidated on the ground of procedural irregularity (IA 1986, s. 6(7)).

Supervisor of composition or scheme

If the proposals put before the meetings are accepted and not successfully challenged, the nominee will become the supervisor of the composition or scheme (IA 1986, s. 7(2)). The supervisor can apply to the court for directions on any matter arising under the voluntary arrangements. An application to the court for the winding up or the making of an administration order may also come from the supervisor (s. 7(4)).

Application to court

Creditors of the company or any person dissatisfied with any act, omission or decision of a supervisor may apply to the court to have this act, omission or decision reversed or modified. The court may uphold or reverse the act of the supervisor, or make such other order as it thinks fit (IA 1986, s. 7(3)).

Variations of CVAs

There is no provision in the *Insolvency Act* 1986 for the variation of a CVA (or an individual voluntary arrangement). The need for a variation can be important, especially where it appears that the CVA may fail otherwise. The Court of Appeal has considered a case involving an IVA and ruled that there was no common sense reason why all those affected were not free to agree an alteration to their rights and liabilities. Section 263 of the *Insolvency Act* 1986 allowed the court to intervene even at the instance of persons not parties to the IVA. The Act did not compel the conclusion that it was not possible for all those interested in a provision of the IVA to agree a variation of the provision when no one else was affected adversely or at all (*Raja v Rubin* [1999] BCC 579). One of the judges considered that this case emphasised the need to include a power to vary in the voluntary arrangement itself.

Failure of CVAs

If a voluntary arrangement is clearly failing, e.g. because the creditor cannot keep up with agreed payments to the supervisor, then it is better to wind up the company compulsorily (*Vadher v Weisgard* [1997] BCC 219). Conversely, if a company subject to a voluntary arrangement goes into winding up, there is nothing in the *Insolvency Act* 1986 or the *Insolvency Rules* 1986 which requires the voluntary arrangement to be brought to an end (*Re Halson Packaging Ltd* [1997] BCC 993).

Where a voluntary arrangement is brought to an end by winding up, that does not necessarily of itself determine or revoke any trust of the funds held by the supervisor (*Re Halson Packaging Ltd* [1997] BCC 993) although, if that trust is terminated, then the supervisor must hand over the assets to the liquidator (*Re Arthur Rathbone Kitchens Ltd* [1998] BCC 450).

¶90-750 Reform of CVAs

The Department of Trade and Industry Insolvency Service has put forward proposals to make company voluntary arrangements more popular, including a 28-day moratorium once a notice of intention to propose a voluntary arrangement has been filed in court. The government stated on 11 February 1998 that it intends to introduce legislation to implement these proposals but no legislative timetable has been set.

ADMINISTRATION ORDERS

¶91-000   Administration procedure

An 'administration' procedure is available under the *Insolvency Act* 1986, which is designed to provide a breathing space for companies in financial difficulties. The role and duties of administrators are outlined at ¶91-100ff. An administrator must be a qualified insolvency practitioner (see ¶91-550).

¶91-050   Application for an administration order

Administration orders are made by the court on an application by the company itself, a creditor or creditors (including any contingent or prospective creditor), the directors or the supervisor of a voluntary arrangement (see ¶90-650, ¶90-700), or by all or any of those parties together or separately (IA 1986, s. 9, 7(4)(b)). Administration orders run for a specified period (IA 1986, s. 8(2)).

The court can make an administration order despite the opposition of the majority creditor: the court has jurisdiction to make the order provided the statutory criteria are satisfied (*Re Structures & Computers Ltd* [1998] BCC 348).

There are conflicting judicial decisions as to the power of the directors of a company to petition for an administration order. In one case it was held that such a petition required unanimity (*Re Instrumentation Electrical Services Ltd* (1988) 4 BCC 301); in another that, once an appropriate board resolution had been passed, it was the duty of all directors to implement it, and accordingly it sufficed that a single director petitioned (*Re Equiticorp International plc* (1989) 5 BCC 599). The distinction turns on whether the directors are acting as individuals (in which case unanimity is required) or there has been a formal board decision (in which case the majority prevails). This in turn opens the question (which is unresolved) as to whether, in the latter case, it is more appropriate to regard the petition as one of the company itself, on the basis that, while in the absence of specific powers in a company's articles of association a corporate petition for winding up requires shareholder approval (*Re Emmadart Ltd* [1979] 1 All ER 549), the same logic may not necessarily apply to a corporate petition for the less final remedy of administration.

The effect of the grant of an order is to transfer the running of the company's business into the hands of an 'administator', who is appointed for the purpose by the court (IA 1986, s. 8(2)).

Two criteria must be satisfied before the court will grant the petition. The first of these is that the company is, or is likely to become, unable to pay its debts (IA 1986, s. 8(1)(a), s. 123). The second is that the court considers (IA 1986, s. 8(1)(b), (3)) that the order is likely:

- to secure the company's survival, and the whole or any part of its undertaking, as a going concern;

- to result in the approval of a voluntary arrangement under s. 1–7 (Pt. I) of the *Insolvency Act* 1986;

- to result in the approval by the company and its creditors of a composition in satisfaction of its debts or a scheme of arrangement under s. 425 of the *Companies Act* 1985; or

- to achieve a more advantageous realisation of the company's assets than would result from a winding up.

The order must actually specify the purpose or purposes for which it is made (IA 1986, s. 8(3)) and there must be a 'real prospect' that one of these objectives will be achieved (*Re Primlaks UK Ltd* (1989) 5 BCC 710). Once presented the petition cannot be withdrawn without leave of the court (IA 1986, s. 9(2)). The court may dismiss the petition, adjourn the hearing, make an interim order or any other order it thinks fit (s. 9(4)). If the company is in liquidation, no administration order can be made (s. 8(4)).

Notice of an application to the court for an administration order must be given to those persons entitled to appoint an administrative receiver. If an administrative receiver has already been appointed, the court must dismiss the petition for an administration order unless the persons who appointed the receiver (or on whose behalf the receiver was appointed) consent, or the court is satisfied that the administrator will be able to discharge, release, challenge or avoid the security under s. 238–240, 242, 243 or 245 of the *Insolvency Act* 1986 (IA 1986, s. 9(3)).

Effects of application

The consequences of the presentation of a petition to the court for an administration order are (IA 1986, s. 10(1)):

(1) no resolution may be passed by the company or order made by the court for winding up the company;

(2) no steps may be taken to enforce any security over the company's property, or to repossess goods in the company's possession under a hire purchase contract, without leave of the court: the court may impose terms before allowing the enforcement or repossession; and

(3) no other proceedings or execution or other legal process may be commenced or continued, and no distress may be levied against the company or its property, without leave of the court: the court may impose terms where it does grant leave.

These restrictions apply from the time of the presentation of the petition, and end with the making of the order or dismissal by the court of the petition.

However, leave of the court is not required for (IA 1986, s. 10(2)):

(1) the presentation of a petition for the company's winding up;

(2) the appointment of an administrative receiver; or

(3) the carrying out by an administrative receiver or any of his functions.

If an administrative receiver was in office at the time of presentation of the petition for the administration order, the above restrictions on winding up and protection of the company's property do not come into force unless and until the consent of the petition of the person on whose behalf the administrative receiver was appointed is obtained (IA 1986, s. 10(3)).

¶91-100   Powers and duties of the administrator

The grant of an administration order will result in the appointment of an administrator who manages the company for the period specified in the order (IA 1986, s. 8(2)). Within three months of the administration order being made, the administrator must draft proposals for achieving the objectives set out in the order which, if approved by the company's creditors, he will then implement.

The administrator has general powers of management in the exercise of which he acts as the company's agent (IA 1986, s. 14(5)). These powers are conferred under s. 14 (the general management power) as amplified in Sch. 1 to the *Insolvency Act* 1986. The powers contained in Sch. 1 are the same as those conferred upon administrative receivers, and are listed at ¶90-400. The administrator can remove and appoint directors and call meetings of the members and creditors (IA 1986, s. 14). He also has the specific powers to sell charged assets and replace the proceeds as the property subject to the charge (s. 15).

Applications to the court may be made by the administrator for directions in relation to any matter which arises in the course of carrying out his function (IA 1986, s. 14(3)).

General duties of the administrator

The administrator takes into his custody and control all the property to which the company is, or appears to be, entitled (IA 1986, s. 17(1)). However, before his proposals are approved, the administrator may only manage the affairs, business and property of the company in accordance with directions given by the court (s. 17(2)(a)). Once his proposals are accepted he must manage the company in accordance with those proposals (s. 17(2)(b)).

Discharge or variation of administration order

The administrator has wide powers of management to achieve the purposes set out in the order under which he was appointed under s. 8(3) of the *Insolvency Act* 1986. However, the administrator may apply to the court for the order to be discharged or varied, or for an additional purpose to be specified (IA 1986,

s. 18(1)). Such an application may be made if it appears to the administrator that the purposes specified in the order have been achieved or are incapable of achievement (s. 18(2)(a)). A majority of the company's creditors may also require the administrator to make such an application (s. 18(2)(b)). On hearing such an application the court may discharge or vary the administration order, or make any other order it thinks fit (s. 18(3)).

Adjustment of prior transactions, etc.

The administrator may apply to the court in order to set aside, or gain relief in respect of, agreements entered into by the company prior to its liquidation which unfairly prejudice its creditors (IA 1986, s. 236–246).

The administrator may be able to demonstrate that a floating charge created in the 12 months prior to the presentation of the administration petition should be avoided (see ¶93-300). The administrator may also apply to the court to obtain declarations avoiding either 'preferences' (i.e. payments by the company to creditors prior to insolvency which place them in an unfairly advantageous position) or 'transactions at an undervalue' (i.e. agreements where the company received little or no consideration) (see ¶93-200 and ¶93-150).

The administrator may apply to the court to have the company relieved from the terms of extortionate credit transactions undertaken within three years of the making of the order (see ¶93-250). The court may set aside or vary the terms of the transaction, and order repayment to the company of sums received by the other party.

¶91-150   Duties of the administrator, etc.

The administrator must summon a meeting of the company's creditors if directed to do so by the court, or if one-tenth in value of the company's creditors request the meeting (IA 1986, s. 17). Notice of the grant of an administration order must be sent to the company immediately, given to the registrar of companies within 14 days, and to all known creditors of the company within 28 days (IA 1986, s. 21). The administrator's name and the fact of this appointment must be displayed on every invoice, order for goods or business letter which bears the company's name (IA 1986, s. 12(1)). If the administrator or any officer of the company permits a default under s. 12(1), he is liable to a fine of up to one-fifth of the statutory maximum.

Statement of affairs to be submitted to administrator

Once an administration order is made, the administrator must request a statement as to the company's affairs (IA 1986, s. 22(1)). The statement must show specific details but also 'such further or other information as may be prescribed' (s. 22(2)).

The persons from whom a statement may be requested are past and present company officers, those persons who have taken part in the company's formation at any time within one year of the date of the grant of the order, current employees or persons employed by the company within the past year, and employees or officers of companies which are or have been officers of the company (IA 1986, s. 22(3)). Once requested, these persons have 21 days in which to submit their statement of affairs to the administrator (s. 22(4)).

¶91-200   The administrator's proposals

A copy of the administrator's proposals for achieving the purpose set out in the administration order must be supplied to the registrar of companies, the members and the known creditors of the company (IA 1986, s. 23(1)). A copy of this statement must be laid before the creditors at a meeting within three months of the administration order being granted. The creditors must be given at least 14 days' notice of this meeting. This period may be extended by the court. The procedure for calling meetings of creditors (with the appropriate period of notice) must be repeated if the administrator makes substantial revisions to these proposals (IA 1986, s. 25).

Consideration of proposals by creditors' meeting

The meeting of creditors may accept or reject the administrator's proposals (IA 1986, s. 24(1)). This result must be relayed to the court and the registrar of companies. The meeting may approve the proposals subject to modifications, but the administrator must approve all the modifications. If the creditors vote against the proposals the court may discharge the administration order and make such consequential provision as it thinks fit, or adjourn the hearing conditionally or unconditionally or make an interim order or any other order it thinks fit. If the court discharges the administration order, the administrator must send a copy of the discharge order to the registrar of companies within 14 days (IA 1986, s. 24(6)).

Creditors' committee

If the meeting of creditors approves the administrator's proposals, a committee of creditors may be set up, to which the administrator may be called upon to report at not less than seven days' notice (IA 1986, s. 26). The administrator must respond to this request within a 'reasonable' time and provide such information about the carrying on of his functions as the committee may 'reasonably require'.

Protection of interests of creditors and members

A right of petition to the court is also conferred upon creditors and members if they believe that the administrator is conducting the company's affairs in a manner which is unfairly prejudicial to the interests of creditors or members generally, or some part thereof, or is proposing to do so (IA 1986, s. 27(1)). On hearing such a petition the court can make any order to grant relief it thinks fit, adjourn the hearing conditionally or unconditionally or make an interim order (s. 27(2)). The order may (s. 27(4)):

(1) regulate the future management by the administrator of the company's affairs, business and property;

(2) require the administrator to refrain from doing or continuing an act complained of by the petitioner or to do an act which the petitioner has complained he omitted to do;

(3) require the summoning of a meeting of creditors or members for the purpose of considering matters as the court may direct; or

(4) discharge the administration order and make such consequential provisions as the court thinks fit.

However, the court must not prejudice or prevent the implementation of any voluntary arrangement approved by the creditors (see ¶90-650 and ¶90-700) or sanctioned under s. 425 of the *Companies Act* 1985 (see ¶80-150) (IA 1986, s. 27(3)). If the application for an order from the court under s. 27 above is made more than 28 days after the proposals of the administrator have been approved by the committee, the court order must not prejudice or prevent the implementation of those proposals.

¶91-250 Effect of an administration order

The effects and consequences of the grant of an administration order by the court are:

(1) the affairs, the business and property of the company are managed by the administrator (IA 1986, s. 17: see ¶91-100);

(2) any petition for the company's liquidation is dismissed (IA 1986, s. 11(1)(a));

(3) any administrative receiver must vacate his office (IA 1986, s. 11(1)(b)); and

(4) any receiver appointed over only part of the company's property may have to resign if asked to do so (IA 1986, s. 11(2)).

Further, for the duration of the order (IA 1986, s. 11(3)):

(5) no resolution may be passed by the company or order made by the court for the company's liquidation;

(6) no administrative receiver may be appointed;

(7) no steps may be taken to enforce any security over the company's assets or for repossession of goods under any hire-purchase agreement, other than with the administrator's consent or leave of the court: the court may impose terms before giving its consent; and

(8) no other proceedings or legal process may be commenced or continued and no distress may be levied against the company or its property except with the consent of the administrator or the leave of the court, and subject to whatever terms the court may impose.

¶91-300   Termination of office of administrator

Administrators may be removed from office by order of the court, or may resign by giving notice of resignation to the court (IA 1986, s. 19(1)). The release from office is then effective from such time as the court may determine (s. 20(1)(b)). From that time, no liability for acts or omissions of his office can attach (s. 20(2)). An administrator must vacate office if he ceases to be qualified to act as an insolvency practitioner or if the administration order is discharged (s. 19(2)).

Should an administrator die whilst in office, his release from office is effective from the date of notification of death to the court (IA 1986, s. 20(1)(a)). At that date, the receiver will be discharged from liabilities arising from his acts or omissions whilst in office (s. 20(2)).

If property has been misapplied by the administrator, or if he has become accountable for any property or has acted in breach of his duty, the court may order restoration by him of the assets or a contribution from him pursuant to s. 212 of the *Insolvency Act* 1986 notwithstanding his release from office (IA 1986, s. 20(3)).

On termination of office, the administrator has a charge on company property which was under his control for his remuneration. Money payable under contracts made or contracts of employment adopted by the administrator whilst in office is charged on property under his control. The latter charge has priority over that for his remuneration (IA 1986, s. 19(5), (6)).

PARTIES IN A WINDING UP

¶91-500   Modes of winding up

Winding up is the name given to distribution of a company's property amongst creditors and members, prior to the company's dissolution.

A winding up may be voluntary (see ¶92-000ff.), or by the court (see ¶92-500ff.) (IA 1986, s. 73). Within the former procedure are the 'members' voluntary winding up' (see ¶92-200) and the 'creditors' voluntary winding up' (see ¶92-250). A liquidation by the court is termed a compulsory winding up.

The distinction between the creditors' and members' voluntary winding up is that a declaration of solvency is required from a majority of the company's directors for a members' voluntary winding up (IA 1986, s. 90). This declaration from the directors expresses their belief that the company will be able to pay its debts in full within 12 months of the commencement of the winding up (see ¶92-200).

The voluntary winding up of a company does not bar the right of any creditor or 'contributory' (see ¶91-700) to have the company wound up by the court (IA 1986,

s. 116). In the case of a creditor, the court will not replace the voluntary winding up against the wishes of the majority of creditors unless there is some special reason to override the wishes of the majority having regard to the 'general principles of fairness and morality which underlie the details of insolvency law' (*Re Falcon R J Developments Ltd* (1987) 3 BCC 146). If the application is by a contributory, the court must be satisfied that the contributories' rights would be prejudiced by a voluntary winding up.

The court may at any time after a winding-up order has been made stay the winding-up proceedings on the application of the liquidator, the official receiver of any creditor or contributory (IA 1986, s. 147). The company would then return to normal operation.

The most important parties in a winding up are the liquidator (see ¶91-550), the official receiver (see ¶91-600), creditors (see ¶91-650) and contributories (see ¶91-700).

¶91-550   The liquidator

A licensing system for insolvency practitioners is contained in the *Insolvency Act 1986*. An individual may act as an 'insolvency practitioner' only if he is authorised to do so by a recognised professional body or by the relevant authority set up by the Secretary of State. Further, there must be a security in force for the proper performance of his duties (IA 1986, s. 390).

An insolvency practitioner is someone who, in relation to companies, acts as a liquidator, provisional liquidator, an administrator, an administrative receiver or a supervisor of a voluntary arrangement under the Act (IA 1986, s. 388). The professional bodies which will be granted recognition by the Secretary of State are those which regulate the practice of their profession and maintain and enforce rules that ensure that any members who are permitted to act as insolvency practitioners are fit and proper persons and meet acceptable standards in education and in practical training and experience (IA 1986, s. 391).

If an individual does not qualify as an insolvency practitioner through his membership of a professional body, he may apply to the Secretary of State himself. The criteria for determining whether a person is fit and proper to be licensed as an insolvency practitioner are contained in the *Insolvency Practitioners Regulations 1990* (SI 1990/439 as amended by SI 1993/221).

Persons not qualified to act as insolvency practitioners

An individual will be disqualified from acting as an insolvency practitioner if (IA 1986, s. 390):

- he is an undischarged bankrupt or if sequestration of his estate has been awarded and he has not been discharged;
- he is subject to a disqualification order under the *Company Directors Disqualification Act* 1986; or

- he is a patient within the meaning of either the *Mental Health Act* 1983 or the *Mental Health (Scotland) Act* 1984.

¶91-600   The official receiver

Official receivers are officers of the court appointed to investigate and administer compulsory liquidations. In practice, the official receiver will occupy the office of liquidator until such time as the creditors or contributories of the company nominate another person to fulfil that role.

¶91-650   Creditors

Although not statutorily defined, a 'creditor' is any person to whom the company owes a debt. A debt is defined as:

- any debt or liability to which the company is subject at the date of the liquidation; or

- any debt or liability accruing after that date but which arises from an obligation incurred before that date; or

- accumulated interest (*Insolvency Rules* 1986 (SI 1986/1925), r. 13.12).

¶91-700   Contributories

Contributories are persons who may be called upon to contribute to the assets of a company in the event of its being wound up (IA 1986, s. 79). However, persons liable for either fraudulent or wrongful trading (see ¶93-400 and ¶93-350) are specifically excluded from this definition. The following persons are specified as contributories on the commencement of a winding up:

- every past and present member, up to the amount outstanding on their shares (IA 1986, s. 74);

- past and present directors, if they have had unlimited liability imposed upon them (IA 1986, s. 75); and

- directors of companies which have made a payment out of capital to redeem shares (IA 1986, s. 76).

In a voluntary liquidation, the liquidator will settle a list of contributories (IA 1986, s. 165). In a compulsory liquidation, this is the responsibility of the court and is delegated to the liquidator (IA 1986, s. 160).

If a shareholder is unable to meet a call on unpaid shares, any person who held those shares within the year prior to the commencement of the winding up may be called upon. However, this is only in relation to debts incurred prior to his transfer of the shares (IA 1986, s. 74).

VOLUNTARY WINDING UP

¶92-000   General

A company may be wound up voluntarily:

(1) when the period (if any) fixed for the company's duration by the articles expires, or an event (if any) occurs on the occurrence of which the articles provide that the company is to be dissolved, and the company in general meeting has passed a resolution requiring the company to be wound up voluntarily;

(2) if the company resolves by special resolution that it be wound up voluntarily; or

(3) if the company resolves by extraordinary resolution that it cannot by reason of its liabilities continue its business and that it is advisable to wind up (IA 1986, s. 84(1)).

A voluntary winding up commences at the time the resolution is passed (IA 1986, s. 86). From that time, the company ceases to carry on its business, except so far as may be required for its beneficial winding up (s. 87). The company's assets fall under the control of the liquidator once he is appointed, for distribution among the creditors and shareholders, and the company is no longer the beneficial owner of those assets (*Ayerst v C & K (Construction) Ltd* [1976] AC 167).

Both forms of voluntary winding up have certain common features. The company's property in a voluntary winding up is applied in satisfaction of the company's liabilities and, subject thereto, distributed to the members. The liquidator has a statutory duty to pay the company's debts (IA 1986, s. 165). The preferential creditors (see ¶93-600) are paid off first, then liabilities, subject to secured creditors unaffected by insolvency claims, are met pari passu. Any remaining assets are then distributed amongst members according to their rights and interests in the company (IA 1986, s. 107).

The liquidator must give notice of his appointment in the *Gazette* within 14 days, and deliver notice to the registrar of companies (IA 1986, s. 109). If there is no liquidator acting, for whatever reason, the court may make an appointment. The court may also replace a liquidator 'on cause shown' (s. 108). Even if no liquidator has been appointed, the directors cannot exercise their powers, except within very tightly defined limitations (s. 114).

Reference of questions to the court

The liquidator or any contributory (see ¶91-700) or creditor may apply to the court for the determination of any question arising in the course of the winding up.

An application may also be made for the exercise of powers available to the court if the winding up were conducted by the court (IA 1986, s. 112). If the court is satisfied that determination of the question will be just and beneficial, it may accede to the application, or make such other order as it thinks fit. Copies of any order which stays proceedings in the winding up must be forwarded by the company to the registrar of companies.

¶92-050 Liquidator's powers

The powers of the liquidator in a voluntary winding up are set out in s. 165 of and Sch. 4 to the *Insolvency Act* 1986. These powers enable the liquidator to collect assets, administer the company and dispose of property, with overriding power to do all such other things as may be necessary for winding up the company's affairs and distributing its assets. Exercise of certain of these powers requires the sanction of an extraordinary resolution of the company (in the case of a members' voluntary winding up) or of the court, or the liquidation committee or meeting of the company's creditors if there is no liquidation committee (in the case of a creditors' voluntary winding up).

Powers exercisable with sanction

(1) Power to pay any class of creditors in full.

(2) Power to make any compromise or arrangement with creditors or persons claiming to be creditors, or having or alleging themselves to have any claim (present or future, certain or contingent, ascertained or sounding only in damages) against the company, or whereby the company may be rendered liable.

(3) Power to compromise, on such terms as may be agreed:

    (a) all calls and liabilities to calls, all debts and liabilities capable of resulting in debts, and all claims (present or future, certain or contingent, ascertained or sounding only in damages) subsisting or supposed to subsist between the company and a contributory (see ¶91-700) or alleged contributory or other debtor or person apprehending liability to the company; and

    (b) all questions in any way relating to or affecting the assets or the winding up of the company;

and take any security for the discharge of any such call, debt, liability or claim and give a complete discharge in respect of it.

Powers exercisable without sanction in voluntary winding up (with sanction in winding up by the court)

(4) Power to bring or defend any action or other legal proceedings in the name and on behalf of the company.

(5) Power to carry on the company's business so far as may be necessary for its beneficial winding up.

Powers exercisable without sanction in any winding up

(6) Power to sell any of the company's property by public auction or private contract, with power to transfer the whole of it to any person or to sell the same in parcels.

(7) Power to do all acts and execute, in the name and on behalf of the company, all deeds, receipts and other documents, and for that purpose to use, when necessary, the company's seal.

(8) Power to prove, rank and claim in the bankruptcy, insolvency or sequestration of any contributory for any balance against his estate, and to receive dividends in the bankruptcy, insolvency or sequestration in respect of that balance, as a separate debt due from the bankrupt or insolvent, and rateably with the other separate creditors.

(9) Power to draw, accept, make and endorse any bill of exchange or promissory note in the name and on behalf of the company, with the same effect with respect to the company's liability as if the bill or note had been drawn, accepted, made or endorsed by or on behalf of the company in the course of its business.

(10) Power to raise on the security of the company's assets any money requisite.

(11) Power to take out in his official name letters of administration to any deceased contributory, and to do in his official name any other act necessary for obtaining payment of any money due from a contributory or his estate which cannot conveniently be done in the company's name. In all such cases the money due is deemed, for the purpose of enabling the liquidator to take out the letters of administration or recover the money, to be due to the liquidator himself.

(12) Power to appoint an agent to do any business which the liquidator is unable to do himself.

(13) Power to do all such other things as may be necessary for winding up the company's affairs and distributing its assets.

A liquidator may, on the company's behalf, assign a right of action vested in the company to another person such as a director who may pursue the action with the benefit of legal aid (*Norglen Ltd (in liq.) v Reeds Rains Prudential Ltd* [1998] BCC 44).

¶92-100   Release of liquidator

Once a voluntary liquidator obtains release from office he cannot be held liable for acts or omissions in the course of the winding up or otherwise in relation to his conduct as a liquidator (IA 1986, s. 173(4)). If removed by a meeting of creditors or a general meeting of the company, release is obtained on notice being given to the registrar of companies, provided that the meeting does not resolve against his release (s. 173(2)). In the case of a liquidator removed from office by a meeting of creditors which does not resolve in favour of his release, or who is removed from office by the court, or who has vacated office on ceasing to be qualified, his release is operative as from such time as the Secretary of State may determine.

On completion of a winding up, the liquidator will be released from liability on notification to the registrar of companies of the final meeting of members or creditors (IA 1986, s. 173(4)). If, however, a final meeting of creditors resolves against the liquidator's release, the release is effective from such date as the Secretary of State determines.

Expenses properly incurred in the winding up (including the liquidator's remuneration) are payable out of the company's assets, in priority to all other claims (IA 1986, s. 115).

¶92-150 Sale of business

The liquidator may enter into a transaction whereby the whole or part of the company's business or property is sold to another company in exchange (wholly or partly) for shares or like interests in the transferee company (IA 1986, s. 110), or the right to participate in profits of the transferee company or to receive any other benefits therefrom (see ¶80-100). The liquidator then distributes the consideration he has received to the members of the company in liquidation. Such an arrangement may be effected by special resolution, in the case of a members' voluntary winding up, and with the additional consent of the court or the liquidation committee in the case of a creditors' voluntary winding up.

Dissent from arrangement

There is a facility for dissent by members of the company in liquidation who did not vote in favour of the proposals. The dissent must be presented, in writing, to the company's registered office within seven days of the resolution (IA 1986, s. 111). The dissenting member may require the liquidator either to abstain from carrying the resolution into effect, or to purchase his interest at a price fixed either by agreement or arbitration between the parties. This mechanism is sometimes used to effect a de-merger.

¶92-200 Members' voluntary winding up

Where it is proposed to wind up a company voluntarily the directors (or, if more than two, the majority of them) may, at a meeting of the directors, make a statutory declaration to the effect that they have made a full inquiry into the company's affairs and that, having done so, they have formed the opinion that the company will be able to pay its debts, with interest, in full within such period not exceeding 12 months from the commencement of the winding up as may be specified in the declaration (IA 1986, s. 89(1)).

The declaration must be made within the five weeks which immediately precede the date that the special resolution is passed, or on the day of the resolution but before it is passed. The declaration must also carry a statement of the company's assets and liabilities at the latest practicable date before making the declaration (IA 1986, s. 89(2)). A copy of the declaration must be delivered to the registrar of companies within 15 days of the date of the resolution for winding up (IA 1986, s. 89(3)).

If a director participates in a declaration of solvency without reasonable grounds for the opinion expressed in it he is liable on conviction to imprisonment, or to a fine, or to both. The burden of proof is upon the director to show that he had reasonable grounds to express the opinion in the declaration if the company is wound up pursuant to the resolution and is unable to pay its debts (IA 1986, s. 89(4)).

Appointment of liquidator

The company in general meeting appoints one or more liquidators to wind the company up. The powers of the directors then cease, except as far as the company in general meeting, or the liquidator, sanctions their continuance (IA 1986, s. 91(2)). If the winding up takes longer than a year, the liquidator is required to call general meetings annually, at which an account of his actions and of the conduct of the winding up during the preceding year is presented (s. 93).

Final meeting prior to dissolution

A final general meeting must be called once the company's affairs are fully wound up at which an account must be given as to how the liquidator has conducted the winding up and how the company's property has been realised (IA 1986, s. 94(1)). This meeting must be publicised in the *London Gazette* (s. 94(2)). The liquidator must send to the registrar of companies a copy of the account, a return of the holding of the meeting and notification of its date, within a week of its being held (s. 94(3)).

Effect of company's insolvency

If in the course of the liquidation the liquidator becomes of the opinion that the company will be unable to pay its debts with interest within the period stated in the declaration of solvency, he must call a meeting of creditors within 28 days (for which at least seven days' notice is given by post), with notice once in the *Gazette* and at least once in two local newspapers, and provide to creditors such information as they may reasonably require about the company's affairs (IA 1986, s. 95(1), (2)). Further, a statement of the company's assets and liabilities, the names and addresses of creditors, securities held by them, the dates when the securities were given and any such further or other information as may be prescribed, must be presented to the meeting of creditors, at which the liquidator must preside (IA 1986, s. 95(3), (4)). The latter statement must be verified by affidavit by the liquidator.

From the date of the creditors' meeting, the directors' declaration of solvency is treated as never having been made, and the winding up becomes a creditors' voluntary winding up (IA 1986, s. 96).

¶92-250   Creditors' voluntary winding up

A creditors' voluntary winding up is a winding up by resolution of the members in which no declaration of solvency is made by the company (IA 1986, s. 90).

A meeting of creditors must be held within 14 days of the resolution to wind up (IA 1986, s. 98(1)). Creditors must be given seven days' notice of such meeting (unless the creditors' winding up was a members' winding up where the company turned out to be insolvent and a creditors' meeting under s. 95 of the Insolvency Act was held (see ¶92-200) (IA 1986, s. 96)). Notice must also be published in the *Gazette* once, and in two local newspapers at least once.

Contents of notice of meeting

The notice sent to creditors must give the name and address of an insolvency practitioner who is qualified to act and who will supply such information about the company's affairs as creditors may reasonably require during the period before the day on which the meeting is to be held, or a local address at which names and addresses of creditors may be inspected free of charge (IA 1986, s. 98(2)).

Directors to lay statement of affairs before creditors

The directors must prepare for the creditors' meeting a statement of the company's affairs, which sets out its assets, liabilities, the names and addresses of creditors, any security the creditors hold, the dates on which the securities were granted and any such further information as may be required. The statement must be verified by affidavit. A director must also be appointed to preside at the meeting of creditors (IA 1986, s. 99).

Appointment of liquidator

At the meeting of creditors, a liquidator may be appointed (IA 1986, s. 100(1)). If the creditors fail to nominate a liquidator, the liquidator appointed by the members in the general meeting remains in office (s. 100(2)). If different liquidators are nominated by the members and the creditors any member, director or creditor may, within seven days, apply to the court for an order that either the members' choice of liquidator should prevail, or that the two liquidators should take the office jointly, or that some person other than the creditors' choice should be selected (s. 100(3)); failing this the creditors' appointment prevails.

Appointment of liquidation committee

The creditors may appoint a liquidation committee of five or fewer persons (IA 1986, s. 101(1)). The company may also appoint not more than five representatives to the committee (s. 101(2)). If the creditors object to all or any of the company's representatives, they cannot remain on the committee unless the court directs otherwise (s. 101(3)).

The purpose of the committee is to safeguard the interests of the company's creditors. It is empowered to request regular reports from the liquidator on how the liquidation is being conducted. In specific circumstances, its approval is required before the liquidator can proceed with various schemes, compromises and arrangements (IA 1986, s. 165, Sch. 4).

Meetings of company and creditors at each year end

If the winding up continues for longer than one year, the liquidator must call a general meeting of the company and a meeting of the creditors at the end of the first year from the commencement of the winding up. Such meetings must be held within three months of each succeeding year-end (IA 1986, s. 105). At the annual meetings, the liquidator lays an account of his actions and of the conduct of the winding up during the preceding year.

Final meetings prior to dissolution

Once the company's affairs are fully wound up the liquidator must call final meetings of members and creditors. At these meetings the liquidator presents an account showing how the liquidation has been conducted, and how the company's property was disposed of, and he gives an explanation of the account. Each meeting must be advertised in the *Gazette* with at least one month's notice. The advertisement should disclose the time, place and object of the meeting. Copies of the account and returns of the meeting are sent to the registrar of companies within one week of the meeting (IA 1986, s. 106).

The detailed procedure for conduct of meetings of creditors and meetings of the committee are set out in the *Insolvency Rules* 1986 (SI 1986/1925).

Right to seek compulsory winding up

If a creditor is dissatisfied with the conduct of the voluntary liquidation, a petition to the court for compulsory winding up can be attempted (IA 1986, s. 116). The court will only interfere with a voluntary winding up if satisfied that the winding up cannot be continued without due regard to the interest of creditors or contributories.

Protection of creditors' interests

A creditors' voluntary winding up is clearly designed to protect creditors' interests in a number of ways. A liquidator may not exercise full powers until confirmed in office by the creditors. Further, the liquidator must report to the creditors' meeting on any use by him of his powers prior to that meeting (IA 1986, s. 166(4)).

Execution against goods, etc.

Execution creditors must not retain the benefit of the execution unless it was completed prior to the commencement of the winding up or receipt of notice of the creditors' meeting (IA 1986, s. 183). A sheriff who has taken goods in execution must return the goods on receipt of notice of a resolution for voluntary winding up if the notice is received prior to completion of the execution or sale of the goods (s. 184).

Directions for remedying defaults

The liquidator must apply to the court for directions in respect of the following defaults (IA 1986, s. 166(5)):

- the company failing to call a meeting of creditors within 14 days of the resolution for winding up or to give the appropriate notice or disclosure; or

- the directors failing to make a statement of assets, debts and liabilities in accordance with s. 99(1) and (2) of the *Insolvency Act* 1986.

COMPULSORY WINDING UP

¶92-500   Petitions

A petition for the compulsory winding up of a company by the court must be lodged with the court and served at the company's registered office (unless the petition is presented by the company itself).

Grounds for winding up

A company may be wound up by the court if a petition is made on any of the following grounds (IA 1986, s. 122):

- the company has by special resolution resolved that the company be wound up by the court;

- being a public company which has registered as such on its original incorporation, the company has not been issued with a certificate under s. 117 of the *Companies Act* 1985 (public company share capital requirements: see ¶22-300) and more than a year has expired since it was so registered;

- it is an old public company, within the meaning of the *Companies Consolidation (Consequential Provisions) Act* 1985 (i.e. it was a public company on 22 December 1980, and has not re-registered as a public limited company or become a private company since that date);

- the company does not commence its business within a year from its incorporation or suspends its business for a whole year;

- the number of members is reduced below two (except in the case of a single member private company limited by shares or guarantee);
- the company is unable to pay its debts (see ¶92-550); or
- the court is of the opinion that it is just and equitable that the company should be wound up (see ¶62-800).

Petitioners

A petition for the compulsory winding up of a company may be made by any of the following persons:

- the company (IA 1986, s. 124(1));
- the directors (IA 1986, s. 124(1));
- any creditor or creditors (IA 1986, s. 124(1));
- any contributory or contributories (see below) (IA 1986, s. 124(1));
- the official receiver (IA 1986, s. 124(5));
- an administrative receiver (IA 1986, s. 42(1), Sch. 1, para. 21);
- an administrator (IA 1986, s. 14(1), Sch. 1, para. 21);
- the supervisor of a voluntary arrangement (IA 1986, s. 7(4)(b)); or
- the Secretary of State (IA 1986, s. 124(4)).

Petitions by contributories

A contributory (see ¶91-700) must demonstrate that he has a tangible (i.e. financial) interest in the company's winding up (*Re Chesterfield Catering Co Ltd* [1977] Ch 373). Further, he must comply with the statutory condition that, unless the number of members has fallen to less than two, he must have been either an original allottee of the shares, or he must have been entered on the register of members for at least six of the 18 months preceding the petition (IA 1986, s. 124(2)).

The above rules do not apply to past directors and shareholders who are exposed to a liability in respect of a share repurchase or redemption within one year of the commencement of the winding up under IA 1986, s. 76 (see ¶51-950).

Just and equitable ground

The court will not grant a petition for winding up on the just and equitable ground presented by contributories if the petitioners have some other remedy, and are acting unreasonably in seeking to have the company wound up (IA 1986, s. 125(2)). Winding up on the just and equitable ground is considered at ¶62-800.

Companies with no assets

The court cannot refuse to make a winding-up order solely on the ground that the company has mortgaged its assets to an amount equal to or in excess of their value, or that the company has no assets (IA 1986, s. 125(1)).

Petition by Secretary of State

The Secretary of State may present a petition for the compulsory winding up of a company either because of a failure by the company to be issued with a certificate under s. 117 of the *Companies Act* 1985 (public company share capital requirements: see ¶22-300), or because the company is an old public company or because it is expedient in the public interest to wind up the company (IA 1986, s. 124A). In the latter case, the court must weigh the factors which point to the conclusion that it would be just and equitable to wind up the company against those which point to the opposite conclusion (*Re Walter L Jacob & Co Ltd* (1989) 5 BCC 244). In *Re Secure and Provide plc* [1992] BCC 405, the court declined to wind up the respondent company on the ground that, although it had committed certain misrepresentations, it had at all times acted in good faith.

Petitions by creditors

Creditors will normally petition for a compulsory winding up on the ground that the company is unable to pay its debts (see ¶92-550).

Wishes of creditors and contributories

In deciding whether to grant a petition for the winding up of a company, the court may have regard to the wishes of creditors and contributories (IA 1986, s. 195). The views of contributories are unlikely to influence the court if the petition is presented by creditors on the ground that the company is unable to pay its debts.

Petition by official receiver

An official receiver may petition for the compulsory winding up of a company which is already in voluntary liquidation, but the petition will not be granted unless the court is satisfied that the winding up cannot be continued with due regard to the interests of creditors and contributories (IA 1986, s. 124(5)).

¶92-550   Definition of inability to pay debts

A company may be wound up by the court if, inter alia, it is unable to pay its debts (see ¶92-500). The company will be unable to pay its debts where (IA 1986, s. 123):

- a creditor to whom the company is indebted in a sum exceeding £750 then due has served on the company, by leaving at the company's registered office, a written demand in the prescribed form (a 'statutory demand') requiring the company to pay the sum due, and the company has for three weeks thereafter neglected to pay the sum or to secure or compound for it to the reasonable satisfaction of the creditor; or

- execution or other process issued on a judgment, decree or order of any court in favour of a creditor of the company is returned unsatisfied in whole or in part; or

- it is proved to the satisfaction of the court that the company is unable to pay its debts as they fall due: hence, a 'statutory demand' is not a pre-condition to obtaining a winding-up order where a company has failed to pay a debt (*Re Taylor's Industrial Flooring Ltd* [1990] BCC 44), though one is normally made.

A company is also deemed unable to pay its debts if it is proved to the satisfaction of the court that the value of the company's assets is less than the amount of its liabilities, taking into account its contingent and prospective liabilities – the so-called balance-sheet test (IA 1986, s. 123(2)).

If a company disputes the alleged debt, the creditor will be prevented from continuing with the winding-up action (*Mann v Goldstein* [1968] 1 WLR 1091). Likewise, even if the debt is undisputed, where the company has a genuine cross-claim in a figure in excess of the petitioner's debt but was unable to litigate the claim, the court may dismiss the petition or, if it has already been granted and a winding-up order made, discharge that order (*Re Bayoil SA* [1998] BCC 988).

Note that the courts do not like it where they are used as a debt-collection agency or where a statutory demand is used just to put pressure on a debtor company. If there is malice involved in petitioning for a winding-up in which the company pays (or is relieved from) the debt, the petitioner may be liable in the tort of malicious presentation (see *Partizan Ltd v O J Kilkenny & Co Ltd* [1998] BCC 912 where, however, the action did not succeed).

¶92-600   Liquidator's functions and powers

The compulsory liquidator will gather in a company's assets, pay creditors and distribute any surplus to members (IA 1986, s. 143). He has custody and control of the company's assets (s. 144). The powers of the directors are therefore superseded. The compulsory liquidator is given wide powers to enable him to protect the company's assets and achieve his objectives (s. 167). However, some of these powers may only be exercised with the sanction of the court or any liquidation committee (see ¶92-050).

Remedies of aggrieved persons

Persons aggrieved by any act or decision of the liquidator may make an application to the court, and the court may confirm, reverse or modify the act or decision and make such order as it thinks just (IA 1986, s. 168).

CONSEQUENCES OF A PETITION AND AN ORDER FOR COMPULSORY WINDING UP

¶92-650   General

The commencement of a compulsory winding up is backdated to the time the petition was presented to the court. If the company is already in voluntary liquidation, the passing of the resolution to wind up is deemed to be the commencement of the compulsory winding up (IA 1986, s. 129). Two dates are of special significance for a compulsory winding up. These are the date of the petition and the date on which the order is made. The relevance of the two dates is summarised in the following table.

Table: Compulsory winding up

Distinction of consequences of date of winding-up petition and date of winding-up order

Date of petition	Comments
Application to court for stay of proceedings can be made by company or creditors (*Insolvency Act* 1986, s. 126.	
Attachment, sequestration, distress or execution put in force against the estate or effects of the company after date of petition is void (*Insolvency Act* 1986, s. 128).	
Issue of execution or attachment of debt is void, unless execution or attachment is: • complete before petition; or • complete before notice is received by the creditor of a meeting at which a resolution for voluntary winding up will be proposed (*Insolvency Act* 1986, s. 183).	Court may set aside in favour of a purchaser of goods from the company in good faith on a sale by the sheriff. Court may set aside the liquidator's right to recover assets attached in a creditor's favour, on such terms as it thinks fit (s. 183). Section 183 does not apply to distress.
Disposition of company property, transfer of shares or alteration in status of members is void unless court orders otherwise (*Insolvency Act* 1986, s. 127).	

Date of order	Comments
Company's employees dismissed.	
No action can be commenced or proceeded with against the company or its property without leave of the court (*Insolvency Act* 1986, s. 130).	Court may grant leave on such terms as it thinks fit.
Ascertainment of preferential creditors (*Insolvency Act* 1986, s. 130).	Alternative is any earlier date on which resolution for winding up was passed or a provisional liquidator appointed.
Foreign currencies converted into sterling for proof of debt (*Re Lines Brothers Ltd* [1982] 2 All ER 183).	

The court may appoint a provisional liquidator after the winding-up petition has been presented (IA 1986, s. 135). The official receiver is usually appointed to this post. No action may be commenced or continued against the company or its property without leave first being granted by the court that made the winding-up order (s. 130).

¶92-675 Appointment of provisional liquidator

The provisional liquidator is appointed to protect the interests of all the parties and to carry out such functions as the court may confer upon him. His powers are accordingly limited. The appointment of the provisional liquidator freezes the powers of the directors and accordingly also automatically revokes the authority of agents appointed to act on behalf of the company by or under the authority of the directors (*Pacific and General Insurance Co Ltd v Hazell* [1997] BCC 400). All actions and proceedings against the company's property are stayed on the appointment of a provisional liquidator: they cannot proceed without leave of the court and may be subject to such terms as the court thinks fit (IA 1986, s. 130(2)). It is possible for the court to appoint a special manager of the company's business or property. This is done where the provisional liquidator considers that the nature of the company's business or property, or the interests of the company's creditors, contributories or members, require the appointment of another person to manage that business or property. The powers of a special manager are as determined by the court (IA 1986, s. 177).

¶92-700 Appointment of liquidator

Once a winding-up order is made by the court, the official receiver becomes the liquidator. The official receiver continues in office until another person, usually selected by the company's creditors at their first meeting, becomes liquidator.

If the winding-up order follows the discharge of an administration order or a voluntary arrangement, the administrator or supervisor may be appointed by the court to liquidate the company (IA 1986, s. 140). The creditors may remove a liquidator so appointed (s. 172).

Once appointed, the official receiver has to determine two issues. The first is whether the company has sufficient assets to cover the cost of the liquidation. The second is whether any affairs of the company require investigation. If the company's assets are insufficient to cover the cost of liquidation, and the company's affairs do not require further investigation, the company may be dissolved. Creditors, contributories (and an administrative receiver, if appropriate) must be informed of the official receiver's decision to dissolve the company by 28 days' notice. The creditors, contributories or administrative receiver may apply to the Secretary of State for directions that the liquidation should proceed as if no notice had been given. If no such application is forthcoming, the official receiver's only duty is to dissolve the company (IA 1986, s. 202).

In the absence of any notice to apply for dissolution, one-quarter in value of the company's creditors may request meetings of all creditors and contributories for selection of a new liquidator (IA 1986, s. 136(5)). If there is no request for the meetings, the official receiver must decide within 12 weeks whether he should call such a meeting; if he decides against this, the court, the creditors and contributories will be informed of his decision. The official receiver may also apply to the Secretary of State for a different liquidator to be appointed in this place (s. 137).

Choice of liquidator

Should the meetings of creditors and contributories take place, each will nominate a liquidator (IA 1986, s. 139(1), (2)). If different persons are nominated, the choice of the creditors will prevail; if the creditors fail to make a nomination, the nominee of the contributories will take office (s. 139(3)). There is a facility for application to the court for appointment of the contributories' nominee, joint liquidators or a third person if the two meetings select different liquidators (s. 139(4)).

Liquidation committee

A mechanism is provided for the creation of a liquidation committee which will assist and supervise the liquidator. A liquidation committee may be elected at the meeting of creditors and contributories. Alternatively, a compulsory liquidator other than the official receiver may summon meetings of creditors and contributories with a view to establishing such a committee (IA 1986, s. 141). One-tenth in value of the company's creditors may also request a meeting.

¶92-725 Release of liquidators

The release of a compulsory liquidator by which he is also discharged from all liability is determined in accordance with s. 174 of the *Insolvency Act* 1986. Where the official receiver is the compulsory liquidator, he obtains his release:

- when notification is given to the court of his replacement by a general meeting of creditors and contributories or the Secretary of State;

- at such time as the court may determine, if the court appoints the replacement; or

- at such time as the Secretary of State determines, if notice is given to him by the official receiver that the liquidation is complete.

If the compulsory liquidator is not the official receiver, his release is obtained:

- if he is removed by a general meeting of creditors that has not resolved against his release or, if he has died, at the time at which notice is given to the court that he has ceased to hold office;

- if he is removed by a general meeting of creditors who have resolved against his release, or by the court or the Secretary of State, or if he no longer qualifies as an insolvency practitioner, at such time as the Secretary of State may determine;

- if he has resigned, at such time as is prescribed by the *Insolvency Rules* 1986 (SI 1986/1925);

- if the liquidation is complete, and the final meeting has consented to his vacating office, at the time of vacation; or

- if the liquidation is complete, and the final meeting of creditors has not so consented to his release, at such time as the Secretary of State determines (if the meeting does resolve to release him, release is effective from when he vacates office).

A provisional liquidator in a compulsory winding up obtains his release with effect from such time as the court determines.

COLLECTION AND DISTRIBUTION OF ASSETS ON A WINDING UP

¶93-000   Repayment out of the company's assets

The assets which are available to creditors and members on a liquidation are those which the company owns at the commencement of the winding up. It is possible that a company has goods in its possession which it does not own and which may be reclaimed by the owners. If goods were purchased by the company under a contract with a reservation of title clause, by which the vendor retained ownership until the goods were paid for, recovery from the liquidator by the vendor may be possible, unless for example the items purchased have lost their identity by being incorporated into another product (*Re Peachdart Ltd* [1984] Ch 131; (1983) 1 BCC 98,920). If the contract with the vendor further provides that the company could sell the goods purchased, but the proceeds were to be held on trust for the vendor until he received payment from the company, the resale proceeds must go to the vendor in priority to general creditors. The company is viewed as a trustee of the proceeds for the vendor in these circumstances (*Aluminium Industrie Vaassen BV v Romalpa Aluminium Ltd* [1976] 1 WLR 676): hence the description of a retention of title provision as a 'Romalpa clause'.

¶93-050   Contributions from shareholders

If the company's share capital is not fully paid up, the liquidator may call for the balance outstanding on the shares from the contributories. The obligation to pay the uncalled capital arises if the company's funds are insufficient to pay the costs of liquidation, the company's debts and liabilities and the nominal amount of the shares (IA 1986, s. 74). Shareholders in a limited liability company are liable to contribute up to the issue price of their shares. If the company is limited by guarantee the shareholder must meet the unpaid portion of his undertaking. Shareholders in an unlimited company have no ceiling on their potential obligation to contribute to the company. The liquidator can also recover unpaid capital from persons who owned the shares in the year preceding the winding up, but only to the

¶93-000

extent of any shortfall after contributions are collected from the holders at the date of commencement of the winding up (IA 1986, s. 74(2)). The former shareholders cannot be requested to contribute to capital for repayment of debts and liabilities incurred after the disposal of their shares.

¶93-100   Setting aside previous transactions

The liquidator of an insolvent company may be able to enlarge the fund from which creditors and contributories are to be repaid by pursuing remedies in respect of previous transactions of the company or avoiding transactions in which the company participated prior to the winding up (see ¶93-150ff.).

¶93-150   Transactions at an undervalue

A remedy is available where a company makes a gift or enters into a transaction with someone for either no or inadequate consideration at a time when the company either cannot pay its debts (for which see ¶92-550), or where it is unable to pay its debts as a consequence of the transaction (IA 1986, s. 238). If the transaction took place within the two years prior to a winding up, an application can be made to the court for return of any benefit conferred. If the liquidation followed the discharge of an administration order, the application can be made in respect of benefits conferred in the two years ending on the date of which the presentation of the petition for an administration order was made.

Orders of the court

The court may make such order as it thinks fit (IA 1986, s. 238(3)). In addition, the court is empowered to make the following orders (IA 1986, s. 241):

- the return of property, or its value, to the company;
- the release or discharge of any security given by the company;
- the repayment of benefits;
- the revival of any sureties or guarantees previously released; or
- the provision of security for the discharge of any obligation arising under a court order, or for such an obligation to be charged on any property (IA 1986, s. 241).

The court may also determine the extent to which any person whose property is vested in the company by the order must prove debts or liabilities in the winding-up process (IA 1986, s. 241(1)(g)).

Further, the order under s. 238 may affect the property of, or impose an obligation on, any person whether or not he is the person with whom the company in question entered into the transaction. However, no order for restoration will be made where the transaction was entered into in good faith and for the purpose of carrying on the company's business and, at the time of transaction, there were reasonable grounds for believing that the transaction would benefit the company.

See further ¶93-200.

¶93-200   Preferences

A company gives preference to a person if:

(1) that person is one of the company's creditors or a surety or a guarantor of any of the company's debts or other liabilities; and

(2) the company does anything or suffers anything to be done which (in either case) has the effect of putting that person into a position which, in the event of the company going into insolvent liquidation, will be better than the position he would have been in if that thing had not been done (IA 1986, s. 239(4)).

Further, the court cannot make an order in respect of a preference given to any person, unless the company which gave the preference was influenced by a desire to produce the result in (2) above (IA 1986, s. 239(5)). This has been judicially distinguished from the former test of a 'dominant intention to prefer' under the *Bankruptcy Act* 1914 (*Re M C Bacon Ltd* [1991] Ch 127; [1990] BCC 78).

If a creditor of a company in insolvent liquidation was put into a better position at a time when the company was unable to pay its debts (see ¶92-550), as a consequence of an act of the company within six months of the winding up (or two years, if the creditor was connected with the company), an application to the court for cancellation of the 'preference' is available (IA 1986, s. 239(2), 240(1)). If the liquidation followed the discharge of an administration order, preferences conferred in the six months (or two years, for connected persons) prior to the presentation of the petition for an administration order are vulnerable.

Orders of the court

The court may make such an order as it thinks fit (IA 1986, s. 239(3)). These powers are amplified in s. 241 of the Insolvency Act, where a list of possible restitutionary orders is set out (see ¶93-150). Further, the persons to whom the section is applied is extended to cover those who did not actually receive the preference (s. 241(2)).

Presumption of absence of good faith

Where a party has entered into a preferential transaction, and at that time he:

● had notice of the relevant surrounding circumstances and proceedings; or

● was 'connected with', or 'an associate' of, the company;

then an absence of good faith on his part will be presumed by the court. A person is connected with a company if:

● he is a director or shadow director of the company, or an associate of such a director or shadow director; or

● he is an associate of the company.

An associate is a spouse, a relative (of either spouse) or the spouse of a relative, a partner of either spouse or relative, or an employer or an employee. A trustee is an associate of any beneficiary if that beneficiary (or any associate of his) may have powers of the trust exercised for his benefit. Companies are associates if controlled by a common group of associated persons. A company is an associate of any person who either alone, or with his associates, exercises control (IA 1986, s. 435).

In *Weisgard v Pilkington* [1995] BCC 1,108, the respondent directors of the company were in breach of the rule against preferences by leasing residential properties from the company at highly preferential rates. The directors fell within the statutory definition of 'connected persons' and were therefore presumed by the court not to have acted in good faith.

Restrictions on orders

Exceptions to the above are provided so that no order under s. 238 or 239 of the Insolvency Act may prejudice any interest in the property which was acquired from a person other than the company in good faith and for value. A person who received a benefit from the transaction or preference in good faith and for value cannot be made to pay money to the applicant unless he was actually a party to the transaction or was a creditor of the company (s. 241(2)).

¶93-250   Extortionate credit bargains

If a company has entered into a credit transaction on extortionate terms within three years of the winding up, an application can be made to the court for an order setting aside or varying the terms (IA 1986, s. 244(2), (4)). Money paid under the agreement can also be refunded to the liquidator.

A credit agreement is extortionate if its terms call for grossly exorbitant payments to be made in respect of the provision of the credit, or it otherwise contravenes ordinary principles of fair dealing (IA 1986, s. 244(3)).

¶93-300   Avoidance of floating charges and unregistered charges

A floating charge over a company's assets may be struck out if created one year prior to the winding up (or to the presentation of a petition for an administration order which was subsequently granted), if the company was unable to pay its debts (see ¶92-550) at the date of creation or became so unable as a consequence of the transaction by which the charge was created (IA 1986, s. 245). If the person to whom the charge is granted is connected with the company, the one-year period is extended to two years, and the company's financial standing at the date the charge was granted is irrelevant. If the floating charge is created in between the petition for, and grant of, an administration order, it may be avoided.

The charge remains valid to the extent that new consideration was provided, on or after its creation, or a debt is discharged or reduced at the same time as, or after, the creation of the charge, or interest is paid in respect of the latter two obligations. Although the charge is avoided, the debt still remains payable.

Charges required to be registered under s. 395–424 (Pt. XII) of the *Companies Act* 1985 (see ¶53-300ff.) are void as against a liquidator or administrator if they are not properly registered within 21 days of the date of their creation. Late registration of the charge is possible, though the court will not generally permit such rectification if it would either prejudice the rights of the parties acquired before the time for registration or where the company has gone into liquidation (*Re Ashpurton Estates Ltd* [1983] Ch 110).

Where the charge is void as against the liquidator or administrator, the whole of the money secured on it becomes immediately repayable on demand (together with any interest).

¶93-350   Wrongful trading

If a director (or shadow director) of a company in insolvent liquidation knew or ought to have concluded that there was no reasonable prospect that the company would avoid going into insolvent liquidation at some time before commencement of the winding up, the court may declare that the director is liable to make a contribution to the company's assets (IA 1986, s. 214). (A disqualification order may also be made against persons found liable under s. 214: see ¶41-800).

The court cannot impose personal liability if satisfied that the director, etc. took every step with a view to minimising the potential loss to the company's creditors as he ought to have taken (IA 1986, s. 214(3)). In ascertaining whether personal liability should be imposed, the court has to apply a statutory test, as to the facts which the director ought to have known or ascertained, the conclusions which he ought to have reached and the steps which he ought to have taken. The test is by reference to a reasonably diligent person having both:

- the general knowledge, skill and experience that may reasonably be expected of a person carrying out the same functions as were carried out by that director in relation to the company; and

- the general knowledge, skill and experience that that director had (IA 1986, s. 214(4)).

Accordingly, a base level standard is imposed, by reference to the 'skill and experience' which would be expected of a person occupying that position. However, a higher standard may be imposed, by reference to the special skill or knowledge of the person involved.

The first case under the wrongful trading provisions was *Re Produce Marketing Consortium Ltd*.

Case example
Produce Marketing Consortium Ltd went into liquidation on 2 October 1987. Accounts for the years 1984–85 and 1985–86 were both only produced in early 1987. The company had continued to trade believing that the best solution for creditors would be to realise the value of perishable fruit in cold storage. However, on receiving the accounts, the directors admitted that liquidation was inevitable.

> The court considered that, notwithstanding the absence of accounts in July 1986 for these years, the directors had such an intimate knowledge of the business that they must have been aware of substantial losses. Further, the actual figures for the accounts of 1985 to 1986 must have been known to the directors, as they were normally capable of being ascertained. As Knox J outlines (at p. 595D–E: 'The knowledge to be imputed in testing whether or not directors knew or ought to have concluded that there was no reasonable prospect of the company avoiding insolvent liquidation is not limited to the documentary material actually available at the given time. This appears from s. 214(4) which includes a reference to facts which a director of a company ought not only to know but those which he ought to ascertain, a word which does not appear in s. 214(2)(b). In my judgment this indicates that there is to be included by way of factual information not only what was actually there but what, given reasonable diligence and an appropriate level of general knowledge, skill and experience, was ascertainable. This leads me to the conclusion in this case that I should assume, for the purposes of applying the test in s. 214(2), that the financial results for the year ending 30 September 1985 were known at the end of July 1986 at least to the extent of the size of the deficiency of assets over liabilities.' *Re Produce Marketing Consortium Ltd* (1989) 5 BCC 569.

In *Re Sherborne Associates Ltd* [1995] BCC 40, the court set out further guidelines for determining whether a director had committed wrongful trading under s. 214. In particular, one should not, with the benefit of hindsight, immediately conclude that what happened was inevitable and clearly apparent to the directors at the time.

While the contribution to assets is such a figure as the court thinks fit, this is primarily compensatory rather than penal. In *Re Purpoint Ltd* [1991] BCC 121, the director of a company that had gone into liquidation was ordered to contribute to the company's assets pursuant to s. 214. These sums were designed to meet the liabilities that the company would otherwise not have incurred. Their purpose was to compensate the company and the unsecured creditors rather than punish the director. Prima facie, the appropriate amount that a director is to be declared liable to contribute is the amount by which the company's assets can be discerned to have been depleted by the director's conduct. However, this statement will not constrain the court from having regard to other factors. The fact that there was no fraudulent intent is not of itself a reason for fixing the amount at a nominal or low figure, but it may be a factor to be taken into consideration. Note that the defence under s. 727 of the *Companies Act* 1985 that a director has acted honestly and reasonably and ought fairly to be excused cannot be invoked to reduce or discharge any liability to contribute to the company's assets arising under s. 214 (*Re Produce Marketing Consortium Ltd (Halls v David)* (1989) 5 BCC 399); this is because the s. 214 test is objective, whereas the s. 727 defence is subjective.

Sums recovered by a liquidator under s. 214 are added to the company's assets, which then become subject to distribution in accordance with the rules outlined at ¶93-600. Importantly, the funds recovered go to all creditors, not just those who suffered direct loss as a result of the wrongful trading. Whether contributions made under s. 214 are caught by a floating charge that has crystallised (see ¶53-300) will depend on the terms of the related charge (*Re Produce Marketing Consortium Ltd*, above).

A liquidator cannot sell the fruits of a wrongful trading action as the contract to do so will be tainted with champerty and the fruits are not 'the company's property' which a liquidator has express power to sell (*Re Oasis Manufacturing Services Ltd* [1997] BCC 282).

The 'contribution ... to the company's assets' for wrongful trading under s. 214 of the *Insolvency Act* 1986 is for the recovery of a sum of money but does not preclude the liquidator accepting property other than money to satisfy the director's liability (*Re Farmizer (Products) Ltd. Moore v Gadd* [1997] BCC 655).

The six-year limitation period in the *Limitation Act* 1980 applies to wrongful trading actions (*Re Farmizer (Products) Ltd. Moore v Gadd*, above).

Where a director is ordered to contribute to a company's assets under s. 214, that is ground for disqualification under s. 10 of the *Company Directors Disqualification Act* 1986 (see ¶41-800).

¶93-400   Fraudulent trading

A liquidator may apply to the court for a declaration that persons who were knowingly parties to the carrying on of a business with the intention of defrauding creditors of the company or creditors of any other person, or for any fraudulent purpose, should be made liable to contribute to the company's assets (IA 1986, s. 213). Directors are obviously within the scope of these rules.

The court may order that such persons should contribute as the court thinks fit. A disqualification order may also be made against persons found liable under s. 213 (see ¶41-800).

Fraudulent trading has been explained as 'allowing a company to incur credit at a time when the business is being carried on in such circumstances that it is clear that the company will never be able to satisfy its creditors' (*Re White and Osmond (Parkstone) Ltd* (unreported, 30 June 1960, Buckley J)).

It is important to note that s. 213 and 214 of the *Insolvency Act* 1986 (see ¶40-100, ¶41-800) are not alternatives: a director may be liable under both to make a contribution to the company's assets.

Where a director is ordered to contribute to a company's assets under s. 213, that is ground for disqualification under s. 10 of the *Company Directors Disqualification Act* 1986 (see ¶41-800).

Punishment for fraudulent trading

Further, whether or not a company is being wound up, where the business is conducted with an intent to defraud creditors, every person who was knowingly a party to that action is liable to a fine or imprisonment or both (CA 1985, s. 458).

¶93-450 Breach of duty

Personal liability may be imposed under s. 212 of the *Insolvency Act* 1986 if, in the course of a liquidation, it appears that any person who is, or has been, an officer of the company, or who has acted as a liquidator, administrator or administrative receiver, or who has taken part in the promotion, formation or management of the company, has retained or misapplied the company's assets or has been guilty of any misfeasance or breach of fiduciary or other duty. The court may order repayment of money or restoration of assets or contribution to the company's assets by way of compensation for misfeasance or breach of duty (IA 1986, s. 212).

In defence or mitigation to a s. 212 action, a company officer can plead that he acted honestly and reasonably and in the circumstances ought fairly to be excused (see *Re Brian D Pierson (Contractors) Ltd* [1999] BCC 26); contrast a s. 214 action.

¶93-500 Acting while disqualified

Personal liability may be imposed upon a person who acts a director of a company in contravention of a disqualification order. Persons who concern themselves with the management of a company after having been disqualified, or who act in the management of a company on the instructions of disqualified persons, become liable for debts incurred by the company whilst they were involved in its management or willing to act on the instructions of disqualified persons (CDDA 1986, s. 15). In such situations, liquidators may be able further to enlarge the assets of an insolvent company (see ¶41-850).

¶93-550 Disclaimer of onerous property

A liquidator may disclaim the company's rights, interests and liabilities in or in respect of any unprofitable contract, any property which is not saleable or not readily saleable or any property which is such that it may give rise to a liability to pay money or perform any other onerous act. This power is often used to disclaim leases. The disclaimer operates from the date of the disclaimer. Persons sustaining loss as a consequence of the disclaimer (e.g. a landlord whose lease has been disclaimed) are made creditors of the company, and prove for the loss in the course of the winding up (IA 1986, s. 178).

Where a liquidator disclaims a lease under s. 178 of the *Insolvency Act* 1986, the disclaimer operates to determine the insolvent company's liabilities in the lease but, except for the purpose of releasing the company, not so as to affect the rights of any other person (s. 178(4)(b)). Three scenarios on the effects of disclaimer of a lease were set out by the House of Lords in *Hindcastle Ltd v Barbara Attenborough Associates Ltd* [1997] AC 70; [1996] BCC 636:

(1) where only a landlord and insolvent tenant company are involved, both the company and the landlord are released from their respective obligations

under the disclaimed lease, the leasehold estate ceases to exist and the reversion accelerates back to the landlord;

(2) where others have responsibilities in respect of *the lease*, e.g. the tenant company's obligations were guaranteed by another party, or the company had taken the lease on assignment from an intermediate tenant who had covenanted to pay the rent, then by virtue of s. 178(4)(b) the obligations of the guarantor or assignor are *not* determined by the lease; and

(3) where others have an interest in *the property*, e.g. if the tenant company had previously assigned the lease to a subtenant, the latter's interest is similarly not determined by disclaimer of the lease by the liquidator of the tenant.

A disclaimer of a waste management licence as onerous property by the liquidator of a company in voluntary winding up has been considered by the Companies Court which held that, although the waste management licence was property for the purposes of the *Insolvency Act* 1986, the provisions of the *Environmental Protection Act* 1990 preventing disclaimer would prevail over the 1986 Act both as a matter of public policy and because of the sequence of the legislation (*Re Mineral Resources Ltd. Environment Agency v Stout* [1999] BCC 422).

On the disclaimer the landlord becomes an unsecured creditor of the company and can prove in its winding up for the contractual right of the future rent and other payments owing under the lease for the residue of its term, but he is under a duty to mitigate the loss suffered during the residue of the term by re-letting the property (*Re Park Air Services plc* [1999] BCC 135) and the sum for proof is subject to discount as an accelerated payment.

¶93-600   Distributions of assets

The distribution of funds of a company in liquidation follows a strict 'pecking order'. Subject to preferential payments, the company's property available for distribution in a voluntary winding up (i.e. excluding property which is the subject of a valid fixed charge) is applied in satisfaction of its liabilities pari passu and, subject to that, is distributed amongst members according to their interests in the company unless the articles provide otherwise (IA 1986, s. 107). The liquidator's remuneration, and other expenses properly incurred in the winding up, rank first (s. 115).

Preferential debts

The first in line are the preferential creditors (IA 1986, s. 175). These rank equally amongst themselves, and in priority to any floating charge. The date for determination of a creditor's status as 'preferential' in a voluntary liquidation is that of the resolution for winding up. Where a winding-up order immediately follows the discharge of an administration order, the relevant date is the making of that order. If neither of the above situations applies, the date is determined by when the provisional liquidator is appointed. If no such appointment was made, the date of the winding-up order itself applies.

The preferential creditors listed in Sch. 6 to the *Insolvency Act* 1986 include:

- debts due to the Inland Revenue: PAYE deductions due to the Revenue in respect of the 12 months preceding the winding up;

- debts due to Customs and Excise: VAT referable to the six months prior to the winding up, and various other taxes and duties;

- Social Security contributions: 12 months' Class 1 and 2 contributions;

- contributions to occupational pensions schemes; and

- remuneration of employees: pay due to employees in respect of the four months prior to the winding up, plus any accrued holiday remuneration.

Ordinary debts, etc.

Once the preferential creditors are paid off, the company's property is applied in satisfaction of the company's remaining liabilities pari passu, excluding sums owed to contributories in that status. Sums owed to contributories in respect of unpaid dividends are termed 'deferred debts', and rank after other debts, in order of payment. Any sums remaining are paid to the contributories in accordance with their rights and interests in the company. Distribution to contributories must be in accordance with the company's memorandum and articles of association.

UNREGISTERED COMPANIES, DISSOLUTION

¶93-800 Winding up of unregistered companies

All the rules relating to the compulsory winding up by the court of a registered company apply to the winding up of an unregistered company, together with certain other specific rules (IA 1986, s. 221(1)). An unregistered company cannot be wound up voluntarily, but must be wound up by the court. An unregistered company may be wound up if:

(1) the company is dissolved, or has ceased to carry on business, or is carrying on the business only for the purpose of winding up its affairs;

(2) the company is unable to pay its debts; or

(3) the court is of the opinion that it is just and equitable that it should be wound up (IA 1986, s. 221(5)).

An oversea company, i.e. one which has been carrying on business in Great Britain, may be wound up as an unregistered company under the *Insolvency Act* 1986 even if it ceases to carry on business in Britain, and has been dissolved or otherwise ceased to exist as a company by virtue of the laws of the country in which it was incorporated (IA 1986, s. 225). Where a foreign company has not established a place of business in Great Britain (and therefore is not an oversea company), it may be subject to winding-up jurisdiction in the UK if it has a sufficient connection with the UK and there is a reasonable possibility of benefit to the creditors from the winding up. The foreign company in question need not have assets within the UK (*Re a Company No. 00359 of 1987* [1988] Ch 210; (1987) 3 BCC 160).

¶93-850   Dissolution of companies

Dissolution of a company by voluntary winding up occurs three months after the registration by the registrar of the final account and return (which explains how the winding up has been conducted).

Dissolution in a compulsory winding up occurs three months after the registrar of companies receives either a notice that the final meeting of creditors has accepted the liquidator's report on completion of the winding up, or a notice from the official receiver that the winding up is complete (IA 1986, s. 205).

Early dissolution

The official receiver may apply for the company's early dissolution where it is clear that its assets are incapable of covering the expenses of the winding up, and that no investigations into the company's conduct need to be made (IA 1986, s. 202(2)).

Court's power to declare dissolution void

The court has power, normally within two years after a dissolution, to declare the dissolution void (CA 1985, s. 651). This then permits such proceedings to be taken as might have been taken had the company not been dissolved. The two-year limit does not apply in the case of a claim for damages in respect of personal injuries or under the *Fatal Accidents Act* 1976, but this cannot effectively override the general law on limitations (CA 1985, s. 651(5)).

¶93-900   Striking off

The registrar of companies may strike the company off the register if it appears to be defunct. Two warning letters must be sent to the company, and a notice placed in the *London Gazette*, before the order will be made (CA 1985, s. 652). Any member or creditor of the company may apply, within 20 years of the striking off, to the court to have the company restored to the register (CA 1985, s. 653).

A procedure has been introduced which formalises the previous practice of allowing private companies to be voluntarily struck off the companies register (CA 1985, s. 652A–652F). An application must be made in the prescribed form by a majority of the directors. Striking-off can then only take effect once three months have elapsed from the date of an advertisement in the *Gazette* (which states that the company's management wish to follow that course of action).

Various safeguards are built into the procedure which prevent it from operating if (CA 1985, s. 652B):

- certain events have taken place in the three months prior to the application being made (i.e. the company has changed its name); or

- the company is subject or potentially subject to a voluntary arrangement, an administration order, a winding up or a receivership; or

- obligations regarding notice to various parties (i.e. members, employees, creditors, etc.) are not satisfied.

INVESTIGATION OF A COMPANY'S AFFAIRS

¶94-200 Investigations by liquidators

A facility is provided for investigating a company's history by 'office holders', who are statutorily defined as administrators, administrative receivers, liquidators or provisional liquidators (IA 1986, s. 234(1)).

Where any person has in his possession or controls any property, books, paper or records to which the company appears to be entitled, the court may require that person to transfer these items to an office holder.

Designated persons must also (IA 1986, s. 235):

- give the office holder such information concerning the company and its promotion, formation, business, dealings, affairs or property as the office holder may reasonably require; and

- attend on the office holder at such times as he may reasonably require.

The persons who must comply with the above duty are:

- those who are or have at any time been officers of the company;

- those who have taken part in the company's formation within one year of the liquidation or date of appointment of a provisional liquidator;

- those who are in the company's employment, or have been in its employment (including employment under a contract of services), within that year, and are in the office holder's opinion capable of giving information which he requires;

- those who are, or have within that year been, officers or in the employment (including employment under a contract for services) of another company which is, or within that year was, an officer of the company in question; and

- in the case of a company being wound up by the court, any person who has acted as the company's administrator, administrative receiver or liquidator.

Failure to comply with a request from the office holder exposes the offender to a fine (IA 1986, s. 235). Liens over the company's books, papers and records are unenforceable if they would deny the office holder access to them (s. 246). However, the above does not apply to a lien on documents that confer proprietary title and are held 'as such' (s. 246(3)). Hence, in *Re SEIL Trade Finance Ltd* [1992] BCC 538, solicitors were permitted to retain security documents because they conferred title and were held 'as such', notwithstanding the fact that they would otherwise have given rise to a lien.

The office holder may apply to the court for an order that certain designated persons submit an affidavit to the court containing an account of their dealings with the company, or produce any books, papers or other records in their possession or under their control relating to the company (IA 1986, s. 236). The persons from whom such information may be obtained are:

- any officer of the company;

- any person known or suspected to have in his possession any property of the company, or supposed to be indebted to the company; or

- any person whom the court thinks capable of giving information concerning the promotion, formation, business, dealings, affairs or property of the company.

The powers under s. 236 are conferred to enable information to be obtained. If it appears to the court, on consideration of any evidence obtained under s. 236, that any person has company property in his possession or is indebted to the company, the court may on the application of the office holder order that the property or debt be recovered (s. 237).

Litigation on the use of s. 236 of the *Insolvency Act* 1986 by insolvency office holders to obtain information has become prolific since 1997 and a distinct jurisprudence is now emerging in this area. A number of principles have been forthcoming:

(1) The provision binds the Crown (*Soden v Burns. R v Secretary of State for Trade and Industry, ex parte Soden* [1997] BCC 308).

(2) On an opposed application under s. 236 the court should first see whether the office holder has made a reasonable requirement for oral or documentary information: if he has, the court must then carry out a balancing exercise weighing the importance of the information to the office holder against the risk of oppression to the witness (in particular the exposure to self-incrimination in possible proceedings against the witness) (*Re Bank of*

Credit and Commerce International SA. Morris v Bank of America Trust and Savings Association [1997] BCC 561).

(3) Section 236 should not be used in a 'fishing expedition' against the witness for possible future litigation against that witness (*Re James McHale Automobiles Ltd* [1997] BCC 202).

(4) The cost of complying with a s. 236 order, particularly of providing and transporting documentation, can be high and may be ordered in favour of the witness (*Re Bank of Credit and Commerce International SA. Morris v Bank of America Trust and Savings Association*, above).

¶94-250 Official receiver's request for statement of company's affairs

When the court has made a winding-up order or appointed a provisional liquidator, the official receiver may require some or all of the following persons to make out and submit to him a statement as to the company's affairs (IA 1986, s. 131):

- those who are or have been officers of the company;
- those who have taken part in the company's formation within one year of the winding-up order or date of appointment of a provisional liquidator;
- those who are in the company's employment or have been within its employment within that year, and are, in the official receiver's opinion, capable of giving the information required; and
- those who are or have been within that year officers of, or in the employment of, a company which is, or within that year was, an officer of the company.

These persons have 21 days in which to provide a statement, verified by affidavit, which shows:

- particulars of the company's assets, debts and liabilities;
- the name and addresses of the company's creditors;
- the securities held by the creditors;
- the dates when the securities were given; and
- such further or other information as may be prescribed or as the official receiver may require.

Where a winding-up order is made in respect of a company, the official receiver has an overriding duty to investigate the company's conduct and determine the causes behind its failure (IA 1986, s. 132). Where appropriate, the official receiver must draft a report setting out the conclusions reached.

¶94-300 Public examinations

Where a company is being wound up by the court, the official receiver may apply to the court for public examination of any person who:

- is or has been an officer of the company; or

- has acted as liquidator or administrator of the company or as receiver or manager; or

- has otherwise been concerned, or has taken part in, the company's promotion, formation or management (IA 1986, s. 133).

The official receiver must make an application for a public examination of any of the above if requested to do so by one-half in value of the company's creditors or three-quarters in value of the company's contributories.

The persons who may ask questions during the public examination of company officers are the official receiver, the liquidator, a special manager, any creditor who has tendered a proof and any 'contributory' (see ¶91-700).

¶94-350 Investigation of criminal offences in relation to a company

If, in the course of either a voluntary or a compulsory winding up, it appears that any past or present officer, or any member, has been guilty of an offence in relation to the company for which he is criminally liable, the following consequences may ensue (IA 1986, s. 218).

In the case of a winding up by the court, in which the court uncovers the suspected offence (either of its own motion or upon the application of any person interested in the winding up), it may direct the liquidator to refer the matter to the Director of Public Prosecutions (DPP) or, in Scotland, the Lord Advocate. If it is the liquidator (and not the official receiver) who uncovers the suspected offence, he must report the matter to the official receiver.

Liquidator's duty to report offences

A liquidator in a voluntary winding up must report suspected criminal offences to the DPP or Lord Advocate and facilitate the investigation of the offence. The DPP, etc. may then refer the matter to the Secretary of State, who must then investigate the matter further (IA 1986, s. 218(4)).

Liquidator's report to DPP, etc.

If it appears to the court in the course of a voluntary winding up that any past or present officer of the company, or any member of it, has been guilty of a criminal offence in relation to the company, and no report has been made to the DPP or Lord Advocate by the liquidator, the court may direct the liquidator to make such a report on the application of any person interested in the winding up or on its own motion. The Director of Public Prosecutions may then refer the matter to the Secretary of State as above (IA 1986, s. 218(6)).

Use of answers as evidence, etc.

Answers given in the course of investigations under s. 218 above may be used in evidence against the individual concerned (IA 1986, s. 219(2)). Further, should the

Secretary of State or DPP decide to institute criminal proceedings, it is the duty of the liquidator and every officer or agent of the company (past and present) to give all assistance in relation to the prosecution that he is reasonably able to give (s. 219(3)).

CASE TABLE

This list directs the subscriber to numbered paragraphs (¶) where a particular case is mentioned.

Bor

How

Per

355

LEGISLATION FINDING LIST

This list directs the subscriber to numbered paragraphs (¶) where particular legislative (or quasi-legislative) provisions are mentioned.

The legislation is listed in alphabetical order of title and references in the provisions column are to section numbers unless otherwise stated.

Provision	Paragraph
Banking Act 1987	70-750
Bank of England Act 1998	23-700
Bankruptcy Act 1914	93-200
Business Names Act 1985	
See generally	14-000; 23-000
2(4)	14-650
3	23-000
4(6)	14-650
4(7)	14-550
7	14-650
Charging Orders Act 1979	
5	51-100
City Code on Takeovers and Mergers	
See generally	45-600; 80-500
r. 8.3	51-450
Civil Procedure Rules 1998 (SI 1998/3132)	
r. 50	51-100; 62-000; 62-050; 90-100
Sch. 1, O. 15, r. 12	62-000; 62-050
Sch. 1, O. 15, r. 12A	62-050
Sch. 1, O. 30, r. 3	90-100
Sch. 1, O. 50, r. 11–15	51-100
Sch. 1, O. 51	90-100
Companies Act 1948	
See generally	60-550
168(2), 172	11-100
Sch. 1	31-000
Companies Act 1967	
See generally	44-300
13(1)	44-300
Companies Act 1980	20-000; 50-250; 51-000
Companies Act 1981	20-000; 51-800; 81-300
Companies Act 1985	
See generally	14-000; 20-000; 20-200; 20-250; 22-750; 30-800; 41-950; 51-800; 54-000; 54-350; 54-500; 80-000; 80-650
1	30-000
1(3)	20-150
2	30-050; 30-450; 50-000
2(2)	13-500
2(5)	50-000

Provision	Paragraph
2(7)	30-450
3A	30-050; 30-700
4	13-500; 30-450
5	30-450
6(3)	14-425
8	30-150
8(2)	20-300
8A	20-450
9	13-500; 30-250; 30-500; 60-600
9(1)	30-500
10	22-000; 41-300
13(7)	22-000; 30-700
14	30-000; 30-250; 50-950
16	30-450; 30-500
17	13-500; 30-450
18(2)	30-450
18(3)	14-425
19(2)	14-625
20(2)	14-625
24	21-050
26(1)	22-750
28	11-000; 13-500; 22-950
28(2)	22-900
28(5)	14-650
29	22-800; 23-000
31(5), (6)	14-650
32	22-850
33, 33(3), 34	14-650
35	30-700; 30-800; 42-500
35(3)	13-500
35A	30-800; 43-500
35A(1), (2)(b)	30-800
35B	30-800
36A	23-250
36C	22-400
42	23-150; 23-550
43	13-500; 22-500
44	22-500
47	22-500
49	30-450
51	13-500; 30-450
53	13-500; 22-600; 51-750
54	22-600
54(10)	14-425
59, 60	54-500
80	50-550; 50-600; 50-625
80(9)	14-900

Provision	Paragraph
Financial Services Act 1986	
See generally	20-000; 23-700; 50-500; 54-150; 54-350; 70-750
47	45-200; 50-500; 54-150; 54-400
61	54-150; 54-400
62	45-200; 54-250
Pt. IV	53-050; 54-000; 54-100; 54-250; 54-400
142–157	53-050; 54-000; 54-100; 54-400
146(1), (2), (3)	54-100
147	54-100
148(1), (3)	54-100
150, 150(1), (3)	54-150
150(4), (6)	54-150
151(1), (2), (3), (5), (6)	54-150
152	54-150
152(9)	30-250
154A(b)	54-150
156(2)	54-100
Pt. V	54-000
158–171	54-000
177	41-700(2); 45-400
177(3), (4)	45-400
178(3)	45-400
199	45-400
Sch. 11A	54-100
Human Rights Act 1998	23-850
Income and Corporation Taxes Act 1988	
767A, 767B	21-000
Industry Act 1975	
11–13	80-650
Inheritance Tax Act 1984	
94–102	21-000
Insolvency Act 1985	20-000
Insolvency Act 1986	
See generally	14-000; 20-000; 70-225; 90-000; 90-050; 90-350; 91-000; 91-550
Pt. I	90-650; 91-050
1–6	52-025
1–7	90-650; 91-050
2(2), (3)	90-650
3	90-700
3(1), (2), (3)	90-650
4(2), (3), (4), (6)	90-700
5(1), (2), (3), (4)	90-700
6, 6(2), (3), (4), (7)	90-700
7(2), (3), (4)	90-700
7(4)(b)	91-050; 92-500
Pt. II	70-225
8(1)(a), (b)	91-050
8(2), (3)	91-050; 91-100
8(4)	91-050
9, 9(2), (3), (4)	91-050
10(1), (2), (3)	91-050

Provision	Paragraph
11(1)(a), (b)	91-250
11(2), (3)	91-250
12(1)	91-150
12(2)	14-575
14	91-100; 92-500
14(1)	92-500
14(3), (5)	91-100
15	91-100
17	91-150; 91-250
17(1), (2)(a), (b)	91-100
18(1), (2)(a), (b), (3)	91-100
19(1), (2)	91-300
19(5), (6)	91-300
20(1)(a), (b)	91-300
20(2), (3)	91-300
21	91-150
22	41-750
22(1), (2), (3), (4)	91-150
22(6)	14-950
23(1)	91-200
24(1), (6)	91-200
25, 26	91-200
27, 27(1), (2), (3), (4)	91-200
29(2)	90-350
30	14-750; 90-050
31	90-050
33	90-050; 90-150
38	90-275
39	90-000; 90-275
39(2)	14-575
40	53-200
42	90-400
42(1)	90-400; 92-500
43	90-400
44, 44(2A)	90-425
45	90-425
45(1)	12-300
46(1)	90-375
47	41-750
47(2), (3)	90-375
47(6)	14-950
48, 49	90-375
66	41-750
73	91-500
74	91-700; 93-050
74(2)	93-050
75	91-700
76	51-900; 91-700; 92-500
79	91-700
84	42-300
84(1)	92-000
84(1)(b)	13-500
85(2)	14-400; 15-025
86, 87	92-000
89(1), (2), (3)	92-200
89(4)	14-325; 15-025; 92-200
89(6)	14-325; 15-025

INDEX

This is the index to the Guide. References are to paragraph (¶) numbers.
See also the Case Table at p. 347 and the Legislation Finding List at p. 355.

Joi